Heart Like a Fakir

Heart Like a Fakir

*General Sir James Abbott and
the Fall of the East India Company*

Chris Mason

ROWMAN & LITTLEFIELD
Lanham • Boulder • New York • London

Published by Rowman & Littlefield
An imprint of The Rowman & Littlefield Publishing Group, Inc.
4501 Forbes Boulevard, Suite 200, Lanham, Maryland 20706
www.rowman.com

86-90 Paul Street, London EC2A 4NE

Copyright © 2023 by The Rowman & Littlefield Publishing Group, Inc.

Cover images:
Front: background detail from artwork: The Remnants of an Army, 1879, Elizabeth Butler, Presented by Sir Henry Tate
Photo: Tate; left: General Sir James Abbott dressed as an Indian noble by B. Baldwin 1841, The History Collection / Alamy Stock Photo; right: public domain.
Back: public domain.

All rights reserved. No part of this book may be reproduced in any form or by any electronic or mechanical means, including information storage and retrieval systems, without written permission from the publisher, except by a reviewer who may quote passages in a review.

British Library Cataloguing in Publication Information Available

Library of Congress Cataloging-in-Publication Data

Names: Mason, Chris, author.
Title: Heart like a Fakir : General Sir James Abbott and the fall of the East India Company / Chris Mason.
Other titles: General Sir James Abbott and the fall of the East India Company
Description: Lanham : Rowman & Littlefield, [2022] | Includes bibliographical references and index.
Identifiers: LCCN 2022036604 (print) | LCCN 2022036605 (ebook) | ISBN 9781538169568 (cloth) | ISBN 9781538169575 (paperback) | ISBN 9781538169582 (epub)
Subjects: LCSH: Abbott, James, Sir, 1807-1896. | East India Company. Army—Officers—Biography. | British—India—Social life and customs—19th century. | India—History—Sepoy Rebellion, 1857-1858—Causes. | East India Company—History—19th century.
Classification: LCC DS479.1.A32 M37 2022 (print) | LCC DS479.1.A32 (ebook) | DDC 954.03/5092 [B]–dc23/eng/20220810
LC record available at https://lccn.loc.gov/2022036604
LC ebook record available at https://lccn.loc.gov/2022036605

For Hannah, TTTMDH

Contents

List of Illustrations ix
Nomenclature xii
Acknowledgments xiii
Introduction xv
Chapter 1: Beginnings, 1807–1824 1
Chapter 2: Baptism of Fire, 1824–1826 23
Chapter 3: Reform and Progress, 1826–1834 60
Chapter 4: D'Arcy Todd and the Revenue Survey, 1834–1838 . . . 94
Chapter 5: A Mission to Khiva, 1838–1843 112
Chapter 6: A New Beginning, 1843–1849 159
Chapter 7: The Man Who Was King, 1849–1853 212
Chapter 8: Endings, 1854–1896 248
Appendix: Abbott the Artist 285
Notes 297
Bibliography 338
Index 358
About the Author 368

Illustrations

Figure 1.1	Detail from the painting *Portrait of Henry Lannoy Hunter*	3
Figure 1.2	Detail from the caricature "The Nabob Rumbled" by James Gillray	5
Figure 1.3	The Paragon, Blackheath, when James Abbott was a child	7
Figure 1.4	*A View of Dr. Benson's School at Hounslow*, by J. S. Stadler	11
Figure 2.1	*An East Indiaman Reefed Down*, by William Knell	24
Figure 2.2	Cabin of a typical East Indiaman for middle-class passengers	27
Figure 2.3	*Indian Army Officer*, by William Havell	32
Figure 2.4	Small boat on the Hooghly River below Calcutta circa 1875	36
Figure 2.5	"A Dandy or Boatman," by Frans Balthazar Solvyns circa 1796	38
Figure 2.6	Detail from *Tom Raw, the Griffin, a Burlesque Poem* by Charles D'Oyly	41
Figure 2.7	*Bengal Foot Artillery 1846* by Henry Martens	46
Figure 3.1	Uniforms of the Bengal Native Infantry circa 1830	65
Figure 3.2	"Titania Lying Asleep," by Arthur Rackham	73
Figure 3.3	James Abbott's handwritten Simla–Khiva diary in oil-skin pouch	76
Figure 3.4	"Tom Raw Is Introduced to His Regimental Commander" by Charles D'Oyly	85
Figure 3.5	*Skinner's Horse at Exercise* by John Gwatkin and "Khitmatgar, Meerut" by S. Murray	87
Figure 4.1	Pen-and-ink sketch of D'Arcy Todd circa 1835	96
Figure 4.2	Indian village map from *Manual of Surveying for India* by Smyth and Thuillier	106

Illustrations

Figure 4.3	"Surveying in India," pen and ink with aquatint, by Walter Sherwill	108
Figure 5.1	The city of Herat, Afghanistan, in the early 1800s	119
Figure 5.2	"Audience with the Khan of Khiva" by Armin Vámbéry	124
Figure 5.3	"Three Khivans Drinking Tea in the Courtyard of Their Home," photograph by Anton Stepanovich Murenko	126
Figure 5.4	"Portrait of Sammud Khan" from *Narrative of a Journey from Heraut to Khiva* by James Abbott	129
Figure 5.5	Map of Central Asia published by A. B. Graham in 1905	131
Figure 5.6	Photograph of British agent Saleh Mohammed and his son circa 1860	135
Figure 5.7	Bronze cast of the death mask of Charles XII	138
Figure 5.8	Portrait of James Abbott in oils by B. Baldwin, London	141
Figure 5.9	Montage of portraits of British men and women living in the East prior to 1860	147
Figure 5.10	Asirgarh plateau and "Jhaur Ghat," pen and ink by James Abbott	155
Figure 5.11	The grave markers of Margaret Abbott in the British cemetery in Asirgarh	157
Figure 6.1	"Budgerow," aquatint by Balthasar Solvyns circa 1796	164
Figure 6.2	Watercolor painting of the mountain pass to Kôt Kangra by Alexander Jack	173
Figure 6.3	The fortress at Kôt Kangra by Charles Hardinge, as it appeared around 1847	177
Figure 6.4	"Portrait of a Hazara Mountaineer, India," pen and ink by Gilbert	181
Figure 6.5	*Hamil Sahib Badahur and Raja Dina Nath*, painting by unknown Sikh artist	185
Figure 6.6	Period painting of Chattar Singh Attariwala by an unknown Sikh artist	205
Figure 7.1	"Glen at Nārā Huzāra," pen-and-ink drawing by James Abbott	215
Figure 7.2	View of the Indus River at Attock from site of Abbott's camp at Sirikot	219

ILLUSTRATIONS

Figure 7.3	British map of the Hazāra region from the 1860s with locations added	221
Figure 7.4	"Study of a Fakir," watercolor over pencil, by British artist John Gantz	237
Figure 7.5	Print of the Black Mountain looking eastward from a tributary of the Indus, 1888	242
Figure 8.1	Hand-tinted portrait photograph of James Abbott as a major in full dress uniform	258
Figure 8.2	"British Lion's Vengeance on the Bengal Tiger," *Punch* cartoon by John Tenniel	260
Figure 8.3	The massacre of British survivors of Cawnpore, lithograph by T. Packer	262
Figure 8.4	Photograph of James Abbott at retirement by Cornelius Jabez Hughes	266
Figure 8.5	Portrait photograph of James Abbott at the time of his knighthood, May 1894	275
Figure 8.6	The last known photograph of James Abbott on the Isle of Wight	278
Figure 8.7	*Rock of Aornos in Huzāra*, watercolor by James Abbott circa 1850	282
Figure A.1	"Jehaz Ke Mhyl, Ruined City of Maandoo in Malwa," pen and ink by James Abbott	291
Figure A.2	Ghats on the riverbank at Maheshwar, Nimarr, pencil and ink by James Abbott	295

Nomenclature

JAMES ABBOTT LEFT A VOLUMINOUS BODY OF WRITING, MOST OF IT unedited and unpublished. His spelling and grammar were exceptionally good, although his writing is liberally dusted with the seemingly haphazard dashes and commas that were popular with Victorian writers. Where these are confusing, I have removed them. The proper names of places in India I have used in the form most common during Abbott's life to conform to his own spellings, a convention I believe will be the least jarring to the reader. The city of Kolkata, for example, is rendered as Calcutta throughout the text. Similarly, archaic transliterations of words in Hindi, such as Sadhoo (for Sādhu, साधु, a wandering monk), have been left as Abbott wrote them, with explanatory notes when necessary to clarify meanings of obscure terms. Contemporary spellings of Hindi words were of an ad hoc nature and varied widely, sometimes even within the same sentence. There was no formal, accepted system for rendering Hindi into English at this time, so Britons in India simply did their best phonetically. This reflects not a disdain for the language but rather full assimilation into it—an internalization of Hindi and Persian into their thinking and vocabularies so complete that mental translations were no longer taking place. Finally, some English words in Abbott's day had different meanings then than they do today. In 1830, for example, "combination" meant a sinister plot. I have provided an endnote where it is important to the understanding of the passage in question.

Acknowledgments

MANY PEOPLE MADE THIS BOOK POSSIBLE, AND I AM INDEBTED TO ALL of them. First and foremost, I would like to thank Dr. Dane Kennedy, my mentor, dissertation advisor, and good friend. In 2005, Dane sized up a retiring Foreign Service officer with no educational background in history and for some reason gave me a chance at a PhD at the George Washington University. He taught me how to be a historian, and I would not be writing this today without his patience, support, and guidance. The flaws in this book are in spite of his teaching me better. I would like to thank the other members of my dissertation committee as well for their improvements to this book: Professor Thomas Johnson, Dr. Benjamin Hopkins, Dr. Ronald Spector, and especially Dr. Muriel Atkin, whose advice and help along the way were invaluable to me as an aspiring historian.

The months of research at the British Library in London would never have been possible without the kindness of my dear friend Dr. Björn Reinhardt, who put up with a guest who stayed far too long and too often with unfailingly gracious hospitality and comradeship. My wife, Yasemin, and my daughter, Hannah, too, were endlessly patient and supportive, and I am grateful forever to my daughter, to whom this book is dedicated, for sharing her father with James Abbott for several years without a word of complaint and encouraging me every step of the way. Thank you, Treasure. My old friend and colleague Harold Ingram always had my back, and his support helped me see this through when I had doubts. Thanks for always being there in this and everything else. I am very grateful also for the support of my brother Ross, who is always there when I need him. Harry Walters and Linda Bernstein kept the home fires burning all the many times I was away and got me through the swine flu with homemade chicken soup on the doorstep. I also want to thank my acquisitions editor at Rowman & Littlefield, Katelyn Turner, both for seeing the potential in this story and for her guidance through the publishing process, as well as production editor Felicity Tucker, whose professionalism kept the trains running on time, and my brilliant copy editor, Jennifer Kelland, who caught and corrected any number of mistakes in the manuscript. I would also like to thank Rowman & Littlefield designer Chloe Batch for her great work on the book cover.

The entire staff of the Asian and African Studies Reading Room at the British Library in London and the archivists at the National Archives in New Delhi were very helpful and supportive of the research that went into this book and remarkably patient with my many pesky questions. In addition, I want to thank Dr. Ron Sela at Indiana University for his help with Central Asian manuscripts, the Royal Society for Asian Affairs in London for allowing me access to their archives, Mr. Mohammed Khan in Abbottabad for his kind assistance with documents and sources, and Professor Omer Tarin for sharing his encyclopedic knowledge of Abbottabad and Hazara as well. Finally, I would like to acknowledge a British scholar who deserves recognition for her work on James Abbott. In the 1950s, British researcher and historian Evelyn Werge-Thomas (1891–1975) did extensive work organizing and cataloging the papers of James Abbott in the British Library and interviewed his last living descendant in 1958. I often felt like I was following a trail of breadcrumbs she left for me, and I am grateful for her scholarship.

Introduction

THE BRITISH EAST INDIA COMPANY'S RULE OVER INDIA CAME TO AN ignominious end immediately after what would be recorded in British history as the Great Indian Mutiny of 1857. "The Mutiny," as it was simply referred to by generations of Britons, was one of the most calamitous events in nineteenth-century British history. It was analogous in the Victorian world, in its level of public shock, policy consequences, and psychological impact, to the terrorist attacks of September 11, 2001, in the United States. Yet thirty years before 1857, when the British in India were more culturally attuned and better understood the contractual nature of the service of their soldiery, it could not have happened. Even before the guns of that terrible summer fell silent, historians began attempting to understand how such a thing became possible in such a short span of time.

James Abbott was an officer in the British East India Company's army, and he lived in British India throughout this entire period of history. He was a keen and sensitive recorder of everything around him, and he left behind more than ten thousand pages of observations of this era in his journals and papers. When interwoven with other primary source accounts and situated within the context of historical events, his observations shed new light on important questions about British life in India in the first half of the nineteenth century, the British East India Company, and the origins of the Great Mutiny itself.

What actually happened in the Bengal Presidency of the East India Company in the summer of 1857? How did matters come to this cataclysm of violence and hate? How was the nature of the British presence in the subcontinent transformed in a few decades from one largely of open curiosity, tolerance, and a remarkable degree of cultural assimilation in the 1820s to almost total cultural apartheid by 1860? Decades beyond the period of William Dalrymple's *White Moghuls*, Britons living in India were still adopting Indian architecture, diet, language, and often dress.

There are hundreds of oil and watercolor portraits from these decades depicting British residents of India going out of their way to appear to have fully assimilated into Indian culture, for example, and comparatively few that do not. From the indigenous perspective, from being seen broadly in the 1820s as rapacious but impartial tax collectors by the relatively small proportion of the peoples of India who actually came into contact with them, the British by 1860 were viewed almost universally with fear and animosity. The rebellion of 1857 marked the end of almost any meaningful cultural interaction between Britons and the people of India for the remainder of the colonial period. Cultural intermarriage was transformed from the norm in 1820 to a taboo in 1860, especially for the officer class. Perhaps most marked of all was the collapse of the military relationship between British officers and their Indian soldiery. Abbott's journals and papers lend a fresh perspective to the questions of how, why, and, importantly, when these extraordinary changes occurred.

The last forty years of British East India Company rule can perhaps best be understood as a collapse of trust in the compact between colonizer and colonized with its epicenter in the Bengal Presidency. (The Bombay and Madras presidencies were largely unaffected by the cataclysm in the north of the subcontinent.) The most common explanation for this collapse is that, beginning in the early 1830s, an influx of missionaries and British women into India gave rise to a narrative of social separation, and a combination of this new social distancing together with misguided legal and economic reforms led almost inevitably to violence. However, the archival record makes this superficial explanation unsatisfying. The reforms were initiated, certainly, but the archival evidence shows that they were not fully or even broadly implemented across the subcontinent by the time of the events of 1857. The number of missionaries and British women arriving in India did increase but overall remained small relative to the population. More importantly, the narrative of cultural separation that begins to be seen in the 1830s was largely just that—a narrative— and it was widely disregarded in practice. It is clear from Abbott's journals and other primary sources that few British men in India in the 1830s and 1840s were actually changing their private lives to reflect this new public discourse of separation—even if they publicly espoused it, and many did

INTRODUCTION

not. Indeed, the witticism that "necessity was the mother of invention and the father of the East" remained true in practice for a majority of Britons serving in India until well into the 1850s and, in many places, particularly Burma, a half century beyond that. Like latter-day "abstinence-only" sex education programs for teenagers, moralizing sentiments were largely a triumph of magical thinking over human nature and represent far more how some Britons wanted to be seen than they do historical reality. The voyage to India undertaken by tens of thousands of Britons was commonly understood, at least until the end of British East India Company rule, as a one-way trip. In a context in which fewer than one Briton in ten survived to return home,[1] many more men were clearly willing to risk the hypothetical social stigma resulting from relationships with Indian women than has generally been assumed to be the case.

This same disconnect between word and deed is also found in the broader interface of Britons and the peoples of India in the first half of the nineteenth century as well. In Abbott's observations and anecdotes, there is a dichotomy between the deteriorating public characterization of the peoples of India in the abstract and the maintenance of close personal friendships with Afghans, Punjabis, and Bengalis as individuals, who are still often described in highly positive terms. The incongruity between what many British officers said publicly in this regard and what they did is often striking. James Abbott's journals suggest that what happened during this period is far more nuanced and much more complicated than is commonly understood. In some cases the breakdown in trust was contested even as it was happening. And infused into this epic collapse of trust were evolving British notions of race, class, masculinity, and the role of gender—changes that influenced the trajectory of the growing doubt and distrust in sometimes obvious and sometimes subtle and less visible ways.

From the beginning of this period to the end, James Abbott was a prolific chronicler not only of his own life but of the people and events around him. The small mountain of journals, unpublished books, monographs, papers, letters, and files he left behind have gone largely unexamined since his death in 1896. Their contents provide both a trove of information about British life in India during this period and a timeline

INTRODUCTION

upon which to plot waypoints in the deterioration in the relationship between Britons in India and the subcontinent's indigenous peoples. Abbott himself often reflects the almost willful blindness of British East India Company officers to the reality of their own army, but his own responses to it were sometimes antithetical. During the forty years he was in India, Abbott continued to interact with the peoples of South Asia in ways that lay outside the growing narrative of segregation, often while also outside the regimental structure of the Bengal Army. His writing provides a perspective far more personal and candid than the typical published memoirs left behind by Indian Army officers of the "My Forty Years in India" genre because he never intended his journals for publication.

Abbott himself was an extraordinary character who did some truly remarkable things. He has never before been the subject of a biography. Contemporary British colonial historian John Kaye described him as "chivalrous, heroic, but somehow or other never thoroughly emerging from the shade."[2] This book is intended to correct that. In one sense, he already has: while many men played the Great Game in Central Asia in the nineteenth century and a great many more struggled to secure India's Northwest Frontier, it is James Abbott's name that lives on in maps of South Asia. At the suggestion of his friend, Herbert Edwardes, the administrative center that grew up around Abbott's base camp in the wilderness of the Hazāra District was named Abbottabad after he left, and it remains so today.[3] The current population is nearly one million. On May 2, 2011, Osama bin Laden was killed by US Navy SEALs in Abbottabad, briefly bringing Abbott's name back to prominence. Ironically, Abbott's last military campaign was against the first radical Islamist group in the Punjab, the so-called Hindustani Fanatics, who shared the same tenets of Islamic fundamentalism as bin Laden and the Taliban who sheltered him in Afghanistan.

James Abbott arrived in India at the end of the *White Moghuls* era and remained for a decade beyond the bloody and ignominious end of the East India Company. His first commander in India was a typical old Indian Army officer of the kind Lord Dalhousie recalled, from his days as governor-general between 1842 and 1844, as "old soldiers with

INTRODUCTION

a native family and half native habits."⁴ His commander smoked a hookah throughout the day in his office and almost literally thought of his sepoys⁵ as his children. By the end of the Great Mutiny thirty-five years later, Abbott would witness British officers striking high-caste Hindus with riding crops in the streets of Delhi. Between those two extremes, Abbott was an active participant in virtually every major aspect of the last forty years of East India Company rule. From the relatively minor sepoy mutiny at Barrackpore in 1824 to the Great Mutiny of 1857, from the siege of Bhurtpore to the First Anglo-Afghan War and both Anglo-Sikh wars, from the Great Game to the revenue settlement of the Northwestern states and the annexation of the Punjab, he was there, recording it all. James Abbott was almost certainly Britain's first guerilla leader. What really sets him apart from his peers, however, are his experiences in Central Asia as an ambassador to the Khanate of Khiva in the Great Game and later his service in the Hazāra District of the Punjab as a district commissioner. Abbott's tenure in the Hazāra in particular was highly unorthodox in the British experience in India. Far from being typical of the officers serving under Henry Lawrence in the Punjab, Abbott was extraordinary not merely among Lawrence's Young Men, as this group was called, but among officers in India in general. None of Abbott's fellow officers in the Punjab attempted to replicate his manner of living among the people, a lifestyle in which he assimilated almost completely into their culture and became known as the King of Hazāra. His unorthodox methods were downplayed to Calcutta by Henry Lawrence until Abbott, like Kurtz in Joseph Conrad's *Heart of Darkness*, became "unsound" and had to be removed despite his remarkable success at pacification.

At the same time that he was recording all he saw around him in his journals, many contemporaries, both British and indigenous voices, recorded their thoughts about and reactions to Abbott as he passed through their lives, providing an unusually reliable means of calibrating his recollections of events. This remarkably rich vein of documents—spanning more than forty years—has been mined for this book to reexamine how and why the relationship between Britons and the peoples of India deteriorated so rapidly between 1824, when Abbott arrived in Calcutta, and 1858, when the East India Company's role as the governing and administrative body for India came to its abrupt and brutal end. This book and Abbott's canon add to our understanding of the last forty years of the British East India Company in two important ways. First, the deterioration often presented in the history of British India as beginning in the late eighteenth century does not appear to have begun, as Abbott's journals demonstrate, to a significant degree until much later. Abbott's extensive observations of the society around him and the research that backs them up suggest that in reality this tragic breakdown occurred more rapidly and over a shorter period than is commonly thought. Nevertheless, by 1858 the assimilation into Indian culture seen in men like Sir David Ochterlony (1758–1825) and Major General Charles "Hindu" Stuart (1758–1828) at the beginning of Abbott's career in India was replaced by a stark, almost impermeable cultural and social barrier that never lifted again during Britain's rule in India.

Second, many of Abbott's observations of particular interest to historians of British India engage with the causation of the Great Mutiny of 1857, the event that brought about the end of East India Company rule. The broad and deep historiography of the Mutiny is the densest body of literature of any aspect of British India. It was the single most traumatic event of Britain's imperial history, and scarcely a year has passed since the events of 1857–1858 without the publication of another study or memoir about them. Yet all of these, when addressing the fundamental question of why the Mutiny happened, have examined virtually exclusively the social and cultural imperatives behind the rebellion from a civilian perspective. Within Abbott's writing lies an important and entirely new argument from a military perspective to be added to the well-known theories of causation, and few men could present better bona fides for putting it forward than James Abbott. He witnessed not one but three sepoy mutinies during his career, and he gave a great deal of consideration to all of them. His keen observations on the corrosive and ultimately fatal impact of the obscure military reforms instituted by Lord William Bentinck as governor-general of India in the 1830s on the good order and discipline of the Bengal Army are persuasive.

From a historian's perspective, the fact that much of the material for this book is derived from the extensive journals that Abbott kept during his career raises several issues. The keeping of such journals was commonplace in his time; yet, unlike many such diaries, his were written for his young daughter and never intended for a wider audience. The access records for most of the Abbott files mined for this study show that they had not been touched for more than a century. Historical sources must always be interrogated, and the question of the purpose of the writer always looms large in research. Thinking about his daughter reading his journals in the future, Abbott himself was not unaware of the question of objectivity. He wrote rhetorically in one early entry, "Who can reveal his secret thoughts without reservation? ... [I]f he reveals only those which will bear the test of light, he may be giving a false estimate of his character."[6] Yet a close reading of all of his journals together suggests that, as a source, James Abbott was a sensitive, candid, and accurate recorder of events, even when they reflected no credit upon himself.

The second problem endemic to his writings is that, like that of so many of the men of his era, Abbott's prose embodies the nearly universal and cloying dogmatism of this period that is so off-putting to the modern reader. As Walter Houghton notes, "Of all the Victorian attitudes the hardest for us to take is dogmatism,"[7] and Abbott's journals have no shortage of it. In reality, what Houghton observes as "the imperious pronouncement of debatable doctrines with little or no argument, the bland statement of possibilities as certainties and theories as facts, [and] the assertion of opinion in positive and often arrogant tones"[8] was simply the fashion of discourse of the day.

Overall, however, these disadvantages are offset by Abbott's truly extraordinary memory. His power of recollection of names and even mundane details of ordinary events beginning in his early school years was remarkable. Taken together, they provide a unique pathway into British colonial India in the first half of the nineteenth century, and the story they tell necessitates a reconsideration and perhaps a reevaluation of part of what has hitherto been accepted as canon about this period.

I

Beginnings

1807–1824

BEFORE THERE WAS AN EAST INDIA COMPANY, THERE WERE ABBOTTS in the East. From the late sixteenth century on, an intrepid British traveler in Damascus, Cairo, or Constantinople could expect to meet an Abbott as a prominent member of the expatriate merchant community.[1] One of the earliest, Morris Abbott, was among the founders of the Levant Company in 1581 and a lord mayor of London.[2] James's father, Henry Aloysius Abbott, was typical of this small world of adventurous British merchants. He was born in Constantinople to a British father and an Armenian mother and grew up on an estate in Ankara.[3] Frederik von Haven, a Dane, met them in 1761. "We again visited Mr. Abot [*sic*]," von Haven wrote, "another English merchant, whose wife is from Angora [Ankara] and speaks no other language than Turkish. But, on the other hand, her daughter, who is a renowned beauty, speaks all the other languages used in Constantinople."[4] When James's grandfather died of dysentery in 1773, James's father was sent to Aleppo to live with an uncle, one of about eighty Britons in the city.[5] Opportunities for trade were now in decline in the Levant, however, and when Henry was old enough, he decided to seek his fortune in India instead. In 1784, at the age of twenty, he arrived in Calcutta from Aleppo aboard the East Indiaman *Neptune* to set up his own business.[6] Within a decade he became one of the most prosperous merchants in Bengal, and by the 1790s, three Abbotts—Henry, his brother William, and their cousin Richard—were

Chapter 1

corresponding regularly from India with family members in Aleppo, suggesting a significant overlap between Levant Company and East India Company trading families.[7]

Henry was exceptional less in his rapid prosperity in India than in finding a British wife in Calcutta, as prior to the 1820s, there were few eligible British women in India. A third of all British men's formal wills in India between 1700 and 1775 left bequests to Indian women.[8] It may be assumed a great many more had Indian wives but died intestate or left no formal bequests. In 1794, at age thirty, James's father met and married Margaret Welsh. It was a socially savvy match for Henry and a prosperous one for Margaret. She was born in Edinburgh, the descendant on her mother's side of Sir William Gascoigne, which gave their children a remote claim to aristocratic ancestry. Although the era of the princely merchants in India was drawing to a close, the couple lived in opulence for eight years at the center of a wealthy social circle. They had had five children in India, three of whom survived, but when Margaret developed a liver problem in 1803, Henry determined to settle his affairs and move the family to England.

In 1804, when Henry was forty, they arrived in London, very wealthy but, as an Anglo-Indian family, socially unacceptable. He was hardly alone as a rich social outcast. All British merchants returning from India were a target of social ridicule and known collectively as "nabobs," a corruption of the Hindi word *nawab*.[9] As Tillman Nechtman notes, "By the second half of the eighteenth century, the term *nabob* had become a ubiquitous insult in Britain." James Abbott's father differed from most nabobs in that he was born in Turkey and went directly to India from there. Until his Scottish wife fell ill, it had been his intention to remain in the East his entire life, as eight generations of Abbotts before him had done. Most nabobs, however, set out from England to make a fortune in India and then return to England to spend it.[10] One wealthy India merchant, Joseph Price, wrote a pamphlet in 1783 reminding Britons that many nabobs were "English gentlemen, who have served the East India Company in Asia, and who, after a long course of years, have returned to spend the remainder of their days amongst their few surviving friends in their native country.... Not ten in the hundred ... return to their native country

Figure 1.1. Detail from the painting *Portrait of Henry Lannoy Hunter in Oriental Dress, Resting from Hunting, with a Manservant Holding Game*, by Andrea Soldi circa 1733–1736. Hunter, kneeling, was a Levant Company factor in Aleppo. His servant is Armenian. His daily attire suggests the degree of assimilation by Levant Company merchants into Ottoman culture. Andrea Soldi (c. 1703–1771) painted numerous portraits of British merchants during his travels before moving to London around 1736. (TATE, PURCHASED WITH ASSISTANCE FROM TATE PATRONS AND THE ART FUND 2004; PHOTO: TATE)

[prosperous] ... and not twenty in the hundred ... ever return at all."¹¹ But the plea largely fell on deaf ears. For the governing class of landed gentry, who saw Parliament as their private preserve, those nabobs in particular who sought seats in Parliament came in for special abuse.¹² At least a half dozen popular stage plays in London made villains or buffoons of Anglo-Indian characters, most notably Samuel Foote's *The Nabob*, which opened in 1776. "What is England now?" Horace Walpole lamented in a letter to Horace Mann in 1773. "A sink of Indian wealth, filled by nabobs, emptied by Maccaronis."¹³ The London newspaper the *Public Advertiser* compared them to common thieves.¹⁴ Britons like the Abbotts returning from India naturally expected to integrate themselves into the society of their native country, regardless of the land of their birth, and in this they were usually disappointed. Not a few were soon homesick for India. Most returned as single men; a few like Henry Abbott, lucky enough to find a British wife in India, returned with British families; and occasionally nabobs and military men returned to Britain with Indian wives and their children.¹⁵

Whether married or not, nabobs invariably brought quite a bit of India home with them, usually in the form of furniture, curios, and recipes.¹⁶ Those who tried to maintain their hybrid Anglo-Indian identities by continuing to wear Indian dress, for example, or by re-creating Indian architecture were the most criticized. But the stereotype of the vulgar nabob was generally greatly overstated. As Michael Edwards suggests, "On the whole, the nabobs were reasonably well-bred and neither boorish nor vulgar. This would not, in itself, have prevented British society from considering them inferior, because their fortunes had been made in trade, if nothing more dubious."¹⁷ It was not until James Abbott had been in India for fifteen years that popular opinion shifted enough to accept a sympathetic portrayal of a returning East India Company servant in *The Nabob at Home* by Mrs. Monkland.¹⁸ In this social climate, many, if not most, nabob families like the Abbotts found themselves living "a life between two worlds."¹⁹ There were some exceptions: William Makepeace Thackeray, for example, was born in India, the son of an East India Company official.

Figure 1.2. A detail from the background of a 1783 caricature by James Gillray lampooning Sir Thomas Rumbold, showing an English "nabob" riding an elephant atop a sack of "Roupees" while shaded by a servant with an umbrella. Thomas Rumbold was the governor of Madras from 1777 to 1780 and infamously corrupt. (YALE CENTER FOR BRITISH ART)

CHAPTER I

It is hardly surprising that Anglo-Indian families created their own social circles and were apt to cluster together geographically. P. J. Marshall notes, "In the early nineteenth century ... returned 'Indians' tended to try to counter their sense of being in a strange land by seeking out one another's company."[20] Abbott's journals bear this out. Literally all of his family's friends and acquaintances were also returnees from India. As a result, service and trade in India ran strongly in families because opportunities were far more readily available to young men with access to the patronage these social connections provided.

When the Abbotts entered Anglo-Indian social limbo in England, they first lived at a rented estate called Little Court in the village of Crawley, Hampshire,[21] southwest of London, but Henry soon bought a house in the Paragon, Blackheath, one of the clusters of nabob families in London, where James was born on March 12, 1807. Soon afterward, the family moved to a larger estate in Blackheath "with beautiful grounds in the same neighborhood."[22] Now forty-three, Henry entered into a business partnership with another Anglo-Indian, Martin Lindsay, which engaged, naturally, in trade with India, and soon his financial affairs were again prospering. Young James was born into the wealth and privilege of upper-middle-class England but excluded from upper-middle-class British society. It was a pampered life: his family engaged fifteen servants in Blackheath.[23]

His mother gave birth a total of twelve times in her marriage. Henry Jr., Clementina, and Margaret were born in India. Augustus was conceived on the long and arduous sea voyage home and was born the year the family arrived in London. Frederick was born a year and a half later. James, born in 1807, was the sixth surviving child in the family. He was followed by his sister Emma in 1808 and his brothers Saunders in 1811, Keith in 1814, and Edward in 1816. Only Margaret, who left India when she was three, and Henry, who left India at the age of eight, did not live in India as adults. Of the five boys who went back East, four of them, Augustus, Frederick, James, and Saunders, retired as generals in the British army. The youngest surviving son, Keith, entered the civil service instead and served as the British consul in Tabriz and Odessa before succumbing to disease in 1873.

The Paragon, Blackheath

Figure 1.3. Two images of the Paragon, Blackheath, where James Abbott was born and lived in his early childhood, as it appeared around 1840. The top image was first published by Rock & Co. in 1864. (TOP: LEWISHAM BOROUGH PHOTOS; BOTTOM: TOSHI HAYASHI)

CHAPTER I

One of James's earliest memories was of being taken into the parlor in Blackheath and lifted up to see images of India mounted on the walls. "These pictures were chiefly colored engravings of ... Calcutta and Madras," Abbott recalled. "One I well remember was a team of buffaloes tugging up a vessel above the sea shore and the figures of the buffaloes were a puzzle to me to the last."²⁴ The household was full of curios and relics from India, and another of James's early memories was of being allowed to handle some of the bows and arrows that adorned the walls.

His first seven years were spent on the estate in Blackheath. After his seventh birthday, like his older brothers Augustus and Frederick before him, James was sent off to boarding school, but unlike his brothers, who attended the prestigious Warwick School, James stayed close to home, and his education was more typical of East India Company officers. As Charles Trevelyan, who joined the East India Company in 1826 and later served as the governor of Madras, noted, "When families are assured of appointments for their younger members ... they are apt to consider it unnecessary to give them an expensive education; and ... the great majority [are] educated at cheap proprietary schools."²⁵ Such education was "characterized by a slavish devotion to the Classics and frequent recourse to the birch."²⁶ The headmasters of these schools were often unsuited to their occupation. The Reverend Charles Delafosse, Richard Burton later noted, "was no more fit to be a schoolmaster than the Grand Cham of Tartary."²⁷ Henry Lawrence recalled that he acquired no learning at school prior to entering the East India Company military seminary at Addiscombe "except a very little history and cyphering."²⁸

James was sent nearby to the Reverend John Potticary's school in Blackheath. He later recalled that "the plunge from the fond affection and tender care of [my] house to the heartless, coarse intercourse of so many young ragamuffins was most painful."²⁹ The schoolmaster, the Reverend Potticary, was a nonconformist. James disliked him intensely because he seldom, if ever, bathed. Anglo-Indian families generally adopted the Indian custom of bathing daily, and Potticary, like most Britons at the time, did so rarely.³⁰ Abbott thought him foul.³¹ Even worse were the tyrannical discipline and the split-and-bound wooden cane with which it was regularly enforced. The school was in fact an unusual choice for

Henry Abbott to make for his son, given his own staunch Anglican convictions. The school at 2–3 Eliot Place, Blackheath, had, among other pupils, several Quaker students and two Jewish boys, who received pastoral care from a visiting rabbi each Saturday.[32]

At school, too, James's associates were virtually all from Anglo-Indian families. Among them were the son of Colonel William Littlejohn of the Bengal Native Infantry; John Greene, the son of a Calcutta merchant; James Sanford, later a colonel in the Bombay Artillery; and the sons of Sir John Garner and Sir John Parnell.[33] Littlejohn and Greene were already friends of the family. So too was Amelius Bond, a nephew of the Abbotts' close friends, the Isaakes.[34] But Abbott recalled "the most remarkable of my schoolfellows was doubtless Benjamin Disraeli." It was a fateful crossing of the stars, because Disraeli and Abbott's reaction to him were to have enormous consequences in later years. Disraeli at the time was about four years older than Abbott:

> *a dark complexioned, vivacious, black-haired lad, full of pretension, with large wild eyes and features very dissimilar from those which appear in his after portraits . . . in person and disposition so like Lord Sothen Lemon, with whom I was afterwards at school, that I find it difficult to separate them in memory. Disraeli had pretensions to be a universal genius—his voice was loudest in every coterie—it mattered not what was the subject; he laid down the law confidently in every case, and being a lad of great talent [he] had considerable influence in all debates. . . . Disraeli slept in the same room with me. He possest . . . the delightful talent of improvising romances and fairy tales. He was a Londoner too and affected knowledge of all the arts which constitute young bucks in town. . . . [A]nyone who knew that he was heir to a fortune might have foretold his future eminence. . . . Disraeli, excepting his pervasive presumption which was offensive to a few, was generally popular without being much liked or respected.*[35]

James spent a considerable amount of his free time in the school library, where his favorite book was Christoph Christian Sturm's *Reflections upon the Works of God*, "a book which gradually interested me deeply and nourished my natural turn for reflection and self-examination."[36] Abbott recalled that he was not of a nature to be bullied: "I had no fear of bullying from any of nearly my own age or size, for my bodily powers were early developed and there was none of my own age who could run, leap, wrestle or box with me."[37] Here, in his recollections of childhood as seen from the age of fifty, are evident the two central pillars of his self-image in adulthood: a "natural turn for reflection and self-examination" combined with combativeness and athleticism—not a warrior poet but a poet warrior.

In 1818, when James was eleven, his family received two severe blows. The youngest child, Edward, died at the age of eighteen months. A few months later the brother of Henry's business partner absconded with £30,000 in negotiable bills from the firm and was never seen again. The loss of a child and a fortune at the same time was devastating. The company was prosperous enough that the loss of this huge sum alone would not have sunk it. However, news of the embezzlement leaked into commercial circles and triggered a run on the firm, which resulted in bankruptcy. It was a common fate of nabobs.[38] Financial ruin of overseas merchants was in fact so frequent an occurrence that a philanthropic organization, the Morden College at Blackheath, existed to help those ruined in the course of trade.[39] The Abbott's bankruptcy forced a dramatic change in their lifestyle. The Blackheath estate was sold, and the fifteen servants were found positions with other families. The Abbotts rented a house on the new and partly developed Euston Square.[40] That year James's older brother Augustus entered the East India Company's military academy at Addiscombe. Mrs. Abbott's sister-in-law, the daughter of an Indian princess and a British officer, came to live with her children in the small rental house as well. James was sent to Doctor Benson's school at Hounslow, a larger and less expensive institution that he greatly preferred over the Reverend Potticary's. "With all its evils of foul language and big oaths," he wrote, "there was a more manly spirit developed—greater justice in all affairs of the fist. There was no sneaking, no spying."[41]

In 1819 there was still worse to come. Henry fell ill while traveling to Marseille in search of business. His health declined, and he died in 1820

Figure 1.4. *A View of Dr. Benson's School at Hounslow*, an aquatint by J. S. Stadler done in 1804. It is interesting that the schoolboys are wearing military-style uniforms, which Abbott does not mention in his memoirs. (BRITISH LIBRARY BOARD)

at the age of fifty-six. The death of the family breadwinner as a cause of middle-class poverty was even more common than bankruptcy.⁴² Widows and orphans had little recourse but to fall back on friends and extended families. The Abbotts were taken in for a time by an old friend whom Henry had set up in business as an indigo planter in India, Mr. Maseyk, who was now retired in London. Mrs. Abbott then relocated the family to a village in Somerset.

The broader social safety net for most of the families of the middle classes, and especially for those in such dire circumstances, was patronage.⁴³ Orphans were among the most frequent beneficiaries. From 1810 to 1854, fully 25 percent of the cadetships to Addiscombe were awarded to young men whose fathers were dead.⁴⁴ Before Henry's death, the Abbotts secured places at Addiscombe for Augustus and Frederick via patronage, and Margaret Abbott did the same for her other sons afterward. The family's annual income was now reduced from around £4,000 at its peak in London to about £200. This was actually an average annual income for a middle-class family in England at this time, although entirely inadequate to maintain the Abbott's upper-middle-class pretensions.[45]

For middle-class families like the Abbotts, the options for genteel occupations were limited. In 1857, Henry Thompson identified just seven careers that were considered gentlemanly pursuits. The first three—the clergy, law, and medicine—required university degrees, which were beyond the means of the genteel poor. The fourth, a posting in the civil service, required political patronage, which was also generally beyond their reach. The remaining three genteel professions were the army, navy, and mercantile marine.[46] The purchase of a commission in the Royal Army was expensive, and an officer's salary was inadequate to cover his expenses, requiring private means to supplement his monthly pay. Families like the Abbotts needed a monthly cash inflow, not a monthly cash outflow. Commissions could not be bought in the navy and required patronage from within the Lords of the Admiralty. Thus, for most of the sons of the many bankrupt nabobs who swelled the ranks of the genteel poor, the only available avenue for retaining their status as gentlemen was a career in the East India Company.[47] For most it was a matter of making a virtue of necessity. Even for families like the Abbotts, with legacies in the East, India generally had little genuine appeal.[48] This dynamic had significant consequences in India itself, where East India Company officers were frequently "imbued with high notions of conduct and ignorant of the high ideals of imperial mission."[49] The same, however, might be said of anyone going out to India in the nineteenth century. Few men or women went to India purely for lofty imperial ideals. It was a place where a middle-class man might make enough money to retire upon or a middle-class woman might find such a husband. Almost no one went as a tourist or simply for the adventure of it.

The East India Company offered its officers a generous pension for life upon retirement, but it was a good bargain for the Company. A man had to serve twenty-two years in India to be eligible to retire,[50] and even by the sterner calculus of the nineteenth century, it was a harsh lottery. In 1838 it was reported that, not counting those still on active duty, only 10 percent of Company officers who had entered the service since 1760 had survived to collect their pensions.[51] The report, prepared by East India

Beginnings

Company agents Edward Dodwell and James Miles, makes for fascinating reading. There are several entries for "Killed in duel," "Cashiered by court martial," "Invalided in India," and "Died aboard ___" followed by the name of a ship inbound to or outbound from India. Battle casualties are indicated by the entry "killed at ___" followed by the name of the action, but these are comparatively few. One man, James Brooke,[52] was "struck off, December 13, 1827, having been absent more than five years in England," and one cadet "did not join but returned insane." But by far the most common is the melancholy entry "Died at ___" followed by the name of a place in India, indicating death by disease or accident.[53] The real graveyard of the British Empire was India, not Afghanistan.

Data are also available for the social backgrounds of Bengal Army officers at the time of Abbott's entry into East India Company service. Of the thirty-five hundred officers who served in the Bengal Army at some point from 1820 to 1834, the occupations of the fathers of approximately two thousand of them are listed in Major V. C. P. Hodson's *Officers of the Bengal Army*. About six hundred had fathers in India, of whom 90 percent served in some government capacity. Among the remaining fourteen hundred, half were sons of clergymen or military officers. The sons of merchants like the Abbotts accounted for 118 of the 2,000, or just 5.9 percent. The sons of clerks, farmers, craftsmen, manual laborers, and other nongentlemanly occupations accounted for only seventy-four officers, or 3.7 percent of the officer corps. An almost equal number came from the nobility and landed gentry, a total of seventy-eight officers, or 3.9 percent of the total. But many of these seventy-eight men were Irish and of considerably less financial worth than their English peers, and virtually all of them were the younger sons of the family. Thus it can be seen that fully 92 percent of East India Company officers came from the middle classes or the genteel poor.[54] About a quarter of East India Company officers were Scots.[55]

The low percentage of officers from working-class backgrounds reinforces the image of an army that cherished the perception of gentility in its officer ranks. But as P. J. Marshall notes, "To pass as a gentleman was not of itself a particularly exacting test in the eighteenth or early nineteenth centuries."[56] Often the only difference between officers and European enlisted men in the Bengal Army was a lack of access to patronage. Thomas Quinney, for example, who enlisted in 1826, found in the army a number of men who had been preparing at school for the study of law, medicine, or the divinity but who had lost all means of support and were forced into the army as a last resort—as indeed were most of their illiterate comrades.[57] Enlisted men in the Royal Army on rare occasions received commissions as officers for acts of great valor on the battlefield, but there is no evidence of this ever occurring in the East India Company Army.

Before his death, James's father had disapproved of the school at Hounslow as being too tolerant of ungodliness, so James transferred to the College School in Taunton, where he rose to the first class and won two prizes in the annual examinations. But the College School at Taunton proved to be no improvement over Hounslow in the godliness department. James found the behavior of the older boys there shocking, noting "the habits of some of the scholars, grown men of one and twenty years, were indecent and immoral beyond anything I had yet seen."[58] He remained at Taunton but a year before transferring to Monsieur Le Vapeur's school back at Blackheath to improve his mathematics.[59] This frequent changing of schools was common for middle-class boys, and East India Company cadets in particular were often "perambulated around different schools in the neighborhood of the metropolis" prior to their arrival at Addiscombe.[60] That year, Augustus passed his examinations for the artillery and sailed for India. At the invitation of family friends in Calcutta, their older sister Clementina went out to India with Augustus to find a husband.

Le Vapeur was French, and the entire course of instruction at the new school was in that language. James found nothing objectionable about the school.[61] Indeed, he took a liking to the eccentric Le Vapeur and recalled that he always pictured him in his mind when imagining the character of Baron Bradwardine in Sir Walter Scott's *Waverly*. Sundays back in Blackheath were depressing, however, as he was required to walk from the school to church past his old family estate.[62] This melancholy weekly ritual was compounded by the proximity to the first great love of his life, Laura Lucas, the daughter of a retired Indian Army surgeon and his former next-door neighbor. She was "a beautiful girl of about 12 years. Tall, finely formed, with beautiful features and large dark eyes—a complexion fair as the snow and a profusion of golden hair." In the manner of teenage boys, he could scarcely manage to speak to her on visits to the Lucas household. Looking back in the 1850s, Abbott observed, "As a consequence of this . . . I was loving a creature of the imagination [about] whose real character and disposition I knew almost nothing and of whose sentiments toward myself even less. . . . [T]his passion grew upon me to an absorbing degree which after preyed upon my spirits. When I left England it was at its highest. Laura . . . probably never suspected it, for before her I was utterly [insensible]."[63] Later, in India, he would have the initial *L* tattooed on his arm. He continued to idolize her from afar for nearly a decade before this first love eventually faded.

Abbott was a sensitive youth who loved reading and poetry and was more introspective than many young men his age. Like many of his fellow officers, he was quick to take insult, real or imagined, and had an exaggerated sense of injustice, which he often dwelled upon. These traits he carried into adulthood, where they landed him in official disapprobation more than once. There is no doubt he considered himself a gentleman and socially above the "lower orders." His descriptions of young men in the streets of Croydon, near Addiscombe, for example, make this explicit. There is an element of overcompensation in his emphasizing his station, and he clearly felt considerable insecurity in his social and financial status. This was almost ubiquitous among East India Company officers.[64] He described himself as shy but possessing inner strengths, "sensible . . . of powers which others did not guess."[65]

In regard to the opposite sex, as his relationship to Laura Lucas suggests, Abbott was also typical of many young middle-class boys of his era. Like virtually all of his contemporaries, he generally considered them unable to function physically or mentally in the male world outside the home.[66] As he did with Laura, Abbott described each woman he met first physically, usually in the order of her figure, her facial features, then her hair, and then rated her degree of refined manners, or "accomplishments." Those who were "fairy-like" he held in highest esteem. Abbott struggled to repress his sexual feelings, as is evident in his relationship in England with another family friend, Susan Sweeting, who was about twenty-five at the time. Of her, he wrote, "There are perhaps few ties so sweet as that which spring up at times between a boy of my age and a lovely woman many years his senior—Her presence is a source of continual inspiration to him. Without any of the fever which ordinarily marks the inter[action] of the sexes ... she is to him as a guardian angel from whose presence every evil passion and debasing thought takes flight."[67] Whether other young men of Abbott's era believed sex to be "debasing" and "an evil passion" is debatable, but the fact that Abbott himself did is clearly not. In contrast, with rare and important exception, the men whom Abbott met were evaluated first on the degree to which they had "proper feelings," then their courage, and finally their intellect, almost as if he were describing a different species altogether. There are few hints of sexual impulses in his journals, but he mentions several infatuations and relationships with women, most notably with Laura Lucas in Blackheath and later, in India, with his second cousin Marianne Abbott and his family friend Fanny de Burgh.

James Abbott's religious views were also typical of many East India Company officers—that is to say, old school Church of England of the early nineteenth century. The Anglican churches of Abbott's youth were austere places, "bare, depressing buildings, their former glories vanished, mutilated or neglected" in which "dust, dilapidation, and debris were everywhere."[68] Abbott, like his father, charted a middle course of austere religious belief between the "High Church," which leaned toward Catholic rites, and the "Low Church," which was the wellspring of nineteenth-century English evangelism. He harbored a lifelong disdain for both what he called the "Romish pretensions" of the High Church and the evangelism of the Low Church. Abbott held his faith to be a private matter between himself and God.

He was physically of compact and wiry build, but athletic, active, and sturdy. He never gained significant weight. Fevers and serious illness are mentioned only rarely in his journals. He early on had an abhorrence of alcohol and was a teetotaler all his life. The physical characteristics of a strong constitution and resistance to disease would stand him in good stead in India, as would his abstinence from alcohol, which in India contributed to the premature deaths of many.

Beginnings

Abbott remained at Le Vapeur's school somewhat less than a year, until in 1821, when, still fourteen, he followed Augustus and Frederick into Addiscombe. By 1821, the Addiscombe seminary's original enrollment of ninety cadets had expanded to 120. The sixty available cadetships each year were highly sought after. At that time, the school was still only for cadets seeking to become officers in the artillery or the engineers, as infantry officers were not then generally thought to require any military training.[69] The awarding of cadetships was a perquisite of the Board of Directors of the East India Company, and they were distributed almost solely by patronage.[70]

Childhood was a much shorter period of a person's life in 1820 than it is today, and in Britain in 1820, by the age of fourteen it was certainly over. Boys of twelve were regularly assigned as midshipmen in the Royal Navy. The age of consent in England for girls was twelve until 1878, when it was raised to thirteen, and it was not at all uncommon for girls of this age to be courted and even engaged. Thus Abbott's infatuation with twelve-year old Laura Lucas, his entry into Addiscombe at fourteen, and his commission at sixteen were very much the norm.

When James entered Addiscombe in 1821, his brother Frederick was in the upper class, and their cadetships overlapped by a full year. Upon arrival the cadet took an examination proctored by the headmaster to ensure he had at least the rudiments of an education. James was examined by the infamous Reverend Dr. James Andrews, the headmaster from the school's founding in 1809 until his forced retirement in 1823. A cadetship could provide a young man with an income for life and a fair chance of securing significant wealth in India if he survived, but its initial investment cost was considerable. Parents or guardians of cadets were required to pay £50 per term,[71] of which there were two a year, in addition to various ancillary expenses. As the Abbott family income was now in the range of £200 a year, the family clearly had assistance from relatives, perhaps James's paternal uncle William, lately returned from Madras, who is listed as his male next of kin on his cadet papers. Considering the mortality rates in India and the heavy debts acquired by officers early in their careers, return on this initial investment was long in coming for middle-class families, if indeed it ever came at all.

Together with general instruction in literature and the classics, the primary subjects taught were mathematics, fortification, topography, drawing, French, Latin, surveying, and Hindustani. Instruction in the last of these was weak at best, and few students thought it was sufficient. Orfeur Cavenagh attended Addiscombe in 1835 and recalled that the cadets "really learned little or nothing" of Hindustani.[72] Abbott entered Addiscombe in 1821, after the retirement of the Hindustani instructor Meer Hassan Ali, who was born in Lucknow and came to England in September 1809.[73] Ali, an excellent example of the counterflow of the peoples of India to Britain in this period, taught Hindustani at Addiscombe from 1810 to 1816, but he retired to Lucknow in 1817.[74] During Abbott's residence, Hindustani was taught by John Shakespear, who had composed the grammar of Hindustani in use at Addiscombe as a text but could not speak a word of the language. In 1844, a Muslim scholar traveling in England named Lutfullah met Shakespear and wrote, "I addressed to him a very complimentary long sentence in my own language. But alas! I found that he could not understand me, nor could he utter a word in that language in which he had composed several very useful books."[75] The quality of language instruction declined even further after Shakespear's departure in 1829, when the position was taken over by Charles Bowles, who was nineteen when he assumed the instructorship, had never been to India, and had never heard a word of Hindustani spoken.[76] Although officers were expected to become fluent in the language of their men upon arrival in India, the declining quality of instruction in Hindustani at Addiscombe did nothing to reduce the growing gap in the 1830s and 1840s between British officers and their sepoys. It is also suggestive of a growing attitude that nuanced communication with their soldiers was declining in importance.

Andrews, whom Abbott ironically describes as "a man of low birth and imperfect breeding,"[77] was a perennial source of cadet discontent and the villain of many contemporary memoirs of Addiscombe. By all accounts he was a martinet. James soon fell afoul of him, wrongly accused by a stable boy of mistreating a horse. He was given two days on bread and water in the "Black Hole," a repurposed pigeon coop. Andrews did not even question him on the matter before passing sentence, which inflamed Abbott's

Romantic sense of injustice and caused him to loathe the headmaster. "Dr. Andrews," he wrote, "knew not the nature of justice."[78] Justice was an objective truth for Abbott, and his exaggerated sense of it formed one of the central elements in his personality. When alloyed with the second element, the poet-warrior of his romantic imagination, this chivalric pursuit of "justice" forged in adulthood the knight-errant he always imagined himself to be.

James excelled in the nonmilitary subjects of literature and poetry. It was at Addiscombe that his love of poetry came into full bloom; his cadet years were marked by his first serious attempts at writing it. The two years passed without incident, with one important exception. He kept a small pistol at the school, which was strictly against standing orders, but which he carried for self-defense on walks in the hills. One evening there was a typical fracas with some local men. Eager for relief from the tedium of the school, James joined the cadets who turned out for it. In the melee, Abbott pointed his pistol at two local farmers armed only with pitchforks. They backed down. Afterward he was mortified that he might have shot at the men, which would have ended his career before it began, but his habit of keeping arms close at hand saved his life more than once in India.

The most important aspect of his cadetship was the friendships made there, which were of far more consequence in India than they were at Addiscombe. In a school so small, virtually all the cadets knew one another. Each gained a reputation that followed him for years. At Addiscombe, Abbott first came to know the two men who were to have the greatest impact on his life, D'Arcy Todd and Henry Lawrence, who thirty-five years later would pass into Victorian legend in the epic defense of Lucknow. It was Todd who would send him to Khiva and Lawrence who sent him to the Hazāra, the two most important periods in his life.

Abbott recalled that he was not very close to either man during his cadetship but knew both well enough to establish a relationship and make an impression that never faded. He remembered candidly that Lawrence "did not excel at anything in particular" at Addiscombe. "Few would at the time have credited any prophecy of his future greatness," Abbott recalled, but "the honesty of Pat [Henry] Lawrence was proverbial.... [H]is love of truth was extraordinary."[79] Most endearing to the like-minded Abbott was Lawrence's "extraordinary enthusiasm for poetry, especially of the romantic kind."[80] It was this shared love of Romantic poetry that would bring them together again on the march to Kandahar in 1839 and cement their friendship for the future.

At Addiscombe, too, lay the roots of his intense friendship with D'Arcy Todd, which lasted until Todd's death. It was to be the greatest friendship of Abbott's life. Here again, the two men knew each other, but because they were in different years (Lawrence was in the class senior to Abbott, Todd in the class junior), they did not move in the same groups. Todd struck Abbott as quite young in appearance, and he wrote in the 1850s,

> *He was at that time and for several years afterwards remarkable for a beauty which was quite feminine—His stature was that of a child—His complexion the most beautiful possible—He had delicate features and large blue eyes shaded with long black lashes.... He had altogether the air and manners of a child and was a kind of pet in his class. I did not like him much at that time, nor probably should we ever have been intimate,*[81] *had not similarity of sentiments united us—He was quick and clever—but not otherwise remarkable—After he had been in India two years, all his delicacy of appearance disappeared and his person was remarkable only for his very gentlemanly appearance and intellectual expression.*[82]

In June 1823, Abbott passed for the artillery and returned to his mother's cottage in Somerset. Cadets were normally granted as much as six months leave in England after graduation, depending on the needs of the service and the season of the year.[83] However, Frederick, who graduated a year before James, was sent after his six-month leave to a six-month course at Chatham Depot, where the East India Company had a base on the Thames estuary. Frederick was now due to embark for India. Their mother decided that James's own leave would be shortened to just a few weeks so that he and Frederick could sail together. Their sister Emma, a year and a half younger than James, was invited to Calcutta to join Clementina, and she accompanied her two brothers on the voyage. Given the cost, risk, and duration of a sea voyage to India at that time, the intent was clearly that Emma should remain in India to find a husband. Such young women sent out to India with chaperones by Anglo-Indian families to find suitable husbands were mockingly referred to as the "fishing fleet"; those who came home unmarried were cruelly dubbed "returned empty."[84] Emma was unsuccessful; she died in England in 1875 having never married.

The portrait that emerges of James Abbott on the verge of sailing for India is thus typical of generations of East India Company Army subalterns in the early nineteenth century. He came from the English middle classes, distinctly a plural concept in English society at this time with many subtle striations and substrata.[85] Like many, his family was thrust into the ranks of the genteel poor by bankruptcy in trade and the death of his father. It was a family with broad and deep connections to the East India Company and ample access to its patronage. James was painfully aware of his poverty and his fragile and attenuated claim to gentility. His family's centuries-long heritage of marriage to Greeks, Italians, and Armenian Turks remained hidden, but his poverty was made worse by his roots in trade and especially in Anglo-Indian nabobery. All of this imbued him with a deep and lasting insecurity typical of his peers.

He was typical, too, of a segment of the "lower upper middle class,"[86] as George Orwell later phrased it, in his Church of England religious beliefs, his awkwardness around women, and his prudery about sex. He was fluent in French, remarkably well versed in the classics, and could read Latin and Greek texts in the original. He was more introspective, perhaps, than most subalterns in the East India Company Army, as fond of the Romantic corpus of Sir Walter Scott as any, and more interested in poetry as a means of expressing the lofty feelings and sentiments that he believed marked a gentleman than all but a few. What set Abbott apart as he prepared to embark for a lifetime in India was the way in which all these factors combined to produce a self-image of a real-world knight-errant. Like a majority of his peers, he was a young man channeled into life in the East by financial necessity and a dearth of options, but his internal compass was guided by notions of medieval chivalry and a deeply held Romantic and moralistic sense of "doing right," which he would never outgrow.

James, Frederick, and Emma boarded the East Indiaman *Mary* in September 1823 and set sail for Calcutta. For James it was not a happy event. Although the die was long since cast, he was having second thoughts about a lifetime away from England and Laura Lucas. Looking back thirty-five years later, he recalled, "I felt that I was departing into perpetual banishment. The fame,[87] the fortune, which others looked to win in the far East were not for me. I entered the vessel that was to bear us away as a living man might walk into his grave."[88] There was a 90 percent chance he was doing just that.

2

Baptism of Fire

1824–1826

THE *MARY* WAS A SMALL EAST INDIAMAN OF 570 TONS[1] WITH A CARGO of 100 tons of spelt.[2] The Abbotts traveled together with another artillery cadet, Ambrose Carden, and his sister Suzanne, who, like Emma, was bound for India to find a husband. In 1823 the voyage took about six months, depending on the winds, sailing south around the Cape of Good Hope and then onward across the Indian Ocean. The vessels were generally three-masted ships of between five hundred and one thousand tons.[3] The parents or guardian of each cadet were required to pay for his passage, which in 1823 cost approximately £110, a significant sum of money, equivalent in 2020 to at least £10,190.[4] The cadet's date of rank as an officer began with the date of his commission, which was important because promotion was based upon it, and this occurred on arrival in India. The sooner a cadet reached India, the sooner he got in the long queue for promotion. In addition, his pay and allowances did not begin until he set foot in India. This clever accounting device enabled the Company to avoid paying nearly half a year's salary to men of no use to it while they were floating on the ocean. It also meant that cadets needed to take with them either sufficient cash or letters of credit to have some means of support until they began receiving their pay.

Chartered ships like the *Mary* had one major advantage over Company-owned ships in that each traveler had a very small private cabin. On some ships, two passengers shared a room. On a Company ship,

CHAPTER 2

Figure 2.1. *An East Indiaman Reefed Down and Riding Out the Gale*, by William Adolphus Knell (1805–1875), oil on canvas. In the 1820s the passage to India was long and dangerous. (WIKIGALLERY)

however, each cadet was only given a hammock and allocated a tiny space in the steerage compartment scarcely larger than the hammock itself. This advantage of chartered ships was well known.[5] As Frederick and James were traveling with their fourteen-year-old sister, Emma,[6] passage on a Company ship under such sleeping arrangements was out of the question, even if, as a family steeped in trade with the East, they had not been well aware of the advantage of having a private cabin at the same cost.

By 1823, when James, Frederick, and Emma sailed for India, the six-month ordeal was somewhat safer than it had been in Clive's day. Prior to the nineteenth century, without the means to calculate longitude, mariners navigated the vast ocean distances between England and India largely by guess and by God. The invention of the first reliable ship's clock by English horologist John Harrison in 1764 and the subsequent development of the mathematical tables necessary to make the complex sextant reductions at last made the calculation of position at sea possible to within ten miles. By the last decade of the eighteenth century, almost all ships plying the waters to India possessed the means to calculate their positions with far more precision than ever before.

Nevertheless, both the crew and the passengers well knew there was still considerable danger from storms, reefs, and piracy. For some travelers, like Lady Eden,[7] who sailed to India in 1836, the greatest additional discomfort was the exhaustion of the coffee and orange marmalade supplies. Others were not so lucky. Many ships foundered in storms or broke apart on poorly charted reefs and shoals. In February 1805, the *Earl of Abergavenny* ran aground off Portland Bill and foundered with the loss of 263 lives out of 402 people onboard.[8] The *Arniston* was wrecked off the coast of South Africa in 1815 with the loss of 372 lives[9]; there were six survivors. In the year between December 1, 1827, and November 30, 1828, the East India Company lost twenty-one officers at sea in transit to India from various causes, a number equivalent to one-third of all the new officers to graduate from Addiscombe during that period. Some ships simply disappeared without a trace, like the 528-ton *Guildford*, which vanished in the Indian Ocean in January 1831.[10] In 1825 the East Indiaman *Kent* caught fire, blew up, and sank in the Bay of Biscay with the loss of eighty-one crew and passengers. There were a number of other spectacular shipping losses in the early nineteenth century, and as late as 1852, the wreck of the troopship *Birkenhead* while rounding the cape took the lives of 450 men, a reminder that a ticket to India was no guarantee of arrival.[11]

Death at sea from disease was commonplace. When Agnes Rankin went out to India in November 1799 aboard the East Indiaman *Charlton*, she had as fellow passengers 130 officers and men, 12 lascars, 9 ladies, 9 gentlemen, 31 cadets, 50 soldiers, 3 enlisted soldier's wives, 3 female servants, and 2 male servants, one of whom was a Bengali named Sabdi who worked for her husband George, the surgeon of the 5th Bengal Native Cavalry, altogether 249 persons.[12] Sixty-six of them died of scurvy.[13] The *Charlton* was subsequently captured by French frigates in 1809, another danger of trooping to India.[14] During times of war with the French, East Indiamen were fair game, and for this reason, all East Indiamen were armed. But even in peacetime, the sighting of another ship at sea was cause for alarm.[15] Piracy was not unknown, and fear of it added to the anxiety of the voyage.

Even under the best conditions, the journey was not pleasant. The East Indiamen were built for speed, not comfort. When new and at dockside, a sailing ship has a strong smell of pitch, salt water, and wet hemp. But at sea near the equator, after several years of service, with the added smell below decks of bilge water, livestock, and dozens of men living in close quarters, some of whom were seasick or suffering from dysentery, the smell was stupefying. Just floating dockside, James Abbott recalled, the smell of the bilge was "utterly sickening."[16] The food consisted mostly of salted beef and hard biscuits, which in their wooden crates were difficult to keep from infestation by weevils. Fresh water was rationed, and a luxury like washing laundry with fresh water was out of the question— hence the need for the great many changes of undergarments recommended in *The Cadet's Guide to India*. The fresh water went putrid in a month or two in its wooden barrels, encouraging many among the officers to avoid it completely in favor of wine and spirits. Additional fresh water could only be obtained by making port or capturing rainwater with rigged canvas. On the *Mary*, rats gnawed into many of the water barrels early in the voyage, rendering that water no longer potable, and the water ration aboard was even further reduced.

Then there was seasickness. A ship at sea moves on three axes: the side-to-side motion is "roll," the front-to-back motion like a rocking horse is "pitch," and the motion around the vertical axis, like the spinning of a compass pointer, is "yaw." While the immense weight of a modern cruise liner mitigates roll, pitch, and yaw, in a small wooden sailing ship they were pronounced and continuous. In any kind of severe weather, the effect was not unlike being inside a can and shaken. Even for experienced sailors the effects were uncomfortable. For men and women who had never been to sea before, they were often debilitating. Some eventually found their "sea legs"; others were confined to their quarters for virtually the entire voyage. Abbott recalled "the *Mary* was the friskiest of the frisky—she pitched until she seemed plunging head foremost to the bottom—She rolled until we thought she had reached her beam ends. She was never quiet—always oscillating like a pendulum.... [T]his was at

Figure 2.2. The bunk beds in a typical two-person cabin on an East Indiaman, seen in the restoration of the East Indiaman *Friendship*, usually docked at the Salem Maritime National Historic Site in Massachusetts. In reality, the cabins were never this well lit, as they were normally illuminated only by a lantern. (PHOTOGRAPH BY AUTHOR)

first very trying to the inner man."[17] Suzanne Carden and cadet Albert Hervey were among those who spent nearly the whole six months confined to their beds. "I suffered horribly from sea sickness," wrote Hervey. "I really thought I should have died."[18]

Nor were the threat of shipwreck and piracy, the ever-present stench, the oppressive equatorial heat, the inability to bathe (even if one were so inclined), the bad food, the lack of fresh drinking water, and the ship's constant motion the only sources of discomfort. There was also the unrelenting boredom of endless hours with no means of communication with the outside world and very limited possibilities for entertainment (reading exacerbates the disequilibrium of the inner ear that causes seasickness). However bad the conditions were for the higher classes of passengers and the ship's officers, they were considerably worse for the crew and any troops traveling below decks. Unwise ship captains often made life at sea even worse by imposing unnecessarily severe discipline on the crew. The captain of a ship at sea was virtually a king. He could not order executions, but beyond that his power was almost unlimited. Arrest in chains, reduction of rations, and flogging were all well within his authority. Because life at sea was grim at best, the men who took to it were generally a rough lot, and many had little left to lose. As army Captain Thomas Williamson noted in 1810, on an East Indiaman it was normal to have a "crew composed of all nations, and often including the most hardened and daring culprits."[19] Floggings were common. Cadet Albert Hervey saw several on his voyage to India.[20] This form of punishment in particular was unpopular, to say the least, and not infrequently led to mutiny. Such was the case on the *Mary*, where Captain Ardley ordered three floggings, each time resulting in an angry reaction from the crew. The young James Abbott, however, found it a great adventure:

> *The crew were unruly and when the captain ordered a man . . . to be flogged they rushed forward with one accord, knife in hand to cut him down—The captain and mates and purser met them sword in hand, and Frederick and myself followed the example. I was delighted to draw out my new sword. It was an exciting spectacle. The captain . . . had sprung upon a pile of cables close to the prisoner and stood with his saber brandished over his head. The purser . . . stood in the midwaist with a cocked pistol presented in [each] hand. . . . The men, 30 in number, a ragged unwashed crew, brandishing knives and marlinspikes and such . . . were wise enough to see that armed as we were they had no chance of success and after much excitement the punishment was carried out.*[21]

In his interactions with the officers and crew of the *Mary*, Abbott's class consciousness and insecurity about his social status were often evident. As his bedside copy of *The Cadet's Guide to India* made clear, under no circumstances was a cadet to associate with the crewmen. "The officers and midshipmen . . . are gentlemen with whom the cadet may freely associate," it advised, "but with the petty officers of the ship,[22] [such] as [the] master-at-arms, carpenter or boatswain, he must avoid all intimacy. . . .

On board licensed ships it frequently happens that the mates have been common sailors, and are consequently unfit society for cadets, but occasionally they are gentlemen who have served in King's or Company's ships as officers."[23]

In the early nineteenth century, the relationship between a gentleman and the "lower orders" was peculiar, to say the least. The author of *The Cadet's Guide* was at pains to point out that his "observations are not intended to sanction pride or assumed consequence, than which nothing is more contemptible, on the contrary, they recommend a pleasant condescending civility as due to every man."[24] In other words, a gentleman did not take obvious pride in being a gentleman, and to affect an air of superiority was contemptible: in Abbott's day a gentleman was to simply exist in the *state of being a gentleman* without apparent arrogance or incivility. Not all succeeded. Sailors and enlisted men were often well aware of the artificial nature of this contrived and frequently flimsy social segregation. Staff Sergeant John MacMullen, for example, an Irish soldier in H.M. 13th Light Infantry, advised potential recruits, "You will have to listen patiently and silently to the contemptuous remarks of a man who, very probably, is your superior only because his father was fortunate in trade and therefore able to pay 450£ for a commission for his son; who has in turn learned to . . . say ''pon his honour,' and look down on you with all the quaint consequence of little-mindedness as a being of an inferior species."[25]

However, while MacMullen and others rejected the notion that the tradesman's son with a purchased commission was superior to a man in lesser circumstances, few rejected the architecture of class itself or its consequences. MacMullen was aware that a man's occupation was one of the chief determinants of social class. He and others accepted not only that the classes themselves were clearly defined but also that the social relationships between them were equally so. He acknowledged as a matter of course that interactions between the classes were rigidly codified, even among friends and acquaintances: "I felt unusually sad on bidding some old and valued friends adieu the evening prior to my departure. The reflection too that I could no longer have intercourse with them on terms of equality as hitherto, was productive of additional pain. I had sunk from their level in society ... and an insuperable bar was placed between our future associating, according to the conventional usages of the world."[26]

MacMullen's account of the barrier between officer and enlisted man and between enlisted man and civilian friends resulting from occupation supports historian David Cannadine's argument that the British in India readily embraced the caste system they found there because many of its social features seemed similar to their own class system in Britain. It was familiar, it was easy to understand, and it meshed exactly with what Mac-Mullen called "the natural usages of the world." Cannadine's contention that the relationship between colonizer and colonized in India at the time of Abbott's arrival was principally based not on race but on class derived from occupation (i.e., a British interpretation of caste) is supported by some of Abbott's observations on the matter. Race per se was not yet a well-developed sensibility in the 1820s.[27]

The Cadet's Guide identified the first mate of a vessel, the captain's right-hand man, as acceptable company, and aboard the *Mary* Abbott struck up an acquaintance with the first mate, "a very noble fellow named Tapley."[28] As he had with his pistol at Addiscombe, Abbott took the precaution of arming himself with a homemade knife. On one occasion, Abbott came to Tapley's aid when a crewman named Neagle drew a knife of his own on the first mate, for which Neagle was later flogged. In his friendship with Tapley, Abbott made an interesting and important distinction between birth and behavior. He focused on "thoughts and feelings," or what he called "sentiments." "Tapley," thought Abbott, "was every inch a sailor and although I believe his birth was somewhat humble, he had the finest and highest sentiments of the Gentleman. I felt a very great regard for him."[29] Here Abbott subtly but perceptibly widens the spectrum of the acceptable origins of gentlemen to include those which were "somewhat humble," although not those from the "lower orders," by emphasizing the refinement of a man's "sentiments." In truth the only real difference between Abbott and MacMullen, both of whom were well educated and the victims of bankruptcy in trade, was that Abbott's family had sufficient patronage in the Anglo-Indian community to secure him an appointment to Addiscombe and MacMullen's did not.

While Tapley was considered by Abbott among the ranks of gentlemen both because he possessed the "finest and highest sentiments of the Gentleman"[30] and his position as first mate, an ordinary member of the crew who possessed the same "high sentiments" would not have been considered a gentleman. Genteel status was a hybrid calculus. Much of what could be said about Tapley could as easily be said of Abbott himself, the partly Armenian son of a nabob with negligible financial means and only the remotest connection to British gentry. Abbott emphasized the intellectual component of gentility while deemphasizing the social and financial aspects. Although he was now on the cusp of being a commissioned officer, he still felt his strongest claim upon being a gentleman lay in having the proper *sentiments* of a gentleman, which he assiduously cultivated. As a result, however, Abbott frequently demonstrated "the self-made man's exaggerated respect for wealth and privilege."[31]

The humbler origins of many East India Company officers were frequently alluded to as a mark of social inferiority by Royal Army officers in India. For Royal Army officers, sufficient accumulated wealth to purchase an officer's commission and maintain oneself as an officer was the most important manifestation of class and status as a gentleman. Yet occupation too, which correlated to some extent with caste as Hindus in India understood it at that time, also remained a critical component of social status. Thus being a "gentleman ranker" meant being a former gentlemen who *became* a ranker, not a ranker who was a gentleman. These were mutually exclusive, as MacMullen makes clear. A hypothetical private soldier who was independently wealthy would not have been a gentleman as a consequence of his occupation. But on the rare occasion when an enlisted man was promoted from the ranks to a commission without purchase, regardless of his financial means, he immediately *became* a gentleman. In such a case, Abbott could not have associated with him one day and the next day he could. On the other hand, real snobs like Lord Cardigan of Light Brigade fame held that merely setting foot in India disqualified a man from being a gentleman.[32] Thus, the concept of gentility in Abbott's day had some *external* coherence, but internally it was inchoate, debatable, and fluid, a complex and shifting formula of education, wealth,

Figure 2.3. *Indian Army Officer*, oil on wood painting by William Havell (1782–1857) in 1822. Havell worked as a painter of portraits and landscapes in Calcutta from 1817 to 1825. The original image measures just eleven inches by thirteen inches. (READING MUSEUM, READING BOROUGH COUNCIL)

occupation, family heritage, personal behavior, and even geography. It did not, however, require the ownership of land.[33]

Aboard the *Mary*, Abbott also demonstrated a disregard for such social conventions, the first signs of an iconoclasm that would later mark his career in India. One of the ordinary crewmen was a lifelong sailor beyond middle age named Monday. Abbott recalled, "He was an old whaler and used to harpoon with great skill and effect—I spoke much to this man about the wild profession in which he had passed his youth." Abbott found him "sensible and well informed," an observation that suggests something unexpected in the "lower orders."[34] Nevertheless, by striking up an acquaintance with a crewman, which, according to *The Cadet's Guide*, was beyond the pale for a gentleman, Abbott showed a willingness to flout some social conventions when it suited him. In his relationship with Monday, Abbott's insecurity did not overwhelm his intellectual curiosity about whaling and life at sea in the eighteenth century. Monday was a trove of old sea stories and nautical lore, and Abbott greatly enjoyed their conversations.

Despite such acquaintances and the rumblings of the surly crew, "the voyage was a very weary one."[35] He at least had his brother and sister on board to pass the long, tedious hours underway. Apart from two days at Tenerife, the entire six months were spent at sea. The most significant event was a storm that caught the *Mary* during her Indian Ocean transit. The waves were so high and the roll of the *Mary* so great that the boom ends of the main mast dipped into the water on each roll. When a mainstay snapped, two of the ship's three masts broke apart and fell into the sea next to the ship in a tangle of cordage, timber, and canvas. This acted like a sea anchor, rapidly pulling the *Mary* hard over to such an extent that she was in danger of capsizing. Only the one hundred tons of spelt deep in the hold as ballast kept her from going over. As it was, pigpens, chicken coops, and bottle bins broke loose on deck, adding panicking birds, squealing pigs, and broken glass to the pandemonium in the darkness. As the crew were always barefoot, the glass slashed their feet and incapacitated many. Abbott recalled, "The confusion and uproar baffled description. . . . No man was killed by the fall of the masts nor in the perilous [efforts] made to clear the rigging . . . [but] for some time, the ship was in considerable danger for much sail had been set . . . and the foremast very nearly followed the others. At length the ship was freed from her broken masts and rigging and became again manageable."[36]

Chapter 2

With no choice but to continue under reduced sail, the *Mary* limped across the remainder of the Indian Ocean toward India. Finally, after six months at sea, land birds were sighted, and several alighted on board. A hawk and a hoopoo[37] were so tired the crew managed to catch them alive. "The next symptom of land, observed about 3 days sail from the sand shoals," Abbott remembered, "was a romantic scent which I have since observed in forest land in India."[38] Finally the sand heads of the Hooghly River and the coast of India hove into sight.

In an age before photographs, television, and film, nothing could begin to prepare a Briton for his first contact with India. Most cadets were from families with some connection to the subcontinent; not a few had been born there. But children were usually "sent home" to England when they were five or six, and only a few had any memories of India. All cadets had read stories, listened to accounts of tiger hunts, and heard wildly exaggerated tales from older boys at Addiscombe about nautch dancers,[39] but a young lifetime of exposure to the lore and foods of India while still in England could not lessen the sensory overload that came with stepping ashore for the first time.

Leaving Emma and Suzanne with Suzanne's brother to continue aboard the *Mary* up the Hooghly to Calcutta, James and Frederick went ashore by local dinghy to make the trip alternately on foot and by small boat. Looking back from the 1850s, Abbott recalled,

> *Every thing was very strange to me at first, some things sufficiently astonishing. As this is not written for Indians I will endeavor to give my first impressions. The first of these [is] the boatmen who came to the ship's side at the sand heads with fruit and various articles of merchandise. Were these indeed men? They were almost naked with black shining skins and yet as Maria Graham naively observed "there was no sense of indecency in their nakedness—One felt quite at home with them as if they were clad." They were indeed in the fullest dress; a complete suit of black—But they were such dark delicate, effeminate looking creatures, some looked like young girls. Was all India peopled by a race so degenerate? We embarked in one of their dinghies. . . . [I]t was made of planks most artfully clinched together by flat nails . . .*

forming perfect seams. Ridiculous as was its figure, there could be no doubt that the carpentry was extraordinary for a people so backward in civilization as to be without breeches or shoes.[40]

Maria Graham, whom Abbott quotes, was a Scottish author of travel and children's books. She married a Scottish naval officer, Thomas Graham, in India in 1809 and published her first book, *Journal of a Residence in India*, after their return to London in 1811.[41] Abbott's quotation is a paraphrasing of Graham's observation: "For the most part they wear nothing but a turban, and a cloth wrapped round the loins, a degree of nakedness which does not shock one, owing to the dark colour of the skin, which, as it is unusual to European eyes, has the effect of dress."[42] A very similar reaction was recorded by John MacMullen, who wrote, "Ladies, in most cases are very much shocked when they suddenly find themselves among them. Habit, however, and the dark skin of the natives soon enables them to look upon the latter with the most perfect nonchalance."[43] Seeing his first indigenous boat crew, Bishop Reginald Heber also noted, "The crew were chiefly naked, except a cloth round the loins; the colour of all was the darkest shade of antique bronze, and together with the elegant forms and well-turned limbs of many among them, gave the spectator a perfect impression of Grecian statues of that metal.... The second observation was how entirely the idea of indelicacy, which would naturally belong to such naked figures ... if they were white, is prevented by their being a different colour from ourselves."[44]

This trope—that indigenous peoples were not nearly naked because of their skin color—is a fascinating ad hoc European improvisation to reconcile their own moral values about "nakedness" with the reality of local culture. Skin color became the modality of adaptation. It was essentially admiring the emperor's new clothes because the emperor had dark skin.

The Hooghly delta was prone to flood, and its frequently shifting banks were devoid of anything but scrub and reeds. The brothers found nothing of interest along the way, walking by day and sleeping on the boat at night. James found the boat quite comfortable and admired it:

Chapter 2

Figure 2.4. "A View of a Local Boat on the River Hooghly Near and to the North of Calcutta 1875," by an unknown photographer. This traditional watercraft is similar to the one James Abbott and his brother hired to get to Calcutta in 1824 after arriving in India. (PUBLIC DOMAIN)

> *This boat, too, rude as it was, afforded shelter which our boats . . . can rarely boast. Frederick and I spread out ship's cots upon the deck beneath the awning of bamboo and could bid all weather defiance. . . . [W]e found that whatever the advantages of civilization, the savage has at least that of independence. . . . [O]ur boatswain lighted an instantaneous fire, and with two earthen gourds for cooking pots had soon made . . . an excellent fish curry; the rice being cooked as no English cook can dress it in one pot and shoes[45] of fish and slices of a radish in the other with green and red chilies, turmeric and kala-jerie[46] in due proportions. So we dined and went to sleep under these strange conditions, serenaded all night by the yells of jackals. It was a new and strange taste of life and not disagreeable.*

Because these are recollections of impressions formed thirty years previously, it is impossible to say with any certainty that they were not influenced by his evolving attitudes over the passage of time. In them are found, however, many of the common first British reactions to India. Certainly the reference to the "effeminate" appearance of the Bengali workers was influenced by the rising trope of the "effeminate Bengali" in the 1830s and 1840s and was likely applied retroactively to this memory. This cliché was present in British commentary on the people of India before Abbott's arrival, but it really began to rise to prominence, and later general acceptance in the 1830s, with the writings of Thomas Macaulay, who used the "effeminacy" of the Bengalis largely to justify British dominion over Bengal.[47] Its appearance in Abbott's description of his arrival in India in 1824 may be taken to be influenced by attitudes developed among British officers in the intervening thirty years before these "memories" were first put to paper.

There is overall a sense of a young man enjoying an adventure with his brother, coupled with the alertness to a new environment common to the first weeks of cultural immersion. Abbott clearly had prior experience with the curries served on their boat. He did not, however, see the obvious connection between the barefoot English crew of the *Mary* and the barefoot Bengali boat crews below Calcutta, although the journal entries are only pages apart. Although the *Mary*'s crew was "ragged," barefoot, and certainly unwashed, they are not described as "backward" by Abbott (although they are certainly of the "lower orders"), while the Bengalis are "backward" despite undoubtedly being much cleaner, better mannered, and more refined people. The conviction that England and Scotland were at a higher level of civilization than India was an article of faith among Britons in the nineteenth century.

Upon arrival in Calcutta, the Abbott brothers were assigned quarters in Fort William and given the standard thirty days to equip and accustom themselves. They met for the first and last time their second cousin, John Abbott, son of their grand-uncle John. James also met up again with Eliza Scott, who had been his playmate in London in his early childhood. His description of her is a typical example of his formula for feminine depiction:

Figure 2.5. An illustration titled "A Dandy or Boatman" by Frans Balthazar Solvyns from *A Collection of Two Hundred and Fifty Coloured Etchings: Descriptive of the Manners, Customs and Dresses of the Hindoos*, published in Calcutta in 1796. It was republished without Solvyns's permission by Edward Orne in London as *The Costume of Hindustan* (1807). Solvyns was a prolific Flemish artist who lived and worked in Calcutta from 1791 to 1803. (PUBLIC DOMAIN)

Eliza has always been beautiful even as a very young girl. . . . About 5 ft. 5 in height with a most graceful figure and bearing—beautifully fair with dark brown glossy hair in abundance and features classically beautiful without any of the stiffness of the Grecian cast, good teeth, a most exquisite mouth—an innocence of manner very charming and a voice of great beauty and compass well moderated—She was then little more than 16 years of age and was without comparison the belle of Calcutta and its neighborhood. The Natives in their admiration called Eliza the "Peri Banon"—Fairy Queen. . . . [H]ad my heart not been engaged [to Laura Lucas] I should have been madly and hopelessly in love with Eliza Scott.[48]

At Fort William, James and Frederick each hired a native *khidmatgar*,[49] two brothers whom they dubbed Budoo Senior and Budoo Junior. "The facility with which an Indian servant provides food for his master early surprised me," Abbott noted. "Indian cookery ... is infinitely superior to what is met with in the country in England, unless the mistress herself takes the trouble to look after the servants."[50] There is no sense of discomfort with the notions of "master" and "servant" between either an Englishman and a Muslim employee or between an English gentleman at home and the working-class employees who did his labor. As Lawrence James notes, East India Company and Royal Army officers were taught to believe that "the exercise of authority came naturally to a gentleman, whether over the British working classes, who filled the ranks of the white regiments, or sepoys."[51] Abbott's journal reflects an ease learned in his family's days of wealth and reinforced at Addiscombe in negotiating the class differences that he and his peers readily transferred to India.

After his thirty days at Fort William, Abbott was sent to the artillery garrison at Dum Dum on the outskirts of Calcutta. He was unimpressed with what he found there. His observations on the officers in his chain of command illustrate the spectrum of relationships between Britons and Indians in 1824. They reveal not one official mind but a deeply fractured military society in different stages of transition. The early 1820s were near the end of the period of cultural hybridity by a majority of Anglo-Indians.[52] Times were changing. Yet Abbott lived among many officers still grandfathered into a lifestyle deeply embedded in the local culture. One such officer was Colonel (later Brigadier General) Alexander MacLeod, the commandant at Dum Dum, who long before had married a Bengali and settled down to family life in India. His love of the hookah, which was nearly universal at the beginning of the nineteenth century, was Abbott's first exposure to the device: "His whole existence," Abbott wrote, "was spent in making a bubbling sound in a glass vase by means of a long tube which his mouth exhausted," adding, "He was said however to be by nature kind, generous and brave [but] was certainly gifted with a native family who added nothing to the attractions of the place."[53] Subedar[54] Sita Ram's first commanding officer in 1814 was another colonel cut from the same cloth, "an old man, very short and stout, without a hair on his face or head, with a skin of a bright red color. He was smoking a magnificent *hookah*."[55] As did Abbott, who had been told his colonel was a brave man, Sita Ram also described his colonel as a legend to his men for having killed no less than seven tigers.[56]

The stereotype of the kindly, Indianized regimental commander at this time was ubiquitous. Far from being the exception, he was in fact the norm. In 1828 Charles D'Oyly[57] published a lengthy satirical poem titled *Tom Raw, the Griffin, a Burlesque Poem*,[58] which was accompanied by twenty-five color plates showing the newly arrived Tom Raw of the Bengal Army in comical situations.[59] D'Oyly, a talented illustrator, was born in India and spent most of his life there. He was a keen observer of the Company scene, and his engravings depict archtypical vignettes of Indian Army life. In the illustration "Tom Raw Is Introduced to His Regimental Commander," the kindly old Colonel Banks is seen seated with his hookah and his senior Indian officer at his left side. An Englishman smoking a hookah seems to present a microcosm of British India. Major General James Lunt noted that the practice was ubiquitous until the mid-nineteenth century, including among some women as well.[60] The first quarter of the nineteenth century was clearly dominated by Anglo-Indian officers at the top of the chain of command still broadly immersed in many Indian customs and still operating within traditional indigenous forms of employment, marriage, and recreation. These old soldiers were slow to fade away: Lord Ellenborough remembered such men "with a

Figure 2.6. A detail from the illustration "Tom Raw Is Introduced to His Regimental Commander" by Charles D'Oyly, published in *Tom Raw, the Griffin, a Burlesque Poem* (London: Printed for R. Ackermann, 1828). The illustration shows the stereotype of the old-school British commander of a sepoy regiment, hookah in hand, with his senior Indian officer right next to him. Over the next twenty years this close relationship would largely become a thing of the past, while its perception remained intact. (YALE CENTER FOR BRITISH ART)

native family and half native habits" still living in India while he was governor-general from 1842 to 1844.⁶¹

Cultural immersion of a different sort formed the basis of the lifestyle of the second of the officers whom Abbott met at Dum Dum, the commandant of ordnance, Captain Richard Powney:

> *Powney [was] quite a character. . . . [I]n height he was 5 ft. 2 inches, pretty well built with black hair, ruddy complexion, large blue laughing eyes . . . and a physiognomy so exactly like that of George the 4th that being born about 9 months after the visit of that Monarch (then Prince of Wales) to his Mothers' house there could be no doubt that he was his natural son. This idea he himself seemed proud of. . . . Lady's society he did not much affect—He loved to have around him half a dozen young boys to whom he might be kind and whom he often kept from worse associates by giving them a home in his house.*⁶²

Abbott is either too delicate or too naive to discuss a rather obvious case of a pederast keeping a small harem of young boys in his home. Powney was hardly alone. The infamous case of Lieutenant Colonel Edward Smythe and Captain Garton, both of the 8th Madras Cavalry, who were accused of homosexual relationships with their *sowars*,⁶³ created a scandal that led to a court-martial when one of the young *sowars* whom Smythe propositioned tried to kill him.⁶⁴ An equally notorious case in Karachi in 1845, involving rumors of three British officers on Sir Charles Napier's staff visiting brothels specializing in pederasty, purportedly led to a clandestine investigation by Lieutenant (later Sir) Richard Burton, possibly the only officer on Napier's staff who could speak Sindi.⁶⁵ In fact, for men of all sexual proclivities, there is more than ample evidence that India in 1824 remained a kind of erotic paradise where sexual desires might be indulged with only a minimum of discretion. British enlisted men also had a full spectrum of relationships with local women (and men) from legal marriage to prostitution,⁶⁶ but the officers' privileged lifestyle, much greater pay, and often private quarters made it far easier to pursue sexual relationships. As the gentleman ranker, Staff Sergeant MacMullen, noted in 1846, "Many in the upper walks of life keep regular harems, and assimilate themselves to their Mahometan neighbors, scarcely preserving even the shadow of Christianity, while the lower grades exceed in sensuality the most reckless profligates of our largest cities."[67]

Many officers, perhaps a majority, maintained a monogamous lifestyle with an indigenous woman at this time. William Dalrymple has presented convincing evidence that a substantial majority of British officers maintained monogamous relations with women in India prior to 1800. If an officer's career notionally lasted thirty years, a majority of senior, old-school officers like MacLeod remained in the 1820s.[68] More than 90 percent of indigenous wives were Muslims, but British officers occasionally found ways to marry Hindus as well. Not a few such wives returned with their husbands to England. Sometime after her arrival in India in 1835, Lady Emily Eden noted the sad case of

> *a native woman of very high caste and very beautiful, who was married both by the Mussulman and Protestant rites to an English Colonel, who took her to England last year, and he died on the passage home. She has never changed her native habits [and] cannot speak a word of English. She came back in the ship that took her out under the care of her eldest boy.... They say it is quite melancholy to see her sitting on the floor as natives do, with a course veil over her head, moaning over her loss. Her children are all brought up at home, as English people, and she will never see them again.*[69]

A third officer of Abbott's early acquaintance represented a step away from sexual engagement in Indian society while still evincing respect for its people:

> *Major Grenshaw [was] a singular character, very reserved, the consequence it was said of a sad accident which befell him soon after entering the service—his bearer was holding the chatta*[70] *over his head so carelessly that it did not screen him from the sun. After speaking to him two or three times, he struck him on the side with the back of his open hand. The blow, which would not have caused a man in health to flinch, fell upon an abscess in the liver. It burst and the bearer died.*

CHAPTER 2

Luckily several persons present had witnessed the blow [and] he was acquitted of criminality, but it preyed upon his spirits the rest of his life, inducing premature old age.[71]

Grenshaw was so devastated by accidentally causing the death of a low-caste Bengali servant that it essentially destroyed him and his career. This was not a man who thought of Bengalis in ethnocentric terms as lesser than Britons. Explicit in this account is the fact that a formal court-martial was held to try Grenshaw for the wrongful death of the servant. Officers in this informal group strove to respect local culture and learn the vernacular language of their troops as a matter of practical governance. These officers often recognized the fragility of British rule in India and sought social coexistence rather than cultural dominance or cultural assimilation. Abbott himself would fit into this category. Officers like Grenshaw and Abbott accepted their status as members of an elite upper class in India but maintained a compassionate working respect for the lives, culture, and beliefs of the people.

A fourth officer in Abbott's chain of command represented the opposite end of this spectrum, the archetype who would come to personify the British officer in India in the minds of many:

Colonel Hopper [was] a tall and rather fine man: very violent, very quarrelsome, very blind and very worthless.... [H]e was standing at the head of his stairs when he got into violent and causeless rage with his bearer. He rushed at him to kick him downstairs. The bearer eluded him and the violent old man kicked himself... to the bottom of the staircase and broke his leg. A gentleman going to see him some days afterwards found him filled with bitterness at the ingratitude of his bearer, who had not suffered himself to be kicked downstairs.... So far as I remember... he never recovered but died of the consequences of this fit of ungovernable rage.[72]

By 1833, this type of officer was already becoming more common, even among newly arrived cadets. Captain Albert Hervey recollected of his arrival in Madras that he was immediately thronged by "naked looking savages, all jabbering away in broken English and Malabar.... [S]ome actually seized hold of me.... I asked the sergeant who was with me for his cane, which being obtained, I laid about me right and left, and soon cleared myself of the crowd."[73]

These four archetypes may be said to represent a spectrum of the interfaces between British officers and the peoples of India around the time of Abbott's arrival. There were surely many interstices along this spectrum, from full immersion and extensive assimilation, to partial immersion including either monogamous or serial sexual relationships, to pragmatic adaptation to cuisine and customs, with a relationship of respect between employer and employee that mimicked such relationships in the metropole but did not generally include sexual contact, to, at the other end of the spectrum, abusive and sometimes violent misuse of power coupled with disregard for the rights and dignity of the colonized. Although there is no way to determine percentages, anecdotal evidence suggests that these four broad categories of engagement with the indigenous peoples of India represented roughly equal numbers of colonial relationships in 1824.

Broadly speaking, the peoples of India for their part seem to have generally accepted the first, tolerated the second, and thought of the third the way employees think of employers almost anywhere. It was the growing number of men like the irascible and abusive Hopper and the angry young Hervey, together with the evangelicals, like Lieutenant Colonel George Carmichael-Smyth of the 3rd Bengal Light Cavalry, who gradually poisoned the relationship. Captain Wredenhall Pogson noted a case, for example, in which he served as an interpreter in an investigation into the mass resignation of the Hindu soldiers of the 5th Bengal Light Cavalry in 1813. It was found that their commanding officer had constantly insulted and verbally abused them.[74]

When Abbott arrived at Dum Dum, the annual artillery exercises were already concluded for the year. There was little to do at the garrison beyond the weekly dress parades on Saturdays in the full gala artillery uniform, which he found both irksome to wear and comical in appearance. "The duties in those days were carried on at Headquarters in a very slovenly manner," he noted, adding that "very little instruction was

Figure 2.7. A detail from the watercolor *Bengal Foot Artillery 1846* by Henry Martens (1790–1868), painted in 1856 for the Ackermann's *Costume of the Indian Army* showing the heavy woolen tunic or coatee worn by artillery officers around the time of Abbott's service. (HENRY MARTENS, "BENGAL FOOT ARTILLERY 1846," PRINTS, DRAWINGS AND WATERCOLORS FROM THE ANNE S. K. BROWN MILITARY COLLECTION, BROWN DIGITAL REPOSITORY, BROWN UNIVERSITY LIBRARY, HTTPS://REPOSITORY.LIBRARY.BROWN.EDU/STUDIO/ITEM/BDR:230733)

afforded to the young officers sent thither to learn."[75] Instead, he wrote, "I spent the greater part of my time in my room, studying, drawing or reading.... I am a being lonely by habit. I met with few that understood me or [could] answer me thought for thought. In every crowd I find myself alone. A slight thing hurts my feelings which another perhaps would not notice. A word or a tone of dissonance drives me back upon my heart."[76] As this was written in the 1850s, it seems this self-awareness came later in life, as his hypersensitivity to criticism and his reactive responses to it were his Achilles' heel in the intervening three decades.

Evangelism among the officers, too, was beginning to be prominent. The 1820s in India saw a rise in evangelism that paralleled its growth in Britain. New generations of officers arriving in India now increasingly imported their proselytizing zeal. Many were wise enough "not to interfere with the superstitions of the natives," as the saying went. The gentleman ranker, John MacMullen, for example, noted in 1846, "Most of the mutinies ... among native troops have been caused by interfering with their superstitions, so tenaciously clung to by all castes of Hindoos."[77] Others were not so reserved, and the first doubts and rumors began to appear among the peoples of India that the British were bent on breaking their castes and converting them all to Christianity. In British garrisons throughout India, too, tensions grew between the evangelizing impulses of many newer officers and the old laissez-faire school. The officers at Dum Dum, as elsewhere, divided themselves socially into three religious groups. Abbott dubbed these "the Religious set," "the Moderate party," and "the Unreligious": "The Religious set ... made what they considered Religion the business of their life. The Moderate party, among whom were many more truly Christian than the first set, but who conceived that religion lay hidden in the heart with God and should be evidenced chiefly by its fruits ... and the Unreligious, who sought to worry and expose to ridicule those whom they termed 'New Lights.'"[78] From his centrist Anglican upbringing, Abbott classified himself in the "Moderate" group. Although privately deeply religious, he shared none of the evangelical fervor of the "Religious set." It was among this group, however, that he found one of his future colleagues in the Punjab, Herbert Edwardes, who throughout his career was among the most unabashed evangelicals in the

East India Company. Like Abbott he was destined in twenty years to become a "Paladin," one of the group of Henry Lawrence's Young Men chosen to administer the Northwest Frontier. Abbott noted laconically that Edwardes had "breathed fire from Heaven."[79]

In 1824, while Abbott was in his first year at Dum Dum, the First Anglo-Burmese War began. It lasted two years, from March 1824 to February 1826, the first of three wars fought with the Burmese over control of northeastern India. It was the longest war ever fought by the British in India. Frederick was keen to go and lobbied for a place in the artillery train, which was granted. James remained at Dum Dum.[80]

After he had been six months at Dum Dum, another class from Addiscombe arrived from England. Among the artillery cadets was D'Arcy Todd, who became the closest friend of Abbott's life. His arrival marked the beginning of a long, exceptionally close, and deeply loving relationship:

> *Of D'Arcy Todd what shall I say? At Addiscombe I had known him as a very small, very pretty and very irritable boy. I imagined it impossible that we should ever be friends. But when we shared together the same house, he was so youthful in manners and mind—so dependent upon me for everything, that he became exactly the kind of friend that my nature requires; something to protect and watch over. There were points, too, where we met on the same ground—I was passionately fond of poetry and he was acquiring a taste for it. . . . We both loved adventure and enjoyed the quiet of our style of life. Our naturally fiery tempers set us frequently by the ears for a few minutes, but it was as soon forgotten. On one point we differed extremely: he loved running about from house to house of friends and acquaintances—I stayed resolutely at home. There was to me no enjoyment in time killed in this fashion.*[81]

A minor incident at Dum Dum at this time reflects well upon Abbott's personal courage but poorly upon his judgment. One night a bull elephant went mad and tore through several villages, destroying homes and killing six civilians. Following the cries of "Hŭtti Hŭtti,"[82] Abbott and his friend Lieutenant Ellis gave chase on horseback. The elephant was hit by a number of musket balls near the Dum Dum garrison but appeared immune to those as well as to arrows from indigenous bows. Abbott several times threw a spear, which stuck briefly in the animal's side, but the elephant plucked it out each time with his trunk. After a long chase, Ellis wisely gave up and returned to the garrison, but Abbott was stubborn. He decided to try hamstringing the elephant's back legs using a sword, a tactic he apparently derived from accounts of elephant hunting in Africa: "I rushed at him and struck a backhanded blow at what I supposed to be his hamstrings—but not knowing the anatomy, the blow was aimed too high [and] it was not near[ly] enough to do more than graze the hock with the sword point. Stepping into a deep hole as I struck, I fell headlong into the water about waist deep.... This probably saved my life."[83] The attempt was exceptionally reckless, and the deep, water-filled hole undoubtedly saved his life, as the elephant turned and trampled angrily over and around the hole before running off and escaping into the jungle.[84] Twice before, at Addiscombe in the episode with his pistol and on the passage to India confronting the knife-wielding crewman Neagle, Abbott showed the same recklessness. In all three cases, a man acting with more circumspection would have avoided incidents that were not remotely his business. But all of them—coming to the defense of a schoolmate threatened by the "lower orders," aiding a "gentlemanly" crewman against a mutinous sailor, and defending helpless villagers against a wild animal—invoked Abbott's sense of the knight-errant. Perhaps more than any other single factor, this sensibility, consciously or unconsciously, continued to shape Abbott's life in India.

Shortly afterward, in November 1824, an incident of signal importance to the relationship between the colonial power and the people of India occurred, one that had a significant impact on both the British narrative of the nature of their rule as well as the subaltern narrative of resistance. Three Bengal Native Infantry (BNI) regiments stationed at Barrackpore—the 26th, 47th, and 62nd—were ordered to prepare to march for service in Burma. The 47th BNI, the first of the three to be ordered to march, rebelled. It was not the first rebellion of sepoy troops in the Indian Army, and it would not be the last. The mutiny at Vellore in 1806, for example, was a serious affair that is widely known. British authorities deliberately suppressed information on other sepoy rebellions, like the one experienced by Staff Sergeant John MacMullen of the 7th Native Cavalry and the 4th, 64th, and 69th Bengal Native Infantry at Shikarpore in 1844, and many of them remain obscure today.[85]

At the heart of these incidents lay very different views of soldiering. The sepoy and the *sowar*[86] considered themselves professional soldiers. Being a soldier was an honorable profession in India, one pursued by as many as one adult male in ten in India at the time of the arrival of the East India Company. The nature of their work was contractual. Contracts between soldiers and employers in pre-British India were usually based on the old Mughal code, the *Seeur ul Mutu ukhireen*, which stated the terms of employment. Contracts naturally could not be altered without mutual consent. Employment as a soldier with the East India Company was popular because it paid promptly, which was often not the case in the armies of the many princely states. But it was a serious error to believe, as the British often did, that the sepoy felt any sense of loyalty to the East India Company itself, much less any patriotism for an island nation six thousand miles away. Their loyalty was to the regiment. Each new sepoy or *sowar* swore an oath upon enlistment of *izzat*, or honor, to the *pultan*, or unit, before the regimental colors. During mutinies, sepoys virtually always kept their regimental colors and their uniforms, demonstrating a loyalty to their *pultan* and their profession, not to their employer.

When the East India Company unilaterally changed the terms of the sepoys' contract—for example, by reducing pay, failing to provide stipulated benefits, or altering the location of the service—it was violating the *Seeur ul Mutu ukhireen*. The sepoys would then occasionally conduct their profession's equivalent of a work stoppage. In the mind of the sepoys, this was a labor dispute. In the mind and the language of the colonial power, it was mutiny. These almost diametrically opposed cultural paradigms of soldiering and acceptable forms of grievance were among the most frequent causes of dissonance between Britons and the peoples of India and contributed much to the deterioration of their relationship in the first half of the nineteenth century.

At Barrackpore the issue was also a labor dispute. Sepoys on the march were to be provided with either pack animals or equipment carriers hired from one of the castes of porters.[87] They were in the caste of soldiers, not the caste of porters, which their contract explicitly recognized. Furthermore, if they were to perform foreign service, their contract stipulated double field rations. The East India Company provided neither of these on this occasion. As Abbott charitably noted, "There was no doubt much mismanagement on the part of the government and of the officers."[88] Finally, and perhaps most importantly, the lengthy transit by land or sea that service in Burma would entail could result in breaking the caste of many of the Hindu sepoys, a calamity that was not to be contemplated.[89] The British officers at Barrackpore could have solved the rations and portage issues but showed no initiative in finding remedies. In fact, they were even unaware that the contract of the men of the 47th stipulated that service across the Brahmaputra River mandated double rations. The British perspective was that the men might have legitimate complaints, but they were soldiers, and like British soldiers they should stop complaining and "get on with it." On the morning the 47th was to begin the march to the transports, the sepoys refused orders but harmed no one. As soon as this happened, the knight-errant in James Abbott again stepped forward, in this case because the Scott family, including his childhood friend Eliza, was at Barrackpore: "A force of Infantry was marched up from Fort William and a battery of Artillery from Dum Dum. I tried hard for permission to join the battery, not from my love of slaying our own soldiery, but because Mrs. Scott and the beautiful Eliza were at Barrackpoor and I fancied I might in some way protect them. But I could not get leave."[90] The British response was swift and uncompromising. The force assembled at Fort William under the command of Major General Robert Dalzell confronted the men of the 47th, who expected some sort of labor negotiation to redress their grievances. A complete lack of cultural understanding on both sides forced the issue to an armed confrontation. The sepoys sent a note in Persian that read simply, "The triple cord, though old, rotten and worn out, is still dear to us."[91] As Captain Wredenhall Pogson noted, to a Company officer attuned to the sepoys' culture, this meant that "although their religious rites and venerated customs were coming into disregard, yet they could not violate them by going on board ship or by passing the natural boundary of their country."[92] Dalzell and his staff, all Royal Army officers new to India, however, had no idea what the message meant.

The sepoys generally saw their officers as honest and fair, in that they did not take bribes or show favoritism, and they expected the British would see their grievances as legitimate and redress them, and then everything would go back to normal. Here *they* did not comprehend *British* culture. The matter might still have come to a peaceful end, but General Dalzell further provoked the sepoys by ordering them to *ground arms* rather than *stack arms*. To ground arms was to surrender; to stack arms was to secure their weapons. An order to stack arms might have been obeyed. Their rejoinder was brave but foolish. They chose instead to load their weapons, a symbolic show of defiance intended to demonstrate the seriousness of their discontent with their employer. However, they did not fire a shot. General Dalzell ordered his artillery to open fire with grapeshot. There was no return fire, which, under similar cannonading by an enemy in the field, their professional duty would certainly have required. Indeed, if sepoys routinely ran away from artillery fire, the East India Company would likely never have gotten beyond Calcutta. But in this case, shocked that the British had opened fire rather than continuing the intricate dance of negotiations, they fell back. Dalzell, not content with breaking their ranks, sent in his infantry, which chased down the sepoys as they fled.

There was no official count of the casualties. Pogson reported that eleven men killed by the volley of grapeshot lay where the rebellious element of the 47th had stood.[93] Perhaps twice as many were killed as they left the field or drowned in the river trying to escape pursuit. Of the prisoners, a dozen believed to be the leaders of the revolt were tried the next day in a drumhead court-martial and sentenced to death. One of the twelve had his death sentence reduced to penal servitude because his identity was not satisfactorily proven. All the remaining prisoners were sentenced to fourteen years hard labor at the penal colony in the Andaman Islands. They were later pardoned by the governor-general, Lord Amherst, and dismissed from the army. The 47th was disbanded, and the sepoys who had not taken part in the dispute were sent to another regiment.

The rebellion at Barrackpore provides a kind of litmus test of British attitudes in India at this time. Under the control of older Indian officers like David Ochterlony, Charles Stuart, or Abbott's commander at Dum Dum, Alexander MacLeod, the massacre would very likely not have happened. Their understanding of the sepoys and their terms of service normally prevented matters from getting nearly this far. Under officers in the second group, who knew Indian customs and traditions and understood that the sepoys' terms of service had to be respected, even if they themselves saw the traditions as "native superstitions"—men like Grenshaw and Pogson—violence would also likely have been avoided by more attentive responses to the grievances and greater willingness to pursue other resolutions. A step further from this position was that of Abbott himself in 1826, who knew that "native superstitions must not be interfered with" but nevertheless set a strict boundary on cultural adjustment and held that disobedience of soldiers to orders was on the other side of it.

The weight of British opinion in India regarding the events at Barrackpore at this time, however, came down heavily on the side of the sepoys, as Abbott notes: "The press was of course very severe upon this massacre as they called it and laid by their insane yelping the foundation for the mutinies that have followed: for the local government has from this time shrunk from doing its duty in cases of mutiny until the Sipâhis have felt that [we] dared not punish them. It is a horrible thing to mow down a regiment with grape shot—but it is the less terrible of the two alternatives."[94]

"The press" in this case was an almost entirely *British* press, as there was at that time only very limited publication of newspapers in vernacular languages.[95] The English-language newspapers served an almost exclusively Anglo-Indian readership, and their editorial views and the slant of their news coverage could not be far out of line with that of their readership if they expected to remain in business for long. From their coverage it may be concluded that a broad majority of Anglo-Indians at this time strongly disapproved of Dalzell's conduct.

Shortly after the events at Barrackpore, Abbott received orders to proceed with the 1st Battery of foot artillery to Agra. This entailed a long, slow movement of men and guns by river as far as possible and then

CHAPTER 2

overland, a journey of many months. In his journal Abbott explained the logistics: "In those days ... [the] train [and] steam boats ... were things unknown.... Edwards, Cookson and myself hired a budgerow[96] together with its cook boat and baggage boat. The life suited me better than being at rest—I was constantly ashore with my gun, not seeing much game certainly, but stretching my legs while the slow budgerow toiled up the river dragged by 16 boatmen."[97]

Even this prosaic form of travel was not safe. Some weeks into the journey, a storm swept up the river, and twenty-two of the boats sank, drowning a European gunner. Such noncombat deaths were so common as to elicit little attention. About 7 percent of all European soldiers in India died each year.[98] The year 1820 for the Bengal Artillery provides a particularly harsh example: The strength on paper was 2,472 Europeans, and in the course of the year 363 men (15 percent) were lost to attrition of all types, including deaths, desertions, insanity, transfers, retirement, and invalid discharges. Of these, 218 men, or 8.8 percent of the Europeans, died.[99]

As the fleet neared Bauhipoor, where his sisters Emma and Clementina and Clementina's husband, James Elphinstone, now lived, Abbott received leave to visit them. He saw his older sister for the first time since childhood. Emma, he discovered, was bedridden with an unknown ailment, which prescriptions of calomel and opium had not cured.[100] An unguarded entry in his journal about this visit dating from around 1860 suggests Abbott's depression and loneliness in middle age: "How happy was that hour!" he wrote, "one of the few moments of sunshine that have cheered the waste void of nearly 40 years."[101]

After a month of leave with his sisters, Abbott set out to rejoin the fleet of boats still toiling their way upriver to Agra. Traveling by *dak*,[102] a kind of stagecoach, he soon caught up with the fleet. When the battery finally reached the waypoint of Cawnpore, he bought a horse and continued by the Mynpoorie road some 175 miles to Agra, which he reached in May 1825. Augustus was already stationed there, and they lived together. The summer heat in Agra was stupefying. "It was now that I discovered the difference between the climates of Bengal and Hindoostan," he wrote. "The thermometer rose in my room to 104."[103] For a year there was little to do, but in 1826 there came at last a chance for war, or "active service," as it was called: a military campaign to offer both relief from the boredom of regimental life and the possibility of distinction.

The battle would take place at Bhurtpore (or Bharatpore), a fortress that had acquired an almost legendary status for the people of Bengal. A British siege there in 1805 failed, making the fort a symbol of resistance and living proof the British were not invincible. George Malleson observed that "Bharatpore was a word to be conjured with in the habitations of disaffected princes and nobles throughout the country."[104] Abbott noted that "Bhurtpoor when I arrived . . . was the British Bugbear and the Native Champion."[105]

The matter in 1826 involved the politics of relations with the princely states. The East India Company had pledged its support to the dying raja of Bhurtpore for the succession of his infant son, Balwant Singh. When the raja passed and Balwant Singh's uncle, Durjan Sal, seized power instead and imprisoned the child, the British Resident at Delhi, Sir David Ochterlony, assembled a siege force and marched on Bhurtpore. At that time the fort was in disrepair and poorly defended. The governor-general, Lord Amherst, feared an overextension of British military power while much of the army was still in Burma and recalled Ochterlony to Delhi. Ochterlony immediately resigned, and he died shortly afterward at Meerut, many said of a broken heart as a result of Amherst's action. Abbott thought Ochterlony "the best general (Wellington excepted) that India had ever produced."[106]

Durjan Sal immediately set about repairing the fort and raising forces to defend it, using its legendary reputation to enhance recruiting. The recall of Ochterlony's force was interpreted by the garrison as a British retreat, which both boosted recruiting and increased the garrison's morale. By the time Amherst recognized his mistake, the fortress was repaired, fully manned, and well stocked with provisions and ammunition. With the opportunity for a quick victory and his best general lost, Amherst assembled an army of thirty thousand men. It had a siege train twenty-four miles long, divided into three eight-mile columns, altogether two hundred pieces of artillery of all sizes and types. Each of the heavy guns and siege mortars required a team of twenty-two bullocks to pull it.

CHAPTER 2

James and Augustus arrived at Bhurtpore with the 2nd Company of the 1st Battalion of Foot Artillery on December 10, 1826. James was temporarily reassigned to the 3rd Company under the command of Captain George Woodrooffe, apparently to keep the two brothers from being killed on the same spot at the same time.[107] Firing positions were constructed, and the artillery went into action the next day. James commanded a mortar positioned about eight hundred yards from the fortress, while Augustus commanded a gun battery some distance down the artillery line to James's left.[108] James's friend D'Arcy Todd was present in the 4th Company of the 3rd Battalion of Foot Artillery.[109] Also present were two officers who had served at the first siege of Bhurtpore twenty-one years before[110] and an enlisted gunner, Bombardier Herbert, who had served under the Duke of Wellington with the Royal Artillery at Waterloo in 1815. The latter unfortunately deserted during the siege, possibly while drunk, and went over to fight for Durjan Sal. He was caught and hanged after the battle. Being a veteran of Waterloo only went so far.

By the early nineteenth century, sieges had become mathematical exercises, conducted along engineering principles laid down by French Marshal Marquis de Vauban (1633–1707) more than a century earlier. The siege guns fired all day, while trenches were advanced toward the fortress being assaulted. As new, closer gun positions became ready, the guns were moved forward, gradually increasing the accuracy and destructive power of their fire. Unless the besieged could stop this process, Vauban had shown, the success of the attack was inevitable.

Like virtually everyone else, Abbott was under fire from the fortress almost continuously, as the defenders used their own cannon to try to destroy the British guns and stop the trench digging process. "In the evening [of the first day]," Abbott wrote, "we were all on the parapet [viewing] the fortress, when a shot came and cut the branches just over our heads and another and another still better pointed warned us that parapets were no safe footing."[111]

As an eighteen-year-old second lieutenant under fire for the first time, Abbott did what he was supposed to do, which was to remain in his mortar pit with the men under his command, direct their fire at the fort, and observe and adjust its effects. Each mortar like Abbott's fired between twelve and twenty rounds per day throughout the thirty-eight days of the siege, a far smaller number than the average forty-eight rounds fired per cannon, because of the slow and cumbersome loading procedure.[112] A single mortar round weighed approximately 108 pounds. The gunners were Europeans, mostly British, with a smattering of Portuguese and French soldiers, the descendants of families from Goa and Pondicherry. The *golandaz*[113] and gun lascars were Indian sepoys. Approximately a third of the overall officer strength of the Bengal Artillery served at Bhurtpore.[114] In all, the artillery element of the army comprised 76 British officers and 2,312 noncommissioned officers and enlisted men, the latter divided almost equally between Europeans and Indians.

When permitted to sleep, officers and men slept next to their mortars and guns; rations were delivered to the men in place. A British veteran of the battle recalled that for thirty-eight days, "the roar, both of cannon and musketry, was like a ceaseless thunder peal, and slackened neither by day nor by night. During the day, our artillery fired into the breach, or to ruin the defences of the place; whilst regular parties of musketeers took it by turns to lie in the nearest trenches, and pour a shower of balls into the embrasures and over the parapets in their front. At night ... grape, canister and shrapnels swept the breaches, with the design of preventing the workmen from filling them up, or erecting traverses behind them."[115]

The officers, in particular, were expected to expose themselves to the full view of the enemy, both to encourage their men by their example and, in the case of the artillery officers, to observe where the shot of their guns was hitting and correct it to the desired target. With so much metal flying through the air, survival under such conditions in any battle in any war is generally a matter of random chance. Several days into the battle, as Abbott was standing on his mortar parapet, keeping a journal of the siege "written faithfully amid all the difficulties attending the exercise of the pen in battery," he noted nonchalantly that his journal "was [s]plashed with the brains of one of my men, whose head a round shot smashed as he was serving the gun."[116]

During the battle Abbott showed a willingness to circumvent orders when they were clearly wrong. As a result of too large a powder charge, his mortar's shots were going completely over the fortress walls and into the city beyond, where the civilian population awaited the outcome of the battle.[117] The size of the powder charge was not at the discretion of the individual mortar commander but rather his immediate superior, Captain Woodrooffe. When Abbott reported the error to Woodrooffe,

> *he looked very black at my presuming to know better than himself, but he gave me no order to alter them and I rather feared from his black looks that had I asked I should have met with a flat denial. I therefore received the charges as they were made up, but went on reducing them until they pitched up the rampart or immediately under or beyond it. Whilst cutting away with my sword the superfluous length of the large powder-bag, from which I had extracted about a third of the powder, I looked up and old Woodrooffe stood before me looking glum. "What are you about Mr. Abbott" he said . . . "you oughtn't alter the charges without my permission." "But I informed you, sir, of the fact and I was sure you could not wish this to continue." The argument was unanswerable, and he was silent but not pleased.*[118]

The second siege of Bhurtpore was soon successful in capturing the fort and restoring British prestige. By January 18, sufficient damage had been done to the walls by artillery and mines[119] to allow a frontal assault by the infantry. The defenders stood their ground but within six hours the British took the city. The cost, however, was considerable: 1,050 British personnel of all ranks were killed, wounded, or missing, including four artillerymen killed and twenty-three artillerymen wounded. British sources estimated that some five thousand defenders were killed on the ramparts and another five thousand died in the fight for the interior of the fort and in the city itself.[120] There was extensive looting,[121] and treasure valued at 41,50,000 rupees[122] was taken by the designated prize officers to be officially distributed according to rank.[123] Enlisted men eventually received £4 each.[124] Two immense bronze guns were taken as souvenirs, one of which is still on display in Woolwich today. A battle clasp for "Bhurtpoor" was struck for the Army of India Medal and subsequently awarded to all participants in the siege. Abbott would go on to fight many more battles, but Bhurtpore was the only set-piece engagement waged by conventional forces of his career and the only one he fought as an artillery officer. The army marched back to its garrisons. On the way home, it detoured briefly to the fortress at Dheeq, which had shown some inclination to take sides with Bhurtpore. But the fate of Bhurtpore caused the Raja of Dheeq to have a complete change of heart regarding his loyalty to the British, and the army was not needed to restore order there after all. In this sense the Bhurtpore campaign achieved its wider aims of subduing the restlessness and insubordination of the petty rajas of north-central India. It was the last major fighting in Bengal for thirty years. At the time, for James Abbott, the end of the Bhurtpore campaign meant only a return to the tedium and penury of regimental life when he and Augustus returned to their bungalow at Agra. But change was coming.

3

Reform and Progress

1826–1834

THE WAR IN BURMA, THE SIEGE OF BHURTPORE, AND THE MUTINY AT Barrackpore were over, but all three events were to have a lasting and corrosive effect on the relationship between Briton and sepoy, and in the decade that followed, it deteriorated badly. In assessing this decline, James Abbott helpfully left two contemporary writings that survive unedited as artifacts of 1832 and 1838, respectively. The first is an article he published in the *United Services Journal* under the pen name of Snellius Schickhardus.[1] The second is an official report on the Bareilly District.[2]

Within the officer corps of the East India Company Army, the swiftness of the victory at Bhurtpore and the relatively low casualty levels in comparison to the long and bloody campaign in Burma caused no little disharmony. Bhurtpore was the kind of success the press in England loved to depict as martial glory, and as P. J. Marshall notes, "By the early nineteenth century, there was a lively public appetite for military success in India."[3] The muddy grind of Burma, on the other hand, lacked, for the most part, both set-piece battles and a clear focus. As it dragged on over two years through many skirmishes in obscure places, it was often difficult even for staff officers in Calcutta to have a firm grasp on what was going on there. The officers slugging it out in the jungles of Burma, where tropical diseases decimated the army, derided the siege of Bhurtpore as a "champagne campaign."[4] They were resentful too that Bhurtpore yielded a significant amount of prize money, while the poverty of Burma offered little hope of the financial reward that formed a goodly part of the motivation of both the officers and the men doing the fighting. The two campaigns had the effect of dividing the officer corps of the Indian Army into two camps, the Burma veterans and the Bhurtpore veterans. This rift created distraction and disharmony at exactly the time when unity was needed to meet the challenges facing the army ahead. Furthermore, the Royal (King's) Army officers snubbed the Company officers by promoting their exploits in the press and downplaying those of the East India Company men in both campaigns. This deepened the existing rift in the relationship between the two elements of British India's security forces, which was already badly strained.[5]

Royal Army officers in India lorded it over Company officers and denigrated both their more modest social origins and the mercenary nature of their service to a "mercantile" concern.[6] In the contemporary novel *Oakfield*, Company officers were depicted as "detested ... and what was worse, heartily laughed at by the [royal] service which they aped; but to this, as is the wont of servility, they were blind."[7] The result was a collective inferiority complex. In the words of historian Peter Stanley, "Their endemic financial anxiety and their efforts to establish security and respectability would prove characteristic of the Company's officers.... [O]ne suspects that at the heart of their individual and corporate existence lay feelings of anxiety, frustration and desperation."[8] The real social distance may not have been as great as King's officers liked to make out, however, as the wealthiest among these men frequently avoided service in India by selling their commissions in regiments deploying to India and buying into regiments staying in England, leaving only those officers of more modest means to take what was generally recognized as a one-way ticket to India.[9]

Both officer corps saw military service first and foremost as a means of maintaining their social position; second, as a potential route to attaining honors and social recognition for acts of valor; and lastly, if they were lucky, perhaps as a way of becoming wealthy. Each of these three goals was inherently more difficult from the outset for Company officers than for King's men. As a result, Company officers were more prone to self-interest.[10] James Abbott was typical of the East India Company Army

CHAPTER 3

officer in this sense. Coming from a background of genteel poverty with a precarious claim to gentility, he embodied the financial and social insecurity that motivated the majority of his peers.[11] The huge debts which Abbott and other Company officers were obliged to incur at the outset of their careers generally frustrated their quest for financial security, and their sense of inferiority to Royal Army officers usually stymied their social aspirations. Neither craving could be satisfied by regimental assignment. Company officers in general tended to see their relationship to the Company as that of employees "rather than that of shareholders-cum-retainers, the customary stance of the royal officer."[12] Ironically, in this sense, Company officers were exactly the same as their sepoys: mercenaries whose social anxieties and class interests outweighed their loyalty to their employer. They never recognized it in themselves, and perhaps for this very reason, they never recognized it in their sepoys either.

The organic contradiction between what its stakeholders wanted and what the Company army per se was structured to provide created a military organization in conflict with itself, especially in peacetime. This is readily seen in the ubiquitous and catty written criticism of senior officers, appointments, and policies in the *United Services Journal* and elsewhere in the press. Perhaps the major driver of this gnawing discontent was the exceptionally long time it took to obtain promotions, which were based entirely on seniority, unlike in the Royal Army, where higher rank could be purchased. Marshall observes that as a result of this stultifying atmosphere, "tables of precedence set this great community of office holders into a hierarchy from the Governor-General to the newest arrived cadet."[13] The Board of Control determined that it took, at this time, fourteen years on average to be promoted from lieutenant to captain and another twelve to reach the rank of major. At the beginning of the 1830s, when Abbott was returning from Bhurtpore to regimental life, an East India Company officer could expect to wait forty-eight years to become a colonel.[14]

The prospects for living so long were bleak. As a result of the report by Edward Dodwell and James Miles, Company officers were well aware that perhaps one man in ten would ever get out of India and return to Great Britain. The best way around the promotion logjam was assignment to positions outside the regimental system, and senior officers were deluged with correspondence from junior officers seeking patronage for these positions. By 1830, only 40 percent of the officers assigned to the Bengal Army were actually with their regiments.[15]

Not only did the aftermath of all three events—Burma, Bhurtpore, and Barrackpore—add to the disharmony between Royal and Company officers and between Company officers who served in different campaigns, it also widened the gap between the British and their Indian sepoys. The Commander in Chief in Burma, Brigadier Archibald Campbell, like General Robert Dalzell at Barrackpore, had little experience of India and nothing but contempt for the sepoys placed under his command, an attitude that neither man did anything to conceal. Campbell deployed them largely in supporting and garrisoning roles, and they protested in vain for an equal share of the dangers and the fighting. Moreover they resented the insult. Indian troops were also falsely rumored to have advanced slowly and reluctantly at Bhurtpore. As in Burma, the commander of the siege of Bhurtpore, Lord Combermere, had placed a European battalion at the head of each of the three columns to advance in the final assault. The reports of sluggishness on the part of Indian troops at Bhurtpore say less about what actually happened and "more about how the British wanted history to be recorded."[16]

Unfortunately, at the same time as demeaning stories began circulating about the lack of courage of the sepoys in battle, the rebellion at Barrackpore resulted in an equally corrosive dialog in the press regarding their reliability and trustworthiness as well. In fact the mutiny at Barrackpore was just the tip of the iceberg of sepoy discontent. Sepoy desertions rose steadily in the 1820s, from 687 in 1822, to 1,041 in 1823, to 5,593 in 1824 and 8,322 in 1825.[17] Incidents of violence between British troops and sepoys were also increasing. There were clear indications by the late 1820s, for those astute enough to see them, that all was not well in the Bengal Army. Some perceptive junior officers saw the deterioration, but few senior officers did, and the broader implications of the Barrackpore mutiny were lost altogether on most senior East India Company officials.

The "cowardly sepoy" and the "untrustworthy sepoy" tropes soon merged into one narrative. Outlandish recommendations were made. One King's Army officer suggested if the sepoys were not replaced by "Arab,

Malay and Cafre[18] mercenaries," Britain's grasp on India would surely be broken.[19] Such a debate would have been scarcely imaginable even twenty years earlier. Most, although not all, aspersions cast upon the sepoys came from Royal Army officers and not from Company officers. Although they had little access to rebuttal, enough indigenous soldiers could speak and read English well enough by this time that many sepoys were aware, to at least some degree, that their British employers were publicly questioning both their courage and their trustworthiness.

A number of Company officers came to the sepoys' defense, including James Abbott, who entered the debate in 1832 with an article in the *United Services Journal* titled "An Apology for the Indian Army."[20] Abbott's defense of the sepoy was as full-throated as it was lengthy. The article is unequivocal evidence of his respect for Indian troops at this time. Abbott wrote of the sepoys, "Of their bravery, there can be no doubt. They are clean, intelligent, tractable, and seldom guilty of drunkenness; their chief vices are extravagance and improvidence."[21] He went on to rebut point for point the arguments of "W.W.," the anonymous writer of an earlier article, noting the sepoy required much less material comfort in the field than the British soldier, was far better suited to the climate, and could march farther, faster, and with a heavier load than British troops for significantly less cost.[22]

However, his twelve-page defense of the Indian soldier also epitomizes two related, fundamental misunderstandings about the sepoy that arose around 1800 and which, by 1830, were held by a majority of Company officers. The first, mentioned earlier, was the willful and counterfactual disregard for the contractual nature of the sepoy's employment. Abbott wrote, "The Sipâhi is not a common mercenary; in the Bengal army he usually is a small landholder, who has an interest in good order and in the permanence of government. He frequently is of a wealthy family, and enters the army for the sake of the influence and privileges it bestows."[23] This paragraph also articulates the second misunderstanding: the ultimately fatal fallacy that because he was a landowner, the sepoy shared with the East India Company a mutual interest in the stability of British governance in India, a classic example of cultural mirroring. Most British officers in Bengal at this time were convinced that the upper-caste

Figure 3.1. Creating a simulacrum of the British army: ignoring the military traditions and uniforms of the Indian soldier, the East India Company worked to recreate in India an image of the British army at home. A nineteenth-century illustration of the Bengal Native Infantry circa 1830 by an unknown artist. (WIKIMEDIA COMMONS)

Hindu Brahmins being recruited into the Bengal Army were analogous to English yeoman farmers, whose ownership of their land gave them a vested interest in stability and made them stakeholders in the permanence of Company rule.

Thus there were two major cross-cultural misinterpretations at work simultaneously: the belief that the sepoy was a soldier akin to the British soldier, in the sense that it was a soldier's duty to obey his officer's orders first and complain about their fairness afterward, and the belief that being minor landholders made upper-caste Hindu sepoys natural collaborators with the British in maintaining the status quo of British rule. Both of these were a direct result of the British tendency to interpret what they saw in India as a social system far more like their own in England than it actually was. This projection of their own culture onto the cultures of India was a natural cognitive bias,[24] and it was reinforced with the visual trappings of England.[25] The deliberate effort to make the Indian Army look exactly like the Royal Army beginning around 1800 is a perfect illustration of this. In the first thirty years of the nineteenth century, this bilateral misunderstanding of the relationship of the sepoy to the Company gradually evolved into dogma that by 1830 was passing largely unquestioned by the great majority of Company officers.

In fact, what the upper-caste Bengal sepoy had an interest in was maintaining his socioeconomic status within his caste, which depended heavily on preserving and enhancing his religious position.[26] Property rights were important to the degree that they preserved Brahmanic privilege. Meanwhile, British policies such as that which allowed the East India Company to take control of princely states whose rajas died without a natural heir, the so-called Doctrine of Lapse, for example, were alarming and infuriating to the landed aristocracy of indigenous society, the rajas and ranis.[27] By the mid-1850s this double fallacy had taken on a fatal, self-reinforcing status in the philosophy of colonial rule, and it played a major role in the Mutiny of 1857.

Cultural assimilation and fraternization also became part of this public debate about the sepoys. In his criticism of them to which Abbott responded, "W.W." argued there could be no bonding or comradeship between officers and sepoys because the latter had "customs and religious prejudices which keep them so distinct from their British officers as to admit of scarcely any ... intercourse beyond that which takes place on parade."²⁸ In the era when officers of the "old school" like Colonel Alexander MacLeod were assimilated into Indian life, this statement would not have had the ring of truth. By 1830, however, the Indian Army officer corps was perceptibly changing, and "W.W." was closer to the mark. Critically, however, while the officer corps was becoming estranged from its sepoys by the 1830s, most officers, like Abbott, were in denial about this estrangement and continued to believe they were as close as they had ever been. A few of Lord Ellenborough's "old soldiers" still were, but a majority by this time now were not. Abbott's robust and paternalistic defense of the relationship in rebuttal to "W.W." typifies this legacy belief:

> *It is not easy to conceive from what intercourse ... they are deterred by their "religious prejudices." ... I do not pretend to determine what ought to be the degree of intercourse between an officer and a private; but this relation in the Indian Army seems sufficiently intimate for all useful purposes. ... [The sepoy] solicits the indulgence of an occasional exemption from duty to perform some religious ceremony; speaks to [his officer] without hesitation on what he considers the most intimate subjects ... generally adding, "to you, Sir, who are my father, I feel no reluctance in talking of a forbidden subject." This is a great mark of confidence. ... In his law-suits, and he or his family are seldom unprovided with one, his officer not rarely acts as his chamber counsel [and] the latter is generally the arbiter of his domestic quarrels. ... In short the intercourse is continual, and upon the sepoy's part is one of extreme confidence.*²⁹

But by the 1830s most of the surviving old-school officers like MacLeod of whom this had been true were going into retirement, and largely only the belief in it remained on duty. Subedar Sita Ram recalled of the 1820s that "in those days the sahibs could speak our language much better than they do now, and they mixed more with us."³⁰ As newer generations of British officers became more dismissive of the "superstitions of the natives" and participated in sepoy life far less frequently, an ever-widening confidence gap grew on the sepoy side, while, critically, among the British the illusory belief in the paternal and professional bond of loyalty between the officer and the sepoy remained in place as a vestigial article of faith from the earlier era.

Defenses by Abbott and others of the sepoy notwithstanding,[31] the damage to the sepoy's reputation and morale was done, and attempts to repair it were ineffectual.[32] In the thirty years since Richard Wesley[33] had transformed the East India Company from a trading enterprise into an imperial power, the broader Anglo-Indian perception of the Bengal Army had changed entropically from a relatively clear understanding of how and why the sepoy fought into a fantasy that now interwove two new, false narratives: first, that the sepoy was a less courageous, less trustworthy, dark-skinned homunculus of the British soldier, and second, that he was akin to the British yeoman farmer—dependent upon British rule for his future and upon British gentlemen for leadership. The result was toxic and led directly to the Great Mutiny of 1857.

The accelerating growth of the "empire of opinion" discourse and the widening gap separating the British from their sepoys coincided with the end of the governorship-general of Lord Amherst and the beginning of that of William Bentinck. The seeds of disaster had been sown in the aftermath of Burma, Bhurtpore, and the Barrackpore mutiny, but this did not mean they would flower by themselves. Discontent and disharmony in the Indian Army would require the right nursery and the right nutrients if they were to grow into broad rebellion. William Bentinck's decade of "reform" and "progress" between the siege of Bhurtpore and the beginning of the First Anglo-Afghan War provided both in ample measure.

All this still lay in the future as the Indian Army settled back into its peacetime routine in 1827, however, and James and Augustus returned to duty at Agra. Soon afterward, in one of the most interesting incidents in Abbott's career, his white campaign horse Lancer was stolen from the artillery stables, and his indigenous groom, whose duties included guarding the horse, set about recovering it. Abbott's account of the episode is remarkable in several ways.

> *The man was a Hindoo and ... he planned his operations with much wisdom. He broke two pieces of reed to the exact length and breadth of the print of the horse's foreshoe and with these in hand he started tracking the animal seventy miles by his hoof prints into the Gwalior Territory and finally into a small mud fort there. Not satisfied ... he determined to make sure of the horse being actually in the fort. He therefore smeared his face and hair and person with ashes, threw aside all clothes excepting that about his loins, and thus disguised as a faqir entered the fort boldly and asked for alms. These were granted and he was allowed to enter the stables, where he not only found ... Lancer but identified him beyond doubt by the scar upon his coronet.*[34] *He then returned in all haste to me and reported the success of his mission ... and the horse was recovered in good condition.*[35]

Abbott's account of the resourcefulness of the groom in the use of simple technology to identify the hoof print, his amazing skill in tracking the animal over seventy miles, and his remarkable ability to adopt an alternate caste identity by shifting between groom and fakir provide an image of the peoples of India almost diametrically opposed to the stereotype by which the British were beginning to portray their indigenous subordinates. It is also an exceptional illustration of how some Indians at different levels of society could have a sophisticated and contextualized understanding of personal identity and could and did see caste not as an impenetrable barrier, as the British understood it, but as a permeable ipseity of religious agency. Thus, in Abbott's writing is seen not only praise and respect for sepoy troops in general but also an honest regard for the intelligence, ingenuity, and courage of ordinary Bengalis as individuals as well.

At Agra, Abbott again recklessly cast himself as the knight-errant in another episode that might have cost him his life: chasing down a rabid dog on foot before it could reach the market area of the city. As it so often did in Abbott's life, chivalry ran far ahead of strategy. Cornering the dog, Abbott soon found himself being attacked by it. The dog leapt at him, sank his teeth into Abbott's arm, and could not be shaken loose. Abbott's friend Lieutenant Edwards caught up with the pair at that moment and struck the dog on the head with a rock, which luckily caused it to let go of Abbott's arm and run away into a wooded area. Abbott gamely joked with Edwards, "I shall go mad now and be biting my neighbors."[36] But it was no joking matter. The bite wounds, consisting of eight deep punctures, were treated by the surgeon, Dr. Thomson, by cutting out all the tissue around and under each puncture, effectively excising the teeth marks by enlarging the holes, then filing them with what was called "lunar caustic."[37] Abbott noted,

> *It was a long operation and not very pleasant. . . . I was left to think of the probability, which appeared to me considerable, of hydrophobia. . . . For years the apprehension returned to me from time to time and shortly afterwards I was present at the death of a native groom from hydrophobia communicated by the bite six weeks previous of a rabid jackal. It was an ugly scene to witness—The man was haunted with the presence of some object which he vainly grasped at within a foot of his face. His countenance was distorted and his reason was gone.*

Abbott had good reason to be apprehensive: the death of Europeans from hydrophobia (or rabies) in India was a common event. As Abhijit Dutta notes, "The annual reports of the Baptist Missionary Society are replete with instances of European missionaries in the mofussil[38] perishing from hydrophobia caused by the bites of jackals or dogs."[39] But for the fourth time in as many years, his remarkable luck held. He also did not contract the cholera that swept through Agra at the outset of what is known today as the Second Cholera Pandemic, which originated in Bengal in 1827 and spread worldwide. It killed hundreds of thousands of people by the time it died out in 1835.[40]

Abbott recalled the monsoon of 1827 as a trying season in which cholera killed at least a dozen Europeans in Agra, including the division adjutant, Lieutenant Blake.[41] Abbott received orders to replace him, a prestigious assignment, but it entailed a transfer four hundred miles east on the Grand Trunk Road to Karnal, where Blake was to have been sent. Abbott could not afford a house when he arrived in Karnal and lived instead in a tent.[42] He found it "a solitary spot and suited [to] the melancholy mood on which I entered upon my new life."[43] Hardly had he arrived, however, than a new order appeared indicating the previous one had mixed up its Abbotts: it was his brother Augustus who was intended to replace Blake. Abbott recalled there were no hard feelings: "When ... Augustus was appointed in my place he of course came to Karnal and I occupied with him a house near the Artillery Barracks. We understood one another better now and got on well together, he going out punctually to visit at 11 o'clock and remaining out until our early dinner and I reading and writing in my own room."[44] At Karnal, James became friends with Captain and Mrs. James Eckford. With the wry humor he sometimes demonstrated in his journals, Abbott found that James Eckford: "was imbued with a notion that the Bible being the Word of the Most High, life was too short to be given to the consideration of any other. And from morning till night, he pored over the Bible; not apparently adding many new ideas to the stack already acquired."[45] In company with the Eckfords, Abbott took leave for his first visit to Simla, then a small hill station with a temperate climate that later became a major garrison. Abbott was deeply affected by the beauty of Simla, and the memory of it never left him. He would later write a great deal of poetry about Simla and sketch and paint its mountains in watercolor countless times:

> *No words can express the delight which the aspects of mountains afforded me. ... In the evening we took a long walk in the illumination of the Dewallie.*[46] *... [T]he purity of the air and immense depth of the glens were all delightful ... [but] when entering the rhododendron pass ... all the beauty of that glorious mountain began to open upon me. No words could express my delight. I was intoxicated with happiness.*[47] *... [T]he glorious scenery has haunted me with its beauty for the rest of my life. ... There was an enchantment about the spot that deeply affected me. It was in my thoughts by day and my dreams by night—Never was there such a paradise on Earth.*[48]

One day in 1827, Augustus received an invitation from an old family friend, Miss Stacy, who was traveling to Simla with Augustus and James's second cousin, Marianne Abbott. Her brother, Major Lewis Stacy, was spending the season at Simla on leave with his family. Augustus secured six months leave to go to Simla to court Miss Stacy. He returned to Karnal after two months, his suit with Miss Stacy unsuccessful, but in the meantime he had built a small house at Simla. When James contracted fever soon afterward, the surgeons at Karnal recommended that he go to Simla for recovery and convalescence. At Augustus's insistence, he went and stayed in the new cottage, with unexpected results: he fell in love with his cousin.

> *Being so near the Stacys I was constantly in their company and in that of my cousin Marianne. The consequence was an engagement which Major and Mrs. Stacy opposed with all their might, but which we referred to Marianne's mother, a widow residing in England. Much misery was the result to me—Whether Marianne suffered, it was difficult to say, for scarcely had her mother's consent been obtained, when she herself wrote to break off the engagement, and soon after she was the wife of a tiny wine merchant in Calcutta named Hadow, who dying, left her in very straightened circumstances with several children to bring up.... I felt the blow severely at the time.... Neither nature nor education had fitted us to be companions. But the close and unreserved intercourse of cousins in a region so breathing of love as Simla had made her fancy that she felt more for me than for others. Marianne was a fine girl and had many good qualities, but there was no stability of purpose in her. Peace to her memory.*[49]

Consciously or unconsciously, Abbott here echoes the sentiments of the narrator of the 1842 poem "Locksley Hall" by Alfred Tennyson: "O my cousin, shallow-hearted! O my Amy, mine no more!"[50] Simla was indeed a very romantic spot, and such romances blossomed there regularly. In the years ahead, it would gain a well-earned reputation as a sort of Shakespearean *locus amoenus*,[51] a space where erotic passions could be freely explored outside the strict social order and tightly regulated behavior of British garrisons.[52] Such spots were a well-known element in British Romantic literature beginning in the Renaissance, so it is hardly unusual that with Abbott's Romantic sensibilities, he would fall under

Figure 3.2. A depiction the Victorian feminine alternative offered by the hill station at Simla to the masculine hierarchies of martial India, as seen in a darkly wooded, overgrown, and mysterious *locus amoenus* by painter Arthur Rackham, titled "Titania Lying Asleep," first published as an illustration in the 1908 William Heinemann edition of *A Midsummer Night's Dream*. (WIKIMEDIA COMMONS)

the spell of one in Simla. Like the forest in Shakespeare's *A Midsummer Night's Dream*, Simla was a feminine place of twilight and faeries and the mysteries of the deep woods. It became notorious eventually as a place where officers' wives, escaping the hot season in the cooler hills, would have affairs while their husbands sweated out their daily lives on the hot plains below.

Abbott's engagement to Marianne in 1827 was not his only romantic affair during this period. The following year in Karnal, he had an intimate correspondence with "F.B.," his boyhood friend Fanny Case, now Fanny de Burgh and the wife of Major de Burgh, a man for whom Abbott had little respect. Their correspondence was maintained by passing back and forth a tiny blue diary approximately two inches by four inches. Much of the minute writing is now illegible, but the word "love" is decipherable often, and in one passage Fanny refers to her lover as "naughty, naughty James." Abbott carried this Lilliputian notebook with him for more than a decade in an oilskin slipcover, using it again in 1840 to record his route to Khiva. His keeping of the little book close to his heart for so long is strongly indicative of the torch he carried for Fanny and the great sentimental value the correspondence held for him. In his journals he was very circumspect about their affair, but his affection for her is clear.

In October 1828 ... Major and Mrs. de Burgh arrived at Karnal from England. ... I had known Mrs. de Burgh in my boyhood as Fanny Case. We were staying together [in England] at the Saunders and a very close friendship had subsisted between us. She was one of the most beautiful creatures I have ever seen. It was strange to meet her thus the wife of a man prematurely old and in every respect her inferior. [He] ... was in fact a fool who had by fast living broken his constitution. To him from first to last she was an angel. He had the sense to know this but his infirmities increased. ... It was to me the most painful part of the ordeal to contemplate. As I knew her in 1828/9, [she] was one of the loveliest creatures in the world, and her friendship was to me all in all for many, many years of exile. ... In the Diana Vernon of Rob Roy *is a vivid picture of this lovely being as I knew her at Karnal.*[53]

Like Laura Lucas, Fanny was one of the great tragic Romantic loves of Abbott's life. His analogy comparing her to Diana Vernon is telling both of his perception of their relationship and his exaltation of Sir Walter Scott. Like all of Scott's heroines, Vernon could not marry the man she loved. Romantic novels of the period did not have happy endings, and *Rob Roy* was no exception. But after his abortive engagement to Marianne Abbott, James undoubtedly found solace in a "sensible" girl like Diana Vernon, who tells her lover, "Boys and girls prate themselves into love.... But you and I, Frank, are rational beings, and neither silly nor idle enough to talk ourselves into any other relation than that of plain honest disinterested friendship. Any other union is as far out of our reach as if I were man, or you woman—To speak truth," she added, after a moment's hesitation, "we cannot marry if we would; and we ought not if we could."[54] Diana and Frank's parting is a classic of the Romantic genre, in which the lovers kiss and say good-bye forever, "a moment never to be forgotten, inexpressibly bitter, yet mixed with a sensation of pleasure so deeply soothing and affecting as at once to unlock all the floodgates of the heart."[55] Diana then rides off into the night, and Frank says, "I had scarce given vent to my feelings in this paroxysm ere I was ashamed of my weakness."[56] This noble pain nobly borne was exactly the sort of stuff after Abbott's own heart. And he had reasons for delicacy in describing their relationship that went beyond gentlemanly sensibilities. In their youth, his brother Frederick had also been a friend of Fanny's at Blackheath. In England, Frederick was more interested in another girl than in Fanny, but in 1833 when Major de Burgh died, Frederick married her.

The year James Abbott's relationship with Fanny de Burgh ended in 1829 was a contentious one in India. After a lengthy trial, the Resident and Commissioner at Delhi, Sir Edward Colebrooke, was found guilty of corruption and dismissed from office after fifty years of Company service.[57] The trial was the talk of India. Historians have often interpreted it as a watershed in the Company's administration from the indigenized practices of old-school Anglo-Indians to the steadily anglicizing values and standards associated with British governance at home, a kind of High Noon "showdown between the Orientalists and the Anglicists."[58] There is considerable evidence that Colebrooke did consider himself a scapegoat

Figure 3.3. These two images show James Abbott's miniature Simla-Khiva diary. This tiny diary was carried in an oilcloth pouch by Abbott for many years, beginning in Simla in 1831. It contains an intimate conversation with "F.B.," almost certainly Fanny de Burgh, a close friend of Abbott's who in later years married his brother Frederick. The last half of the diary is comprised of Abbott's route sketches of his journey to Khiva in 1840. A one-pound coin is shown to indicate size. (PHOTOGRAPHS BY THE AUTHOR)

for "new reformers" of the "separation school" of administration.[59] And nuances of meaning in conflicting translations of evidence in Persian were the source of considerable legal debate at the trial and later did have a significant influence on Bentinck's landmark decision in 1832 to transition to English as the official court language of India, which it became by law in 1835.[60] But in general the argument that the Colebrooke affair marked a profound turning point in the relationship between Britons and the peoples of India is overstated. The trial did not end the "entanglements between British and Indian culture"; nor did it significantly change the political calculus of the relationship.[61]

Of far greater importance in this regard was the passage four years later of the Government of India Act of 1833, which terminated all of the East India Company's commercial functions in India.[62] Removing all commercial interest from the portfolios of Company officials did much more to reduce influence peddling and personal enrichment on the epic scale engaged in by Edward Colebrooke than Utilitarian-inspired admonishments to Indian civil service cadets at the Company's academy at Haileybury to "resemble English gentlemen" and see "themselves as ... Britons" rather than nabobs.[63] With the Government of India Act in 1833, the Company's original purpose of mercantile profit with an Indian army to protect and expand it became, virtually overnight, a mission of outsourced colonial governance with an Indian army to enforce it. It was a nineteenth-century mercantile version of "mission creep," from pure commerce to nation building and administration.

Nevertheless, while the Colebrooke trial was not transformative, the relationship between Britons and the indigenous peoples they came into contact with *was* undoubtedly changing as a result of the impetus to reform transported to India by Bentinck and "fresh recruits imbued with utilitarian and evangelical attitudes."[64] The overall extent of British impact on the culture of India in general, however, is debatable. In 1830, some twenty-five thousand British troops, approximately a quarter of the Royal Army, were in India, including about one thousand officers. The East India Company Army contained another fifteen thousand Europeans, of whom just under four thousand were officers.[65] The number of civil servants was well under eight hundred men, as was the number of missionaries, planters, and other nonofficial Britons. Thus, including British women at a ratio of 1:3 in the genteel occupations and a lesser percentage among enlisted men, far fewer of whom were allowed to bring their wives to India, there were not more than fifty thousand Britons in India at this time, the majority of whom were clustered in major cities.

Given an indigenous population at this time of roughly two hundred million, the ratio of the indigenous population to Britons was never less than 4,000:1. The sepoys numbered some 250,000 men, and even if six servants were employed as sweepers, grooms, water carriers, porters, cooks, and other laborers for every sepoy and *sowar*, and each middle-class Briton employed ten local civilians in his household establishment, the number of indigenous persons who had any significant contact with Europeans relative to the general population can scarcely have been higher than one in a hundred. The historical reality is that the vast majority of the peoples of India in the nineteenth century lived their entire lives without ever seeing a Briton, much less being influenced by one to change their culture or beliefs in any significant way.

In fact, Britons tended in general to be more influenced by Indian culture than the other way around, as one might expect given a population ratio of 4,000:1. As P. J. Marshall notes, "In a way that was entirely different from colonies of extensive British settlement ... British society in India was shaped by Indian society."[66] Virtually all Anglo-Indians in the first half of the nineteenth century assimilated into the culture of the subcontinent to some degree in terms of language and diet. Many also adopted all or part of Indian dress, and a few, like Major General Charles Stuart, adopted Indian religions. But this did not mean they integrated into local society. With some notable exceptions, Britons rarely "went native." Instead they formed their own tribe and clans and had their own social strata. For example, the Anglo-Indian officer and enlisted classes had virtually no contact with one another outside the performance of military duties.[67] Apart from commercial and labor interactions, and except in unusual cases at isolated stations, Anglo-Indian officers and civil servants also lived apart from the indigenous people of India and formed their own social circles wherever they went.[68] But so too in a sense, it should be noted in fairness, did the indigenous people of India, who at this time also seldom had meaningful friendships or even regular social contact with people outside their own castes, extended families, or tribes and literally never married outside them. The barriers to true cultural understanding between Britons and the peoples of India were indeed high and seldom breached. But it could be argued that Anglo-Indians—especially enlisted soldiers—while relatively small in number, intermarried with and, when living on the local economy, mingled with other ethnicities and people of other social strata on a more frequent basis and perhaps more broadly than any other group on the subcontinent.

Even for officers, intercultural marriages and families continued to be the norm.[69] Abbott's observations of British life, as well as the extensive writings of his contemporaries throughout this period, show that this remained a standard fixture of Anglo-Indian life well into the nineteenth century. The 1830s, and sometimes earlier, have sometimes been portrayed as a decade of change in the nature of physical relationships between Britons and the peoples of India. Historian Durba Ghosh summarizes this portrayal with the observation that other historians of British India "have commonly asserted that the early period of colonial rule was reasonably free of racial and cultural prejudice, that British officials had an appreciation for India and its heritage, and that it was only after the 1830s that Britain started to see itself as distinctly superior."[70] One of the most common reasons given for this purported shift and for locating its timing in the 1830s is the free entry of missionaries into India beginning in 1813. In this historical view, the increasing numbers of missionaries steadily introduced expressions of religious disapproval of marriage and concubinage with the indigenous population, while at the same time bringing increasing numbers of eligible Englishwomen into India—and with them, the changing views of race in Great Britain in this period. The memsahibs,[71] this narrative suggests, not only gradually replaced local women as wives and sexual partners but also began to re-create mixed-gender British social circles in India. Historian Kenneth Ballhatchet was one of the early proponents of this argument. "These [Englishwomen] were important not merely as wives for officials, and so opposed to *bibis* as rivals," he wrote, "but also as the nuclei of inward-looking European social groups in every city and town, as well as in smaller 'stations.'"[72]

There are a number of problems with this historical view, however, which go well beyond Abbott's broad portrayal of British society at this time and those of his contemporaries. One of them is that the argument has limited empirical evidence to support it. Ballhatchet's own influential work, for example, focuses almost entirely on Burma, citing only a single example of official disapprobation of an incident of concubinage in India—and that from 1868. Another is that the argument is structured almost entirely on the behavior of the officer class, which made up a tiny fraction of the overall British population in India.

In fact, there were never enough eligible Englishwomen in India in the nineteenth century to come close to the number of officers who wished to marry, let alone the enlisted soldiery. At no point in the century was the ratio of British men to British women less than 3:1.[73] And as P. J. Marshall notes, the great majority of British men in India were in their twenties and thirties, the prime of their sexual lives.[74] The depiction of decreasing intercultural relationships between British men and indigenous women is simply not borne out by period statistics or by Abbott's writings and other period journals. Disapprobation of such relationships *was* increasingly present in public discourse, but the reality on the ground was different. Ghosh notes that "visual and textual representations suggest that the process of intercultural amity and friendship was much more uneven and contested.... By the early nineteenth century, almost one in three Europeans in the presidency towns was Eurasian or mixed race, suggesting that while there was little documentary proof of interracial liaisons, the mixed-race population was growing, as there were six times as many Eurasians being born in India than 'pure' Europeans."[75] Abbott's journals show that British men, and occasionally women, were clearly able at this time to disaggregate platitudes from passions. In fact, British officers and enlisted men routinely married Indian women and women of mixed heritage well into the 1850s and even beyond. The very last strand of cultural hybridity to be broken was the sexual thread, which yielded slowly and stubbornly. It was not completely dissolved until the Great Mutiny of 1857, and in some cases, particularly in Burma, not even then.[76]

There is also little evidence that this practice caused any great antipathy or resentment from the indigenous perspective. Indeed, there is some reason to believe the opposite was true, that this drew the sepoys closer to their officers, improved the officers' language skills, increased the avenues for indirect communication among them, and perhaps fostered a sense that the British respected them and their culture.[77] Some officers do appear, like Abbott, to have genuinely abstained from sexual relations with the women of the subcontinent, but most did not. As Richard Holmes observes, "Although there were many monkish warriors who mortified the flesh with long rides or cold baths, the majority of British officers and men in India found sexual abstinence an unreasonable challenge."[78]

Several contemporary guidebooks for young officers in India contained practical advice on selecting and maintaining concubines. One in particular refutes the notion that these were generally exploitative relationships in which British men held power over Indian women without agency. Captain Thomas Williamson pointed out that although "concubinage" was interpreted as a form of prostitution in Western sensibilities, it was in fact an accepted and respected form of legal marriage in Muslim culture:[79] "According to the Mohamedan law, there are various degrees of connubial attachment, from the strictest and most formal union down to what we should call a very loose kind of left-handed marriage. These are, however, sanctioned by that law, if performed according to enjoined ceremonies.... [B]eing Mussulmans, and ... very scrupulous in the observance of whatever forms are ordained respecting viands [and] contracts ... it may be reasonably concluded that they rather deem themselves to be [married] than as retained prostitutes."[80] Williamson refers here to *Nikāḥ al-Mutʿah* (Arabic: نكاح المتعة). In Islamic law, *Nikāḥ al-Mutʿah* is a complex form of temporary legal marriage most commonly practiced among Shi'a Muslims. At least 90 percent of marriages between British men and Indian women were to Muslims, and from the prevalence of legal wills, it can be assumed that these were legal arrangements.[81] In addition, a high proportion of Royal Army enlisted men who survived their twenty years in India opted to remain with their Indian families rather than return to England.

In one case, the widow of a staff sergeant who died in India subsequently married a lieutenant general, demonstrating a degree of social mobility that British women in the metropole could not dream of. In an era two hundred years before Bollywood, popular music, the internet, and social media even introduced the notion of romantic marriage to India (to which it remains remarkably resistant[82]), virtually all indigenous marriages were arranged, and marriage to a European brought many advantages as well as social mobility where it was otherwise impossible. In fact, records show that Muslim women in India in this period adroitly used *Nikāḥ al-Mutʿah*, a perfectly legitimate form of contract marriage within their culture, to their social and financial advantage. When critics of colonial intermarriage in India consider the practice exclusively from a Western perspective, they are ironically guilty of practicing exactly the kind of Eurocentric cultural hegemony imagined by Edward Said in *Orientalism*.

Abbott noted numerous examples of British officers married to indigenous women during this period. His account of the first of these, his commanding officer at Karnal, Captain Blake, is a remarkable expression of cognitive dissonance. It suggests a struggle to reconcile the new public narrative in regard to Blake's character, based on his intercultural marriage, and what Abbott knew to be true of his personal behavior:

> *Blake was quite a character.... [H]is merit, his talent and imagination fulfilled all its promise. But his great talents were turned to no account. He was connected with a Native woman by whom he had a daughter, almost as black as a Native and utterly uncouth and uncivilized. People looked upon him as somewhat lax in the moral obligations, yet when a mercantile house in Calcutta in which he had lodged his whole fortune was about to fail and he had timely notice, he nobly refused to withdraw a farthing from the house.... He lost every farthing he possessed. It is refreshing to meet with such traits and especially where they are exhibited by men whose moral culture has been imperfect.*[83]

This was recollected in the 1850s, by which time Abbott was clearly immersed in the discourse which held that marrying a local woman was evidence of Blake's "imperfect moral culture." Yet Abbott viewed Blake's behavior as a gentleman, in allowing himself to be bankrupted as a matter of honor, as exemplary. Abbott struggled with but could not reconcile this apparent contradiction, reflecting again the same ambiguity between received and perceived values that he had expressed about the old whaler Monday on the voyage to India.

Writing of the 1850s, Isabella Burton, the long-suffering wife of explorer and diplomat Sir Richard Burton, also observed,

> *The Bibi (white woman) was at that time rare in India; the result was the triumph of the Bubu (colored sister). I found every officer in the corps more or less provided with one of these helpmates.... [She] teaches him not only Hindostani grammar, but the syntaxes of native life. She keeps house for him.... She keeps the servants in order. She has an infallible recipe to prevent maternity, especially if her tenure of office depends on such compact. She looks after him in sickness, and is one of the best of nurses, and, as it is not good for man to live alone, she makes him a manner of home.*[84]

As the population of mixed-heritage offspring increased as a result of such liaisons despite "infallible recipes," so naturally did marriage with them. So-called half-caste ladies were very much sought after as wives. Durba Ghosh notes that the female Eurasian orphans at the Lower Orphan School established by the East India Company were highly sought after as wives in the early nineteenth century, describing them as the "Cinderellas of the establishment."[85]

Intercultural marriage was also perhaps the most common theme of period Anglo-Indian novels, a case of art mirroring contemporary social realities, as Anglo-Indians struggled to come to terms with this dichotomy and their own social insecurities.[86] *The Baboo and Other Tales Descriptive of Society in India*, a novel by Augustus Princep published in 1834, tells the story of Lieutenant Colonel Henry Forester, who has been reported dead but is later found living with a Muslim woman: "He married a Mohummedan girl—or at least lives with her as if married; and some say he has turned Moosulman to please her."[87] Abbott himself left fragments of an unfinished novel about an English officer, "Captain Adam" of the Shah's Contingent, who was left behind in Kabul at the time of the British retreat and nursed back to health by "Begum Gool

Behar," the beautiful daughter of an Afghan prince. In wooden prose and dialogue, Adam struggles to convince her to marry him, but she refuses because she does not want to burden him with an Afghan wife: "Let me not become a curse to him I would fain have served," the girl tells him. "Let me not see him truly pining over a lot forced upon him by circumstances; and envying every man he sees happy in the possession of an English wife." Abbott's contribution to this long-running trope in Anglo-Indian literature regarding mixed-heritage marriages was reflective of his own deep-seated anxiety over the contested space between romantic love and social order.[88]

Such desires sometimes also made their way into visual depictions. In the satirical illustration "Tom Raw Is Introduced to His Regimental Commander" by Charles D'Oyly,[89] described earlier, for example, the kindly old Regimental Colonel Banks is being introduced to Tom Raw, with Banks's Indian wife standing on the right and his comely daughter Charlotte peeking out from behind a curtain *en dishabille* behind Tom's left arm. Charlotte Banks is the belle of the station, described as "a girl of sixteen, pretty too, though brown," who is ardently courted by all the officers at the garrison. D'Oyly's satirical poem makes clear that the daughters of mixed marriages at this time (1828) were considered eminently suitable wives. Lieutenant Robert Wallace also noted their popularity, while also repeating the increasingly common agitprop about social consequences, a lever no doubt intentionally deployed against the social insecurity that was the East India Company officer's psychological Achilles' heel.[90] The practice itself, however, remained ubiquitous and unaffected. Ultimately, British society in India was better at presenting a narrative of a decline in cross-cultural relationships than in actually achieving one.[91]

Although the sexual dimension remained largely impervious, however, the relationship between the peoples of India and Britons *was* changing in other spheres, including the Indian Army, commerce, and, especially, administration and governance. Nothing illustrates this change more dramatically than a remarkable incident in which Abbott got into a brawl with native troopers in 1828. While visiting Simla, Abbott paid a visit to Mrs. Lockhart, the wife of the political agent in Bhurtpore and

Figure 3.4. An expanded detail from the illustration "Tom Raw Is Introduced to His Regimental Commander" by Charles D'Oyly, published in *Tom Raw, the Griffin, a Burlesque Poem* (London: Printed for R. Ackermann, 1828) (seen in figure 2.6). The colonel's Indian wife is depicted standing on the far right, and their daughter Charlotte is seen in the background *en dishabille*, peeking out from behind the curtain in the doorway behind Tom Raw's left elbow. D'Oyly describes her as being ardently courted by all the British officers in the colonel's regiment.
(YALE CENTER FOR BRITISH ART)

a friend of his sister Emma. Sharing the house with Mrs. Lockhart was Mrs. Johnson, whom Abbott describes as "a Eurasian Lady,"[92] the wife of Colonel Johnson,[93] the commander of a corps of irregular cavalry (*sowars*). Mrs. Lockhart's sister was ill and being nursed in the house. Abbott went outside to quiet a commotion in the yard: "I allayed the uproar and was reentering ... the house when a native drest like a khitmatgar began to roar aloud in defiance of me. After vainly ordering him to hold his peace I walked up to him put my hand on his shoulder and threatened to push him over if he did not desist. He said insolently, 'What, will you lay hands upon a sowar?' 'Are you a sowar?' I said and released him."[94] This makes clear that British officers did not normally make any physical contact with Indian troops. As soon as Abbott learned that the man he was touching was a *sowar*, he withdrew his hand. What happened next, however, was disgraceful and reflects no credit on any Briton in India:

As I left the house I saw the sowar with two others. . . . They threatened me for having laid hands upon one of the party. . . . I knew something of the insolence of which men of Irregular Cavalry were capable from some encounters with them at Karnal,[95] *so that now I fully expected they would fall upon me. . . . I was half way down the hill when I heard a native calling me to return. I did not condescend to turn my head or to alter my pace. Presently footsteps were heard and one of the sowars was at my left elbow ordering me to return and saying that his mistress (Mrs. Johnstone)* [sic] *had sent for me.*[96]

Although Mrs. Johnson had sent the *sowars* to ask Abbott to return, he did not consider this course of action. The reason is unclear. The irregular cavalry were notorious for their relatively lax military discipline, however. One British officer named his cat "Indian Cavalry" because, he said, when it wasn't eating or sleeping, it was playing games or fornicating.[97] Abbott clearly expected them to assault him. However, although the *sowars* may have been angry about deep cuts in the numbers of irregular cavalry around this time, even irregular cavalry troopers would not have initiated a fight with a British officer. Abbott seems to have wanted a fight and started one.

A hand was laid upon my collar and like lightening I smote him full in the face, repeating the blow right and left until he fell flat on his back. I turned just in time to meet another sowar . . . who came rushing and roaring at me. . . . Him I [also] pummeled in the face. . . . Meanwhile the first fellow . . . was clinging around my legs and trying to throw me, and the second assailant had taken off one of his heavy shoes and with one arm clinging around my neck was battering my face with the . . . shoe. . . . When the [first] sowar found that he could not stir me from my feet, he took a cowardly advantage of me[98] *which rendered me utterly powerless, and at the same moment the third sowar came rushing to their assistance.*[99]

Abbott did not believe they were calling him back on Mrs. Johnson's orders, but his behavior in not replying to the *sowar* was arrogant, and

Figure 3.5. Left: a detail from *Skinner's Horse at Exercise*, painting by John Gwatkin, circa 1840, shows the conical hat worn by Skinner's Horse and the flowing yellow *shalwar*, or tunic, which earned them the nickname "Yellow Boys." Right: a detail from the photograph "Khitmatgar, Meerut" by S. Murray, circa 1891, depicting a waiter in the traditional dress of his occupation, shows how Abbott could have initially mistaken the irregular cavalrymen at Simla for household staff. (LEFT: NATIONAL ARMY MUSEUM; RIGHT: HARAPPA.COM)

throwing the first punch was the behavior of a ruffian, not a gentleman. It might perhaps be explained as the sort of outburst of anger that typifies posttraumatic stress disorder in combat veterans. He had no choice but to go back with them to the house, but he immediately reported the altercation to the adjutant general. By fighting back, the *sowars* had unfortunately crossed a military Rubicon unfamiliar to the rough Muslim hillmen who made up the irregular cavalry. Nevertheless, what followed can only be described as a travesty of justice of the type that did much to loosen the bond of trust between Briton and sepoy.

Despite the fact that by his own admission Abbott had thrown the first punch, all three *sowars* were sentenced to eight hundred lashes and dismissed from the army. Mrs. Johnson's role was not introduced in the court-martial; nor were the men allowed to use her orders in their defense. Enlisted men in any army, at any time and place in history, are for obvious reasons prohibited from assaulting their officers, so these *sowars* could not afterward have remained in Company service, but a sentence of eight hundred lashes was an act of cruel and vindictive brutality, not justice. Abbott subsequently recorded another incident in 1829 involving a brawl between European artillerymen and some sepoys of the 37th Bengal Native Infantry that took place in the bazaar at Karnal. Both fights would have been unthinkable twenty years earlier.

Into this increasingly hostile relationship between Britons and the people of India stepped William Bentinck in 1828 as governor-general of India. The arrival of a man thought to be more resolute and energetic than Lord Amherst was eagerly anticipated by many Britons in India.[100] They got far more than they bargained for. Bentinck arrived with a simple mandate from the Board of Directors in London—staunch the red ink and make the East India Company pay for itself—but he rode in on a wave of enthusiasm for "progress" and "reform" in India that had already gained currency and momentum in the metropole from the Utilitarian movement.[101] Austerity and reform were perhaps inevitable given the economic and political climate of the day, but the way Bentinck went about both certainly hastened the Company's demise.

To implement reform, Bentinck required the support and cooperation of the "military garrison state."[102] The officers of the East India Company greatly outnumbered civil servants and were in a position to support or undermine Bentinck's agenda. Nevertheless, he chose as his first major order of business the implementation of a measure crafted by his predecessor, Lord Amherst, to reduce by 50 percent the field allowances, known as *batta*, of the Company's officers. In terms of the overall budget, the savings the measure would actually achieve were infinitesimal, but it is hard to conceive of any action better calculated to infuriate and alienate the Indian Army officer corps. The reductions in *batta*, which formed a considerable fraction of officers' remuneration,[103] fell disproportionately on artillery officers, who were clustered at the stations where *batta* was to be cut. As Douglas Peers notes, "The total [annual] savings of the half-*batta* order was about £6,000, which amounted to 0.05% of the total military budget of £10,773,966," but "the political and military consequences were enormous. The half-*batta* issue caused irreparable damage to relations between Bentinck and the army."[104]

Bentinck's zeal for cutting costs and increasing revenues sometimes reached absurd extremes and gave rise to persistent rumors about his cultural insensitivity and even his honesty. Still in Agra at this time, for example, was the famed Agra Gun.[105] Bentinck's appropriation of it for recycling infuriated Abbott, who shared the minority view that Bentinck was personally corrupt. The enormous gun weighed an estimated ninety thousand pounds. Bentinck proposed hauling the gun away and melting it down for scrap metal. "This was done to the great indignation of European and Asiatic," Abbott noted, adding, "It is said that the same worthy tried to sell the Taj [Mahal] to be broken up for material but could get no sufficient bid—such are the Goths who bring disgrace upon a nation."[106]

Far more important than the Agra Gun and rumors about the Taj Mahal, however, was Bentinck's passion for "reform," which led to a wide-ranging effort at social engineering in India in the 1830s. The chief elements were sweeping changes in the judicial system, including the switch from Persian to English as the language of higher courts and the suppression of sati.[107] The reforms alarmed Hindu elites, particularly upper-caste Brahmins, some of whom began to take seriously the bazaar rumors that the British were bent upon breaking their religious and financial power and Christianizing the country. While Bentinck's progressive zeal in India's social sphere is well known, far less well documented are his controversial army reforms, which Abbott believed were a leading cause of the Great Mutiny of 1857. Mutiny historians have paid little attention

CHAPTER 3

to the fundamental changes Bentinck effected upon the Indian Army in the early 1830s, perhaps because their impact appears at first to be of a technical nature. In fact, their effects in the decades that followed them were devastating, as will be seen.

From 1833 until his departure in 1835, Bentinck focused his energies on the subject of Indian Army reform, declaring, "I fearlessly pronounce the Indian Army to be the least efficient and the most expensive in the world."[108] He rightly believed Indian troops had no real attachment to their British employers and recommended the number of British troops in India should be roughly doubled, to comprise one-third of the army.[109] This was prompted, however, not by a fear of mutiny by sepoy troops but rather by fear of a foreign invasion of India and his conviction that only European troops could successfully repel one. He therefore moved the majority of the British troops in India to its frontiers. If Bentinck's fear had been of internal rebellion and not external invasion, he would hardly have denuded central Bengal of British troops, a disposition that was not reversed by his successors and weighed heavily in the early weeks of the Great Mutiny of 1857.

While Bentinck was a visionary in some respects, in particular in regard to the need to foster a limited indigenous capability for self-governance through education and clerical capacity building, he was also deeply prejudiced against the peoples of India, particularly so against lower castes. He fully subscribed to the simplistic mirroring of British class strata upon Indian caste structure and the fantasy narrative in particular of the Bengal sepoy as a yeoman farmer.[110] For this reason, Bentinck endorsed and accelerated the recruitment of upper-caste Brahmin sepoys into the Bengal Army and promoted the primacy of the Bengal Army as the East India Company's premier fighting force. These policies brought together the essential ingredients necessary for a widespread rebellion in north-central Bengal in 1857.[111]

The fundamental misunderstanding of Hindu culture on the part of Bentinck and most Bengal Army officers reached its peak at precisely the same time that changing British interpretations of caste were beginning to enter Anglo-Indian consciousness in a significant way. Under Bentinck's reforms, the portion of the Bengal Army comprised of upper-caste Brahmins and recruited from a relatively small area of the Gangetic Plain—already at 60 percent before Bentinck's arrival—would reach a critical mass of 85 percent of the Bengal Native Infantry by the time of the Mutiny. It was precisely this segment of the Indian Army, not the lower-caste sepoys of the Madras and Bombay armies, the Sikhs, or the Gurkhas, who mutinied in 1857. So convinced was Bentinck of the importance of high-caste Hindus in the army, he not only sharply increased their recruitment, he also outlawed the flogging of indigenous troops as offensive to upper-caste Hindus (while retaining it for European troops), increased sepoy pay, and established offices in the Gangetic Plain to improve pension delivery for retired Bengal Army sepoys.[112]

Not everyone was convinced of the wisdom of this policy. A few British officers began at this time to argue, rightly as it transpired, that the upper-caste Hindu sepoy was more concerned with preserving his religious status than with his military duties. In the 1830s a small but growing unease first formed within the Bengal Army that the high-caste Brahmin sepoy was the problem, not the solution. The sepoy's caste obligations were seen by a small minority as interfering with, even trumping, his military duties. On two occasions in 1830, for example, Sir John Malcolm, the governor of Bombay from 1827 to 1830, warned Bentinck against replacing "pride of corps" with "pride of caste," arguing that the Brahmin sepoy could not be trusted because of his religious obligations.[113] Charles Grant, the Company director who signed Abbott's cadet appointment, warned his colleagues, "This whole fabric [of Hinduism] is the work of a crafty and impervious priesthood, who feign a divine revelation and appointment, [in order] to invest their own order in perpetuity with the most absolute empire over the civil state of the Hindoos, as well as over their minds."[114]

This remained a minority view for twenty years but was still present in 1850, when General John Hodgson argued that high-caste Brahmin sepoys were using their religion covertly to corrupt other sepoys into dereliction of duty.[115] Sir Charles Napier declared in 1853 that the Bengal sepoy could not be relied upon because he had "two commanders to obey, caste and captain."[116] For many, this realization came too late. Major General Richard Birch testified in 1859 he could not "conceive the possibility of maintaining discipline in a corps where a low-caste non-commissioned officer will, when he meets off duty a Brahman Sipâhi, crouch down to him with his forehead on the ground. I have seen this done. The Sipâhi thus treated is the master of the [sepoy noncommissioned] officer."[117]

Increasing the number of high-caste Hindu sepoys by 25 percent was not the only major change cited by Abbott to have momentous consequences. The disempowering of the Native Officers and Bentinck's marginalizing of the British regimental commanders deeply undermined the chain of command. Every unit in the Indian Army had Indian officers (subedars), who were senior to all enlisted sepoys but junior to all British officers. The Indian officers performed the same function as the noncommissioned officers of modern armies today, which is leadership at the squad and platoon level. Efficient military organizations rely on strong leadership at this level of the chain of command. Prior to the 1830s, subedars were *the* critical link between the sepoys and the British officers in each unit. Orders were given through them, their power within their units was extensive, and they possessed a more intimate knowledge of what was going on inside the sepoys' barracks and minds than British officers could ever hope to have, no matter how assimilated to local languages and customs they had become. Furthermore, because attaining these ranks was also purely a matter of seniority, as it was for the Company's British officers, many, if not most, of the subedars were close to the age and number of years of service required for a comfortable annuity upon retirement. Thus, ironically, it was they, and not the high-caste Brahmin sepoys, who were vested in the continuity of British rule. They were, in essence, the lynchpin of the entire relationship between Britons and enlisted men in the Indian Army, the critical "middle ground between the European officer and the sepoys."[118]

Nevertheless the power of the "native officers" was eroded throughout the first third of the nineteenth century, until they possessed little authority and commanded virtually no respect from those beneath them.[119] Humiliated and powerless, they largely withdrew from any active interest in their units and the welfare of their men. The critical link between British officers and sepoys was severed. With only 40 percent of the regimental officers present and the subedars largely marginalized, real leadership and influence shifted to the religious authority of the highest-caste Brahmins in each unit.[120]

Most critically of all, Abbott points out, Bentinck's military reforms also stripped the British regimental colonels of most of their authority over their regiments. Prior to Bentinck's army reforms, regimental commanders held the power of promotion and demotion in the enlisted ranks, as well as sole authority for punishment of infractions not requiring formal courts-martial. Everything from who went on leave and for how long to who received rewards for good performance and who was punished for indiscipline had been the prerogative of the regimental commander. Bentinck's reforms wrecked that system by effectively stripping these powers from the regimental colonels and placing them higher in the chain of command. Sepoys accused of minor infractions could now appeal to higher headquarters and routinely did. Bentinck's reforms completed the internal collapse of British and Indian leadership within the Bengal Army. The results would be catastrophic.

4

D'Arcy Todd and the Revenue Survey

1834–1838

IN EARLY 1829, JAMES ABBOTT'S FRIENDSHIP WITH D'ARCY TODD WAS renewed when Todd was transferred to Karnal and the two men built a bungalow near the Horse Battery lines. Soon after they moved in, Todd fell dangerously ill with fever.[1] Over many weeks, Abbott nursed him back to health, as Todd recorded in a letter to his brother, Colonel Frederick Todd: "My dearest of friends, James Abbott, was unceasing in his brotherly attention. He never left my bedside. Oh! The goodness of God in giving me such a friend to smooth my pillow and to cheer me by his presence. He is the dearest friend of your brother. From the time we left Bhar—the foot of the Hills—he attended me on foot until we arrived here; and when he departed my heart was agonized."[2]

Abbott and Todd came from very similar backgrounds. Todd's mother, who is best known as Samuel Coleridge's first love, Mary Evans, was also widowed when he was quite young. She too faced straightened financial circumstances as a result and also managed to secure appointments to Addiscombe for her sons through family connections. Both men shared a sense of the Romantic spirit and enjoyed writing poetry. Todd was socially outgoing and more religious, spending a considerable amount of his time in Bible reading and prayer circles at the garrison. Abbott was always very introverted, preferring to remain at home, and although his own faith was absolute and heartfelt, he did not share it with others.

Abbott's devotion to Todd was boundless. Todd's fever soon recurred, and he was sent to the hill station at Dehradun to recover. In October 1829, six months after their new bungalow was finished, Abbott was ordered to command of the 3rd Company, 1st Battalion of the Bengal Artillery and ordered to Mhow, 625 miles south. Before leaving Karnal for Mhow, he rode one hundred miles in three days to Dehradun, day and night in the saddle, to visit with Todd for a single day, writing, "I got leave to run up . . . to see him. . . . I found my friend greatly recovered and enjoyed one happy day with him sitting on the mountain side, talking over the past and dreaming of the future."[3]

Interpreting the relationship between Abbott and Todd requires considerable unlearning. Beginning with Sigmund Freud, the last century sexualized virtually everything. But the last century was anomalous "in its automatic post-Freudian suspicion of intense emotional friendships between men."[4] The nineteenth century was steeped in the Greek and medieval revivals and a spiritual rebirth of Christianity, which stressed the search for spiritual perfection. This Christian spiritualism taught that sex was an impediment to this quest and specifically that manly love was superior to and "exceeded the love of women" precisely because it was free of the sexual dimension and consisted of "the non-sexual friendship between equals, men of similar age, rank, habits and sentiments, attracted by each other's character."[5]

This was also a part of the medieval revival of the late Georgian period, which stressed the twelve knightly virtues, defined by Alain Chartier as faith, loyalty, honor, righteousness, prowess, love, courtesy, diligence, cleanliness, generosity, soberness, and perseverance.[6] These essentially define Abbott's self-image. They also dovetail neatly with Abbott's love of Sir Walter Scott and Scott's contributions to medieval revivalism in the first half of the nineteenth century, where "courtly love between knight and lady could exist side-by-side with manly love between knights."[7] The reimagined Middle Ages, in the words of Bryan Fone, "stressed knightly comradeship and chivalry and told of a largely all-male world . . . in which the real life lay in the close bonding of men in manly valor and honor."[8] The influential French Renaissance philosopher Michel de Montaigne and British authors Percy Shelley and Charles Metcalfe all wrote of

Figure 4.1. Pen-and-ink sketch of D'Arcy Todd by an unknown artist circa 1835. (THE BRITISH MUSEUM)

the pure, platonic male bond of friendship.[9] Almost the entire ethos of early-nineteenth-century British manliness was based on this ideal. Boys' schools stressed and amplified its importance. Jeffrey Richards notes that "manly love [was] a central strand in the definition of manliness [and] was one of the qualities which the public schools sought to inculcate."[10] Abbott and Todd's friendship was the epitome of this ideal.

Late in 1829 Abbott departed Karnal for Mhow. The company under his command consisted of eighty-five European gunners and their cannons, twenty sepoys to guard the guns, and twenty gun lascars, who helped move the artillery and ammunition.[11] Accompanying him also were his second in command, Lieutenant Saunders, and Dr. Christopher Bryce, the medical officer. Setting out, Abbott noted, "I was anxious about the conduct of the men.... We were to pass a somewhat wild track and I hoped I might meet with some adventure."[12] He got more than he expected.

The route of march took Abbott through Jaipur, one of the most picturesque cities in India. It was home to an observatory built by Jye Singh, which Abbott visited, noting in his journals that the instruments were of great interest. He added he was "struck with the costume of the petticoated Rajpooties" and thought Jaipur probably the "handsomest city in India."[13] Soon thereafter a journal entry highlights the comradeship and mutual respect that could still be found between British officers and their sepoys: "It was I think at the second march beyond Jypoor that my table servants sent on ahead took the wrong road and I found myself on my arrival in a fair way to fast for at least twenty four hours. The Jemandar[14] of my guard of Sipâhis, a fine veteran, learning this insisted upon dressing and sending me Kurie and rice—the most delicious I have ever tasted."[15]

The march tested Abbott's leadership and his talent for improvisation. The route to Mhow was not well known at this time, and there was confusion about supply points. The upshot was that his company's food supplies were sent to locations that were not on his assigned route of march. To feed his European troops, he had to resort to slaughtering cattle, but this had to be done discreetly because a treaty existed with the Rajput states prohibiting the killing of cows (and, oddly, peacocks) by Company personnel. Despite precautions, his company butchers were caught literally red-handed in the early dawn one morning by a local man, who came to Abbott in horror of the scene.

This was a difficult situation. First Abbott asked the man how he knew they were cows, inquiring whether he saw butchered cows often and if they might not be buffaloes instead. The man was silent. Abbott realized this ruse was not working, so he tried another tack. He asked the man what he was doing in a British camp, whether he had an official pass, and, in the absence of one, whether he was a spy or a thief. Knowing he needed time to remove evidence of the slaughter and get his men on their way before the tale was told, Abbott ordered the man detained (on the invented grounds of his being either a spy or a thief) and kept under guard overnight. Once his men had covered several miles of their march the next day, he released the witness with an apology.

On another occasion, the dromedary of his *shootur sowar*[16] was stolen from the company lines at night and tracked to a nearby fortified village. Abbott's eighty-five Europeans were armed with modern Brown Bess muskets and bayonets, the twenty sepoys were armed with older muskets, and the twenty gun lascars were armed with cutlasses. A siege of the village could be improvised, but Abbott hardly had the authority to go to war over a camel. Nor could he allow a government camel to be stolen by the chieftain of a rural village. He tried a bluff: "I sent for the Jemadar, told him what had happened, [and] desired him[17] to get under arms [the sepoys] and the lascar detachment and march down to the city gate, insist upon seeing the Kotiwal[18] and explain to him that the camel must be immediately surrendered. That I was reluctant to bring my European artillery, as once they entered the city, it would be difficult to save the honor of his women or the property and lives of the citizens." It was a ruse that could have gone badly wrong. The guards manning the town walls might have fired on the sepoys or the *jemadar* delivering the message, and Abbott was well aware that would leave him no choice but to fight. British troops could not ignore such a provocation. "We were more than a hundred miles from any British station," Abbott wrote, adding, "We could have knocked down the gate and ... entered the town. But such a fracas might have lost me my commission."[19] Again his luck held. The camel was surrendered with apologies. Abbott had demonstrated good judgment, a cool head, and an ability for lateral thinking in avoiding the binary choices of fighting or losing the animal. He had also controlled his own emotions. He was aware of his shortcomings in this regard, noting, "My notion of resenting insults promptly was very deep rooted."[20] On this occasion, he mastered them. Unfortunately for his career, he would not always do as well in the future.

When he arrived in Mhow, he bought a small, imbricated bungalow and, in the belief that D'Arcy Todd was soon to be transferred there, decided to enlarge it, which turned out to be a poor investment when Todd was not assigned to Mhow after all. Here Abbott became even more reclusive. "The separation from my friends [at Karnal] left me very lonely," he wrote. "I do not easily find those with whom I can assimilate and at Mhow I formed scarcely an acquaintance of any kind."[21] Time spent like this in the *mofussil* could be very psychologically taxing. As a fellow officer, I. H. T. Roberdeau, noted, "Country life in India is dull, gloomy, spiritless and solitary, and a man doomed to it is much to be pitied if he has not lasting amusements and resources within himself. The man whose happiness depends upon foreign and external circumstances will experience weary hours which he knows not how to employ, and from which he cannot fly."[22] Abbott in this sense was fortunate in being an introvert who enjoyed time alone. Nevertheless, he was not a hermit. He made friends with the de Montmorency family, an acquaintance that was to have fateful consequences in later years, but after they left, there was no one at the station with whom he felt comfortable.

Instead, he did something quite remarkable for a British officer: he began spending all his days in the nearby village of Patalpanie,[23] which was to become his first full immersion in South Asian culture:

> *My solitary habits at Mhow brought me into acquaintance with the peasantry of the pretty village of Patalpanie, which I haunted morning and evening. This was of use to me, showing the natives as they really are and not as we find them debased and degraded in our cantonments. I had received from several of them kind attentions, such as the offer of fruit, milk and [so on], and wished to make them some return. As they were men whose duties required them to keep a watch*

> *at night over their valuable crops, I bought half a dozen good blankets and had them carried down to Patalpanie and begged their acceptance of them. Nothing however could persuade them to comply.... If I would make each of them a pouch for tobacco, would they accept it as a remembrance? I ... made them pouches and they were greatly pleased.*[24]

It was at Mhow that his *khidmatgar*, seeing how drowsy he was in the evenings, suggested he have a cup of coffee after dinner, to which he eventually consented. The change it wrought was profound. "I found the effect of the coffee in brightening up my faculties and preventing drowsiness so delightful," he wrote, "that I looked forward the whole day to my solitary evening."[25] He took to writing poetry with great intensity. He was working on his book-length poem *Constance* at the time, and the stimulation of the coffee made possible the writing of some fifty lines a night. "Under the influence of this inspiration my fancy took flight to the realms of the fairy and my power of giving words to my visions was developed.... [T]he excitement under which [*Constance*] was written was most delightful."[26] He got less and less rest, however, as when he went to bed around midnight, he was unable to fall asleep.

It was at this time too that Abbott was struck by what, from his description, was clinical depression, which began with a panic attack:

> *A sudden sense of horror crept over me—A terror of I knew not what—A dread to be alone. A doubt of my own power of volition. No words can describe the misery which ensued—and which haunted me afterwards more or less for more than 20 years.... I dreaded lest I should infect other minds with the terrible faculty mine had acquired of looking as it were inwards and discovering all its hidden machinery. I struggled with it in secret, hour after hour, day after day, month after month, year after year. Solitude had become terrible to me, yet I could not go into society. I applied to the doctor who recommended me to drink wine and gave me medicine—But nothing afforded relief. It was some time before I discovered that I was laboring under*

dispression[27] *caused by over-exercise of the mental faculties under the action of strong coffee.*[28]

In the first half of the nineteenth century, depression was commonly referred to as "melancholia," a term that became increasingly associated with women as the century progressed. Aristotle associated melancholia with a sensitive temperament, excessive mental activity, and writing poetry, asking, "Why is it that all men who have become outstanding in philosophy, statesmanship, poetry and the arts are melancholic?"[29] Indeed, melancholy fascinated the Romantics, Keats in particular, who wrote "Ode on Melancholy" in 1819.[30]

The seminal medical work on depression during Abbott's lifetime was Robert Burton's *The Anatomy of Melancholy*,[31] first printed in 1621 but reprinted frequently and a book Abbott would certainly have been familiar with. Abbott was literate in Greek and classically schooled, such that he was quite likely aware of Aristotle's views on depression, but Burton's *Anatomy* also covers Aristotle's work on melancholia in some detail. It is surely not a coincidence that Abbott first mentions his struggle with depression in the context of his late-night work on the poem *Constance*.

Although he wrote at this time that he often envied those who died, he did not entertain suicidal thoughts. "I have since gone through great suffering of various kinds," he wrote, "but in comparison [to this] terrible affliction, all were as nothing.... The prospect of life was terrific[32] yet I never despaired—I knew that One Eye pitied me [which] watched the resolution with which I resisted all temptations to give way."[33]

Abbott spent six years in garrison duty at Mhow, writing poetry and increasingly immersing himself in village life at Patalpanie. He doggedly sought an appointment in the Revenue Survey of India, which was then painstakingly mapping and registering every individual plot of land in the North-Western Provinces. Work in the survey entailed detachment from the Indian Army and temporary assignment to civilian employment, which was far better paid. Meanwhile, Abbott deployed a novel strategy for getting out of debt: writing for publication. In 1833, while at Mhow, he wrote *The Private Centinel* [sic], which was first published in serial form in the *East India United Services Journal*: "Mr. Stoequeler had

CHAPTER 4

offered 1£ per sheet for contributions. I was then at Mhow in Malwa, burdened with debt incurred on first landing in India. This [debt] the papers of Snellius Schickhardus, the Johdpore Countermarch[34] and other essays enabled me to discharge, leaving me the means of making my first remittance to my Mother."[35] Abbott's submissions to the *United Services Journal* under various pseudonyms often contained veiled criticism of official policy couched in a "humor in uniform" vein. Peter Stanley notes, "Officers customarily expressed freely their views in newspapers over anything concerning their profession, including, for example, the fitness of officers nominated for senior staff positions, questions which in Britain would have been the subject of private comment."[36] Governors-General Lord Ellenborough (February 1842–June 1844) and Lord Hardinge (July 1844–January 1848) both complained about the manner in which officers used the press to question and criticize their superiors.[37] Abbott availed himself of this channel for expression freely, though anonymously, in a manner that seems all but unimaginable within the confines of military discipline today. Anonymity in such criticism was prudent: official frustration with this behavior escalated from efforts to suppress it by official regulation to courts-martial. In 1850, Captain Christopher Hassell was tried for publishing sharp criticisms and writing disrespectful complaints to his superiors. In 1852, Captain George Thompson was tried but acquitted for publishing disrespectful newspaper articles.

Abbott and Todd corresponded regularly and sent each other poems. Early in 1835, D'Arcy received a coveted assignment to the Political Department with orders to proceed to Teheran as a trainer for the Persian artillery. In October that year, Abbott too managed to escape stultifying regimental duty by securing a position in the Revenue Survey of the North-Western Provinces from Major James Bedford, the Deputy Surveyor General. By that time, the Revenue Survey had undergone significant changes since its inception in 1822.[38] In 1832, after a decade of slow and precise work encumbered by the collection of vast amounts of extraneous data, Governor-General William Bentinck personally intervened to streamline and expedite the process. He increased the number of surveyors and reduced the amount of data collected.[39] This zeal on Bentinck's part gave Abbott his first opening for a position outside the

Bengal Artillery. The number of survey groups was increased from four to nine between 1833 and 1836, and Abbott got his first break as the leader of one of the five new teams.[40] Between 1833 and 1842, a total of twenty-seven districts were surveyed, including Bareilly and Shahjahanpoor, which were completed by Abbott.[41] When it was finished, the survey covered seventy-two thousand square miles and encompassed a population of twenty-three million people.[42]

It has become de rigueur in recent years to ascribe the basest discernible motives to colonial British administrative actions and, in so doing, to oversimplify what were in reality complex and earnestly contested matters of social policy. The revenue settlement of the North-Western Provinces is one such issue. While it would be difficult to argue that maximizing the efficiency of land tax collection was not the primary purpose of the survey, the broader land policy issue of which it was a part was far more complex. The debate over the nature of landownership in India illustrates the struggle during the 1830s between reformers like James Mill, acting through William Bentinck, and the "paternalists" like Thomas Munro, Mountstuart Elphinstone, John Malcolm, and Charles Metcalfe, who in 1830 famously referred to the villages as "little republics."[43]

For decades the paternalists urged that traditional land tenure systems be maintained to avoid destabilizing a society over which British control was fragile at best. But by the 1830s traditionalism was crumbling under the new passion for reform in which land tenure was only one aspect of a broad spectrum of progressive changes that also encompassed the legal system, the military, education, and religion.

Mill and Bentinck were strongly opposed to the old system of *zamindars* and *taluqdars*, the local administrators and tax collectors established by the Mughals. The zamindars and taluqdars lived by collecting rents from the *ryots* (or *ryuts*), the peasant farmers of the land. Bentinck and British administrators of the 1830s like Holt Mackenzie and Robert Bird believed this system had become irretrievably corrupted by earlier policies established under Governor-General Charles Cornwallis. They were proponents instead of reverting to an even earlier system of communal ownership of village lands. In theory, this would not only eliminate an existing but still inchoate aristocracy of landowners but also help prevent or retard a system in which outsiders could gradually buy up parcels of agricultural land from debtor *ryots* and become absentee landlords. The debate was complex and nuanced. Some accepted that the existing system was flawed but believed it should be maintained because the *ryots* were now accustomed to it and any change would be destabilizing. The Mackenzie and Bird camp wanted to set the clock back to the system in existence before Clive, while still others wanted to sweep it all away and replace it entirely with a more progressive landownership system.

On this issue, Bentinck was in the middle camp. He was, as noted earlier, a firm believer in the growing British meme of the Brahmin landholder as a direct parallel with the British yeoman farmer. He also believed in the basic principle espoused by John Stuart Mill that only those who worked the soil had a lasting interest in it. As a result, Bentinck and his reformers decided in favor of the pre-Cornwallis system of communal peasant proprietorship at the village level. Thus social policy was inextricably interwoven with revenue policy, resulting in a complex tapestry of motivations for the survey. Many officers believed they were performing a lasting good for the people of India. This was frequently tied to a growing British sense of paternalism. Henry Lawrence, Abbott's school friend from Addiscombe and now a fellow surveyor, for example, wrote that he wanted to "give up ... firing large guns at the black people. ... I would now much prefer preventing them breaking each other's heads, and be instrumental in leading them into the paths of civilization."[44]

The establishment of the North-Western Provinces coincided with Bentinck's administration and became a kind of showcase for these reforming principles. The North-Western Provinces were made a separate administrative entity with its own judicial system in 1832, the height of Bentinck's reforming energies, and remained so until just before the Great Mutiny of 1857, when Oudh was annexed and the area was renamed the "North-Western Provinces and Oudh." Not coincidentally, these provinces were the epicenter of the Mutiny. The reforming land tenure principles were incorporated into the survey, and "wherever possible the right [of proprietorship] was vested in the village community and all superior tenures were extinguished."[45] The blowback from this policy was the alienation and disenfranchisement of powerful and wealthy upper-class landowners dispossessed of their land claims by the new system, and this social group was a leading instigator of the rebellion in 1857.

Nevertheless, for the decade of the 1830s, a politically ascendant group of colonial officials crafted land policy from a genuinely held belief that they were improving the lives and futures of millions of peasants in India by substantially strengthening their land tenure. This quest against injustice naturally appealed to James Abbott, in whom the knight-errant was always ascendant. He too adhered to the view that the system of tenure prior to Clive's reforms had been fairer to the *ryots*, and he was a strong advocate of the traditionalism of Metcalfe and the paternalist ethic of "not interfering with the natives' superstitions."

Abbott's Romantic sensibilities also mirrored those of Munro and Malcolm in viewing earlier times in India's history as its halcyon period. Bentinck's land reformers, in particular James Mackenzie and Robert Bird, who was charged with carrying out the survey, were convinced that the proof of the failure of Cornwallis's policy was self-evident in Bengal, where a group of disinterested absentee landlords now controlled a large proportion of the arable land. Ireland at the time was an unpleasant contemporary analogy. The prevailing sense among British officers in Bengal was that justice was under siege from the venal landlords in the North-Western Provinces, and a return to the kind of imagined historical Romantic ideal of pre-Cornwallis India was exactly the kind of knightly quest that Abbott was drawn to. Because of Bird's work to put the land back in the hands of the villagers who worked it, Abbott considered him "the greatest benefactor the people of India have ever known."[46] Abbott's use of the word "benefactor" conveys clearly the sense that the officers working for Bird were on a kind of mission to save the peasant farmers.

The disenfranchisement of a powerful upper class of landholders, however, which was not an unintended consequence of the survey in the North-Western Provinces—as it had been in Madras, for example— added greatly to the growing alienation in the 1830s in Bengal between Britons and Bengalis. For if the British thought they were incurring the gratitude of the *ryot* for their efforts, they were gravely mistaken. Peasant loyalties remained firmly with the former landlords for a host of practical reasons grounded in the political economy of the village. Thus, at

CHAPTER 4

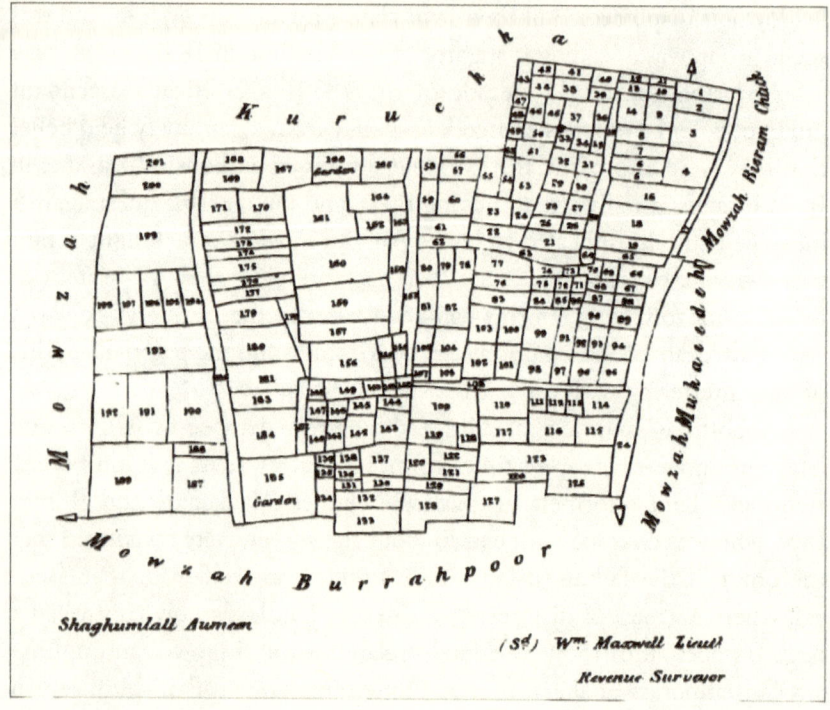

Figure 4.2. A detail from Plate XIV of Ralph Smyth and Henry Thuillier's *Manual of Surveying for India* (Calcutta: W. Thacker & Co., 1851). It shows a typical village map of the plots of farmland in a rural village. The surveyor's name, Lt. William Maxwell, appears in the lower right. (PUBLIC DOMAIN)

the outbreak of the Great Mutiny in 1857, if compelled to take sides, most *ryots* followed the bidding of their former landlords. Like a majority of military officers of his day, Abbott considered the Great Mutiny to be purely a military matter. He never connected the consequences of his Revenue Survey work in the rebellious provinces to the events of 1857.[47]

The technical survey process itself became the vehicle for implementation of Bentinck's reforming land policy. In establishing the village (the *mauza*) as the foundation for *how* the land was to be mapped, Bentinck's new surveying regulation of 1833, "Regulation 9," superseded previous assumptions about land tenure and privileged the village as the primary and enduring tenured agricultural entity. As B. A. Michael notes, "Villages could be treated as permanent entities, unlike estates which varied in shape and could disappear entirely over time.... [T]he village became the basic unit of surveying and formed the building blocks out of which administrative divisions such as the *pargana*[48] were to be reconstructed on maps."[49]

The cadaster process was straightforward in theory but difficult in practice. In consultation with the village chiefs, the local district officer marked out the boundaries of each village with stones. British officers and British or Eurasian assistants used a theodolite to demarcate the village boundaries and record them in a field book (*khasra chitta*). Indigenous surveyors then mapped and numbered every individual plot of land within the *mauza*. The *khasra chitta* listed the plot numbers, together with the names of the proprietors, their total area in square yards, the type of soil found there, and the crops usually grown on that particular plot. During Abbott's tenure, the process was further improved by two other Bengal Artillery officers, Captains Ralph Smyth and Henry Thuillier.[50] A really good survey team could complete one thousand square miles in a survey (i.e., non-monsoonal period) season.[51]

After a brief training period, Abbott reported to Bareilly District to take over from the departing Captain Fraser. Here he soon demonstrated the kind of leadership that would make him loved by many. He had two British civilian assistants, a Mr. Wyatt and a Mr. Dumbleton. He immediately obtained a promotion for Wyatt to a higher rank and pay grade. Dumbleton was handicapped by a belief that he suffered from epilepsy. Abbott had seen similar nocturnal seizures in his friend Arthur Conolly, and he took a solicitous interest in Dumbleton's case. He soon discovered that, like Conolly, Dumbleton was the victim of nightmares, compounded in his case by quackery. Abbott convinced him to stop the bleeding treatments and bizarre potions he was being treated with and allow himself to sleep through the night. He was quickly cured. Abbott then wrote the surveyor general, explained the error that had held up Dumbleton's promotion, and secured a promotion for him as well.

Abbott threw himself into the work, determined to prove his selection had been justified. His survey team, in addition to the two Britons, was comprised of three indigenous subassistants, fifteen indigenous surveyors, and twenty-five *mootsuddies*, or "chain men."[52] When the monsoon

CHAPTER 4

Figure 4.3. A detail from the print "Surveying in India," pen and ink with aquatint, by Walter Sherwill in 1855. Sherwill was a revenue surveyor and geologist working with the British East India Company. (PUBLIC DOMAIN)

set in, Abbott retrained his team to use the newer and faster field book method over the old board system. The next season he and his team completed over one thousand square miles, an excellent achievement. This completed the Bareilly District survey, so they moved on to the neighboring Shahjihanpoor District. The next season in Shahjihanpoor they accomplished 1,150 square miles, which was a record at the time. In his final season as a surveyor, they completed the district with an astonishing sixteen hundred square miles recorded.

Abbott found the work much to his liking. He remained a surveyor for almost four years, until 1838, writing that "the life suited well with my habits and temperament. I was eight months of each year under canvas, marching generally to a new encampment once every month and from there surveying and inspecting the operations around the new centre."[53] It is in Shahjihanpoor in 1838 that Abbott's first use of the word "race" is found, and the word is capitalized. However, Abbott employs it in a manner entirely opposite to how some scholars have suggested the British were already interpreting racial difference in India, using the term not to differentiate between peoples but to suggest a kind of monogenist universal humanism: "In [Shahjihanpoor] are found some noble specimens of the Rajpootie tribe. In Meerpoor especially there were some of the finest specimens I have seen in India of the human Race—countenances and figures that were models of manly beauty—the females I did not see."[54] The debate among scholars as to whether racialism entered British thinking in India at the turn of the nineteenth century or was a post–Charles Darwin phenomenon[55] in the mid-nineteenth century is a heated one, but the writings of James Abbott, who was as curious an intellectual and as interested in the latest developments in scientific thinking as anyone in India in the first half of the nineteenth century, certainly support the latter view. Abbott's first use of the word "race" to convey the idea of separate races rather than one holistic "human Race" dates to the mid-1850s.[56]

The second of the two artifacts of his writing in this period, his report to government on the Bareilly District, is also significant in this regard. Its format follows the regulation template of what information was to be gathered, including the size and type of local buildings, the diet and produce of the people, and the nature and possible causes of diseases,[57] but again there is no mention of "race" in either the format of the report or its contents.

Instead there is an emphasis on cultural anthropology, and extensive data are presented on castes, occupations, religions, and tribes. Abbott's report provides pages of detailed information, including a nuanced discussion of the most minor elements of the ethnographics of the district, such as the Bunjara[58] and the Kalandars[59] then present in very small numbers in Bareilly. His report reflects a startlingly comprehensive understanding of Indian ethnography and is a classic artifact of the British colonial knowledge project.[60]

Landownership arguments frequently arose as parcels of land were measured and boundaries established. The various types of land tenures and relationships between cultivators and owners were extraordinarily complex. As Tapan Raychaudhuri observes, "162 revenue terms were used to describe the various tenures and subtenures. Between the proprietor and the actual cultivator, there might be eight to twenty grades of intermediary tenures."[61] Local residents sometimes attacked and beat the

CHAPTER 4

*Tehsildars.*⁶² Armed gangs usurping the land sometimes even threatened the surveyors themselves, as Abbott found one afternoon:

> *The Tehsildar . . . a tall stout Brahmun of great courage had been several times set upon by Rajpooties. . . . He had been desperately wounded on one occasion and bore some ghastly scars. . . . Yet being a Brahmin he was protected in great measure from outrage by the superstitions which regard the slaughter of a Brahmin as an unpardonable crime. When I came to survey this village, being determined to sift to the uttermost the claims of the aggrieved, I carried pistols in my holsters and a sensible cudgel in my hand. . . . [O]n my return from a stormy investigation, I perceived a posse of armed men of the village gathering ahead of me. . . . As only eight or ten of them were assembled on the spot, I thought it probable that they would be unprepared to attack me. . . . I rode right through the group; who were greatly disconcerted, some beginning to handle their arms but hesitating, while others stood wholly undetermined.*⁶³

Interestingly, here Abbott attributed local behavior in not murdering Brahmin tax collectors to a religious principle, but he failed consistently to make that same connection in regard to the behavior of sepoys.

By living out of doors in each district, where he had to adjudicate disputes on the spot and rely primarily on his wits to protect himself, this assignment prepared him well for new duties that lay in the future. While the gulf between Britons and the peoples of India in general was growing in this decade, Abbott himself was moving in the opposite direction, drawing closer to the people. In living part of every day in Patalpanie near Mhow and now in the survey of hundreds of villages, he showed a keen and genuine curiosity about Indian life, found an unexpected talent for local languages, and demonstrated an ability for lateral thinking in the field.

In the meantime, war drums were beating in Calcutta. Lord Auckland, who replaced Bentinck as governor-general in 1835, decided to go to war in Afghanistan. The Army of the Indus, as it was styled, was being assembled in Karnal with the objective of seating the tractable Shah

Shuja ul Mulk on the throne in Kabul in place of the uncooperative Dost Mohammed. Upon learning of this, Abbott immediately wrote to join the Army of the Indus. His request and his orders directing him to do so crossed in the mail. Abbott's brother Saunders, who had been surveying in Cawnpore, came to take over his survey team. In November 1838, James marched to Karnal to rendezvous with Augustus and go to war again.

5

A Mission to Khiva

1838–1843

WHEN JAMES ABBOTT LEFT SHAHJIHANPOOR, HE HAD ONLY A VAGUE notion of the reasons why he was going to war, but he was eager to go. As Byron Farwell notes, "The Victorian-Edwardian professional soldier often went to remarkable lengths and made extraordinary personal sacrifices to take part in fighting."[1] There was a trade-off: the survey appointment was a long-sought coup, and the salary and lifestyle Abbott now had from it were a huge improvement over the tedium and lieutenant's pay in regimental garrison, which could follow on the heels of any war, as it had after Bhurtpore.[2] Yet the chance to go to war trumped that in spades. Seeing combat and perhaps distinguishing oneself under fire were for most East India Company officers the sine qua non of career advancement.

As he traveled from Mhow to Karnal and then on to Ferozepore, Abbott could not have guessed that the East India Company was about to commit one of the most memorable follies in British history. The road to the First Anglo-Afghan War had twists and turns, but the cause boiled down to British concerns about Russian intentions in Central Asia and what the British perceived as Russian territorial designs on the subcontinent. In 1838, rising British paranoia over the possibility of a Russian accord with the ruler of Afghanistan, Dost Mohammed, crested the banks of rational thought.[3] Lord Auckland in India and Lord Palmerston in London were acutely alarmed by the presence of a single Russian officer, Captain Yan Viktorovich Vitkevitch, at the court of the dost.[4] One

Russian officer intriguing in the Afghan court was one Russian officer too many. When Dost Mohammed refused a peremptory and insulting British demand to deport Vitkevitch, Auckland made the decision to depose the Afghan ruler by military force.[5]

A number of influential men were opposed to an invasion of Afghanistan, including the Duke of Wellington, his brother Henry Wellesley, Charles Metcalfe, and Mountstuart Elphinstone,[6] who knew Afghanistan better than most.[7] William Bentinck, Auckland's predecessor as governor-general, was astonished when he learned of the invasion. "Lord Auckland and [William] MacNaughten gone to war in Afghanistan?" he exclaimed at the news, "the very last men in the world I should have expected of such folly!"[8] Junior officers too had reservations. D'Arcy Todd also thought it foolhardy. "It does not appear to me," Todd wrote presciently, "that the country ... would submit without a struggle to the power of strangers, infidels and invaders."[9] Governor-General Auckland, however, had the ultimate authority. Under the peculiar rules in effect, even the Court of Directors of the East India Company could not change Auckland's decision.[10] Auckland was badly advised by a number of hawks around him,[11] particularly the Secretary to the Secret and Political Department in India, William MacNaughten.[12] Where courteous and respectful diplomacy might have yielded a better outcome, MacNaughten especially seemed bent on confrontation. MacNaughten was the drafter of the insulting ultimatum, which no sovereign could possibly accept, that launched Britain on its first ill-advised attempt at regime change in Kabul. For the purpose of installing on the throne a cousin of Dost Mohammed who would be more amenable to British interests—the uninspiring Shah Shuja—Auckland began assembling the Army of the Indus at Ferozepore in the spring of 1838,[13] initially organized into a Bengal column, a Bombay column, and Shah Shuja's own forces.[14]

Before the army began its march northwest, news was received that the Persian siege of Herat was finally lifted, due in no small part to the exertions of Lieutenant Eldred Pottinger, a British officer present in the city who on his own authority took over and conducted its defense with such skill that the Persians gave up. This news prompted Auckland to reduce the British forces in the Army of the Indus by half to a single

CHAPTER 5

division, the Bengal column, in addition to Shah Shuja's motley collection of mercenaries.[15] The Bombay column was sent home. There remained two troops of horse artillery and four companies of foot artillery. One of the four was commanded by Captain Garbett, and James Abbott was one of the three lieutenants assigned to it. Another was commanded by Augustus. One of the three lieutenants in Augustus's company was Richmond Shakespear, who would later be detached to Herat with Abbott. D'Arcy Todd, just returned from his assignment to Persia as an artillery trainer, was attached to the Political Department and accompanied the army.[16]

When Abbott arrived at Karnal, he typically made his personal preparations carefully. Throughout the nineteenth century, while enlisted men were provided for, officers were generally expected to make their own personal arrangements and organize their own provisions for a campaign. Abbott was by nature a careful planner, and he was good at such logistics. His preparations for the Afghan campaign were no exception: "Foreseeing that a march of 1300 miles through a desolate country, a great part of it hostile to us, would require considerable management, I built a set of tents for myself and servants of the smallest dimensions, reduced my baggage to the lowest space and purchased six camels to carry three half camel loads ... and thus succeeded in bringing the whole safely and in good heart to Candahar."[17]

In addition to his brother Augustus, Abbott also found Henry Lawrence in camp at Karnal preparing to march to Ferozepore. Lawrence had been summoned to the campaign from an adjoining district in the Revenue Survey. Abbott and Lawrence immediately renewed their friendship. "His society had always a great charm for me and he seemed to like mine," Abbott wrote. "[O]ur views of most subjects were congenial."[18] This friendship, begun at Addiscombe, was to have far-reaching consequences in the years ahead. For the moment, with little to do either while on the march or while waiting for the full army to assemble, Abbott and Lawrence launched a literary journal to be assembled by Lawrence's wife, Honoria. Abbott was the only one who ever contributed to it, however, so the project soon collapsed. Abbott later collected his contributions and published them anonymously under the title *Tales of the Forest*, which he admitted "w[as] manifestly unsuited to separate publication, [as it was] abounding in allusions familiar only to East Indians."[19]

Sir Henry Fane, Commander in Chief in India and now also Commander in Chief of the Army of the Indus, was one of the most vocal opponents of the invasion. With the halving of the army to a single division, Fane took this opportunity to step down from its command, correctly citing military protocol that a force of a single division did not call for leadership by the Commander in Chief in India. Command devolved to Sir John Kean, the Commander in Chief of the Bombay Army, an adroit political move to assuage ill-will at the entire Bombay force being returned to garrison. Abbott privately thought Fane "an accomplished officer" but believed Kean to be "quite incompetent to the duty."[20] In the event, Kean carried out the operational aspects of the campaign competently and with a minimum loss of life. It was at the strategic level of war that the campaign was fatally flawed. As Todd had predicted, the Afghans did not react well to having their ruler imposed by infidel foreigners.

The reduced Army of the Indus got underway for Kandahar on December 10, 1838. The march was arduous, especially for the enlisted gunners who had to move the heavy cannons over rough terrain and through narrow passes, but it was largely uneventful. Baloch horsemen kept up steady raids on any supplies and livestock left momentarily unguarded: rarely did such a smorgasbord of plunder present itself in that barren region. For sport and wealth it was much too good an opportunity to miss, and the British cavalry was kept busy chasing them off. Kandahar was occupied against only light resistance in April 1839,[21] and for their participation in the campaign, Abbott and the other officers later received from Shah Shuja the Order of the Durrani Empire Third Class.[22]

Far more importantly, however, at Kandahar Abbott was detached from the Bengal Artillery and posted to the Political Department. This was a pinnacle of advancement for East India Company officers in terms of prestige and pay. Assignment to the Political Department took an officer far from his normal duties in the infantry, cavalry, or artillery, but it could be very career enhancing and, at times, elevate the name of a relatively junior officer from regimental obscurity to the attention of senior officials. Such assignments were highly sought after and difficult to come by. Abbott's posting was arranged by D'Arcy Todd. Because Todd spoke fluent Persian and had observed the siege of Herat from the Persian side, he was selected to lead a small delegation to Herat, and he chose his friend Abbott as his secretary of legation and assistant political officer.[23] Such political officers were often quite junior in rank and not infrequently vested with significant power and authority. For this reason "Politicals," as they were known, had their detractors. Sir Charles Napier, for example, wrote to Lord Ellenborough in 1842, "The chief cause of our disasters is this—when a smart lad can speak Hindostanee and Persian, he is made a political agent, and supposed to be a statesman and a general."[24]

Todd's brief was to assist Lieutenant Pottinger in the city and maintain friendly relations between Britain and Herat. Abbott may not have been as eager as some to join the Political Department. Although he was determined to make the best of his new assignment, he seems to have had serious doubts as to its wisdom and its chances for success: "The whole scheme," he wrote, "appeared to me from the outset unsound and rash, and nothing but a desire to share the fortunes of my friend ... induced me to accept."[25] Within months it was to prove an even more momentous turn of events than he imagined that summer outside the walls of Kandahar.

The small party led by Major Todd departed Kandahar for Herat in June 1839. Besides Todd and Abbott, the legation included Lieutenant Richmond Shakespear, who ironically, as events would transpire, was nominated by Abbott himself at Todd's request for recommendations. Also attached were Lieutenants Saunders and North, both engineers; two medical officers, Doctors Login and Ritchie; and Lieutenant Edward Conolly of the Bengal Cavalry, the brother of Captain Arthur Conolly.[26] The engineers had a detachment of thirty sappers from the Bengal Pioneer Corps to help repair the siege damage to the city. There was also an escort of sixty Afghan irregular cavalry. Abbott, already no fan of irregular cavalry, thought the latter "were not of much account ... if they could be persuaded to fight at all," but their presence no doubt discouraged small roving bands of thieves and raiding parties.[27]

Todd was in his element. Abbott noted, "My friend ... enjoyed himself much.... His thorough knowledge of the Persian idiom and of

Eastern manners made him quite at home with Asiatics, in whose society he found much solace."[28] Todd was another example of Company officers who, given a choice of socializing with other Britons or with locals, often chose the latter. Abbott added that Todd had no misgivings about his mission: "His sanguine temperament caused him to undervalue the difficulties of the game he had been sent to play[29]—And long and intimate intercourse with Sir John MacNeil had caused him to adopt to the fullest the line of policy which Government had assumed."[30]

Nothing of significance occurred on the journey, and the redoubtable Eldred Pottinger soon joined them outside Herat. He had fully adopted Afghan dress. Pottinger's legend preceded him, and Todd's party, including Abbott, held him in considerable awe:

Of this young officer we had all heard much. One of our party had I think known him at Addiscombe . . . and Todd had met him at Heraut during the siege. The rest of our party, myself included, were full of curiosity. . . . He came dressed in Afghaun costume in a cloak of camel's hair and a large white muslin turban. [It was] one of the most becoming of costumes and in which he looked well. . . . He was of low stature, but stoutly built with plain manly countenance. . . . [T]he very important part he had played in the defense of Heraut caused us to treat him with marked deference.[31]

Todd's party entered Herat in early July 1839 and found the city in a pitiful state. The siege and the indifference of the city's leaders to the plight of their people had decimated the population. Abbott noted,

The entire remaining population of the hapless city were collected in [the] street, to stare upon the strangers who had come, they hoped, to feed them—Such emaciated faces and forms I had never beheld previously. Their whole number did not exceed two or three thousands, though previous to the siege the population had been reckoned at 60,000. Death, disease, flight, famine and . . . their own ruler, who had sold them into slavery to fill his coffers had . . . all but annihilated the people of Heraut. . . . [I]t was like threading that region of Hades *reserved for the ghosts of evildoers*³² . . . *under the shattered vaults and thro' the twilight gloom.*³³

When Abbott and Todd reached Herat in July, what came to be called the Great Game was already well underway. Imports to and exports from India formed a significant part of Britain's economic growth and made it, in the words of Abbott's schoolmate Benjamin Disraeli, "the jewel in the crown of the British empire."³⁴ Fear of losing India to a Russian invasion, a paranoia adroitly manipulated by France, was a British bête noire throughout the nineteenth century. After losing its colonies at Mahé, Pondichéry, Chandernagor, and elsewhere on the coast of India to the British, France concocted a number of fanciful schemes to push the Russians into the subcontinent, each of which alarmed British leaders. A French advisor to Catherine the Great urged her to invade India, and the mad Tsar Paul I actually dispatched a force of Cossacks in that general direction in 1801 with vague orders and a quixotic plan. He was murdered, and his son Alexander ordered them back.³⁵ Meanwhile, relentless Russian territorial expansion into Central Asia and the Caucasus throughout the eighteenth and nineteenth centuries was steady fuel for British angst about India's security.

The year between August 1839 and August 1840 was to be one of the most tumultuous in Abbott's life, though he little expected what lay in store when he rode past Herat's famed minarets. The Romantic poet's love of medieval ruins was piqued. Abbott found the famous tiled mosque of Herat "far the grandest and most noble of the religious edifices of the Muhammedans that I have ever seen. The dimensions are gigantic, the proportions are faultless and the finish is perfect."³⁶ The Romantic fascination with ruins and the Anglo-Indian trope of fallen Indian civilization are ever-present in Abbott's writing from this period. He noted, for example, that the tiles of the Jama Masjid, the Great Mosque of Herat, "might have been objected to [for] their gaudiness when new [but] are now touchingly beautiful in their shattered and mossgrown condition . . . reminding us of departed glory in the vivid richness of their dyes."³⁷

In early December, news of a Russian invasion of Khiva—a vague region of unknown boundaries north of Herat called "Khaurism" from the

Figure 5.1. Herat in the early 1800s prior to the Persian siege of the city, which caused significant damage to the citadel walls. Pen-and-ink drawing by an unknown artist circa 1830. (*HARPER'S WEEKLY SUPPLEMENT*, NOVEMBER 1, 1879, P. 877)

old name of the area, Khorezm—reached Herat.[38] The news was brought by an ambassador of the Khan of Khiva seeking help against the invaders. The Khivan ambassador reported the Russian force was a hundred thousand strong.[39] An invasion was indeed underway, though with a force of only ten thousand, under the command of General Vasily Perovsky, a redoubtable Russian commander of proven skill in expanding Russia's boundaries.[40]

Such was the state of British knowledge of Central Asia in 1839 that they did not actually know where the city of Khiva was. Most of the vast area of the Asian landmass was literally terra incognita. Khiva, once a major commercial center on the old Silk Road, was thought to be roughly six hundred miles north of Herat, but what lay in between no Briton knew.[41] Abbott's friend Arthur Conolly had attempted to reach Khiva in disguise as a Persian merchant a few years earlier but was turned back by bandits, lucky on that occasion to escape with his life.[42] That the region was inhabited by robbers, slavers, and homicidal xenophobes was known from his report. Yet Todd was alarmed enough about the threat he perceived from the Russian approach toward India that he determined to do what he could to stem the invasion. He sent messengers to Kabul, where the Army of the Indus was now attempting to consolidate the control of Shah Shuja, and to Tehran, the nearest British diplomatic mission, to alert his superiors to the Russian invasion.

As he could not personally leave his post, Todd decided instead to send his deputy Abbott to respond in person to the Khivan ambassador's message. Abbott's mission was to travel across the six hundred miles of unknown wilderness roamed by hostile nomads and bandits, become the first Briton to reach Khiva, and, once there, forestall the Russian army by means of negotiation.[43] Specifically, he was ordered to make contact with the Khan of Khiva, respond to the message of the khan's ambassador to Herat, assure the khan of Britain's friendship (but promise no military support), and offer to intercede diplomatically with the Russians to stop the invasion.[44] Whether the intent of the Russian invasion was territorial annexation or simply a punitive expedition to free the several hundred Russians being held in slavery in Khorezm is unclear. Todd, steeped in British paranoia about Russian intentions from his service in Persia, feared the former. Nevertheless, he reasoned that if the khan could be persuaded to release all the Russian slaves in his domain preemptively, Perovsky might be satisfied and turn back.[45] This was a slender reed, and it appears to have occurred to neither Todd nor Abbott that any British envoy might himself be believed to be a Russian and treated accordingly, since few Khivans had ever seen an Englishman. Indeed, as it turned out, few Khivans for that matter had ever heard of England at all. Still, it could be the opportunity of a lifetime for a junior officer just given a political assignment. Abbott recognized it was almost suicidally dangerous but, like most British officers of his day, was eager to demonstrate the qualities of honor and duty and accepted such risks with a complacency that is difficult for modern observers to fathom.

No Britons could be spared from the Herat legation to accompany him, so Abbott left the city on December 24, 1839, with a party of five Afghans. The first was Sammud Khan,[46] whom Abbott called his steward and who became the most widely traveled Afghan of his time.[47] The second was a representative of the Emir of Herat, Pir Mohammed Khan, a relative of the vizier.[48] Mohammed Khan's role was to advise Abbott along the route and act as his passe-partout in the emir's lands. Abbott found him "a very handsome man" who startled him by his "resemblance to our best portraits of Edward the Third."[49] Yar Mohammed, the vizier to Emir Kamran,[50] was generally acknowledged to be a dangerous, villainous, Machiavellian usurper by both Britons and Afghans alike,[51] so Abbott assumed Mohammed Khan's true purpose was to sabotage the mission and possibly have him arrested in Khiva, as Lieutenant Colonel Charles Stoddart had recently been in Bokhara.[52] Mohammed Khan, however, was the only member of the group who could speak proper court Persian and was the best companion during the long days in the saddle to help Abbott learn the language, which he would need to speak in Khiva.

The third member of the party was an elderly Afghan whom Abbott called "the Meerza," a phonetic rendering of *mirza*, a title of Persian origin once denoting nobility or high birth but by Abbott's time having a variety of meanings, including simply scribe, which was his occupation on the expedition.[53] The *mirza* was a Shi'a Muslim, which was common in Persian-influenced Herat at that time but much less so along the route northward to Khiva. Abbott usually referred to him as "my old Meerza." He thought of him fondly but did not hold him in any great intellectual esteem, noting on one occasion, when the *mirza* made a humorous play on words, that he "had not suspected the old fellow of mettle sufficient for so bad a pun."[54] Nevertheless, Meerza received forty rupees a month more than Sammud Khan. Abbott found Meerza's spoken colloquial Persian impossible to understand, but Meerza could understand Abbott's, and he could write the language, which neither Abbott nor Sammud Khan could do. The fourth man was an Afghan Pashtun named Nizaum, whom Abbott had also hired in Kandahar. Abbott described him as "my Farish, or body servant,[55] [who] attended to my dress and cooked my food and took a general superintendence of the establishment."[56] He also referred to him as "my Nazir."[57] "Nizaum," Abbott wrote, "whom I found the dirtiest of Feraushs (or porters), has since become by the usage of the country, the most slovenly of Nazirs (or chamberlains)."[58] In practice, Nizaum

CHAPTER 5

acted variously as a groom, mess steward, cook, and spy. The last member of the party was another Afghan Pashtun named Ali Muhammad, who acted as an interpreter between Persian and the Khivan dialects. Ali Muhammad had been a slave in Khiva for fifteen years before purchasing his own freedom.

Abbott's four men were all from Kandahar and had accompanied him from there to Herat. They were paid a good wage but no higher for going on to Khiva than their previous salary. They could have returned to Kandahar and found similar work for another British officer there under far less dangerous circumstances. If they had asked for letters of recommendation from Abbott, he would have written them without hesitation. With such a letter from a British officer, obtaining similar employment in the British garrison at Kandahar close to their homes and relatives was a likely prospect for all of them. Ali Muhammad, in particular, had already been enslaved once in this same territory and had every reason to hesitate in going back. His last trip north of Herat had cost him fifteen years of his life as a slave. An interpreter's wages seem hardly sufficient motivation for his going back into the lion's den. That instead all four chose freely to undertake an obviously dangerous journey into unknown country with an infidel foreigner suggests that Abbott already possessed a degree of what Henry Lawrence would later call "a peculiar power of attracting others, especially Asiatics, to his person."[59]

Various local inhabitants along the way joined the group for differing periods, including a man Abbott refers to as "Birdler Beeg," a misunderstanding of the title *begler beg*, meaning "*beg* [chief or commander] of *begs*." The *beg* was a Turkmen who helped Abbott navigate safely through the Turkmen lands in the steppe north of Herat. He was a Sunni Muslim who would not speak to Meerza, an interesting indication of Sunni-Shi'a relations in this part of Central Asia at this time.

For defense, Abbott carried a carbine and a single-shot pistol. He wore Afghan dress for the journey to make himself less conspicuous from a distance but did not try to pass as a local or pretend to be a Muslim, as Captain Conolly and Lieutenant Pottinger had attempted unsuccessfully to carry off.[60] "I was dressed in the Affghaun attire," Abbott wrote, "consisting of a double set of stiff petticoats."[61] He made careful notes about indigenous dress along his route, and changed his headdress from a turban, to a black woolen Turcoman cap, to a tall black cylindrical fez of Uzbek origin as the occasion required.

When he set out on Christmas Eve 1839, Abbott was thirty-three years old, and, he hoped, following a less-traveled and extremely dangerous trail to imperial glory that had been blazed by a handful of British officers before him. Abbott was certainly aware that completing and surviving such a mission would boost his career: Alexander "Bokhara" Burnes, for example, had merely traced the steps of William Moorcroft, Edward Stirling, and Charles Masson[62] to Bokhara in 1832 and published an account of his travels.[63] Burnes was no pioneer of Asian exploration, but he had style, panache, and a gift for self-promotion. He was lionized by London society and knighted in 1839 by the new monarch, Queen Victoria.[64]

Abbott also knew that a majority of British expeditions into Central Asia were not ending well. "I was sent to execute what might well appear to be an impossibility," he wrote later, "and my fame [i.e., reputation], as well as [my] life, was staked upon the venture."[65] In addition to Pottinger's and Conolly's lucky escapes, it was well known that the British explorer William Moorcroft and his companion George Trebeck had never returned from Central Asia, although their exact fate remained a mystery for some years after Abbott's mission.[66] In August 1839, news reached the British in Afghanistan that Lieutenant Colonel Charles Stoddart, sent to assure the Emir of Bokhara of Britain's friendship, had been arrested and thrown into a rat-infested dungeon. Stoddart would be beheaded in 1842, together with Arthur Conolly, who had volunteered to try to effect his release. But Conolly, like Burnes, had already attained a measure of celebrity by traveling in Central Asia and publishing an account of his travels in 1834, and these two positive outcomes weighed heavily on the plus side of the scale.[67] Moreover, Conolly was no stranger to Abbott personally; the men were in fact good friends who had explored the ruins at Mandu together in 1831.[68]

Abbott, his four Afghans, and the Herati court representative Pir Mohammed Khan set out in a snowstorm on Christmas Eve 1839 into the lands of the Jamshidis, one of the four tribal groups which comprise

Chapter 5

Figure 5.2. "Audience with Khan of Khiva," circa 1863, pen-and-ink drawing by the Hungarian Turkologist Armin Vámbéry, published in *Sketches of Central Asia* (London: Wm. H. Allen, 1868). Armin Vámbéry, born Hermann Bamberger or Bamberger Armin (1832–1913), traveled to Khiva in the early 1860s disguised as a Sunni dervish named Reshit Efendi and met the Khan of Khiva, then Khan Sayyid Muhammad. (PUBLIC DOMAIN)

the Chahar Aimaq people of modern-day Badghis, Ghor, and Herat Provinces. The party wound its way north with the intention of covering thirty miles a day. Abbott suspected Pir Mohammed Khan was under orders to delay him because of long-standing animosity between Herat and Khiva.[69] The *pir* found many reasons to spend extra days in camp on several occasions. The weather was miserable, as usual in Central Asia in January. The party traveled in two groups, with Abbott, the *pir*, Sammud Khan, and Ali Muhammad riding ahead on sturdy Turcoman horses, while Nizaum and Meerza wrangled the slower camels carrying the camping gear and supplies behind them.

When they reached the de facto limits of the Emir of Herat's jurisdiction, Abbott was glad to have an excuse for sending Mohammed Khan back to Herat. Abbott had found him knowledgeable, educated, and intelligent but seemingly determined to make the trip last several years rather than several months. The party now entered a wilderness, a vast ungoverned steppe sparsely populated by a mixture of nomadic Uzbeks, Turkmen, and Kazakhs. All were known to buy, sell, and own slaves, many of whom were Afghans kidnapped from Herat or captured from caravans. The travelers had only small indigenous tents and blankets, in which they rolled themselves up at night to afford some protection from the snow and freezing rain of January in Central Asia.

After the departure of the *pir*, the group made better time and reached Khiva without incident by early March 1840. Here Abbott encountered an entirely unexpected difficulty: the Khivans had little idea who the British actually were and were deeply suspicious of Abbott, believing him to be a Russian spy.[70] Several of the members of the Khivan court believed England to be a small vassal state of Russia, as this is what Russian agents had told them. In a series of audiences with the Khan of Khiva, however, Abbott managed to win, at least partially, the khan's confidence. The Khan of Khiva had never traveled outside his kingdom and asked Abbott many odd and quaint questions. He wanted to know whether the British had a telescope that could see through walls, as he had heard. Did they have ships that could travel underwater? Did people elsewhere put cannons aboard ships, and did they ever fight at sea? Did the British possess the alchemist's secret of turning lead into gold? Was it true his king was a woman? And how many cannons did England have? He himself had twenty-one cannons, he told Abbott.

Abbott answered these questions and many more as honestly as he could. The khan asked Abbott how, if the English and Russians spoke different languages, they could communicate with one another. Abbott explained it was done in French, another European language. The khan had never heard of Europe and was surprised that there were some thirteen languages spoken there. In particular, Abbott was repeatedly questioned about Russia, and it was clear that he was never entirely free of suspicion of being a Russian himself. Several members of the khan's court remained convinced of it and urged the khan to put Abbott to death. The khan's spiritual adviser suggested burying Abbott up to the neck in the desert.[71] Yet the khan and his court had heard of Colonel Stoddart, now a prisoner in Bokhara, and he was definitely English, whatever that was,

Chapter 5

Figure 5.3. "Three Khivans Drinking Tea in the Courtyard of Their Home," a photograph by Anton Stepanovich Murenko. Murenko was an officer in the Russian army attached to the photographic service who accompanied the Russian diplomatic mission to Khiva and Bukhara in 1858. (PHOTO ARCHIVE OF THE INSTITUTE OF MATERIAL CULTURE HISTORY OF THE RUSSIAN ACADEMY OF SCIENCES)

not Russian. During Abbott's stay in Khiva, the khan proposed a rescue mission to free Stoddart, offering to send a body of his horsemen with Abbott in disguise. Abbott was tempted, but his orders were to blunt Russian anger and aggression toward Khiva, not to rescue Stoddart, so he declined the offer. Abbott and the khan often spent hours in discussion. The khan was indeed deeply concerned about the Russians and interested in getting help from wherever he could find it. That it would not come from his archenemies in Herat and Bokhara was clear enough to the khan. Abbott was not authorized to offer a formal alliance or even any material support in the form of guns or advisers. In fact, he had very little to offer the khan at all apart from some modest gifts from the British treasury in Herat.

What stopped the Russians that winter was not Abbott or the khan's forces but the most brutally cold winter on record.[72] General Perovsky's soldiers suffered almost unimaginable hardships in trying to force their way through unrelenting snowstorms and snow drifts often five to six feet deep. They ultimately had to turn back with a loss of much of their force. Unaware of this, Abbott offered to meet the advancing Russians and negotiate with their officers. He told the khan that if he were to free all the Russians slaves in Khorezm, this would remove the Russian pretext for invasion, and the khan agreed to do so.[73]

Exactly what Abbott offered the khan may never be known. Rumors circulated in India in the early 1840s that he had exceeded his authority by offering a defensive alliance with Great Britain. This speculation was fueled by a book by John Marshman, son of the renowned British missionary Joshua Marshman.[74] Without naming Abbott in the first edition, Marshman claimed in 1842 that "the envoy [i.e., Abbott] exceeded his instructions, and proposed an alliance, offensive and defensive, which Lord Auckland immediately disavowed."[75] However, Marshman was employed by the British government only as a Bengali translator, and his account was certainly based on hearsay. His reliability as a source is further discredited by the fact that he got virtually every other detail of Abbott's mission wrong, beginning (in the 1869 edition) with misspelling Abbott's name. Marshman went on to claim in 1842 that "the envoy" (Abbott) was "recalled from Khiva" as a result of his offer of a treaty, when in fact Abbott was already in England before anyone in India knew he was still alive. The source of the rumor that Abbott exceeded his authority in Khiva, which he vehemently denied throughout his life, will never be known with certainty. But the only other Briton to visit Khiva prior to the publication of Marshman's book (and for many years thereafter) and to be in a position to report to (or be believed by) the Indian government was Lieutenant Richmond Shakespear. Shakespear may only have been reporting what was told to him in Khiva of Abbott's conversations with the khan. The Khivans may have had their own reasons for exaggerating the scope of Abbott's mission or the nature of his offer. Or Shakespear may have intended to enhance his own reputation at the expense of Abbott's while forcing him to defend himself against scurrilous charges instead of receiving credit for his accomplishments.

According to Uzbek historian Quwāmidden Munirov, Khivan court records do purportedly substantiate the claim of a treaty offer, recording,

> In Ogahi's Riyozud-davla, *Abbott's arrival to Khiva is mentioned in this way: "Also that on the 15th day of Zulqa'da, 1255[76] from Hindustan came Haibat sahib, an English ambassador on horseback, who was greeted respectfully. . . . Bayoniy[77] writes that Abbott spoke thusly to Khan of Khiva Olloqul: 'The Russians . . . in another fifty years will take your province. If you want that your province should remain in your hands, [and] no one could object to that, sign your province over to us. Let Khorezm humbly find itself among the English peoples, and then it will be free from worry. Our word to you is such that, not from self-interest but of pure friendship, our intention is not to block the Indian road to Russia. We will make you a profit, in no way will it harm you, confer your preferred treaty and we will accept it." But Abbott's words turned out to be hollow. Olloquli, the Khan of Khiva, definitively refused Abbott's offer and gave this answer: "At the present the Russians do not walk on top of us. In fifty years who knows? With all prudence regarding the coming fifty years, we will not today give up [from our hands] our people to someone. That which our successors wish to do, let them decide."*[78]

But Munirov was publishing in the Soviet Union at a time when interpretations of historical texts were being routinely manipulated or altered to comply with Soviet ideology, and this account, like all Soviet official histories, is highly suspect. In a footnote to the text in the first volume of *Narrative of a Journey from Heraut to Khiva*, Abbott was testy about the subject, writing tersely, "I must observe, once and for all, that I do not feel authorized to publish the explicit terms by which I found it necessary to make my meaning understood at this simple court."[79] In the

Figure 5.4. Sammud Khan, James Abbott's traveling companion in Khaurism, Russia, England, and Europe. The drawing was the frontispiece to Abbott's book *Narrative of a Journey from Heraut to Khiva, Moscow, and St. Petersburg* (London: William H. Allen, 1843). (PUBLIC DOMAIN)

CHAPTER 5

final analysis, it seems unlikely that an intelligent, reserved, and introspective brevet captain of artillery would propose a sweeping alliance with a Central Asian state more than a thousand miles from India against his explicit instructions.

Weeks of delay and deliberation followed, but ultimately Abbott was asked by the khan to negotiate with the Russians and express the khan's willingness to exchange all the Russian slaves in his kingdom for the Khivans being held hostage in retaliation by the Russians. Abbott knew he had secured the release of the slaves in principle but was disappointed that none would accompany him to the negotiations with the Russians. That fell to Lieutenant Richmond Shakespear, accompanied by a *sowar* of Skinner's Horse, Fazil Khan, who arrived in Khiva three weeks later believing Abbott dead and escorted the slaves freed by Abbott to freedom. He subsequently claimed the negotiations were his, to great acclaim in London and a knighthood. Abbott could have waited for the slaves to be assembled, but the Russian army was still believed to be advancing on Khiva, and Abbott felt meeting it before it reached the environs of the city was imperative if war was to be averted.

On March 8, 1840, Abbott set out for the nearest Russian garrison at Astrakhan, with his original traveling party, dwindling funds, a letter from the khan stating his mission, and a Khivan guide, a Turkmen chief named Hussun Mhatoor. Hussun Mhatoor was the leader of the Chowdoor Turkmens, a tribe of some sixty thousand people. He did not trust Abbott, and Abbott was warned by a British agent in Khiva, Umeer Beg, not to trust him either. Umeer Beg was now enslaved in Khiva, and Abbott purchased his freedom with a gold watch given to him by his late elder brother Henry. Umeer Beg told Abbott that Hussun Mhatoor's protection as a guide went no further than the extent of his own tribal lands—a prescient warning, as it transpired. Yet Abbott had no choice: Hussun Mhatoor was the guide assigned by the Khan of Khiva.

Their first stop was a visit to Hussun Mhatoor's home village. Only after several days was Abbott able to get him to move forward. Abbott felt a sense of urgency shared by no one else in his party, least of all Hussun Mhatoor. When they reached the shore of the Caspian early in April to signal a Russian ship bound for Astrakhan, Mhatoor held his escort

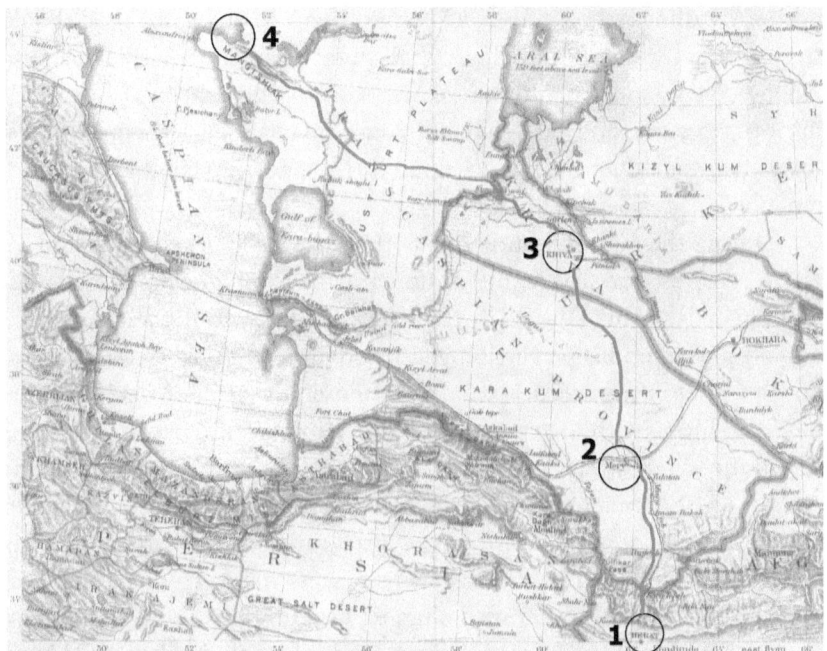

Figure 5.5. Detail of a map of Central Asia published by A. B. Graham in 1905. It shows considerably more knowledge of the region than was available when Abbott set out in 1839 from Herat (1, bottom right). He and his small party traveled north to Merv (2) and then on across the Karakum Desert to Khiva (3). From there he set out across the Ustyurt Plateau in hopes of meeting a Russian ship at Mangyschlak Bay on the Caspian Sea (4). (LIBRARY OF CONGRESS)

duty fulfilled and departed, as Umeer Beg predicted. The Russian ships that Mhatoor had promised would be waiting at Mangyschlak Bay, however, were nowhere to be seen. Abbott now faced an acute dilemma: wait with dwindling supplies of food and fodder for Russian ships that might, or might not, visit that desolate section of the Caspian coastline, or switch to an ad hoc plan to skirt the shore two hundred miles northward to a small Russian fort at Dahsh Gullah. Rather than wait and starve, Abbott chose the latter.

By mid-April, their situation had deteriorated badly. On the route north they fell in with a large group of armed Turkmens, who clearly did not believe Abbott was an ambassador of the khan, the reach of whose

Chapter 5

notional authority had ended far behind them in any case. They shook free of the Turkmens, but their local guide was acting suspiciously in Abbott's view, and Abbott believed he would betray them. It was raining continuously, and he could not rouse his waterlogged companions to greater watchfulness. He distributed the few weapons they had and remained alert, sleeping little.

During the night of April 22, 1840, they were attacked by a band of Kazakh bandits or slavers, in league with their guide, who all believed them to be Russians. Alerted by the sounds of men within their campsite, Abbott picked up his percussion pistol and jumped to his feet. At least a dozen figures in the darkness were overrunning the camp. As in his previous encounters with angry men, including the farmers at Addiscombe, the mutinous crewman Neagle, and the irregular cavalrymen at Simla, Abbott's first instinct was to fight, not flee. He raised the pistol to shoot the closest shape, but a sword stroke struck it from his hand before he could fire. He lunged at the swordsman, drew his dagger, and stabbed him in the throat. Another man charged him from his right, slashing at him with a long, curved sword. Armed now only with the dagger, Abbott deflected two or three sword cuts in the darkness and confusion and was wounded in both hands. A third Kazakh felled him from behind with a heavy club, and the fight was over.

When he came to his senses, Abbott found himself lying on his back in several inches of mud on a slight rise, still dazed from the blow to his head, splattered in blood and soaking wet. Sammud Khan lay next to him. Abbott became aware that his right hand was bleeding, and he bandaged it with a rag and kept the hand up in the air. He felt blood running out of the grimy rag and down his arm, thicker and warmer than the rainwater dripping off his sodden clothes. Recovering from the shock of the attack, Sammud Khan asked him about the wound. "I think the fingers are gone," Abbott replied. "I can feel them dangling." His companion unwrapped the rag and examined the wound. The index finger had been almost completely severed below the first knuckle by a sword cut and hung now only by a strip of muscle. The middle finger was cut more than halfway through, including the bone, just above the first knuckle, and also hung useless. "One, nay two," Sammud Khan said, "have been spared," referring to Abbott's ring and little fingers, "but the first must come off." The only tool Abbott had for the purpose was a small pen knife, which he gave to Sammud Khan. In the darkness, Sammud Khan held Abbott's right hand on a muddy rock and cut off the remainder of the first finger, then bound the hand back up in the rag, and handed back the knife.

The rain, which had been falling steadily for a week, tapered off to a drizzle. As soon as the brief fight ended, the Kazakhs had immediately begun ransacking the camp and were now spreading out to find the other men. During the melee, Nizaum, Ali Muhammad, and Meerza had all escaped into the darkness, but all three were tracked down and captured over the next two days. The wet ground made tracking them easy, and there was nowhere to run or hide in the steppe from mounted men.

In addition to the sword cut that maimed his right hand, Abbott had deep lacerations on his left hand and had suffered a concussion and possibly a fractured skull from the blow to his head.[80] He was fully lucid as long as he held his head still, but if he tried to sit up, he became dizzy and lost his balance, a condition that lasted more than a week.[81] Abbott and Sammud Khan were soon joined in captivity by their three companions. They were held for nearly three weeks, while their captors argued about what to do next. As Abbott's identity gradually emerged and his bona fides were confirmed, most of the attackers seemed to think the best course of action to avoid retribution from the khan was to quickly eliminate the evidence of their mistake. Within the first few days, Nizaum and Meerza were sold into slavery and taken away. Apart from the ad hoc surgery right after the fight, Abbott's wounds went untreated. The pen knife Sammud Khan had used for the impromptu amputation was soon stolen from him, along with all their other belongings. The temperatures soon dropped below freezing. The remaining three men, Abbott, Sammud Khan, and Ali Muhammad—now a slave for the second time—were held in Kazakh tents under guard. They were given no blankets and subsisted on the Kazakh diet of goat's milk and curds.

Abbott wrote afterward that he had resigned himself to death. If he did not stand defiantly at the precipice, as Arthur Conolly by all accounts later would, he nevertheless faced it calmly. His account is emotionally candid enough to have the ring of truth.[82] He mostly lamented failing

Chapter 5

to complete his mission. "To have gone so far," he later recalled with the typical all-or-nothing style of the period, "to have struggled through so much ... and upon the brink of success to lose all ... this was bitter indeed.... Desperate as my mission now appeared, death was the sole thought that afforded anything like peace. On earth I saw but dishonor."[83]

Each day in captivity, the three prisoners divided their food portions evenly. When Ali Muhammad produced a small number of Abbott's silver coins hidden in his undergarments, Abbott divided them also into equal shares, so that each man might have some help in escape if the opportunity presented itself. They were heavily guarded at all times, however, and the ground of the steppe after weeks of rain was still soft enough to make following the trail of a fugitive across it easy work for skilled trackers, as the quick recapture of Nizaum, Ali Muhammad, and Meerza had shown.

Abbott sized up his captors and went to work on the likeliest one, a man named Cherkush Bae, trying to create a protector among them. Abbott tried to convince him to release them with no hard feelings, to no avail, but Cherkush Bae did subsequently protect them to some extent. Communication was difficult. Their captors did not speak Persian, and none of the three prisoners could speak Kazakh. A couple of the Kazakhs could speak some Uzbek, however, so Abbott would speak in Persian to Ali Muhammad, who would then translate Abbott's words into Uzbek. One of their captors who spoke some of that language in turn translated into Kazakh for the rest. But they appeared destined for slavery on the steppe if not a shallow grave.

Then their fate took an extraordinary turn. They were rescued by a courageous, plucky, and resourceful young Afghan named Saleh Mohammed whom Abbott had met in the city of Merv on his way to Khiva and asked D'Arcy Todd by letter to hire as an agent.

While the party was briefly in Merv, Abbott had met this remarkable young man, the son of the chief judge (*qazi*) of Herat. He was struck by his intelligence and charisma and had sent off a letter to Major Todd in Herat asking Todd to hire the young man and direct him to proceed to Khiva to join the diplomatic mission. They had parted ways in Merv long before an answer could be received back from Herat far to the south. Their relationship is one of the most remarkable elements of Abbott's life story.

Figure 5.6. Photograph by an unknown photographer of the British agent Saleh Mohammed and his son during a visit to James Abbott in Delhi in 1860. (BRITISH LIBRARY BOARD)

Chapter 5

As the son of the *Qazi* of Herat, Saleh Mohammed was a member of the highest class of Herati society, the scion of one of the city's wealthiest and most important families. For a young man in his elite position, there was no limit of opportunities for safe, well-paid, career-enhancing employment and little need of any income in any event. Furthermore, Saleh Mohammed and his father the *qazi* had every reason to demonstrate their loyalty to the Emir of Herat, who was by now barely tolerating the presence of the annoying British legation in order to extract as much money from its treasury as possible. Yet, in spite of all this, Saleh Mohammed chose to work for James Abbott. He did not need employment or the modest salary, least of all from infidels who were obviously out of favor with the court of the emir. Whether from a sense of adventure, or a connection with Abbott, or perhaps both, Saleh Mohammed accepted the position with the British in Herat and set off across Central Asia alone to find Abbott as soon as D'Arcy Todd's letter of appointment reached him in Merv.

Saleh Mohammed first tracked Abbott over hundreds of miles north to Khiva. There, having missed him by several days, he then tracked Abbott alone all the way to Mangyschlak Bay and from there to the Kazakh slavers' tents, an extraordinary act of courage, tenacity, and devotion to his assignment to find a foreigner and a Christian he barely knew.

With clever bluff, a cool head, and a letter from the Khan of Khiva, Saleh Mohammed prevailed on the Kazakhs to release Abbott, Ali Muhammad, and Sammud Khan. He purchased back Nizaum and Meerza from slavery with his own money and even had a few of Abbott's looted belongings returned to him, including some of his papers.[84] He then guided them all to the Russian fort at Novopetrovskoye on the Caspian.

If Abbott's tale of ad hoc exploration and diplomacy in the Great Game has a hero, it is the Afghan, Saleh Mohammed, as Abbott's own account fully acknowledges. In fact, Munshi Akundzadah Saleh Mohammed went on to a long and adventurous life as a British agent, and he and Abbott became lifelong friends. After leaving Abbott, he returned to Herat. In 1841, he acted as a courier between Herat and Kabul, where Abbott's brother Augustus gave him an engraved gold watch as a memento.

Saleh Mohammed later served with Arthur Conolly on his subsequent mission to Bokhara, where he was imprisoned in a dank unused cistern with eighty other prisoners for two months on bread and water. Freed from the well after a mock execution, Saleh Mohammed was permitted to leave Bokhara but chose to remain with Conolly. After Conolly's murder by the emir, he traveled to Kabul via Khiva, Merv, and Meshed. He was offered Conolly's and Stoddart's severed heads to take with him.[85] When Yar Mohammed confiscated his family's land on the outskirts of Herat and sought to kill the whole family, the British arranged the evacuation to Kandahar of Saleh Mohammed and his "father, uncle, brothers, and cousins."[86] He subsequently worked for British intelligence in Kabul, where he remained at the time of the ill-fated British retreat toward the Khyber Pass in 1842.[87] In 1846, he is recorded as having been sent on a mission by Colonel Justin Sheil, the British Minister in Tehran, to investigate a report by a former French officer traveling in the region that some survivors of the retreat from Kabul in 1842 had been sold into slavery in Turkistan and were still alive there.[88] Abbott and Saleh Mohammed remained lifelong friends, and their paths crossed again several times in the years ahead.

The rest of Abbott's trip was a journey back from his first *Heart of Darkness*. The loss of his fingers,[89] at first subsumed in the greater calamity, now weighed on his mind: "The loss of my hand ... when hope returned became a most bitter and humiliating thought to one who from childhood had loved every species of romantic adventure, and had often trusted to that hand in the extremist emergency."[90] Over time, however, he learned to compensate well for the loss of his two fingers, as attested by his skill as a painter and sketch artist in pen and ink in later years. Although it was ruled that he had been on political service and not military service at the time of the injury, he was eventually given an annual wound pension of £50 from the East India Company.[91] Abbott never mentioned the wound again in his journals.

At Novopetrovskoye, the party split up. Saleh Mohammed, together with Nizaum, Ali Muhammad, and Meerza, returned to Kandahar via Herat. Saleh Mohammed and Abbott met again many times, but Abbott never saw Nizaum, Ali Muhammad, and Meerza again. Umeer Beg, the

Chapter 5

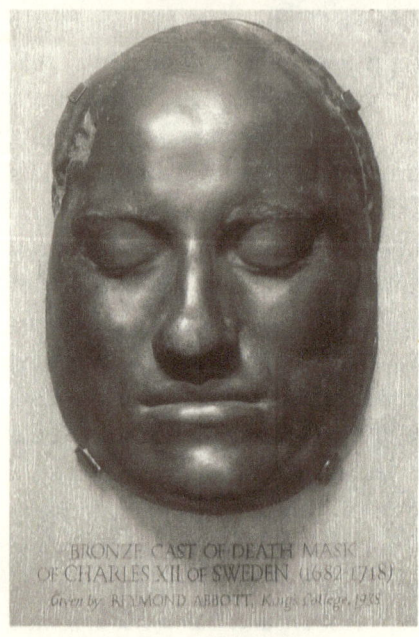

Figure 5.7. The bronze cast of the death mask of Charles XII given to James Abbott by Russian General Vasily Perovsky in 1840. The mask was donated to Cambridge University by Reymond Abbott while he was at King's College in 1938. ("DEATH MASK OF CHARLES XII OF SWEDEN [1682–1718]," FITZ-WILLIAM MUSEUM, HTTPS://DATA.FITZMUSEUM.CAM.AC.UK/ID/OBJECT/14069)

enslaved British agent whose freedom Abbott purchased with the gold watch given to him by his late brother Henry, returned to Herat. Abbott, accompanied by Sammud Khan, now made his way by carriage north to Orenburg and eventually St. Petersburg, where he met with Russian officials about the situation in Khiva.

The Russians treated him with great courtesy and respect. If they were angry about British meddling in what they considered their sphere of influence in Central Asia, they had an odd way of showing it. At Orenburg, the commanding officer in the region, General Perovsky (the leader of the recent ill-fated expedition against Khiva), met Abbott with enormous kindness. "He treated me from the first to last as a brother, although I had come to traverse all his designs upon Khiva,"[92] Abbott wrote, adding that the Russian general "insisted upon my wearing while in Russia a beautiful watch of his." Perovsky presented Abbott with an expensive map of Russia and lent him his own clothes, as virtually all of Abbott's were stolen while he was a prisoner of the Kazakhs. Most grandly, Perovsky gave Abbott bronze casts of the death masks of Peter the Great and his archrival, Charles XII of Sweden.[93]

In St. Petersburg, Abbott was invited by Tsar Nicolas I to two formal reviews of the Imperial Guard comprising some fifty thousand men.

At one of them, the emperor himself "galloped up to me on the review ground, and, singling me out from the crowds of ambassadors and guests, rode straight up to me and greeted me."[94] Ironically, Tsar Nicolas I was the only sovereign who ever greeted Abbott in recognition of his dangerous mission and sacrifice for Britain. Abbott met twice with the tsar's minister of foreign affairs, Count Karl Nesselrode. They negotiated the release of the Khivan prisoners in exchange for the Russian slaves being held in Khorezm, whose release Abbott had already arranged. Alerted by the British Ambassador to their arrival, the Foreign Office sent orders for Abbott to proceed to London. In August 1840, after an absence of nearly seventeen years, he landed back in England together with Sammud Khan.

Abbott arrived home in London when Parliament was not in session, which was unlucky. The government ministers were out of town. Abbott applied for audiences with Lord Palmerston, the Minister for Foreign Affairs, and Sir John Hobhouse, President of the Company's Board of Control. After several weeks, Abbott was granted a short interview with Palmerston. He was apparently too shy to mention his freeing of the slaves in Khiva. Palmerston quizzed him briefly about his experiences and thanked him for his service. That was it. There was no other official recognition of his mission.

Hobhouse invited Abbott to spend a week at his country residence at Erlestoke Park in Wiltshire in October. Hobhouse, as president of the Board of Control, was the highest-ranking official in England directly responsible for oversight of the East India Company. This was a great mark of favor to a young captain of the Bengal Artillery. Abbott might have used this visit also to advance his career, but he was again too shy and too obsequious around gentry to bring it off well. Nevertheless, on October 8, 1840, Abbott made a good impression on Hobhouse at their first dinner on his estate:

> Captain Abbott, our envoy at Khiva, dined with me. His singular adventures accord well with his manners and appearance. He came down to dinner in full uniform of a sort of Turkish or Russian pattern, and with large mustachios, and spurs on his boots. His manners were most formal and rather submissively ceremonious. He never spoke except to answer a question, but all he said was much to the

point, and there was a determined gravity about him, very useful, I should think in his intercourse with such men as the Khan of Khiva. He gave me some dreadful accounts of the state of society and manners of the Afghans of Herat.[95]

Abbott was privately tortured by a trivial bureaucratic matter, an addition he had made to his passport at Khiva to permit his own travel to Russia for negotiations. He refers to it repeatedly and was obsessed with what appears to a modern reader to be a minor and rather obvious necessity under the circumstances. He wanted to raise it with Palmerston, but the interview was too brief to bring it up.

In fact, only three men alive even knew of the matter: Abbott himself, General Perovsky, who asked Abbott about it in Orenburg but was far too busy to make an issue of it and was not a pettifogging man in any event, and D'Arcy Todd, to whom Abbott wrote explaining the necessity and who concurred entirely. This minor matter should have been completely forgotten. No one was ever going to bring it up, but it loomed large in Abbott's imagination for some reason, and at Hobhouse's estate, he did something quite bizarre. He wrote a kind of confession in a letter to Hobhouse and left it for him to find in his guest quarters when he departed the estate on October 13, 1840. Hobhouse recorded finding the letter:

> *Captain Abbott left me, and I found a long letter from him in which he confessed that, when leaving Khiva for Orenburg, he had interpolated the passport given to him by Major Todd, and instructed himself to proceed to the Russian headquarters. The Russian General Peroffsky, at Orenburg, discovered the forgery and charged Abbott with it. The Captain confessed at once, but he did not say a word of the transaction either to Lord Palmerston or myself; and his whole letter to me, when obliged to speak of it, savoured much of cunning or craziness. I had previously promised Abbott to get him employed at Herat; but this discovery, of course, made such appointment impossible.*[96]

Most men would not have given it a second thought; Shakespear almost certainly had no such instructions in his passport when he escorted

Figure 5.8. Portrait in oils of James Abbott by B. Baldwin. Abbott sat for the portrait in London after his mission to Khiva. It is one of hundreds of portraits of Britons in the East in local dress. In this portrait Abbott's left hand is visible but his maimed right hand is not. He is wearing the same robe and dagger as his friend Sammud Khan in figure 5.4. (NATIONAL PORTRAIT GALLERY)

the freed slaves to Novopetrovskoye a few weeks later. It suggests a profound sense of insecurity in Abbott, a self-doubt that manifested itself most visibly in social environments. Whatever Abbott's reasons for leaving the letter, however, it poisoned his reputation with Hobhouse and put a petty and sour punctuation mark at the end of a grand adventure that ought to have been remembered otherwise.

Chapter 5

While in London, he sat for a painting in Afghan dress. It is the earliest known likeness of him. The face is that of a sensitive, even gentle man, his expression thoughtful and somewhat remote. For the sitting, Abbott borrowed Sammud Khan's shirt, waistband, fur cloak, and dagger. The turban is of a golden cloth ornamented with small jewels and looks more like a costume piece for *The One Thousand and One Nights* than anything he wore in Central Asia. It was likely a studio prop, since it is unlikely anything like this survived the robbery on the Caspian. His wounded right hand is conspicuously hidden in the image.

During his year in England, partially on medical leave, Abbott published his first book, the *T'Hakoorine, a Tale of Maandoo*, first written in Bengal in the 1830s. Abbott believed it was lost in Herat, and he rewrote it from memory in London.[97] Criticism of *T'Hakoorine* was muted, but the critics were less kind to his account of the Khiva mission when it appeared in 1843. Abbott had kept a journal of his travels from Novopetrovskoye back to India and recorded all his recollections of the journey prior to the events on the shore of the Caspian. Some of his papers and notes were returned to him on the steppe, through the efforts of Saleh Mohammed with the Kazakh slavers, including his daily logbook. The route maps in the tiny notebook he carried from his affair with Fanny de Burgh also survived. His account of his travels, *Narrative of a Journey from Heraut to Khiva*, was published in Calcutta in 1843 in two volumes, but it did not go over nearly as well as Alexander Burnes's *Travels into Bokhara: The Narrative of a Voyage on the Indus* had when it was first published in 1835. Where Burnes's account had been lively, Abbott's was lugubrious, and he was stung by some of the criticism leveled against it. In his preface to the second edition, he wrote, "As I conceived that the personal narrative of a traveler through the steppes of Tartary could only be interesting by drawing largely upon his sensations and emotions; I noted roughly every thought and fancy that could yet be recovered, intending to select carefully from the mass such as were suitable for publication. The selection has, I feel, been injudicious."[98] This is revealing of both his own Romantic sensibility and his belief that the public still shared this taste for "sensations and emotions." In this he ignored the changing literary tastes of the 1840s. The Romantic prose of his youth was being replaced by more a more down-to-earth style influenced by Utilitarianism and a growing public sense of modernity. On a visit to England in 1837, for example, American author James Fennimore Cooper captured this change in male behavior from the "feminine" emotionalism of the Romantic era to the new stoic manliness when he noted, "The men, as a whole, are simple, masculine in manner and mind."[99] Abbott's Romantic style, typical of the Regency period and couched in what Jeffrey Richards terms "the extravagant emotionalism of the age," was outdated by the early 1840s.[100] The *Monthly Review* for July 1843 panned his book, noting, "This is a singularly unsatisfactory narrative. It is almost entirely destitute of interest and value in a diplomatic point of view, and even of facts of any importance."[101] The critics' primary objection was that it was too emotional, calling the author "a bundle of emotions and sensations."[102] The critics even accused Abbott of "exaggerating the difficulties of the mission on which he was sent."[103] This claim was absurd, but Abbott's fear that the editing was injudicious was well founded.

Another officer with more political and literary savoir faire would have left out the Romantic emotionalism and made a shorter and better story of it, emphasizing his leadership in freeing the four hundred Russian slaves from Khiva and his negotiations with General Perovsky and Count Nesselrode to free some six hundred Khivan slaves from Russian captivity in exchange, and thus have won wider public acclaim. Abbott lacked such instincts. Nevertheless, the book sold well enough over two decades to go into another printing. The preface to the second edition was a self-effacing mea culpa, in which, in his usual florid style, he apologized to his readers for the "defectiveness" of the book and for "instances of egotism of which I was not aware until I saw the work in print."[104] The book, he noted, contained many "of the most unreserved confessions ... that should have been reserved exclusively for the eyes of friends."[105] However, the raw honesty and lack of self-censorship add credibility to his account of events. It is hardly the work of a man trying to portray himself as heroic.

Some players of the Great Game were much better at self-promotion. Where Burnes used an orientalist portrait of himself in Afghan dress as the frontispiece for his book, for example,[106] Abbott sat for just such a portrait but, too shy to publish his own image, used an illustration of Sammud Khan for his frontispiece instead.[107] Shakespear, too, had the instinct for self-promotion. He greatly exaggerated his role in the freeing of the Russian slaves just a few weeks after Abbott's departure from Khiva and either innocently or, more probably, deliberately misconstrued what had transpired between Abbott and the khan. In Great Britain in the 1840s, few officers lacked jealous and petty enemies somewhere within the system who were eager to insinuate damaging gossip about them or to promote themselves at their expense.

That Abbott negotiated the release of the Russian slaves with the Khan of Khiva and concluded arrangements with Count Nesselrode for the reciprocal release of the six hundred Khivans held by Russians is beyond historical doubt. Shakespear was only sent to Khiva because Todd believed Abbott was dead, and Shakespear's completion of Abbott's work in Khiva was achieved essentially by showing up. The slaves who he escorted to freedom shortly after his arrival had taken many weeks to assemble from all over Khaurism. While in Khiva, Abbott also effected the release of twenty female Afghan slaves who were transported back to Herat and purchased the freedom of the British agent, Umeer Beg. Abbott gave Umeer Beg most of the gold coins he had before leaving the city. Altogether more than a thousand people lived in freedom because of James Abbott, a fact for which he was never recognized.[108] Shakespear might easily have acknowledged this and shared the recognition for the accomplishment with Abbott, but he claimed it all for himself.

In the bigger picture, however, Abbott's journey had not done anything to advance Great Britain's geostrategic interests, although that is certainly a high bar of judgment. In the final analysis, if Abbott's mission was quixotic, that was not his fault. Nothing in the thirty-three-year-old artillery captain's life up to that point had prepared him for traveling across hundreds of miles of unexplored wilderness and establishing diplomatic relations with a kingdom no one in Britain had ever seen, in a language no Briton spoke. Abbott did what he was ordered to do and demonstrated in the process that he was a resourceful and determined representative of Her Majesty's interests in remote places and difficult situations. Once again his remarkable good luck and strong constitution seemingly made him almost impervious to infection and disease. To the mutinous crewmen, mad elephants, rabid dogs, cannon balls, and cholera on the list of dangers he had survived, he had now added heavy blows to his head, deep saber wounds to both hands, the amputation of two fingers, and exposure to a Central Asian winter for three weeks without blankets or warm clothing. James Abbott was not an easy man to kill.

On August 4, 1841, he was promoted from brevet (temporary) captain to (permanent) captain.[109] Burnes and Shakespear were knighted for less, but this was Abbott's sole tangible recompense for nearly a year of hazardous service and hardship. It was not enough to perform heroic deeds in Victorian times: one also had to promote them with a certain self-aggrandizing panache.[110]

One of the most fascinating aspects of Abbott's account of his travels is the rare description of the cultural counterflow to British imperialism occasioned by Sammud Khan's visit to Europe. He was almost certainly the first Afghan to visit England. Abbott wrote that Sammud Khan "was far from being uncultivated" and was "a shrewd observer whom nothing escaped."[111] But his stubborn refusal to learn any English or adopt any European habits caused Abbott considerable trouble. He refused to try silverware, for example, and caused a scene on several occasions by eating with his hands Afghan-style from a serving bowl. He maintained his Afghan robes, turban, and green cloak throughout his travels, and everywhere he went, he was a source of fascination. Virtually all the Britons and other Europeans he encountered thought him a Turk, a fascinating reflection on the state of European knowledge of the East in the middle of the nineteenth century. The French even addressed him as "Monsieur le Turc." When Abbott explained he was an Afghan, this descriptor almost universally had no meaning either on the Continent or in Britain. The latter is especially surprising considering Britain was at that time occupying Afghanistan. While Britons traveling to India almost universally adopted Indian cuisine, Sammud Khan would not break his *halal* diet, subsisting on pastries and milk whenever Abbott was unable to find a butcher who would slaughter a sheep or chicken in the prescribed manner. Abbott remonstrated with him to adapt a little to local ways, but Sammud Khan only replied, "I cannot peril my soul, even for your sake."[112]

Sammud Khan maintained his prayers with the aid of a compass that Abbott bought him, found British public drunkenness abhorrent, and was horrified by the English love of pork. On one occasion, Abbott took him to the famous Indian bathhouse of Dean Mahomet in the fashionable St. James neighborhood. He twice attended a production of *A Midsummer Night's Dream* at the Covent Garden Theatre and was delighted with the singing, dancing, and special effects. Of these Abbott noted, "The machinery of the Faeries we have ourselves borrowed from Asia, and it was easily comprehended by him. . . . He still declares that of all the wonderful and delightful things possessed by the English, their Play of the Faeries is the most marvelous."[113]

Sammud Khan also enjoyed his visits to the church at St. Pancras, which he attended often with Abbott. Interestingly, this was the one place where Sammud Khan adapted himself to local customs, following the motions of the congregation exactly. Overall, his yearlong experience of England hardly suggests any grand orientalist project of cultural hegemony underway in Britain in 1840, as has been suggested. What there actually was, in fact, was complete ignorance of the East combined with a naive and universal curiosity. Sammud Khan's comportment in England also presents a fascinating contrast with the British in India, who routinely adapted to Indian food, not infrequently wore Indian dress, learned vernacular languages, and often took great pride in incorporating this acculturation into their public and private identities in the 1840s.

The mainstream historical narrative holds that the 1830s and 1840s in India saw a cultural shift among middle-class Britons toward more "British" cultural mores. Raymond Schwab suggests, for example, that this "anglicization" stemmed from a need to justify and rationalize British imperial expansion as a means of spreading the benefits of a superior culture and religion, and "the conquerors felt obliged to defend their conquest, which meant exalting their own race and religon."[114] Apart from the rise of evangelism, however, little of this "anglicization" is evident in the India that Abbott voluminously recorded. Up until his writing in the mid-1850s (some of which looks back on earlier experiences), there is no mention whatever of race as the term is understood today in Abbott's

Figure 5.9. A montage of period portraits in various media of British men and women living in the East prior to 1860, including James Abbott, upper right. (MONTAGE CREATED BY AUTHOR FROM PUBLIC DOMAIN SOURCES)

journals. Intermarriage with indigenous women and women born of intercultural marriages clearly remained the norm.

Moreover, having oneself immortalized for posterity in Eastern attire in portraiture was very popular with Britons in the Middle East and in India in particular up until paintings were gradually replaced by the medium of photography. While some Britons chose to sit for portraits in British dress and uniform, many others in the nineteenth century went to the trouble and considerable expense of having portraits painted in Indian attire, not infrequently by leading (and expensive) artists like Thomas Hicks, Louis Gallait, and George Chinnery. They are frequently depicted sitting cross-legged and in relaxed poses, which of course was partly necessary for long sittings for the painter, but which also suggests an intent to show that the subject not only understood Indian culture and was adapted to it but that he or she was relaxed and comfortable in it as well. One has to wonder why, if Britons in India were now trying to define themselves in alterity to Indian culture, so many of them had the only portraits ever painted of them made depicting themselves fully assimilated into it.

Chapter 5

In 1841 Abbott and Sammud Khan began their return voyage to India. It was by this time practicable to avoid the journey around the Cape of Good Hope by traveling through Europe to and across the Suez. Their journey was a recreation of the Grand Tour of Europe once thought an essential part of the education of upper-class youth in the eighteenth century. They traveled via Paris, Lyon, and Avignon to Marseilles, then by steamer to Rome, Athens, Cairo, and Suez. In Paris, Abbott was invited to dinner with the British Ambassador, Lord Granville, and, ever morbidly sensitive to the most minute aspects of his social status, noted that Lord Granville "received me with much courtesy and paid me marked attention."[115] This was always psychologically very important to Abbott, who seldom failed to record this kind of self-affirming reception. His accounts of his encounters with gentry almost always reflect a painful emotional insecurity, excessive class consciousness, and a sense that he was somehow not worthy of being present, as Lord Hobhouse's account of his dinner with Abbott in England suggests.

A dinner with the British Ambassador in Athens, Sir Edmund Lyons, evoked one of the most telling passages in Abbott's writing of his perception of British imperialism in India: "[The French ambassador] observed in conversation, that he could not understand why it was that British colonies were so successful [and] the French such failures. I could have told him; but of course did not: that it is because the French do not sufficiently respect the rights and the prejudices of the foreign peoples who they rule. They are accordingly both despised and hated by their subjects."[116] Abbott here reflects the pervasive Anglo-Indian narrative that British colonial possessions prospered because Britons were enlightened imperialists who had captured the love and admiration of their subjects and, conversely, that the French lacked this colonial savoir faire. Otherwise volume 2 of *Narrative of a Journey from Heraut to Khiva* is primarily interesting for the depth of knowledge Abbott demonstrates of Greek, Roman, and Islamic lore.

In Aden, Abbott purchased passage for Sammud Khan to Kandahar via Karachi, and the two men finally separated. The British government allocated Abbott £40 for Sammud Khan's return to Afghanistan, but Abbott's "commonplace books" show the actual expense exceeded

£140, which Abbott paid out of his own pocket rather than send Sammud Khan by himself around the Cape. The difference of £100 paid by Abbott in 1841 is equivalent to approximately £11,000 in 2021,[117] but Abbott was sure that if Sammud Khan traveled alone, "he would die of misery on the voyage."[118] Abbott had become quite attached to Sammud Khan despite what Abbott perceived as his obstinacy on cultural matters. "I parted from him with regret" he wrote, "for we had seen and suffered much together."[119]

Abbott never saw Sammud Khan again, but he continued to receive reports of his whereabouts. When Sammud Khan reached Kandahar, he was surely the most widely traveled Afghan of his time. He subsequently worked for the British army at Kabul, as did Saleh Mohammed. They both escaped the massacre of the British garrison during its retreat through the Khyber Pass. In 1854 Abbott learned from Saleh Mohammed that Sammud Khan had remained in British service well after the First Anglo-Afghan War and was given a pension by the British government, which was continued to his family after his death in Peshawar in 1852.

Abbott sailed alone for Bombay. The voyage to India via Suez was shorter than the trying voyage around the Cape but still dangerous. En route, the monsoon broke, and Abbott's ship encountered a storm at sea, which, exactly like the one on his first journey to India around the Cape in 1823, also tore away the fore and main topmasts of the vessel and nearly capsized it. To repair the damage the ship made port at the former Dutch colony of Cochin,[120] and Abbott found the town retained much of its original Dutch architecture and flavor. He took a great interest in the local Jewish culture,[121] visiting the Cochin synagogue and observing with curiosity that the "scriptures are kept in scrolls, wound around a spindle and enclosed in a case." A local Jewish family held a wedding while Abbott was there, and when he expressed an interest in the proceedings, the family invited this complete stranger to join them. This and other references make clear that, unlike most Britons at this time, Abbott was quite philosemitic. More typical of British officers visiting Cochin was the reaction of Captain Albert Hervey, who referred to the Jewish Quarter as "Jew-Town" and described the Jewish settlers there as "a dirty, squalid set."[122]

CHAPTER 5

Abbott was aware of the prevailing stereotypes of Jews but was outspokenly sympathetic. In Merv en route to Khiva, he had sought out a Jewish merchant in the city, a vestigial remnant of the ancient and powerful Radhanite financial and trading network based in Jewish identity that once spanned all of Asia.[123] Abbott and the merchant found much to talk about. "The condition and history of this people have deep claims upon public sympathy," Abbott wrote, noting that the Jewish population in Mashhad had recently fallen victim to a pogrom.[124] While Abbott was conversing with the merchant, there was a knock at the door. When the man answered it, he was literally struck over the head and carried away. Abbott was outraged and had Nizaum follow the kidnappers. He petitioned the governor of Merv immediately and got the unfortunate man released. Here again was the knight-errant protecting the innocent and the helpless. But such treatment and worse was a common fate of Jews in much of Central Asia during this period.[125]

During a later visit, he met the merchant's son. Abbott thought him "of the most prepossessing countenance," noting "features beautifully regular, and an eye corresponding in beauty of form and in lustre, the most clear and guileless that could be conceived."[126] Abbott clearly subscribed to none of the ugly stereotypes regarding Jewish features and appearance. "I looked upon him with much interest. This was a son of Israel. How lovely must not her daughters be!" he wrote in the 1850s, adding, "This was one of that scattered and persecuted race, erst the chosen of Heaven, and now the scorn of the world."[127] In *Narrative of a Journey from Heraut to Khiva*, Abbott recounted his conversation with the merchant and included it in a strong defense of the Jews:

> "We know that the English are everywhere kind to the Jews, and we have heard that your people are striving to collect together our scattered people, to restore them to their kingdom" [the merchant answered].... I replied that the English did indeed feel a strong interest in all relating to the Jews.... [W]e granted them all the rights of free citizens, including a share in offices of state and legislation. That ... they form a most respectable and powerful body, and are amongst the richest of

mankind. That we believe the Jewish Scriptures, and that Jesus Christ was of the house of David, and of the family of Israel.[128]

Whether this conversation is embellished is beside the point in considering Abbott's philosemitism: what is significant is that he chose to include it in his published memoir and took a strongly pro-Jewish stance in public when this was distinctly a minority view in Britain. In Khiva, Abbott again sought out the Jewish community. Learning of this, the khan asked him whether it was true that the British protected the Jews. Abbott answered that indeed it was and that many leading personages in England were Jewish. Abbott's interest in and robust defense of Judaism prior to 1845 make his future contretemps with Benjamin Disraeli all the stranger and more difficult to understand.

After repairs to the ship were completed, Abbott sailed on from Cochin and arrived in Calcutta in September 1841 without further incident. Lord Auckland invited him to dinner. Abbott thought him "rather of amiable mind than of polished manners," adding ironically that "he [lacked] self-esteem to fit him for the high position he held."[129] He now learned what had befallen D'Arcy Todd after he left Herat for Khiva. Emir Shah Kamran was now being held a virtual prisoner in his own palace by his vizier, Yar Mohammed, who had made himself the de facto ruler of the kingdom. Todd had taken his instructions directly from MacNaughten in Kabul when his own communications with Calcutta were cut, instructions that Todd assumed would be copied to Calcutta. MacNaughten, for whatever reason, neglected to do so and did not live to clarify the situation. As a result, there later appeared to be irregularities in the account ledgers of the Herat legation where Todd followed MacNaughten's instructions for disbursements of cash that Calcutta had not been made aware of.

Auckland was never a man to admit error, as his correspondence with MacNaughten shows, and he would not reverse course and order a withdrawal from Afghanistan and Herat while it could be done in an orderly manner and in good weather.[130] The force in Kabul was thus doomed. What was possible in Afghanistan in the spring of 1841 was impossible by December. The British army retreating in chaos from Kabul was completely destroyed in January 1842 before reaching Jalalabad.¹³¹ Responsibility for the disaster fell upon Lord Auckland. Auckland was informed, as soon as the news of the catastrophe reached London, that he was being replaced as governor-general by Lord Ellenborough.

The men in Herat, meanwhile, were lucky to escape with their lives. When Todd refused to disburse more money without a promise from Yar Mohammed to stop conspiring with Britain's enemies, the vizier made clear that the delegation would be killed if they remained in the city, and they withdrew. Auckland was furious.¹³² Without giving Todd a personal hearing, Auckland censured him, dismissed him from the political service, demoted him to lieutenant, and ordered him to return to the Bengal Artillery.

Many men had predicted the outcome in Afghanistan of what is known to history as Auckland's Folly, but most were now dead or beyond Auckland's reach. Todd, however, had publicly added to Auckland's embarrassment by predicting the outcome as a young major in his memorandum of 1837, a report that reached the Board of Directors and Parliament.¹³³ Todd made a convenient whipping boy. Many officials expressed to Abbott privately that Todd was treated unfairly, but knowing Auckland's bloody-mindedness, they also thought Todd should wait and make his case to Auckland's successor Lord Ellenborough, who would replace him as governor-general in February 1842. As George Pottinger and Patrick Macrory note with understatement, "On any appreciation, Todd was harshly treated."¹³⁴ Abbott was naturally distressed by the injustice and was indefatigable in his unsuccessful attempts to intercede on Todd's behalf.¹³⁵ When Todd returned to Calcutta, he was no longer his old, happy-go-lucky self. Other officers might have kept their distance from a man under Auckland's black cloud, but not Abbott. The two went to the theater together in Calcutta and sat in full view of Lord Auckland, his sisters, and his staff.

Now thirty-five years old, a full captain, and a political officer earning one thousand rupees a month,¹³⁶ Abbott was in a position to think of his marital prospects. While in Calcutta, he fell madly in love with Margaret Ferguson, the daughter of a Scottish merchant.¹³⁷ She was Abbott's vision of earthly beauty: blond, blue-eyed, "small and delicately formed," he wrote, adding, typically, "[with] a figure suited to a faery."[138] It was not all installing her upon an angelic pedestal. He wrote that her lips "were full and it seemed impossible to resist the impulse to kiss them."[139] But there were rules to be observed in courtship in the 1840s: Abbott had to write Margaret's brother, John, and ask permission to court her. Alas Margaret could not return his affections, Abbott learned, because she was informally engaged to another man. John told Abbott his suit was hopeless. Abbott wrote Todd that "Margaret is a perfect angel, but I don't have a hope in the world."[140] Ever the Romantic, however, Abbott carried a torch for Margaret long after he left Calcutta in January 1842.

Abbott now resumed his career in the political branch.[141] He was initially appointed assistant to Colonel Dixon, the superintendent of Murwara in central India. This was a modest posting, but when Alexander Burnes returned to India in 1835 following his knighthood and triumphal visit to London, he was given a similar assignment as Assistant to the Resident at Cutch.[142] It was in fact a typical posting for a captain in the Political Department. When Dixon's anticipated transfer from Murwara was cancelled, Abbott was appointed Assistant to the Resident at nearby Indore instead, with charge of the Nimarr District.[143] His assignment as district magistrate and collector of Nimarr was his first experience of ordinary political work.[144] Nimarr was 930 miles of rough country due west of Calcutta. During the month of January 1842, Abbott traveled west by day, staying overnight at British stations along the way, where an officer would invariably offer him a bed for the night and provide all the hospitality available. He stopped for a night at Dinapore to see his old friends from Mhow, Captain and Mrs. Reymond de Montmorency. Only their youngest daughter, Anna Matilda, was then with them in India. She was Abbott's goddaughter and just walking. Abbott wrote that "she was a little, sweet girl" who "flitted about incessantly."[145] It was their first but not their last meeting.

The district of Nimarr comprised approximately nine thousand square miles, about the size of New Hampshire. Abbott settled into his new job and took a house on the Asirgarh plateau, eighteen hundred feet above sea level. The plateau is the highest point in the district and the site of the ruins of a massive Moghul fort, a green and picturesque place with large

Chapter 5

natural pools, the Mama-Bhanja Talaos, near the commissioner's house. Abbott found it ideal. He learned Nimadi, a local dialect of Hindi, and made many good pen-and-ink sketches of the local area. In July 1843 his account of his journey to Khiva was published in the prestigious *Asiatic Journal*.[146] On a day-to-day basis he was his own boss, and the life suited him perfectly. It was one of the happiest periods of his life.

Abbott's first official duty in Nimarr was to inspect the district jail, which held two hundred convicts. He found the closed cells suffocating and immediately ordered the installation of a barred window in each. Abbott was a man who paid attention to detail. He was suspicious by nature and not easily fooled. When he learned of a plan for a jail break, he put a guard on the main door and had a stout iron bar made by the local blacksmith to reinforce it. Abbott tested the new bar by placing it over two large rocks and jumping on it. It snapped like a twig. After a conversation with the blacksmith about the penalties for aiding prisoners in escape, he ordered another bar made and tested it too. The second bar passed.

Each day in Nimarr Abbott held *kucherry* to adjudicate petty crimes.[147] The largest group of cases he encountered dealt with witchcraft. "No reasoning could shake the belief of the people in witchcraft as of almost daily occurrence," he wrote.[148] In areas outside British jurisprudence, the standard trial for witchcraft consisted of setting the accused afloat on a raft made of dried cow dung. If the woman sank, she was not a witch; if she floated, she was burned or stoned to death. Since few women could swim, the accused usually died either way, to the general satisfaction of everyone except the defendant.

After two years at Asirgarh as district magistrate, Abbott learned from friends that Margaret Ferguson's suitor had married another woman. He immediately requested permission from her brother to resume his suit, and in January 1844 Margaret accepted his marriage proposal. He left at once for Calcutta. In the 1840s, eligible British women, especially young and attractive ones, were still a rarity, and Margaret had no lack of suitors. She undoubtedly still felt considerable affection for James too, and, as Jane Austen's Romantic novel *Pride and Prejudice* had shown in 1813, for example, second proposals were not infrequently more successful than first ones.

Figure 5.10 Two views of Asirgarh. Top: A modern photo shows the ruins of the British station on the Asirgarh plateau. The house in the lower left of the photograph was probably the district commissioner's residence. Bottom: A pen-and-ink drawing by James Abbott of the ruins of a nearby Hindu temple, titled "Jhaur Ghat," done in 1842. (BRITISH LIBRARY BOARD)

Chapter 5

They married in Calcutta on February 15, 1844. As officers could not get leave for longer than ninety days, given the lengthy travel to and from Asirgarh, their honeymoon in a waterfront bungalow on the Hooghly near Calcutta was brief. Just six months before their nuptials, in August 1843, D'Arcy Todd had also married, wedding Marian Sandham, daughter of the surgeon of the 16th Lancers. In February 1844, the two couples met at Dum Dum "to spend a day and how happy a day!"[149] It was the culmination of the two friends' dreams, twenty years since their friendship blossomed on that very spot in 1824, to be happily married and together with their wives, a moment James would never forget. He never saw D'Arcy again. Marian died in early December 1845, and D'Arcy left her graveside to rejoin the horse artillery for the First Anglo-Sikh War. At the Battle of Ferozeshah on December 21, 1845, he was killed far out in front of his guns by the Sikh cannons, his death essentially a suicide by enemy fire.[150]

James and Margaret traveled by steamer around the tip of India to Surat, thence overland 270 miles by palanquin in seventeen days to Asirgarh, the least arduous route for a young woman accustomed to life in the big city and 660 land miles shorter than going overland from Calcutta. Once they had settled, life in Nimarr was a lonely one for Margaret. The nearest British station to Asirgarh was some miles away at Mundlaisir, where a surgeon, Dr. Stover, and two subalterns of the Bengal Native Infantry were assigned. The surgeon's wife, Mrs. Stover, was the only Englishwoman for many days in any direction. Despite the better salary of a political officer, Abbott still had debts and could not afford a horse and carriage for Margaret. She became so lonely that Abbott was actively considering a request to return to regular military duties at a large garrison for her happiness.

Three months after arriving at Nimarr, the Abbotts conceived a child. Their daughter, Margaret Ann, was born in Asirgarh on February 10, 1845, a year after their wedding. But tragically, the most joyous day in Abbott's life was followed immediately by the worst: Margaret died the next day, on February 11, from complications of childbirth.[151] She was buried in the small cemetery in Asirgarh. A pair of pen-and-ink drawings done by Abbott of her gravesite show his grief and devotion; sometime

Figure 5.11 The first grave marker for Margaret Abbott erected by James Abbott in the British cemetery at Asirgarh is seen in the top drawing (indicated with the number 1). Sometime later, Abbott had this grave marker replaced by a tall spire, seen in the drawing below (indicated with the number 2). The grave marker on the far right of both drawings, the final resting place of Captain Gilbert Grierson Maitland, who died there in October 1820, was still there in 2009. Both drawings were done in pen and ink by James Abbott in the 1840s. (BRITISH LIBRARY BOARD)

after leaving Nimarr, he had the first monument removed and erected a spire for his wife on the site. In later years Abbott wrote, "It seems [incredible] to me that my reason survived the blow."[152]

6

A New Beginning

1843–1849

EVENTS OCCURRED IN THE ELEVEN MONTHS FOLLOWING MARGARET'S death in February 1845 which dramatically changed the course of James Abbott's career, events that took him from Bengal to the Punjab and the Northwest Frontier of India and set the stage for the most remarkable chapter of his life. This turbulent year also brought out some of his worst shortcomings. His social insecurity and hypersensitivity to criticism merged now with a new sense of his own correctness. Margaret's death, in particular, seems to have brought about a change in his personality and given rise to an obduracy that was not present before.

The loss of one's wife after just a year of marriage would be a stunning blow to any man. James Abbott was steeped in the Romanticism of Walter Scott and the *Poetics* of Aristotle, and both literary sources had had a profound influence on him. Scott and Romanticism taught him that everything had a tragic ending, and man's lot was to accept it stoically. He was also infused by the *Poetics* of Aristotle. Already, while at Mhow, Aristotle's thoughts on melancholia and poetry appear to have led Abbott to realize he was suffering from depression. The marked change toward pedagogery in Abbott's personality following the tragedy of Margaret's death hints at what he read in Aristotle as *anagnorisis*, a recognition resulting from a shocking reversal of fortune that creates "a change from ignorance to knowledge."[1]

Chapter 6

In more contemporary, scientific terms, this certitude of one's own correctness is not uncommon among middle-aged men in any circumstances, as social scientists have often pointed out. A besetting sin of late middle life, it has been observed, is the tendency to "become impervious to contrary evidence [and] resentful of criticism," and this was only amplified in Abbott by the dogmatism of the Victorian era.[2] This unfortunately also caused irascibility and impatience with his immediate chain of command, a testiness that did not endear him to British authorities either locally or in the halls of government in Calcutta. It was a flaw in his character that he recognized but was often unable to moderate.

It also reinforced the remarkable blind spot in his understanding of the Indian Army. While his knowledge of Indian cultures, both Muslim and Hindu, was by 1845 nearly encyclopedic, his appreciation of the essential nature of the service of the sepoy and *sowar*, which had been wrong when he was a young lieutenant in 1824, had, remarkably, become even more wrong in the intervening twenty years. His newfound confidence in his own correctness established a blind conviction about the sepoys that was no longer susceptible to intellectual self-review. Much has been written in the history of the Great Mutiny of 1857 about the fatally misplaced British confidence in the loyalty of the sepoys and the power of British leadership to control them as their own children, a belief that was part and parcel of the "empire of opinion" narrative. But of all the many causal factors in the Mutiny, perhaps the least considered is this deeper underlying disconnect between the British narrative of why and on what terms the Indian soldier served and the reality, a decoupling that Abbott demonstrated repeatedly.

Already, in the mutiny at Barrackpore, Abbott had evinced the consensus perception among Company officers that the basis of the Indian soldier's professional personality was essentially the same as that of the British soldier. And this may perhaps have been more the case with the soldiers of the Madras and Bombay presidencies, where men at the harsh lower rungs of society with little to lose might join the army and go where it sent them to get a roof over their heads and three meals a day, as was often the case among the enlisted ranks of the British Royal Army. The Madras and Bombay armies sought to downplay caste by deliberately recruiting from castes not traditionally thought of as professional soldiers. Bombay and Madras army sepoys generally did not, for example, insist on preparing their own food to prevent caste contamination; Bengal Army sepoys did. This egalitarianism created a more professional soldiery in the Bombay and Madras armies, as evidenced by the fact that neither army mutinied when the Bengal Army did in 1857.

The Bengal Presidency took the opposite tack of emphasizing and strengthening caste sensibilities. This privileging of caste in the Bengal Army was systematically reinforced by its leaders as a means of enhancing the morale of the army and giving it a sense of being an elite. Instead of impressing upon them that caste did not matter to their officers, as was done in the Madras and Bombay armies, Bengal Army sepoys were told that it was, in fact, the very reason they were good soldiers. Not only were men from the highest castes being recruited almost exclusively, but the Company was now also assimilating a corollary assumption of the Bengal sepoys' loyalty to Britain itself—and with it a belief that what was good for Britain was, by extension, also good for the Bengal sepoy. It is one of the great ironies of British colonial history in India that an empire so deeply engaged in a project to collect knowledge about its subjects, which included the comprehensive gathering, assembly, and classification of information about castes, tribes, and culture, should fail so completely to understand its own soldiery.

Great change was now afoot in India. About the time the Abbott's daughter was conceived in 1844, the East India Company annexed the entire Sind region in what its conqueror, General Charles Napier, famously called "a useful piece of rascality."[3] This tectonic shift within its foreign policy sphere alarmed the neighboring Sikh Empire. It was already in turmoil from internal succession struggles after the death of Raja Ranjit Singh in 1839, and the British conquest of Sind made Sikh leaders wonder if they were the next target of British expansion in India. Both the British and the Sikh empires were inherently expansionist and shared the same economic rationale of increasing tax revenues by means of increasing territorial holdings. The Sutlej River formed an uneasy border between the Sikh Empire and the princely state of Bahawalpur, which was under subsidiary alliance to the East India Company. It was

Chapter 6

a boundary that the British annexation of Sind did nothing to stabilize. Conflict was almost inevitable, and it was not long in coming.

On a personal level, the annexation of Sind brought Governor-General Lord Ellenborough and the British Resident in Sind, James Outram,[4] into direct conflict, and the ripple effects from this animosity changed Abbott's life. Outram's vocal and public opposition to the annexation did not sit well with Ellenborough, who was a notoriously vindictive man both in England and in India.[5] In retaliation for Outram's public opposition to his policy, Ellenborough wanted to deny him another political assignment altogether, but Outram had important friends in London and prevailed on them for protection. Thus Ellenborough found himself in need of a new political assignment for Outram to comply with the letter of the law from the Duke of Wellington to do so.

A momentary clamor for Bengal artillery officers to return to their regiment provided Ellenborough with the opportunity to appear to comply with Wellington's instructions while damaging the careers of two people he disliked in one stroke. As the Resident in Sind, Outram's salary was five thousand rupees (£500) a month, while Abbott's minor political position in Nimarr, in comparison, paid just one thousand rupees (£100) a month. Ellenborough used the momentary recall of artillery officers to send Abbott, whom he did not like, back to his regiment and replace him with Outram, whom he liked less, with an 80 percent cut in salary. When offered the position in Nimarr, Outram wrote Abbott to ask his advice, indicating he was leaning toward declining the position as an obvious demotion. Abbott, as a matter of honor, advised him to accept it on the grounds that refusal would give Ellenborough an opening to accuse Outram of unseemly mercenary motivations.

Outram accepted and relieved Abbott in Nimarr.[6] Abbott's chief concern now was the logistics of moving his infant daughter, Margaret Ann, together with Margaret's sister, a wet nurse, and Margaret's aunt, Miss Petrie, 930 miles through the jungle to Calcutta. Traveling the entire route overland with an infant was impracticable, so he moved the party from one British station to the next, traveling 330 miles overland to Bombay and from there by ship to Calcutta. In Calcutta, the two British women and Abbott's newborn daughter took up residence with his

A New Beginning

brother-in-law, John Ferguson. In 1845, a widower raising a newborn by himself in India was not considered an option. At her request, Abbott entrusted Margaret Ann's care to her great aunt, Miss Petrie. He was posted briefly to Dum Dum, which gave him time with his daughter, but in October 1845 he was ordered to march a half battalion of foot artillery upcountry to Cawnpore.

Abbott was now more deeply in debt than ever, and unable to afford a horse, he made the march to Cawnpore on foot. One day on the road, Abbott was approached by an upper-caste Brahmin who was in great distress because a stray dog had run off with his turban. Always the knight-errant upon the road to aid the helpless and bemused by the disconnect between the loss of a few inexpensive yards of cotton and the man's grief-stricken behavior, Abbott sent for the local village *thanadar* (police chief) and soon discovered the reason: in the nineteenth century, at least, an Indian's turban also served as his wallet. As night was falling, Abbott and his half battalion of foot artillery made camp near the village. His morning tea was interrupted by the sound of gunfire. During the night, his sergeant major quickly informed him, a dog had entered one of the British tents and made off with a man's forage cap, and Abbott's troopers had cracked the mystery: an ingenious traveling Fagan had trained dogs to be pickpockets by running off with whatever headdress they found, and Abbott's men were reacting rather unsportingly by shooting any canine Artful Dodger that now approached the camp.

When he arrived at Cawnpore, he signed the half battalion over to the artillery officer awaiting his arrival. Also awaiting Abbott was news of his appointment as the superintendent of the sea embankments at Hidgellee. This was arranged through the intercession of a friend, Captain Godfrey Greene, who at the time was the Secretary of the Military Board. Abbott was not enthusiastic about the position after being deprived of his assignment at Nimarr by Ellenborough, as it was not a political position; nor was it very well paid. Its primary advantage was that it would keep him near his daughter in Calcutta, so he accepted it with the understanding that if war should break out, the position would not preclude him from volunteering.

Chapter 6

Figure 6.1. "Budgerow," aquatint by Frans Balthazar Solvyns from *A Collection of Two Hundred and Fifty Coloured Etchings: Descriptive of the Manners, Customs and Dresses of the Hindoos*, published in Calcutta in 1796. The *budgerow* was a relatively comfortable if leisurely means of travel in India before the advent of the railroads. They were propelled upriver by teams of oarsmen. (WIKIMEDIA COMMONS, COLUMBIA UNIVERSITY)

Now not having a horse turned to his advantage, as he was able to hire a *budgerow* for the return trip and within a month was back in Calcutta, though not without considerable psychic trauma. "The cholera was raging along the course of the river," he wrote of the voyage.[7] In accordance with Hindu custom, the bodies of thousands of cholera victims were being cast into the river daily. During the month-long voyage from Cawnpore to Calcutta, Abbott was subjected to an appalling and macabre phenomenon. Among the tens of thousands of corpses floating in the river, one particular burial haunted him for most of the trip. At a village he put into for supplies, the bodies of an elderly couple were put into the river together. During the day, under sail, his boat traveled faster and outpaced their corpses. But at night, while the boat was at anchor, the bodies caught up to it again. For nearly a month, the horror of the same two decomposing corpses, floating face up, seemed to await him each morning as his boat set out into the current, "until I really thought we should never part company."[8] This kind of sustained horror so soon after his wife's death must have been mentally taxing to say the least. Not a few British officers went insane in India.[9] Surviving forty years still sound in mind as well as in body required not only physical resistance to disease and infection and a sustained run of luck but a hardness of mind as well.

On the trip downriver in December 1845, Abbott paused for a day at Allahabad to visit again with his friends Captain and Mrs. Reymond de Montmorency. Six years had passed since he last saw them, and Abbott's goddaughter, Anna Matilda, was now seven, "very fair, with blue eyes and light hair, and a step never at rest." Abbott remembered her as "a sweet tempered little thing full of intelligence and affection. Her parents had taught her to love me and during my mission to Khiva, she had daily prayed 'God bless dear Godpapa and save his life from naughty men.'"[10] Anna Matilda, or Maud as she was known, never ceased her adoration of James Abbott. They would meet again in England twenty-three years later, when Abbott was sixty-one and Maud was thirty.

Abbott reported to Hidgellee.[11] There at the mouth of the Hooghly River, the East India Company had built over a thousand miles of sea embankments to a height of eighteen feet to protect the inland area from daily tidal flooding.[12] This rendered thousands of square kilometers arable to rice production. When Abbott arrived, the formerly uninhabitable region was home to sixty thousand farmers and laborers, many of whom worked at the profitable salt works, which produced an annual revenue for the East India Company of sixty *laks* of rupees.[13] Abbott's daily duties consisted of touring the embankments to look for damage or sections in need of maintenance. He found the assignment tedious. The embankments were a complex network of enclosed plots that allowed streams and smaller rivers to run out to the sea through a series of dykes. Much of the region was comprised of rice paddies, so the embankments themselves were usually the only paths. From January to June 1845, Abbott walked them daily. During the monsoon season, which runs roughly from June to September in India, he was permitted to live in Calcutta, as the air of Hidgellee was considered "unhealthy" during this period, meaning that it was highly malarial. The British did not yet know what caused malaria, but they had learned when and where it seemed to be worst and avoided those areas when possible.[14]

Meanwhile, on the other side of the subcontinent, the Sikh and British empires were now in extremis. The prolonged power struggle between

CHAPTER 6

the two major power blocs in the Sikh Empire, the Sikh Sindhanwalias and the Hindu Dogras, following the death of Ranjit Singh in 1839, had given rise to political chaos and near anarchy in the Punjab. The alarm caused by the annexation of Sind and bellicose British behavior led to a spasm of Sikh expansionism to keep the powerful and hegemonic Sikh army employed. On December 11, 1845, it began crossing the Sutlej into British India.

Thus began a mad dash by James Abbott to cross the subcontinent before the resulting war ended. The Military Board was deluged with letters from officers eager for a combat assignment. Abbott was fortunate in that artillery officers were always in short supply. His request to get into the fight crossed again in the mail with his orders to rejoin the Bengal Artillery at Dum Dum, just as it had for the First Anglo-Afghan War seven years earlier.

As so many officers were trying to go in the same direction, however, someone to relieve him could not be found immediately, and there was some delay before a man was assigned to take his place in Hidgellee. As soon as the new officer arrived, Abbott wrote his brother-in-law James Ferguson in Calcutta and asked him to arrange a *dak* (palanquin relay) immediately for the cross-country trip. Ferguson did so, but there were so many officers rushing toward the Punjab that it was twelve days before Abbott's turn came. He arrived in Umballa to find a dozen officers ahead of him waiting for some means of traveling onward. Resourceful and determined, he procured two horses captured from the Sikh army and started out toward Ferozepore 150 miles to the northwest. At Patiala, thirty miles from Umballa, he found sepoys pitching a British tent by the side of the road. When he asked whose it was, the "answer was Captain Abbott Sahib."[15] It was the camp of his brother Saunders, wounded in the shoulder by grapeshot at the Battle of Ferozeshah. Saunders soon arrived, bringing with him the news of D'Arcy Todd's death in the battle, another shocking blow for James. "Death no doubt was welcome enough to him," Abbott wrote when he learned of his friend's death. The deaths of the two people he loved most in less than a year caused him to add, "How welcome [death] would have been to me at any hour since I [too] lost all that made life dear."[16]

Saunders had no way of helping his brother with faster transport to the front, as all the available *dak* bearers were employed by the army, but he gave him two camels. Abbott continued on through increasingly hostile territory. "I pushed on upon the camel through a country the Sikh population of which was in violent excitement," he wrote. "At several places the excitement was so great and the people were so insolent, that I thought I should have to defend myself from their attacks."[17]

Stopping to rest one night at a small town, he asked for a bed in the local guardroom and was shown to a charpoy[18] by the *jemadar* of the guard. It was a medieval setting: the old stone walls were hung with the arms of the guard, faintly illuminated by a single guttering cresset lamp. "As the night wore on," Abbott recalled, "the *Jemadar* made no sign of retiring to rest. He seemed to be watching me, which put me on my guard."[19] Abbott lay awake, covered by his horse cloak, with one hand on his double-barreled pistol and the other on his dagger. After several hours, the *jemadar* got up from his charpoy, took his sword down from the wall, and drew it from its scabbard while looking intently at Abbott. Abbott opened his eyes to let the man know he was awake. The *jemadar* waved the sword around for a minute before sheathing it and putting it back on the wall. Abbott remained awake the remainder of the night.

As he rode toward the front, the Battle of Sabraon was being fought, resulting in another tactical victory for the British force commanded by Sir Hugh Gough, whose old-school tactics of frontal assault against massed Sikh artillery were almost universally criticized.[20] The victory at Ferozeshah had been costly: 694 men killed and 1,721 wounded. Most of the losses were blamed on Gough's tactics. Abbott noted that in the battle, Gough had arrayed his forces such that "there might be a British soldier to stop every bullet the enemy might fire.... As [the British regiments] closed upon the [Sikh] entrenchment ... one overlapp[ed] the other, and as the dust and smoke arose, the rearward corps fired into the rear of the corps in its front so that it was calculated that we had lost more men by our own fire than by the enemy's."[21]

After the Battle of Ferozeshah, Lord Hardinge commented that "India has been saved by a miracle.... [A]nother such victory will cost us the Empire."[22] Even after Ferozeshah, however, Gough remained a firm believer in the power of the bayonet and still not much interested in artillery preparation. Again at Sabraon, he planned a frontal assault against entrenched Sikh positions on the south bank of the Sutlej.

The Sikh army was now understood to be a far cry from previous opponents of the East India Company. This was not going to be a walkover. The Sikhs were as disciplined, well trained, and resolute as the British, and their artillery was modern and well served. Most of the Sikh artillery corps was in fact trained and led by European officers.[23] Sir Henry Hardinge, the governor-general, yielded operational command at Sabraon to Gough, although he held seniority in rank and thus was technically entitled to command. Hardinge nevertheless prevailed on Gough sufficiently to place his initial emphasis on a flanking maneuver on the Sikh left, which rested on sandy soil where deep entrenchments were not possible. On February 10, 1846, General Robert Dick led the flanking attack, but after initial success it was unsupported and driven back by a counterattack in which Dick was killed. The Sikhs bayoneted British wounded on the recaptured ground, a tactical mistake because word of the killing of their wounded raced through the British lines and enraged both sepoys and British troops. The massacre naturally filled them with a consuming desire for revenge. Sabraon was another bloody affair, but the British again prevailed. After the earlier bayoneting of their wounded, they did not take prisoners. An estimated 20,000 Sikhs were killed, while the British suffered 230 killed and just over 2,000 wounded. "So ended successfully the battle of Sabraon," Abbott recorded, echoing the common view that "but for the presence of Sir Henry Hardinge," the battle "must almost certainly have proved a defeat to the British, so strong was the position, and so insanely bent upon slaughtering his own troops was Lord Gough."[24] In fact, Sabraon was not a fair fight. Perfidious Albion had been at work in the form of Governor-General Hardinge, who before the battle had persuaded the Sikh prime minister, Gulab Singh, to contrive to lose it, an act of treason for which he was subsequently allowed to purchase Kashmir and elevated to maharaja.[25] In addition, the leadership of the Sikh generals Tej Singh, Commander in Chief of the army, and Lal Singh, commander of the cavalry, was contemptible if not also treasonous: both men fled the battlefield at Sabraon, Lal Singh taking his cavalry with him.[26]

A New Beginning

Several days after Sabraon, dirty and exhausted, Abbott reached the front, but the war was over. He had traveled twelve hundred miles in six weeks from Hidgellee to the Punjab and missed the final battle by three days. Now just thirty miles from Lahore, the British closed on the city rapidly, and the Sikhs sought terms. Hardinge demanded that the young Maharaja Duleep Singh submit in person; on February 18, 1846, he did so at Kussoor. The army then traveled with him to Lahore, where the peace treaty to end the war was signed.

The terms consisted of reparations in the amount of £1.2 million and the cession to the East India Company of all lands in Malwa and the Jullundur Doab, a triangle of territory formed by the Sutlej and Bias Rivers. The Sikhs were forced to allow a British Resident at Lahore who had a de facto veto over all major policy decisions within Sikh domains. The size of the Khalsa (Pure) Army of the Sikhs was reduced. Political agents and assistants appointed by a British Resident at Lahore now indirectly governed the Punjab through Sikh *sardars* (leaders) appointed by the *durbar* (high council) in Lahore. As a reward for his treachery, the Raja of Jammu, Gulab Singh, was allowed to buy Kashmir from the Sikh state and add it to his existing territory in Jammu by paying £750,000 to the East India Company.[27] He was subsequently invested as a maharaja. Thus, three governing entities were established in the formerly Sikh region of the Punjab: the East India Company's new lands in the Jullundur Doab and Malwa, the rump Sikh state under British oversight (now minus Kashmir, Malwa, and the Jullundur Doab), and the independent state of Jammu and Kashmir.

The British certainly knew they had not heard the last from the Sikhs. Musket for musket, gunner for gunner, and saber for saber, the Khalsa Army was as good as anything the British had, Briton or sepoy. The East India Company had very nearly lost the day at Ferozeshah. But for a poor tactical choice by the Sikhs to defend a bridgehead across the river from their camp at Sabraon and Gulab Singh's perfidy, the British might well have lost there as well. The British military position in the Punjab was dangerously depleted, the bulk of the Khalsa Army was intact, and the war had been expensive. The Treaty of Lahore gained time, money, and territory for the East India Company, provided a flanking position on the remaining Sikh state, and, it was thought, imposed a financial burden on the Sikh treasury from which it might take some time to recover. But few believed the Sikhs were permanently beaten or content to live within their shrunken territories. The question was really when, not whether, the Sikhs would rise again.

Abbott arrived at Lahore in February 1846 with one camel, no tent, and no money. Being slower than the camel, the captured Sikh horses he had borrowed from the army at Umballa arrived after a few days, but without saddles or tack. The army lent him a tent, but the horses remained bareback, as the pay system was far behind the leading edge of the army, and Abbott could draw no pay to buy a saddle. His brother Frederick soon arrived at the main British encampment outside of Lahore much better equipped, and thereafter the brothers shared Frederick's tent.

Far more importantly for Abbott's career, he also found in camp his old friend Henry Lawrence. Lawrence, now a senior advisor to Lord Hardinge, became the agent of the governor-general in charge of political relations at Lahore.[28] The new treaty boundaries had to be demarcated. Henry Lawrence was looking for an experienced political officer and surveyor who could supervise a mapping survey, adjudicate the local land disputes that would inevitably arise from new boundaries, and handle himself in wild tracts of land far from any immediate support. In James Abbott, he found exactly the man he was looking for. Abbott had been a political officer and a successful surveyor, and his experiences in Central Asia had given him a modest reputation in the Bengal Artillery as a hardy and resourceful officer. That Lawrence considered work as a revenue surveyor the best apprenticeship to political assignment, and thus that Abbott was well suited to this position, is evident from a letter by William Hodson, who wrote that he was learning the basics of surveying from Lawrence "that I may get employed in the Surveying Department, after two years of which, he says, 'I shall be fit for a Political.'"[29] Lawrence offered Abbott the position of boundary commissioner with the task of marking out the boundaries between the remaining Sikh state, Jammu and Kashmir, and the newly acquired East India Company lands, and he accepted immediately. Abbott spent the next eight years in the Punjab, and they would be the pinnacle of his active life.

A New Beginning

Within two months of arriving at camp in Lahore, in April 1846, Abbott was at work on the boundaries. In addition to the private journals he subsequently wrote between 1854 and 1857, he also now maintained a journal for the government, which he was required to submit at monthly intervals as a combined progress report and expense account. His day-by-day journal from April 5, 1846, to June 26, 1849, survives in the government archives in Lahore and was published in Allahabad in 1911.[30] In addition, a considerable body of correspondence between Abbott and the Resident at Lahore survives in the Government Records Office in New Delhi.

Abbott was given command of a company of sappers, who would do the physical labor of setting up the boundary markers at regular intervals, and two assistants from the Corps of Engineers, Lieutenants Daniel Robinson[31] and Ralph Young. Also on the commission were the *diwan*,[32] Adjiodhen Persand, as the Sikh member of the Boundary Commission, and Vizier Rooss Chunda to represent Jammu and Kashmir. Abbott got along well with both men.

They had barely started surveying, however, when Abbott was called to Amritsar to meet Henry Lawrence, now Resident of the Board of Control over the Punjab. The fortress of Kôt Kāngra had refused to surrender with the rest of the Sikhs. Because Abbott had been at Bhurtpore, which was of similar construction, Lawrence wanted his advice on what would be required to besiege it. Lieutenant Alexander Cunningham of the Engineers had reconnoitered the fort and reported it to be in such disrepair that artillery would not be required. Abbott disagreed, citing several instances, including Bhurtpore, where field artillery had little impact on wooden and earthen fortifications. He convinced Lawrence to include four 18-inch siege guns in the assault force. Abbott and Lawrence shared the view that the commander of the fortress was not acting on his own initiative but rather had been ordered to refuse to surrender by Gulab Singh, the ruler of Jammu and Kashmir, as a test of British strength and resolve, although Lawrence was much more cautious in saying so. It was a professional diplomatic caution that was ever to elude the outspoken Abbott over the next decade.

Abbott had no sooner resumed work with the Boundary Commission field party than he was recalled again and ordered to take his sappers

CHAPTER 6

and join the besieging force at Kôt Kāngra at the foot of the mountains on the Buhassi River. He reached the mountain pass ahead of the rest of the army and discovered that the road at the summit was impassible for ordinary field artillery, much less for the heavy siege guns. Nothing in Abbott's orders said anything about route clearance work en route to Kôt Kāngra. Many officers would simply have continued on to their destination, but Abbott was always the type to see a problem and stop to fix it. He had the men, and he had tools nearby in their baggage train, so Abbott immediately put his sappers to work clearing the pass. He also sent a dispatch back to Colonel Hugh Wheeler, commanding the main column, and explained the situation ahead of him on the road. Abbott recommended to Wheeler that he halt his advance until the pass could be cleared but requested he send up any elephants in the siege train to help with clearing the heaviest rocks from the road.

Wheeler sent the elephants but disregarded Abbott's advice to hold back the rest of the siege train until the route was cleared. As a result, the narrow mountain path was soon blocked, and the road for miles behind the lead wagons was choked with a backlog of animal-drawn carriages. There was no water or forage for the animals stuck in the pass, as Abbott had warned, and the draft animals began to die in harness, adding to the chaos.

The huge blocks of stone in the pass proved too heavy even for elephants to move and had to be split with sledgehammers or blown apart with gunpowder, which was far back down the clogged mountain trail. There followed an incident that left a deep impression on Abbott and is particularly illuminating of the state of the Bengal Army in 1846, eleven years before the Great Mutiny of 1857. Under the exceptional circumstances, Abbott appealed to the nearest infantry regiment, the 12th Bengal Native Infantry (BNI), for a working party, which its commanding officer promptly dispatched to the mountain pass. But when Abbott ordered the infantrymen to work, they refused to a man. They were infantry, they told Abbott, not sappers or coolies, just as the men at Barrackpore had said they were not porters nearly twenty years before. Abbott sent for British officers from the 12th BNI, who repeated Abbott's orders to the men to get to work. The men still refused. Following the maxim given to young

Figure 6.2. "Showing Part of the Road by Which Guns Were Taken above the Town of Milkera (1847)," by Lieutenant Colonel Alexander Jack (1805–1857) of the Bengal Infantry. Jack was instrumental in bringing up the 18-pounder guns for the siege of Kôt Kangra. The fortress is seen in the background on the left. Jack was a victim of the Cawnpore Massacre in 1857. (ALEXANDER JACK, *SIX VIEWS OF KOT KANGRA AND THE SURROUNDING COUNTRY* [LONDON: SMITH, ELDER & CO., 1847])

officers never to give an order that one is not certain will be obeyed and fearing outright mutiny on the spot, the BNI officers did not push the matter to the breaking point.

Here, as at Barrackpore in 1824, although now deeply attuned to Indian life and the complexities of the caste system in other respects, Abbott still had a complete blind spot regarding the sepoys. He did not grasp the basis of their employment and their views of caste in their profession. Like so many of his peers, Abbott persisted in viewing the sepoys as the counterparts of British soldiers, as military men who preferred fighting to moving rocks, certainly, but who were bound to obey the orders of officers. It was an extraordinary, almost inexplicable intellectual failure.

The sepoys of the Bengal Army regarded themselves essentially as mercenaries of a fighting caste, and in the interpretation of caste that the British had developed and reinforced within the Bengal Army, they could not do manual labor. Demonstrating a remarkable collective agency, they effectively convinced the British leadership that manual labor would be demeaning, as would, for example, doing the work of street sweepers or laundry men. This stands in contrast to the armies of the Madras and Bombay presidencies. There are no cases on record of sepoys from the Madras and Bombay presidencies ever refusing manual labor, and tellingly, virtually none of them mutinied in 1857. This incident shows that in placing such exceptional emphasis on caste in the Bengal Army and interpreting its meaning in this way, by the mid-1840s the British authorities in Bengal were well on the way to being hoisted by their own petard.

In the meantime, Abbott was left with an increasingly chaotic situation. For an officer who had been in India twenty years, he took a peculiar tack with the Bengal infantrymen: he took up a pickaxe, rolled up his shirtsleeves, and set to work himself, while "making cutting remarks upon the effeminacy of men calling themselves soldiers, but who, I said, should have been left at home to be suckled by their own wives. Natives can stand anything better than ridicule."[33] The last sentence in particular is telling of Abbott's changing attitudes. The sepoys are for the first time in his writing referred to as "natives," a term here seemingly conveying a sense of cultural superiority, while his idea that they could be taunted into working by insults hints at a cultural perception of childishness about them not previously seen. After a time, an older Sikh *naik* (corporal), whose name Abbott remembered as Ranooman Singh, picked up a pickaxe and began working with him. Then a *jemadar* took an axe and began working as well, followed by three sepoys. It may well be that these five men were Sikhs and Muslims and thus not proscribed from manual labor by the Bengal Army's exaggerated narrative of Hindu caste. Bengal Army units were predominantly but not exclusively Hindu in composition. Most contained a mixture of 15 to 20 percent Muslims, Gurkhas, and other groups, a formula that would later come under heavy scrutiny in the investigations of the Great Mutiny of 1857. The remainder of the men, however, didn't budge, absorbing in sullen silence the insults being directed at them by Abbott, in excellent Hindi, and the taunts of the *jemadar* and *naik* as well. Particularly telling of the attitudes of many British officers in the 1850s are Abbott's remarks on the incident in his journal written prior to the Great Mutiny:

> *The rest of the louts sat lazily upon the rocks, setting their officers at defiance.... To such a pass had the native army been reduced in the course of 18 years by Lord Bentinck's cowardly and insane measures of centralization. It was the first proof I had had of the disorganization of the native army, but it was a startling one. These men were soldiers in dress and name alone. In all other senses, they were* mutineers, *not merely a useless burden to the State, but a most dangerous mine under its very foundations. I duly reported the startling circumstance to Henry Lawrence and he mentioned it to Col. Wheeler [but] ... nothing was said of their mutiny. Such things had become so common, apparently, as scarcely to attract any notice.*[34]

Here were two similar incidents that Abbott had observed personally in which Bengal sepoys refused to do manual labor on the grounds that it would break their caste and was not part of their military contract; yet he never saw the obvious. This suggests how detached from reality the British view of the Bengal sepoy had become.

Chapter 6

After working with his sapper escort for several days, Abbott and his men rendered the mountain pass serviceable to heavy artillery and instilled order on the road. He then proceeded to the camp before Kôt Kāngra, where he found Henry Lawrence and his staff. Abbott went out to reconnoiter Kôt Kāngra, making sketches from various points while being sniped at ineffectually by men with matchlocks along the walls of the fort.

Some months before, Abbott had created a dossier on the major forts in the Punjab, including Kôt Kāngra. His intelligence had disclosed the existence of a concealed postern.[35] Abbott scouted until he found the hidden gate, sketched it, and delivered his findings to Lawrence and Colonel Richard Baird Smith, the senior engineering officer present.

Lawrence convinced Smith to include an attack on the postern as part of the attack plan. Abbott was assigned to lead it, aided by another artillery officer, Lieutenant William Olpherts.[36] Meanwhile, Abbott discovered that his *munshi* (scribe) was an agent of Raja Deena Nath of the Sikh Durbar in Lahore. He described the man as "a native of Cashmere ... *a plausible, oily tongued rascal, like many of the Muhammedans of that valley*.... I was therefore not astonished at the curiosity he showed to know my opinion of our chances of success in the attack ... and as I knew that all I said would go straight to Raja Deena Nath's ear ... I answered that we had taken places ten times stronger and had not thought much of the work."[37] Lawrence summoned Raja Deena Nath from Lahore to order the commander of the fort in person to surrender so that there could be no doubt of the authenticity of the order. Nath entered the fort ostensibly to convey the order, but Abbott, more suspicious than ever of Sikh intentions, believed Nath told the commander of the fort exactly the opposite.

In the event, no attack was required, which was just as well. The siege guns arrived late in May 1846, and within a few hours, the commander of the fort surrendered, which Abbott believed was due in no small part to his use of his *munshi* to convey disinformation to Deena Nath about the ease of capturing the fort. About 150 older men trooped out of the fort in surrender. Afterward, when inspecting the fort and its approaches close up, both Abbott and Lawrence realized that storming the castle

A New Beginning

Figure 6.3. A nineteenth-century lithograph of the fortress at Kôt Kangra titled "Kangra Fort in 1847" by Charles Hardinge suggests how difficult it might have been to successfully besiege this stronghold. Originally published in London as Plate 2 from *Recollections of India. Part 2. Kashmir and the Alpine Punjab* by James Duffield Harding in 1847. (BRITISH LIBRARY BOARD)

would have been very costly, even with such a small garrison present. They discovered that the frontal walls that Smith planned to assault were made of blocks of squared stone four deep, clamped together with iron, making a wall ten feet thick. The 18-pound siege guns would have had very little effect on such a wall.

The siege force before Kôt Kāngra was broken up, and Abbott returned to his duties as boundary commissioner. These consisted first in determining where the boundary between the Hill States and the Plain States ran, as there were no reliable maps. Then, disputes between the villages had to be adjudicated with the assistance of the commissioners of Lahore and Jammu and Kashmir based upon whatever written evidence was available, sometimes calling on arbitration by native *panchayats*, courts of five arbiters selected by the contending parties. Then records of settlement had to be drawn up and executed in triplicate, with copies being dispatched to the offices respectively of the British Board of Control, the Lahore Durbar, and the Maharaja of Jammu and Kashmir. Next, temporary earthen boundary pillars were erected by the sappers, which were then surveyed by the two lieutenants. The exact bearing and distance of each pillar from the next was calculated trigonometrically using a sextant and a theodolite and working from a baseline running through the Indus Valley at Cutch.[38] Finally, permanent stone pillars five feet high and two and a half feet in diameter were erected by the pioneers to replace the temporary earthen pillars used for the survey work.

Frequently, the boundary between two states was a river. As these changed course often, establishing more reliable boundary markers that could not be washed away in seasonal flooding was a challenge. Land that changed sides by such natural alterations in a river's course were deemed to change in state ownership but not in personal ownership, so that a plot of land still belonged to the same individual afterward, but his land became part of the other state. In all, Abbott and his party surveyed three hundred miles between the Ravi and Indus Rivers.

One morning, a *sowar* of the escort interrupted a conversation to interject his own opinion on a boundary dispute. Abbott rebuked him and sent him to the rear of the column. Soon afterward the same man drew his pistol and galloped toward the front of the group, pretending to be hunting a partridge. Abbott guessed he was about to be shot "accidentally" and drew his own pistol. He played along with the hunt, pretending to be looking for the bird but never taking his eyes off the *sowar*. After a bit of this, the man "trembled, turned pale, uncocked ... his pistol and rode back to the ranks crestfallen."[39] The next day Abbott received news of the Prema Conspiracy to murder the British agent at Lahore, Henry Lawrence.[40] The *diwan* immediately replaced all twelve of the Sikh horsemen in their escort squadron as a precaution.

On June 1, 1847, Abbott made his first visit to Hazāra, the district that was to become synonymous with his name during the next seven years.[41] In the period following the First Anglo-Sikh War, Hazāra briefly became a part of the newly created state of Jammu and Kashmir, which placed it under the rule of Gulab Singh, now the Maharaja of Jammu and

A New Beginning

Kashmir. This left Hazāra initially outside the zone of British oversight of the remaining Sikh state completely.[42] At the time of Abbott's first visit, Hazāra had been a part of the state of Jammu and Kashmir for just over a year. It was a predominantly Muslim region unruly under Sikh rule and even more so under that of Gulab Singh. The Hazārawals generally saw British oversight as the lesser of two evils and were not slow in petitioning the nearest British authority, Captain Abbott, to bring the Hazāra into the British sphere of influence.

During the First Anglo-Sikh War, Hazāra was in open rebellion, and partisans had temporarily occupied a number of smaller Sikh garrisons. The *diwan*, Adjiodhen Persand, was thus uneasy about security for Abbott's visit to Hazāra and arranged for a heavy mounted guard. Abbott normally traveled with a guard of twelve horsemen, but on this occasion Sikh cavalrymen were everywhere along the route. In his account of his first visit, written sometime after his final departure from the district, Abbott's affection for the Hazārawals is apparent. His first impression of the people there was of "the noble spirit of independence of the mountaineers."[43] He took a correspondingly dim view of the Sikhs' frequent punitive expeditions sent in retaliation for local uprisings. Abbott, mounted on an elephant, was soon met by a dozen village *maliks* (appointed spokesmen for their respective villages) on horseback. They told Abbott they sought the protection of the British government against Gulab Singh, their new ruler. Abbott had no choice in his present position but to tell the *maliks* he would represent their grievances to British authorities in Lahore. It was a vague and meaningless-sounding response, and he knew it.

He then visited the remains of the village of Haripur, which had been destroyed in recent fighting. The town, named for Hari Singh Nalwa (1791–1837), the great Sikh military leader, had been inhabited mostly by Hindu merchants, and it now lay in ruins. Abbott suggested he act as a mediator between Gulab Singh's government and the three khans, or chiefs, of the Nārā region—Kyum Khan of Punnia, Hussum Khan of Kyah, and Ahmed Khan of Kôt Najibullah. The local *sardar*[44] of Jammu and Kashmir accepted this proposal, and Abbott's Kashmiri *munshi* conveyed an invitation for a meeting to the chiefs. Writing in the 1850s, Abbott noted his *munshi* "[was] *one of the vainest of a race famous for vanity,*

[and] was determined to do the thing in style, so, unknown to me, he borrowed for my elephant a howdah of solid silver worth about £4,000 from the Sirdar and some rich Cashmere shawls from the Diwan.... [W]ith a small party of horse, [he] rode over to Nārā, distant 6 miles."⁴⁵

Waiting for the chiefs to arrive, Abbott's Sikh *mehmandar*⁴⁶ coached him for the meeting and advised him not to let the chiefs get close enough to his body to strike. Sikh officials routinely not only took this precaution but also had multiple doppelgangers and changed their tents often. Abbott was suspicious by nature but was not about to follow this advice. He did, however, keep his pistol loaded and primed on the table in front of him, hidden beneath a pile of papers, just in case. He awaited the chiefs of Nārā in his tent.

> *The first to enter was Mir Zeman Khan, a man of noble countenance and great breadth of chest and shoulders. The instant our eyes met, all distrust vanished, and from that moment, we were friends. Kyum Khan with his open kindly countenance and tall frame came next then ... Hussum Khan and some others. All crowded close to me as if my touch could save them. I was deeply affected by their confidence and by the recital of all the wrongs they had suffered—They entreated the British Govt to take the people of Huzāra under its protection. They declared they would die rather than submit to Maharaja Gulab Singh, whose cruelties were worse than death.*⁴⁷

The chiefs believed that the hand of British governance would be lighter than that of Gulab Singh, who treated Hazāra as an outer colony of Jammu and Kashmir. Muslims and Sikhs had been in conflict in the Punjab for nearly two hundred years at this point, with much cruelty by both sides. Muslims in the Punjab were not sealed off from the rest of India and were aware to varying degrees of the relative tolerance and lesser greed of British suzerainty compared to what they could continue to expect from Gulab Singh. Land taxes were lower under the British, they knew by now, and freedom of religion was not curtailed.

Abbott was moved by the pleas of the chiefs and agreed to argue their case to British officials in Lahore. When his preliminary sketch of

Figure 6.4. "Portrait of Hazara Mountaineer, India," a drawing by Gilbert, from a photograph by the French explorer Guillaume Lejean (1828–1871). At this time, book publishers had not yet devised a means of directly reproducing photographs in books. The drawing was published in *Le tour du monde* (LONDON: LIBRAIRIE DE L. HACHETTE ET CIE, 1868; AN ANNUAL COMPENDIUM OF MONOGRAPHS BY TRAVELERS AND EXPLORERS. THE 1868 EDITION CONTAINED THE ARTICLE "LE PANDJAB ET LE CACHEMIR" BY LEJEAN, BUT THE MATERIAL IN IT AND THE IMAGE PROBABLY DATE TO 1845.)

the district was completed, he rode back to Lahore and met with Henry Lawrence, recording, "I ... represent[ed] in the strongest terms the cruelty to the people of Hazāra inflict[ed] upon them by the rule of the Maharaja Gulab Singh."[48] Abbott was no fool. He did not see the Sikhs as inherently cruel or the Muslims as inherently peaceful victims. His references to Sikh "cruelty" in his journals are caveated with commentary that the current situation was contextual and resulted from years of bad blood on both sides. However, he was ever a knight-errant. He saw this as a grand chance to liberate an entire people. Abbott proposed to Lawrence an exchange of territory—the Hazāra District for a section of land in the Jammu Jhelum area inhabited by Sikhs, who would be more amenable to Gulab Singh's rule.[49] The foremost consideration for Gulab Singh was how much annual revenue in taxes could be squeezed out of the land in question, an equation that included a calculation of the expense involved in preserving his rule and collecting the taxes. In the case of Hazāra, between six and ten regiments were required to keep the district in submission at any given time, so for him Hazāra was a losing proposition. Over three days, Abbott convinced Henry Lawrence, and Lawrence agreed to put the proposal before the Lahore Durbar, while Abbott returned to his boundary duties.

Although Abbott found a group of indigenous inhabitants he was sympathetic toward, his larger relationship with India and its peoples was deteriorating. The preceding anecdotes show the extent to which Abbott's relationship with ordinary sepoys and civilians had been devolving since his return from Khiva. Disparaging remarks, previously absent from his writing, became almost frequent. For the first time, he used the term "Natives," whom he now occasionally described with pejoratives such as "ruffianly fellows" and "louts." One of his employees was deemed "an oily-tongued rascal, like many of the Muhammedans of that valley," and another was "one of the vainest of a race known for vanity." In his writing from this period, reconstructed in the 1850s, Hindus, Muslims, and Sikhs alike are sometimes disparaged in terms suggesting that their faults are genetic and generalized, not those of individuals. Only his meeting with the chiefs of Nārā suggests a sympathetic, personal connection with indigenous peoples during this time.

A New Beginning

Abbott's official reports show he spent from June to December 1846 predominantly in the Hazāra District, first leading the boundary survey and then revising the revenue settlement. With his extensive experience in these matters, Abbott could see that the Sikh revenue demands in the Hazāra had been set too high. On September 30, 1847, he submitted his initial assessment of the revenue situation in Hazāra to Henry Lawrence in Lahore:

> *The whole of the Hazāra . . . is assessed in a fixed rent, which is supposed to be half the gross produce. . . . [O]ver and above this, under the title of Russoom*[50] *and Nuzzerana,*[51] *about 15 percent [more] was taken previous to my coming; and the two laws, Mussulman and Sikh, prevailing in the land left a wide gap for extractions under the name of fines. . . . I abolished at once all Russoom, Nuzzerana and c, and took off 5 per cent universally. . . . In order to realize your view of taking only one-third gross produce (a view in which I most heartily concur), I [would have had to] reduce the assessments 50 per cent, which was beyond the limit [you] allowed me.*[52]

As his ranking at or near the top of the annual Revenue Survey results every year while at Bareilly shows, Abbott was as good a revenue surveyor as there was in India. Henry Lawrence had been a neighboring survey team leader in the North-Western Provinces and was familiar with Abbott's surveying ability. Abbott also knew his business when it came to assessments. He quickly found a loophole around the Lahore proscription against reducing the rents (i.e., taxes) by an amount greater than 5 percent. Assessments were always based on a fixed *estimate* of how large a harvest a given piece of land would normally produce in an average year. So Abbott simply reduced all the future harvest estimates for Hazāra by 20 percent across the board. Then he rescinded a recent Sikh order levying "transit duties" of an additional 8 percent on the remaining harvest after taxes. Thus where the farmer had previously been paying a tax of sixty-eight bushels of corn per year out of every one hundred, after Abbott's survey, he was now paying thirty-seven bushels, an effective reduction in his taxes of nearly 50 percent.[53] Needless to say, cutting everyone's taxes in half enhanced Abbott's reputation in Hazāra.

Chapter 6

The period from 1846 to 1854 in the Punjab was the epoch of "Henry Lawrence's Young Men" as they were known, the group of officers selected by Henry Lawrence to pacify and administer the entire region.[54] This type of grouping of protégées was hardly unique to Lawrence. Victorian society, as Ronald Hyam has pointed out, celebrated tight-knit, all-male groups under the aegis of a respected leader. These included, in addition to Lawrence's Young Men, Howe's Boys in Calcutta, Wolseley's Staff Ring, the Cambridge Apostles, Rhodes's Lambs, Milner's Kindergarten in South Africa, and Kitchener's Cubs.[55] It was not a coincidence that these social groups closely resembled the medieval legend of King Arthur and the Round Table. In time Lawrence's Young Men became known as the "Paladins of the Punjab," a depiction that perfectly reflected Abbott's own sensibilities. Henry Lawrence's philosophy of governance was famously a kind of gentle but firm paternalism, which eventually became known as the "Punjab School."[56] He enjoined his subordinates to lead by gentlemanly moral example, fully embodying the idea of the "empire of opinion."

During these years Abbott worked with many officers whose names became household words in the decade to come. Lieutenant John Nicholson, who became a frontier legend and a Victorian martyr, was assigned as Abbott's deputy for much of 1847; the two men became close friends. Herbert Edwardes, Reynell Taylor,[57] and Lieutenant Harry "Joe" Lumsden[58] were also regular comrades in the field. Covenanted civil servant Patrick Vans Agnew traveled frequently with Abbott until the events at Multan.

By early June 1847, Abbott was already moving out into the hinterlands of Hazāra. His official journal entry for June 11, 1847, provides one of the earliest recorded impressions of a British officer's encounter with the indigenous governance structures of the people of the Northwest Frontier, which would eventually collectively come to be known as *Pashtunwali*, or "the way of the Pashtuns": "The Dhoonds and Kurrals, two tribes occupying the strongest country of Huzāra and separated by blood and hereditary prejudices from the Pathan, Mogul, and Gukka tribes of that country, live in a state of equality, acknowledging at present no ruler and being amenable to no authority; they settle their political dealings by

Figure 6.5. Painting by an unknown Sikh artist titled *Hamil Sahib Badahur and Raja Dina Nath*, circa 1850. Henry Lawrence's initials were H. M. L. He liked to use these to convert his Christian name to the more indigenous sounding "Hamil." (PUBLIC DOMAIN)

assemblies called jirgahs."⁵⁹ Abbott here initially mistook the Dhoonds and the Kurrals as tribes not Pashtun (Pathan) in origin, but the comment is an accurate description of the acephalous, group-consensus process that still characterizes decision making at the village and occasionally supra-village level in the parts of South Asia dominated by Pashtun tribes today. (Then Afghan president Hamid Karzai called a *jirga* in November 2013 in Afghanistan, for example, to decide the fate of a security treaty with the United States.) At about the same time, Abbott recorded his impression

CHAPTER 6

of "the noble spirit of independence of the mountaineers."[60] This trope of independence and equality among the Pashtuns and other peoples along the Afghan frontier drew heavily on Romantic portrayals of Scottish Highlanders in the works of Sir Walter Scott, which were extremely popular with British officers in India. They would form the backbone of the British narrative of the frontier tribes for the next century. Three months later, Abbott noted, "The Kurrals and the Dhoonds are accounted a treacherous race,"[61] for the first time sounding the second dominant theme in the British Pashtun canon, which would form a corollary to the noble mountaineer theme in the years ahead. This core narrative of the Pashtuns as "noble," "independent," and "treacherous" would morph over the next hundred years, adapting itself to the needs of a British philosophy of rule on the Northwest Frontier that evolved from governance to a fractious coexistence.

Abbott's only map of Hazāra was one he sketched himself by traveling up and down each of its four main valleys and taking multitudinous cross bearings with his compass, a primitive method of surveying. Inaccessible side valleys he filled in based on local reports. During his tenure in Hazāra District, an area larger than Massachusetts, no survey map was created. Not until 1855 was a reliable map of the district produced.

Some of Abbott's early Revenue Survey work in Hazāra, accompanied always by local Sikh revenue officials, consisted of trying to get rebelling tribes to reconcile with the Sikhs by asking them to present themselves for negotiations in Abbott's camp. Abbott acted as a kind of lead negotiator in these meetings in order to maintain civil order, which was always the primary mandate of all of Lawrence's Young Men. This mediator role was initially between the agents of Gulab Singh, and later those of Chattar Singh Attariwala, and the Muslim tribesmen who were generally unhappy, sometimes violently so, about their sovereignty. This was not easy, as there were numerous disaffected tribes with long-standing grievances. Abbott noted, "When I entered on my new duties, the Tarkhailies of Gundgurh Ischaudad Khan, Chief of the Tanawals, the Pathans on the Indus, the Kurrāls, the Syeds of Khagan in a remote [and] formidable valley, and the Dhoonds and Sutties were all in open rebellion."[62] Notionally at Abbott's disposal were five regiments of regular

Sikh infantry, each of about eight hundred men, plus one regiment of cavalry and eight field guns. But "the Sikh troops had an almost childish terror of the mountains of Hazāra," Abbott observed, "where their bravest had been so often defeated with terrible slaughter. It remained to be seen whether they would follow ... the lead of a British officer against these mountains."[63] Abbott here is not claiming to be braver than the Sikhs but rather questioning whether they would follow him at all at this juncture, as opposed to one of their own Sikh officers, to a place they had learned to fear.

In the summer of 1847, Abbott went to the Goojjar mountain village of Bukhur, which had just been attacked by a war party of Simulkundi tribesmen. The attack was in revenge for an incident between the Simulkundis and a different Goojjar group a few days before. The Goojjars of Bukhur were not connected to the original incident, but in the world of mountain tribal feuds governed by *Pashtunwali*, any village of the enemy clan would serve as a focus for revenge. In the attack, many of the people of Bukhur were slaughtered in their sleep. When Abbott arrived, the ruins were still smoldering. He found there a wounded Mashwari tribesman named Hussan Shah. Hussan Shah was not from Bukhur but had gone to the village when he learned of the Simulkundis plan to attack it, hoping his influence as a *Syed*[64] and a member of the respected Mashwari tribe could prevent the raid. In the dark, however, the Simulkundis did not recognize him. He was set upon as an ordinary Goojjar villager, and his hand was nearly severed from his arm by a sword stroke. Abbott, by now no stranger to the carnage of war, was appalled by the devastation he found:

> *I ... did all that lay in my power to alleviate the sufferings of the survivors, many of whom were wounded, and as soon as [Hussan Shah] was well enough to present himself, I sent for him and thanked him warmly for his humanity. [I] gave him a dress of honor*[65] *and procured for him from the Sikh government a gift of land, in recognition of his humanity and courage. I also obtained for the widows and orphans rendered such by this outrage life pensions. For a government which receives taxes for protection, if it cannot protect, is bound to provide for sufferers.*[66]

Chapter 6

From this incident, the legend of Abbott's chivalry began to grow in Hazāra, especially among the Mashwaris and Goojjars.

On August 2, 1847, Abbott and Nicholson mounted a military attack on the Simulkundi heartland in an effort to catch the Bukhur murderers, but Simulkundi scouts reported their approach, and the area was deserted, an aspect of warfare still common to military operations in that part of the world today.[67]

In several cases during his preliminary Revenue Survey, Abbott succeeded in having lands, confiscated by the Sikhs in punishment for rebellion, restored to their previous Muslim owners. One of these men was Khan-i-Zamman, a chief of the Tarkhaili tribe. As the Tarkhailies were in open rebellion against the Sikhs, Abbott summoned the khan to appear in his camp for resolution of the dispute, allowing him three days to present himself. Khan-i-Zamman's own father had been murdered decades earlier by Dost Mohammed after appearing under just such a promise of safe conduct. Reflecting on that, Abbott considered Zamman unlikely to respond to the summons, but on the afternoon of the third day, he did indeed arrive in Abbott's camp: "I went to the door to receive him and led him in by the hand, a grace I had never shown to any other chief. But I was touched by his confidence in me [and I was] very uncertain whether I should be able to get his lost jaghirs restored.... He had committed no overt act of violence since British authority in the Punjab had commenced, and it was not our cue to rake up past offenses."[68] Zamman's lands were later restored to him by the Lahore Durbar at Abbott's recommendation.

Observing from Lahore, Henry Lawrence declared that he was entirely satisfied with Abbott's work. On November 13, 1847, he reported to Calcutta, "Captain Abbott is going on judiciously, and will, I doubt not, soon tranquilize his charge. He has completed [the construction of] three forts, and is daily receiving the visits of chiefs and Zamindars hitherto recusant; some of the Simulkund murderers have even been given up, and others have surrendered."[69]

In early December, Abbott led a brief expedition against another rebellious tribe over a narrow mountain pass, only to be trapped in the pass at the summit by a dense fog. During the march in the fog, Abbott agreed with his Sikh troops about a curious superstition. The Sikhs enjoined him not to blow any bugles or beat any drums "whilst this dense fog should last, lest [the noise] should bring down the snow. I smiled, but gave the permission, for it is better to work with [rather] than counter [to] the prejudice[70] on such occasions. And indeed, upon consideration, I thought the precaution not amiss. For in particular states of the atmosphere it is very possible that the vibratory action of sound may precipitate the crystallization of vapor in the air."[71] This precaution against noise was in vain, however, and snow began falling heavily. The bullock-drawn supply wagons could not reverse on the narrow mountain trail, and splitting up the force went against the basic precepts of military strategy, so there was no choice under the circumstances but to pitch tents in the pass and wait it out. The snow continued unabated for four days. The Sikh troops on the expedition took it in stride; they had good tents and knew how to build fires that would stay alight in these conditions. Abbott's Indian sapper detachment, however, was another story. They had never seen snow before. The sappers lost their tent earlier in the expedition and were now "aghast and utterly disconcerted."[72] They could not be left out in the snow to freeze; nor would they agree to share tents with Sikhs. So Abbott brought them all into his own tent:

> [A] wood fire was burning night and day to the exceeding torture of my eyes. For five days and nights they could eat nothing but parched pulse,[73] for they could not dress their food in the open air whilst the snow fell and as Hindoos, could eat nothing dressed by others. The Sikh soldiers all the while were comparatively comfortable. They lighted a fire in each tent and there the bread was baked upon a huge iron shield placed over the fire. They laughed and chatted and seemed rather to enjoy the fun.[74]

This passage in his journals is important because, in noting that the Hindu sappers "could not eat food dressed by others," Abbott repeats the exaggerated interpretation of caste fostered in the Bengal Army regarding food preparation and caste pollution, indicating that he fully subscribed to *this* particular aspect of caste limitations among the sepoys, while remaining blind to its corollary proscribing manual labor. It was an astonishing myopia.

Shortly after this expedition, Abbott and John Nicholson met again and shared camp in the field on Christmas Day 1847. Abbott wrote at length about many things, often including the personalities of the indigenous peoples he interacted with. In his journals he also not infrequently criticized civilians and senior officers. And in retirement, he was fulsome in his praise of the courage of Herbert Edwardes in the Second Anglo-Sikh War.[75] He seldom wrote any sort of contemporary comments about the personalities of his East India Company peers, however, including Nicholson. In later years, Abbott likened Nicholson to Swedish King Charles XII, whose death mask he had been given as a gift in Russia by Count Vasily Perovsky. Charles XII was, like Nicholson, a fearless warrior who was most comfortable in battle. Both men were unusually tall for their time, were never married or engaged, and died at the front of their troops during a siege battle. Abbott thought Nicholson even resembled Charles XII a little in appearance.[76]

Because of their military campaigns in the field together, Abbott spent a good deal of time with the troubling figure of John Nicholson. Abbott preserved all the letters Nicholson sent him, and the tone of the correspondence is friendly and collegial.[77] However Nicholson appears to have been closer to Herbert Edwardes and Henry and Honoria Lawrence than he was to Abbott.[78] The two men could scarcely have been more different in temperament. Nicholson was known widely as an angry and brutal man in his dealings with the indigenous peoples of the Punjab, "the very incarnation of violence."[79] Abbott was quiet and introspective, eschewing violence. Except for his brawl with the three irregular cavalrymen in 1828, there is no evidence that Abbott ever struck anyone. Whereas Nicholson hated India, writing his mother in 1845, "I dislike India and its inhabitants more every day," Abbott did not.[80] This dichotomy was not lost on the small cult in the Punjab that came to worship them both as the God of Valor and the Lord of Generosity, respectively.[81]

George Pearse, then a young lieutenant assigned to create an experimental battery of mountain artillery in the Hazāra District in 1851, was an eyewitness to the Nicholson-Abbott cult. Their followers were known as Nicholseynites, and Nicholson and Abbott formed a kind of yin and yang. "Nicholson," Pearse wrote, "was a hard, unpoetic, unimaginative man." He had a colorless face, Ensign Reginald Wilberforce said, "over which no smile ever passed."[82] Nicholson "flogged, imprisoned and tortured" the cult followers and was worshipped by them as "the God of Valor." Abbott, on the other hand, Pearse recalled, was the feminine deity of this ditheistic sect. Pearse described Abbott as "a beautiful character, the soul of chivalry . . . a poet and poetic, sensitive, [who] felt too deeply, and all his long life had to think deeply and sadly." He added that "Abbott was worshipped as the Lord of Generosity" by the fakirs who followed Nicholson and were driven by him into exile in neighboring Hazāra District as *kafirs*, whereas Abbott protected them.[83] In describing the cult, Pearse wrote,

> [W]hen the Nicholseyni fuqueer chiefs saw and knew James Abbott, they were at once as much impressed by his singularly pure, good, noble and above all generous nature as they before had been by the hard, violent brave one of Nicholson. Soon James Abbott was raised to the godhood: he became the "Lord of Generosity." The fuqueers . . . who as a rule were good Sanskrit, Hindi and Gooroomookhie [Gurumukhi] scholars, now took to heavy reading, to deep meditation, to much consultation. . . . [T]hese fuqueers . . . wore the largest of Sombrero hats, to them the badge of western civilization. . . . They wore long saffron robes with sandals; they went about far and wide singing the praises of the new avatars, Nicholson and Abbott: warning all people in beautiful Sanskrit "slokas," or verses, that avatars of a new and pure revelation had come.[84]

Nicholson was responsible for a time for the administration of the area known as the Sindh Sagar Doab (written by Abbott as Sind Sagur Doaba),[85] a district of the Punjab south of and adjacent to Hazāra District. He made his headquarters at the town of Hassan Abdal[86] in the Attock District at the head of one of the several renowned natural springs of the town, which Nicholson called Bendemeer's Stream.[87] Abbott visited Nicholson there in 1847 and observed the leader of the cult for the

CHAPTER 6

first time. In later years Abbott wrote that the founder of the sect was a Hindu *gosyne*[88] and that they were "five or six in number," dressed in robes the "color of faded leaves."[89] Later, after being flogged and sent away by Nicholson, the same man came to worship Abbott in Hazāra. Abbott was too diffident to acknowledge the obvious fact that the *gosyne* was now praying to him, recording only,

> *After experiencing several rebuffs from his adopted Deity, [he] determined to try his luck with the Deity's old comrade. And one morning at daybreak, while I was engaged in writing ... I was disturbed by the chanted prayers of the Nicholsynie Priest, who was squatted opposite my window, and with all the power of his lungs was offering adoration to Nicholsyne Sahib. ... I was at first amused by this evidence of Nicholson's high appreciation by the people of the Punjaub. But when this matutinal din became a daily infliction, I rather winced under it and tried to persuade the Chief priest to resort to the haunts and government of his god.*

Abbott could not persuade the holy man to return to Nicholson, so, typically, he tried to find a nearby hut or shed where he and the other cult members would be sheltered from the elements. Later the same man prevailed upon Abbott to give him an old beaver skin hat, which when Abbott finally relented and presented to him, he used to stop foot traffic on the nearby roads and collect alms, much to Abbott's embarrassment and annoyance. Abbott then *ordered* him to go back to Nicholson. "When I last heard of the sect," Abbott wrote around 1887, "it was flourishing and increasing."[90] It survived in the region until the 1980s.[91]

Despite their differences in temperament and personality, Abbott and Nicholson got along well in the field as comrades in arms. For all the time they spent together, however, Nicholson's appearances in Abbott's journals are almost entirely of a tactical nature and not of a personal one. During their Christmas Day camp in 1847, they talked of Sir Henry Lawrence's approaching departure from the Punjab on sick leave to England and of the arrival of his replacement, Sir Frederick Currie. Abbott wrote later in his journal, "Nicholson asked [me] what I thought of Currie. My knowledge of him was not intimate. That he was a man of considerable talent, I allowed, and of experience in Bengal politics. But I held him to be exactly the man that would not suit the Office of Governor to the Punjab in its present condition of a scarcely slumbering volcano, and in the sentiment Nicholson concurred."[92]

Indeed, there were hints that winter that all was not well in the Punjab. There were rumors of plots and conspiracies, especially in Lahore, where the Prema Conspiracy in February 1847 had generated alarm. The Paladins, as Lawrence's Young Men came to be known, had their ears to the ground, and gradually the hints and reports added up to growing unrest within the Sikh state. In January 1848, a surveyor in Hazāra, Lieutenant Daniel Robinson, sent Abbott a report relating an incident among Robinson's troops. One of Robinson's Hindu sappers had an argument with a Sikh trooper, and the sapper threatened to report the Sikh to Robinson. As the incident was relayed to Abbott, the Sikh replied, "What do I care for any British officer? Just wait until the month of *Jayt* [May/June][93] and you will see." When the sapper asked what he would see, the Sikh reportedly replied, "You will see that we will kill all your officers and drive you all out of the Punjab."[94] This is a clear indication that as early as January 1848, plans for the rebellion of the Sikh state against the British were already at least a common rumor, even down to the lowest Sikh enlisted ranks.

Abbott worked most often with Patrick Vans Agnew and had mixed feelings toward him, perhaps partly because he was a civilian. Relations between the army and the civil service in India were often strained, if superficially polite. As is frequently the case between diplomats and soldiers, in general neither side of that equation in the East India Company understood or greatly respected the views of the other. Military officers commonly believe civilians cannot be expected to understand the complexities of a military situation, and diplomats tend to feel, as Georges Clemenceau noted, that "war is too important to be left to the military."[95] The marriage between them in British India was often a rocky one. Abbott noted that "Vans Agnew always wore the Asiatic dress,"[96] an indication that he himself probably did not at this time. In late March 1848, Abbott

CHAPTER 6

and Vans Agnew worked together for the last time. He recalled Vans Agnew as being a

> *somewhat overzealous exposer of the peccadilloes of the Sikh Governor,*[97] *whose authority we now overshaded. . . . [C]onsidering our position, I deemed it inexpedient to rake up past offenses, excepting to redress permanent injuries. It created great alarm in the minds of all [Sikhs] who had ever exercised authority, for all [of them] had been more or less corrupt and tyrannical. . . . He appeared to me to be a man of generous disposition and strong sense and passions [but] his judgment did not seem to me the best. At best he did not seem to me to understand the people of Hazāra.*[98]

The last sentence is telling of Abbott's growing conviction that he did, in contrast, "understand the people of Hazāra."

In early April 1848, the exact date is unclear, Abbott was informed by letter that the Lahore Durbar agreed to his proposed exchange of land. Abbott's petition to Lawrence and Gulab Singh's own desire to rid himself of an expensive hornet's nest had struck a sympathetic chord in the Durbar. After exactly two years as a part of Jammu and Kashmir, Hazāra now reverted back to the remaining Sikh state under British supervision. The Sikhs assigned Chattar Singh as governor of the territory. Chattar Singh was one of the most powerful members of the inner circle of Sikh ruling elites. Abbott was appointed assistant to the Resident in Lahore to act as the first district commissioner of Hazāra:

> *I entered upon my new duties [in] Hazāra with some diffidence. . . . Its length North and South was about 160 miles; Its breadth varied from twenty miles to sixty, giving an average of about 40 miles. The surface was formed of the most rugged mountains, permeated . . . [by] the valleys of Hazāra proper. . . . The mountains had an altitude above sea level of from 3'500 to 14'000 ft. They were occupied by Pathans, Mashwaries, Janawulies, Sohanties, Goojjars, Kurrāls, Dhoonds and Sutties—all armed and warlike, who it was supposed could muster twenty thousand strong and who occupied some of the strongest of mountains.*[99]

A New Beginning

Whatever uneasiness Abbott felt was brief. Perhaps uniquely in the history of British India, he was literally in the position of being popularly seen by the people of Hazāra as a kind of savior of an entire district. He had already cut their taxes nearly in half. Now it was Abbott in their eyes who had championed the exchange of territory and brought Hazāra under nominal British oversight. The "bush telegraph" worked well in these lands, and virtually every Hazārawal knew of Abbott's promise to the Nārā chiefs at the *durbar* in Hurripore. He had promised them he would argue their case for relief from Gulab Singh's rule before the Lahore Durbar, and it came to pass. (The fact that Gulab Singh himself was only too glad to be rid of the territory did not form part of the popular narrative and is not mentioned in Abbott's writing.) Few, if any, district commissioners ever had such an auspicious start. Within days, however, the Punjab fell off the knife's edge, and war was afoot again. Shortly after his last meeting with Abbott in late March, Vans Agnew was dispatched from Hazāra with Lieutenant W. A. Anderson on a diplomatic mission to the town of Multan, where on April 20, 1848, they were murdered soon after their arrival.

The *diwan* (prime minister), Mulraj of Multan, had for some time been seeking permission to resign his post and retire. This was eventually granted by the British after some delay. Vans Agnew and Anderson were sent to meet the *diwan* in Multan to take receipt of his account ledgers and the treasury. After being greeted and led inside the city walls by the *diwan* and his escort on April 19, 1848, they were both set upon by the crowd and seriously wounded, escaped briefly to a nearby mosque, and the next day were murdered after an artillery barrage fired at the mosque by the *diwan*'s forces. In the interval, Vans Agnew managed to get a letter out of the city to Lieutenant Herbert Edwardes in Bannu. Edwardes received the letter from Vans Agnew on April 22, assembled a force of Pashtun irregulars, and was on the move toward Multan within a day, sending dispatches from horseback to other nearby officers to do likewise. He had not gotten far, however, when he received the news that Vans Agnew and Anderson were dead and Multan was preparing for a siege.[100]

Meanwhile, the situation in Lahore had changed dramatically. Three months earlier, on January 15, 1848, as Abbott and Nicholson discussed

CHAPTER 6

at their Christmas campfire, Frederick Currie had replaced Henry Lawrence as Resident. Currie was a covenanted civil servant who had never served in the military. The Paladins of Lawrence's circle instinctively distrusted him as a civilian outsider and had little respect for his military decisions in particular. Currie had previously served in minor posts in Calcutta before becoming the district commissioner in Benares and was later a judge in Allahabad, but apart from serving as the lead negotiator and drafter of the Treaty of Lahore, Currie had no experience of the Punjab or of the Sikhs.

Lawrence, a Bengal Artillery officer, like Abbott, who gained a detailed understanding of the Punjab, its nuanced politics, and the complex relationships between the players in the Lahore Durbar, had operated his Young Men as a close-knit and rather informal network of district officers who were encouraged to use his home and office in Lahore as a kind of open hostel. Currie could hardly have been more different. He immediately put a stop to officers using his residence as a caravanserai and instituted a relationship that was far more formal and, to the Paladins, officious. Lawrence's Paladins were a freewheeling group who typified the "man on the spot" stereotype of local British officers embedded in their respective local cultures. They were trained by Lawrence in the principle that, when in doubt, it was better to seek forgiveness afterward than to wait for permission beforehand. Abbott's Christmas campfire conversation with Nicholson is ample evidence that they considered Currie a Calcutta "office-wallah."[101] Lawrence granted his officers a great deal of discretion in handling local matters as long as their districts remained tranquil, but Currie embodied Calcutta's habitual concern that such men had too much discretion and were making up policy on the fly with potentially binding consequences and no prior vetting by government. Each side had a valid point: the local officers believed they knew the local situation best, and furthermore they faced immediate problems that required improvisation. In an age when correspondence seeking guidance from higher authority might take a month to be answered, they believed they needed the flexibility to improvise policy on the spot. The central government, for its part, was covetous of its role as the policy maker and saw the district officers strictly as policy implementers, in part certainly to protect its own bureaucratic raison d'être, but also because injudicious decisions by local officers might be contrary to larger policy considerations that the field officers were unaware of. And precedents could be hard to walk back once established.

Thus, at a time when the Punjab was a powder keg and the events at Multan the spark, the relationship between the officers in the field and the Resident at Lahore was already plagued by mutual distrust and disdain. As diplomats not infrequently are, Currie was disposed to find his new charge peaceful and orderly, as it was his job to ensure that it was. He was equally indisposed to consider evidence to the contrary, which often reinforced his perception of loyalty and tranquility, a cognitive bias known as the "backfire effect."[102] Abbott nicknamed Currie "Sir Fiddlesticks."[103] Nicholson dubbed him "The Rosy One." When Currie received the news of the initial events at Multan and the wounding of the two officers, however, he immediately took the correct military action, in consultation with the Lahore Durbar, and dispatched the available moveable columns toward Multan to aid Vans Agnew and Anderson. (Upon learning soon afterward of their deaths, he recalled them.) Currie's writing shows a man with a great deal of patience toward the Paladins. To judge from his correspondence, he was a master of the correct gentlemanly forms of bureaucratic writing in favor in Calcutta, but he was not a mean or vindictive man in the mold of Ellenborough. Although Abbott had given him ample provocation, and he had no reason to like Abbott on a personal basis, at this time he believed Abbott was doing an excellent job in the Hazāra, writing to Calcutta, "He is beloved—in fact, almost worshipped—by the people. All persons that I have conversed with, who have come from those parts, are unanimous in their estimation of him. They say he has gained such an influence with the inhabitants of the province that he can do what he pleases with a race the Sikhs could never control, and whom the wily and shrewd Maharajah Gulab Singh was glad to get from under his government on almost any terms."[104]

Currie's comment in 1848 on Abbott's relationship with the Hazārawals would be repeated a dozen times over the next five years by indigenous and British sources alike, by men and women, by Abbott's friends and, like Currie, by his antagonists, and some of them, like Lady

Honoria Lawrence, by astute and frank observers who believed their personal impressions of Abbott in their private diaries would never see the light of day. Furthermore, recorded accounts over the next seventy years by indigenous correspondents, separated in time and space by decades and hundreds of miles and who never knew of each other's existence, are all remarkably similar in describing Abbott's magnetic personality. For his part, Henry Lawrence wrote of Abbott around this time, "He was made of the stuff of the true knight-errant, gentle as a girl in thought, word and deed, overflowing with warm affection, and ready at all times to sacrifice himself for his country or his friend. He is at the same time a brave, scientific, and energetic soldier, with a peculiar power of attracting others, especially Asiatics, to his person."[105] It is particularly noteworthy that Lawrence described this ability to draw the people of Asia to him as a "peculiar power." In 1850, "peculiar" did not mean "strange" or "odd," as it does today, but rather "singular; particular; special," as in "something peculiar to a person or thing." "Singular," in turn, was defined as "single, remarkable, eminent; rare."[106] The 1919 *Oxford English Dictionary* clarifies the British meaning of the word a century ago further as a trait "belonging exclusively to; particular, special." Not until 1919 did the word begin to take on the sense of "strange, odd" as a secondary definition.[107] In other words, Lawrence ascribed this "power of attracting others, especially Asiatics, to his person" not as a trait common to British officers or even to his Young Men but rather as unique to Abbott. Lawrence found this trait of Abbott's so singular and unusual that he was obliged to comment on it. Because Lawrence handpicked all his officers for a set of characteristics—ruggedness, independence, vigor—if he believed them all to possess this kind of power, he would hardly have described it as "peculiar" to Abbott. Indeed Lawrence does not ascribe this "power" to any of his other Young Men or to anyone else anywhere else in his writing, not even to John Nicholson, who together with Abbott became a deity of the indigenous cult that grew up in the Punjab to worship them.[108]

It is de rigueur today to reject such descriptions of relationships between Britons and the peoples of India as forming part of a broad self-serving British narrative of paternal colonialism. Certainly there is a legitimately questionable historical vein of such constructions running throughout the British narrative of India. This is conveyed in the sense of shock caused by the "betrayal" of such "loyalty" and "affection" in the brutality of the Great Mutiny of 1857, for example, when many British officers and even their wives and children were killed by the sepoys whom they believed thought of them as their parents.

However, when even indigenous accounts are unanimously consistent with such a representation, transcribed by interlocutors who never knew Abbott personally and which were recorded decades after the events when no possible self-interest could be served by persisting in testimonials of friendship, it must be considered that Abbott did, indeed, have considerable affection for the people of the Hazāra and that it was in fact returned by much of the population. There are simply too many similar and internally consistent accounts to discount this, such as this encounter recorded by British officer Richard Warburton in the Khyber Pass in 1897:[109]

> *I happened to be walking one morning from Kuldanna to the post office at Murree. Two very old men were walking ahead of me, and hearing the name Abbott repeated time after time, curiosity induced me to join in their conversation, and ask of whom they were talking and who they themselves were. They were both residents of the Hazāra District, and one had been in the police at the time when James Abbott was Deputy Commissioner, and the second man had also been in the service in some capacity. To my inquiries they both said, "Abbott Sahib was loved in the district, and the old people reverence his memory even now." The elder of the Hazāras then spoke of his own accord: "Abbott Sahib's heart was like a Fakir's; he was always thinking of and for his people."*[110]

To suggest that a man like Warburton, whose mother was Pashtun and who was bilingual in Pashto, simply invented this conversation, misinterpreted what had been said to him, changed the words, or enhanced the reverence the old men felt for Abbott a half century after they were with him is simply not credible. It is particularly interesting that the elder of the two Hazārawals used the word "fakir" to describe Abbott, meaning a Muslim ascetic who rejects worldly possessions and may perform feats of magic and healing. A remarkably similar account of Abbott's personality and healing powers was recorded by a British traveler in Central Asia twenty-two years earlier in 1875. Captain Frederick Burnaby did not know Abbott, but he knew of him. He traveled to Khiva about forty years after Abbott and encountered an elderly mullah in Merv:

> *He remembered Captain Abbott's visit to Khiva, forty years before. "He was such a nice gentleman," observed the moullah, alluding to Abbott. "He was a medicine man too, and cured several sick people. We heard afterwards that he had been killed by the Russians. Was that the case?" And on being informed that Captain Abbott had returned in safety to England, the old man gave praise to God. "Your compatriot was with us about the time that the Russians were attempting to reach Khiva," continued the old moullah. "People here then thought that an army from Hindustan was coming to help us. But we did not require any assistance; the winter killed the dogs by the thousands, praise be to God!" And this expression, which is the same in Tartar as in Arabic, was devoutly repeated by the rest of the company.*[111]

The last sentence makes clear that the mullah was speaking among a group of people and not to Burnaby alone. Anything a religious leader would say then, as today, among a group of other Muslims in that part of the world would be given considerable weight by his listeners and would be remembered within the community. Thus it cannot be said that the man was speaking solely for Burnaby's benefit or saying something intended only for the ears of an Englishman for some purpose of self-aggrandizement. His words were heard by his compatriots, and he had nothing to gain from the comment apart from what his parishioners would think. This is another account of a chance encounter with another elderly Muslim who describes Abbott in strikingly similar terms, as courteous and honorable (sahib, gentleman) and having healing powers (fakir, medicine man). These accounts are separated by a quarter century in time and a thousand miles in distance, recorded by two men who never knew Abbott or each other but which give powerfully consistent descriptions of him. This consistency among disparate sources not only validates these accounts but also makes the remainder of these two indigenous reports credible. The issue of Abbott's relationship with the people of Hazāra and with other Muslims who knew him will be taken up again in greater detail in the narrative of his later years there as the district commissioner after the Second Anglo-Sikh War.

By the end of June 1848, Herbert Edwardes, acting on his own in assembling a small scratch force of Pashtun irregulars, Dogras, Gurkhas, and the other non-Sikh troops scattered in small numbers throughout the northern Punjab, succeeded in isolating the town of Multan. Pitched battles were fought with the *Diwan* of Multan's Sikh troops, who were joined by a body of so-called Hindustani Fanatics.[112] The besiegers drove the *diwan*'s forces back, but Multan's fortifications were robust. While the British troops outside the city could prevent small numbers of forces from going in or coming out, they had no siege artillery and no realistic means of storming the walled town. It was a stalemate. Only at this point did Currie send a stronger body of troops toward Multan under the command of British General William Whish.[113] Currie also ordered the Sikh Jaghirdari Horse, with a body of infantry and artillery under the command of Raja Sher Singh, son of the Governor of Hazāra, Chattar Singh, to march to Multan.

It later emerged that the rising at Multan was the first stage of a planned pan-Sikh revolt to drive the British from the Punjab in May, just as Lieutenant Robinson's Hindu sapper had reported in January. At the end of April, however, British officialdom was virtually unanimous in the opinion that Multan was an isolated, local uprising, one that the Paladins believed had to be immediately suppressed. The British officers in the field in the Punjab, most vociferously George Lawrence,[114] Herbert Edwardes, John Nicholson, and James Abbott, strongly urged Currie to assemble and dispatch a powerful siege force at once to recapture Multan and dispense justice to the murderers of the two Britons. Evidence gathered after the Second Anglo-Sikh War indicated the plotters anticipated this denuding of British forces from Lahore to create just such a relief force, which would have left the city open to a sweep into the capital by Sikh troops from Hazāra and Kashmir, bringing about a kind of coup de main. Henry Lawrence, more sympathetic to the plight and pleas of his officers and more bound by the conventions of military comradeship, might perhaps have done just that and left Lahore vulnerable. But Currie was a civil servant, cautious by nature, and not apt to hasty military action. To the incredulity of all the officers in the field, who felt they were being hung out to dry, Currie decided that because it was the hot season and the monsoon was close at hand, the recapture of Multan would have to be postponed until after the rains. Governor-General Lord Dalhousie deferred the question of whether to move at once against Multan or wait until the end of the monsoon to Currie and subsequently endorsed Currie's decision. Dalhousie, however, was not without reservations, and like a clever bureaucrat, he hedged his bets: "The Government of India are fully alive to the effect which the inactivity of the British power for several months, under such insult and injury, will have on the minds of the people of the country. His Lordship in Council does not question the existence of danger to British influence in the course which has been determined on. It is but too possible that the flame, kindled at Mooltan, may spread into conflagration throughout the Punjab."[115]

Although the Paladins were beside themselves over the delay, and history has generally taken their side, on closer analysis Currie's decision was based on sound military considerations. While the weather in May was fair, the siege would likely not have been concluded before the monsoon in June. Moreover there were natural signs the rains would break early in 1848. At this time, it was considered impossible to conduct a military campaign during the monsoon, and a siege force sent to Multan immediately prior to the onset of the monsoon would be forced to suspend all operations when it began. The siege troops would then become that many more waterlogged men to feed outside Multan. This decision to postpone the siege was not based on the miserable and debilitating conditions for the soldiers camped in the field, however, whose lot was to suffer such privations, but rather on a realistic assessment of the extreme difficulties that rivers in flood would pose to provisioning them.

The military maxim in this case holds that "amateurs talk tactics and experts talk logistics." Given the primitive transport conditions in the Punjab in 1848, the logistics issue involved in the decision to wait until October ought not be evaluated from a twenty-first-century perspective.

The virtual impossibility of bringing up supplies of everything from food and medicine to dry powder and shot across multiple rivers in flood was the key factor. Cholera, too, among the densely packed besiegers would always be a danger. Lawrence's Young Men seethed at Currie's perceived inaction, but in the final analysis, his military judgment was sound, and theirs was not.

Dalhousie expressed concern for the Paladins still in the field, instructing Currie, "The Governor General in Council regards with much anxiety the position of Lieutenant Edwardes. His Lordship in Council trusts that the measures you have taken may secure the safety of that gallant officer, and of the other officers who are employed on detached service."[116] Indeed, no one had more on the line than the isolated British officers in the field in the Punjab, who were daily surrounded by Sikh troops and could very easily share the fate of Vans Agnew and Anderson. To a man they believed British prestige and future Sikh allegiance to the Lahore Durbar hinged on a rapid and robust British response. When Currie's decision, backed by the governor-general, was known, the Paladins wrote strongly worded letters of protest against the delay. Senior among the writers was Major George Lawrence. Abbott's own letter to Currie on May 10, 1848, in support of Lawrence's arguments reflected his frustration with the decision to wait until October to reduce Multan. The tone was impertinent, disrespectful, and insulting:

> *The extreme weight and importance of . . . Lawrence's arguments have induced me to send you a copy of his last note lest the original be intercepted. My advice upon the subject has not been required. Yet, as a public servant . . . zealous of the honor of my country and acquainted with the present disposition of the Sikh Army, I consider it a sacred duty to express my opinion. . . . I consider the immediate advance of a British Army upon Mooltan as the only measure that can save the Punjaub. . . . A moment's hesitation after so barbarous an outrage will expose us to the scorn of even our well-wishers. There is no physical difficulty to be weighed against the moral eclipse which our reputation must suffer from delay. . . . Let me entreat you, Sir, as you are the representative of a great and honourable Government, to think of the*

Chapter 6

consequence attending [the] similar delay at Cabul. And whether you could survive the disgrace of being assailed in the Capital. Our honour rests in your hands.[117]

Seldom in the history of British India has there been a more stark and more seemingly clear-cut example of the perennial conflict between the officers at the sharp end of the bayonet, where minutes could seem like hours, and leaders in government forced to take a longer view of a crisis. Currie was not insensible to the very real danger that his decision put his field officers in. They may not have liked him, respected him, or agreed with him, but they were Britons, and he was responsible for their lives. Yet, ironically, while his military judgment was better than that of the military men in the field, his political instincts were worse than theirs. He fundamentally misread what was happening around him.

Currie did not on this occasion rebuke Abbott or any of the other Paladins for their intemperate correspondence, but neither he nor the governor-general was any more disposed by it to rush British forces and siege artillery to Multan. The British officers scattered around the Punjab who were not attached to Edwardes's Field Force would have to sweat it out and hope for the best.

That best would be that the rebellion of the Sikhs at Multan would remain an isolated mutiny and that the remainder of the Khalsa Army would remain loyal to the orders of the Lahore Durbar. And at first it seemed to many Britons that this uneasy state of affairs would prevail. But the Sikh polity was in fact rife with plots and intrigue. Like any state, it had power blocs and power brokers. Maharani Jindan Khaur, mother of the son of Ranjit Singh, Duleep Singh, and regent until his majority, had twice been caught red-handed in schemes to incite rebellion in the Sikh army. After the second instance (the first being the Prema Conspiracy), Currie overruled the unanimous disapproval of the Council of Regency and exiled her to Benares for life, with a sharp reduction in her annuity. Most in the Sikh government or its orbit were loyal to her and her son and wanted an independent Sikh state, not one controlled by the British. Gulab Singh, ruler of Jammu and Kashmir and ethnically a Dogra, was a powerful third force and a wild card with perhaps the most to lose

Figure 6.6. A period painting of Chattar Singh Attariwala, the Sikh governor of Hazāra District and Abbott's nemesis in the Second Anglo-Sikh War, by an unknown Sikh artist, circa 1840. (WIKIMEDIA COMMONS, SIKH HERITAGE)

CHAPTER 6

by making war on the British and possibly the least to gain, because he already had an independent kingdom free of British rule or even a British Resident. Wealthy and influential families, like that of Chattar Singh, sought to solidify or enhance their positions within the royal court, in Chattar Singh's case by betrothing his daughter to the young Duleep Singh, who would become the maharaja upon reaching the age of eighteen. Other Sikh families representing other power blocs within the Khalsa also vied for position. A few may have considered the British to have the upper hand and therefore collaborated with British authorities in peacetime. But when open war broke out again, no major Sikh military leaders or members of the court sided with the British.

Currie's exile of Maharani Jindan Khaur to Benares had caused considerable resentment on the part of the Sikhs, who obviously saw it as disrespect of their regent. The relationship of the British to the Lahore Durbar deteriorated sharply thereafter.[118] Currie certainly gained little but her increased distance from Lahore by this action, as couriers continued to move between the maharani and the Khalsa after her removal to Benares, and the deep reduction of her annuity did nothing to improve her disposition toward the British. This step against the maharani hurt the fortunes of the Attariwala clan the most of all the important Sikh families. The patriarch of this clan, General Chattar Singh, was the *nazim* (governor) of Hazāra District. The planned marriage of his daughter to Duleep Singh had recently been delayed indefinitely by British authorities. Chattar Singh's son, Sher Singh, sat on the Council of Regency in Lahore in addition to being a senior military leader now commanding the Sikh force encamped outside Multan. He believed the British had no intention of allowing Duleep Singh to take the throne when he came of age and thus make his sister the new rani.[119] Thus no one in the Sikh Empire now believed he had more to lose from continued British rule than Chattar Singh, the governor of Abbott's district and patriarch of the Attariwalas. Yet Currie astonishingly believed the exact opposite to be true.

Evidence coming in to Abbott of Chattar Singh's intention to join the rebellion began to mount in May 1848. Because virtually all the Muslim residents of Hazāra hated the Sikhs, Abbott had no trouble establishing an informal network of what he called "voluntary collectors of intelligence."[120] Much information that those around the Sikhs picked up was reported back to him. The Sikh Pulki Brigade, under Chattar Singh's command, was quartered in Hurripore and was especially vulnerable to intelligence gathering by Abbott's spies. Everything from daily food deliveries to the garrison at Hurripore to the contracting of livestock to pull the wagons necessary to move the brigade from place to place found its way to Abbott's ears. Suspicious now of Chattar Singh, Abbott at this juncture substantially increased the number of Muslim irregulars in his personal security detachment and saw to it that they were armed with matchlocks. In June, Chattar Singh used a forged letter bearing a false report of a Pashtun uprising to try to lure Abbott back to Hurripore, but Abbott was called away on other business, and the trap could not be sprung.[121]

Abbott reported the growing evidence of Chattar Singh's disloyalty throughout May and early June, but Currie refused to believe any of it. Currie was not a poor administrator—indeed, he carried out his duties as a district commissioner in Benares and a judge in Allahabad efficiently—but apart from these assignments, most of his career was spent in Calcutta, and, significantly, he was newer to the Punjab than his officers. As Bengal officers so often did in their delusional belief that upper-caste Brahmins naturally supported British rule out of self-interest, Currie believed this equally of Chattar Singh as an article of faith. Chattar Singh would not betray British rule, Currie believed, because British rule was in his best interests. In fact the antithesis would prove to be true in both cases.

For his part, Dalhousie was a strong advocate of expansion of the East India Company's territory. He did not dread the possibility of another Sikh war, which would provide the opportunity to annex the Punjab in its entirety. He was, however, an astute politician and content to let matters in the Punjab take their course in Currie's hands without his fingerprints on them. If things went well, he could take the credit; if they went badly, he could lay the blame on Currie.

By the second week of June 1848, the mutiny of the majority of Chattar Singh's brigade was imminent. Abbott sent more warnings to Currie of the pending mutiny, which Currie continued to blithely dismiss as rumor. Currie assured Abbott that overall the Punjab was calm. Abbott's impatience with Currie's obstinacy crossed the line from impertinence to disrespect again in a letter on June 17. He quickly realized he had gone too far and wrote again the next day to amend it. The letter of June 17 is no longer extant, but Abbott's next letter to Currie reflects his second thoughts:

Upon rereading my letter No. 13 of yesterday's date, it appears to me that my anxiety to impress upon you my own convictions has led me beyond the limits of propriety, considering that I have already more than once explicitly stated my opinions. Could I indeed reasonably hope by repetition of these arguments to effect any change in the arrangements of the campaign, I should the less regret my imputation of failure in defense. But as maturer consideration deprives me of this hope, I would willingly cancel the concluding paragraph of the letter aforesaid, as being under the circumstance uncalled for and as savoring of presumption.[122]

As the Punjab teetered on the edge of war, Currie forwarded Abbott's letter of June 17 to the governor-general's office in Calcutta and censured him in response:

Your letter No 13 was received and replied to two days ago, and the correspondence has been forwarded to Government. . . . As I have said before, I have for the reasons stated forborne hitherto to notice with the reproof of which it may be considered to merit, your taking upon yourself to censure the measures of your official superior and that in inflated and offensive terms entirely as I feel unbecoming your position. . . . Your present communication is not more becoming than the one a portion of which it proposes to cancel. Personally, I feel not the slightest anger at your strictures; but it may perhaps be thought that my forbearance has been carried too far to an extent scarcely compatible with the vindication of my official position, and the extraction of due respect and subordination from my Assistant.[123]

A New Beginning

It was eloquently worded, in the perfect gentlemanly Calcutta prose, but Currie left no doubt, by forwarding Abbott's letter to Calcutta, that he was reprimanding Abbott and that Abbott could expect further censure from the governor-general's office as well. The very next day, the bulk of the Cherenjeet Regiment mutinied exactly as Abbott had warned. In response to Abbott's news of the mutiny, Currie professed himself unmoved and unsurprised by what he considered a minor setback in stabilizing the Punjab and remained firm in his conviction that Chattar Singh was loyal to the Durbar. On June 20, 1848, Currie wrote to the governor-general's office, "I do not expect that the example of the [253 men of the] Churunjeet regiment will be generally followed; there may be more desertions from Sirdar Jhunda Singh's force, but I hope to prevent them. And as the Peshawar, Hazāra and Bunnoo forces have not risen hitherto ... I do not expect that they will do so now."[124] On June 22, 1848, Currie repeated his conviction to William Elliot, the Secretary to the Government of Lahore in the Foreign Department at Fort William, that there would be no further defections: "In continuation of my letters ... regarding the defection of the Churrinjeet Regiment of Cavalry ... [t]he example of the 253 Traitors has not been followed hitherto by the rest of the Regiment or by any of the soldiers of the other forces and it is not likely now, I think, that it will be."[125] Currie was in a state of deep denial.

In the midst of this crisis, in reaction to Abbott's disrespect toward Currie on June 17, the wheels of government in Calcutta continued to grind exceedingly fine. On July 22, 1848, William Elliot sent to Currie Governor-General Dalhousie's response:

> *I am directed to acknowledge the receipt of your two dispatches dated 22 and 24 ultimo [June] No. 134 and 138, submitting a copy of a correspondence with your Assistant, Captain Abbott regarding [illegible] Troopers of the Churrinjeet Regiment, and in reply to request that you will inform Captain Abbott that the Governor General in Council expressed much dissatisfaction with his intemperate and disrespectful letters to you, couched in language inadmissible in any subordinate and which no circumstances could justify.*[126]

CHAPTER 6

During the month of July, Abbott's sources reported that Chattar Singh was inciting rebellion and preparing for a major campaign. Despite being stung by the rebuke, Abbott continued his reports to Currie of Chattar Singh's duplicity, to Currie's evidently increasing frustration. Currie began to consider relieving Abbott and replacing him with someone who shared his conviction of Chattar Singh's loyalty. In early August, matters came to a head. Abbott received intelligence that the remainder of the Pulki Brigade had sold off its surplus stores, engaged wagons and drivers, and packed out its camp in Hurripore for a march to Multan. Abbott raised five hundred additional tribal levies and ordered them to try to block the movement of the Pulki Brigade through the pass at the southern foot of the valley on the road to Multan. On August 12, 1848, Currie wrote to the governor-general,

> *I am afraid from the report I have received, that a serious collision has taken place in Hazāra between the armed Mahomedan population and the Sikh troops in that province, and that this collision has been occasioned by the measures taken . . . by Captain Abbott, in consequence of the belief with which he is impressed, that Sirdar Chattar Singh, Attariwala, the Nazim of the province, is at the head of a conspiracy for the expulsion of the English from the Punjab, and was about to head a crusade against the British forces at Lahore. . . . That the Pulki brigade has been, for some time, in a state of excitement, I have no doubt . . . but that Sirdar Chattar Singh, an old and infirm man, the father-in-law of the Maharajah, and with more at stake than any man almost in the Punjab, should have taken the leading part in an affair of the kind described by Captain Abbott, is altogether incredible.*[127]

Currie also advised the governor-general's office of his decision to replace Abbott: "If it were possible for me to leave Lahore (which it is not, at the present moment, with the brigades advancing on Multan, under my instructions) I should at once go off to Hazāra, where I am satisfied that I could, at once, settle this untoward affair. As it is, I have deputed my chief assistant, Mr. Cocks, with full powers on my part, to make such arrangement as he thinks fit, after a full investigation, for the settlement of the district and the administration of the Hazāra province."[128] This is diplomatic language for "I am sending Mr. Cocks to relieve Captain Abbott." By that time, however, the entire Pulki Brigade under the command of Chattar Singh had already joined the Cherenjeet Regiment in mutiny, Chattar Singh had come out openly in support of the mutineers at Multan, the Second Anglo-Sikh War had begun, and Abbott was in the mountain passes with his tribal levies. Chattar Singh's son Sher Singh, encamped with his force outside Multan, joined the rebellion on September 14, 1848.

What saved Abbott's career on this occasion was that the East India Company was now at war again with the Sikh Empire, with Chattar Singh at its head, and Abbott was trapped deep behind enemy lines in the Hazāra. He was entirely correct from the beginning about the intentions of Chattar Singh and the Sikhs, while Currie was purblind. As Captain Lionel Trotter later observed, "The wily old traitor had at length thrown off the mask which Abbott alone among our politicals had learned to see through."[129] This, on December 18, 1848, Currie himself was forced to admit, writing to government,

> *From all that has come to my knowledge since I have been at Lahore, I am quite convinced that long before the Multan outbreak there was a plan for an insurrection which was to take place during the current year, in which nearly all the Sirdars were to join and of which the Ranee was the prime mover. I would refer to the papers of Captain Abbott in Huzāra passim for the evidence obtained by him of the intention of a general rising of the Sikhs, incited by the Sirdars for the expulsion of the British from the Punjab.*[130]

7

The Man Who Was King

1849–1853

JAMES ABBOTT WAS NOW DEEP INSIDE TERRITORY UNDER THE CONTROL of the Sikhs and far from any British forces. His position in the district transformed overnight from being the officer assigned to advise the district governor Chattar Singh Attariwala to being his military opponent. Abbott, two young British lieutenants, an uncovenanted assistant surveyor named James Ingram, and two British corporals assigned to the sapper detachment on the geographical survey team were the only Britons in the district.

Abbott was probably the first British officer to engage in what would today be recognized as guerilla warfare as the leader of a force of irregular soldiers. In military terms, the purpose of guerilla warfare is to employ armed civilian irregulars in enemy-occupied territories to harass enemy forces and oblige the enemy to deploy a significant number of regular troops to rear areas to protect against and react to guerilla attacks. If a force of one hundred irregulars can make an enemy divert one thousand regular troops to deal with them, those are one thousand fewer troops available at the front lines for combat. British forces observed such tactics by the Spanish against Napoleon in the Peninsular Wars, and the word "guerilla" entered the English language as early as 1809 in the Duke of Wellington's comments. Until 1848 in the Punjab, however, there is no record of another British officer in the nineteenth century employing them.

Abbott's success in Hazāra during the Second Anglo-Sikh War was attributable more to his enemy's inaction than to feats of arms by his tribal forces, but they did harass, worry and delay Chattar Singh's army, which could certainly have done the British more harm elsewhere. Most of the Second Anglo-Sikh War was fought further south by conventional forces. Since the end of the First Anglo-Sikh War, the army of the Khalsa had lost little of its professionalism or its fighting strength. As a result, the Second Anglo-Sikh War was a bloody affair, made worse by General Hugh Gough, the aging commander of the First Anglo-Sikh War, who continued to disdain artillery and whose principal military tactic was still the bayonet charge straight up the middle.[1] As has so often been the case in British military history, the British troops in the Punjab were lions led by a donkey.[2]

Abbott remained at his post in the Hazāra throughout the war, the only British district officer in the Sikh Punjab to hold his ground. He fought with his Hazārawal irregulars to harry the Sikhs and delay Sikh troops in the Hazāra from joining forces with the main body of the Sikh army in the south. Little could have appealed more to Abbott's self-image of the knight-errant than this kind of warfare, and few settings could have better evoked his Romantic sensibilities. He was immersed now in a military world which his imagination could readily transpose onto his Romantic construction of the Middle Ages. It was complete with warriors "clad ... in black and speaking only the Pushtoo tongue," horsemen in chain mail with spiked helmets in the Persian *Kulah Khud* style, and characters like Jafir the Dagger Hand, a chieftain turned bandit who, upon losing his right hand, had attached a ten-inch dagger to the stump, which he would unsheathe before battle.[3] The core of Abbott's forces was formed by the Mashwari tribesmen of the Gundgurh hills, whose leader, Hussan Shah, Abbott had aided after the attack on the village of Bukhur. They were the first men to answer his call to arms in the district, and they always had a special place in his heart afterward. They were augmented by two hundred men from the Suttri tribe of Kashmir. The two hundred Suttris were the closest to real soldiers Abbott had, as they had served in Gulab Singh's infantry and understood the basics of conventional maneuver.

Chapter 7

For some of the time, Lieutenant Daniel Robinson, who worked with Abbott on the boundary survey in 1847, and Lieutenant John Nicholson served under his command in the district. They fought a frustrating guerilla campaign in which their forces generally either fled from the field or made their own local nonaggression pacts with the Sikhs. During the campaign, Abbott was aided by his enemies and hurt by his friends. Chattar Singh was, as Frederick Currie had noted, elderly and infirm, and he moved his forces about in a series of meandering and desultory maneuvers for months. Abbott's record of the actions shows that his own lieutenant, John Nicholson, made a number of tactical errors, two of which resulted in Singh's troops being able to force narrow mountain passes. On one occasion, Nicholson decided to act as his own messenger, and his gallop from his forward position to get reinforcements was interpreted by his irregulars as the signal for a precipitous retreat.

In August and September 1848, Frederick Currie remained in a state of denial about Sikh intentions and was still sending optimistic dispatches to Governor-General Lord Dalhousie in Calcutta that it was all just a misunderstanding. The commander of Chattar Singh's field artillery in Hazāra was an American named Kennedy fighting under the nom de guerre "Colonel Canara." Abbott thought him "an uneducated man of coarse habits, but brave and loyal." When Canara refused to move his artillery batteries without British authorization, Chattar Singh ordered him murdered and paid his assassin a bounty of one hundred rupees.[4] Astonishingly, Currie even accepted Chattar Singh's account of Canara's murder over the factual report forwarded to him by George Lawrence, Abbott's direct lines of communication with Lahore having been cut. After the war, Abbott had a stone pyramid constructed over Kennedy's grave in Haripur, which remains today.

Initially Abbott had high hopes for his irregular forces and chose a location for his base in the center of Hazāra, from where he could readily maneuver his forces and fight large engagements. His first headquarters was near the ruined village of Nārā in Mashwari tribal territory less than ten miles from Chattar Singh's base at Hurripore, the central town in the district. It soon became clear, however, that most of his guerilla forces were not ready to put up much of a fight even in favorable terrain.

Figure 7.1. Pen-and-ink drawing by James Abbott from 1848 titled "Glen at Nārā Huzāra Bivouack of My Armed Levies in 1848 2nd Sikh war." (BRITISH LIBRARY BOARD)

Abbott scaled back his ambitions and moved his camp to a mountaintop at Sirikôt, writing of the new location, "The transition from the burning heat, the noise, the dust, the filth and flies of my huge bivouac at Nara to the cool pure atmosphere and repose of the mountain summit had been as an escape from purgatory to paradise; for I had left all my levies in the valley, being confident in the courage and fidelity of the gallant Mashwaries for my own personal security. From my new position, the Sikh Army cis-Indus was visible, varying in strength from 6,000 to 16,000 disciplined troops."[5]

Chattar Singh outfoxed Abbott in September 1848 with a feint and linked up with a large force of troops under Jundial Singh, and the combined force began a march toward Hassan Abdal, the town that had once been John Nicholson's headquarters. On three occasions in August

Chapter 7

and September, at Margulla, Motí, and Duntour passes, the great majority of Abbott's Hazāra irregulars proved unwilling to fight them. Chattar Singh's forces moved through the passes without a shot being fired, despite Abbott's men having ideal ambush positions high above them. After this, Abbott conceded, "Of their mode of fighting ... Nicholson and myself evidently knew nothing."[6] But Abbott also understood such men could not contest Sikh regulars and knew that even the more reliable tribes like the Mashwaries "valued their households and crops more than their allegiance to me."[7] Abbott's chiefs confided to him that he was doing it wrong. The only way to get them to fight was to stand behind them, they told him, not in front of them, so that if any man skulked, he would be seen doing so: "In all our actions hitherto, Nicholson and I had headed our levies, and in every action we had been deserted by them without them attempting to fight. The chiefs and mulliks assured me, that the same results would ever follow our taking post in front. . . . [I]f I wished them to fight and not run, I must have them throughout the fight under my own eye."[8] Abbott tried again at the Battle of Simulkund on October 18, 1848, when Chattar Singh brought his forces to the fort in the village of that name to relieve and evacuate its Sikh garrison. The village was at the base of a wooded mountain, making the location ideal terrain for Abbott's irregular hillmen, snipers, and mountaineers. This time Abbott selected a position in consultation with his chiefs on a prominent ridge of red rock on the mountain overlooking the fort. He made himself as conspicuous as possible. "I sent for a chair, a small table and an umbrella, and fixed my bivouack at the spot I was to occupy on the morrow," he noted.[9] On the morning of the battle, he took his position under his umbrella in plain sight of his own men and the Sikh gunners. At a range of about twelve hundred yards, the Sikh gunners unlimbered their four 8-pounder guns from the elephants transporting them and took aim at the umbrella. Abbott remained in his chair throughout the entire engagement, while the Sikh artillery tried to hit him. Either they were not very good shots, or their guns were not able to elevate high enough. During the hours he spent sitting in his chair watching the Sikhs maneuver, Abbott observed "the shot generally falling just short of my feet."[10]

Abbott stationed eight hundred of his matchlock men above a narrow pass leading to the fort. From there they could pour fire down into the Sikh troops advancing toward it. He fanned out his remaining one thousand men in a semicircle around the fort on the wooded high ground where they would be in their element and watched the results:[11]

> *As the left column of the enemy approached the [fort] ... I watched them through my telescope in breathless anticipation. Now they seemed to be parallel with the cliff; yet not a matchlock spoke. Their distance from me might be about two miles, but the intervening ground being hollow and my glass a Dollond,[12] I had a perfect view of their movements. Now they were halted under the cliff. I expected every moment a cloud of grey smoke to tell of the fire of the defenders. Even if the Mashwaries, to save their crops from destruction should refuse to fire, I felt assured that Kulhunder Khan would have no scruples and his three hundred men ... should have made great havoc in the Sikh ranks.... It proved afterwards, that when Kulhunder had ordered his men to fire, the Mashwaries had threatened to fire upon him and his party, should they molest the enemy. Had those matchlocks fired, nearly every one must have brought down its man. For more than half an hour, the forces lay thus confronted. Then the enemy resumed their march up the ravine ... and I felt a sickness stealing over my heart in this proof that the men I had most trusted were faithless.[13]*

The Sikhs pressed forward, forcing Abbott's Tarkhaili skirmishers back up the hills, fighting "rock to rock and bush to bush."[14] The Sikhs were soon in possession of the fort and evacuated their garrison in good order, now out of range of any of Abbott's matchlocks. The Tarkhaili chief of Simulkund, Ata Muhammud Khan, and five of his men charged with swords into a body of Sikhs near the castle and momentarily drove the Sikhs back before being cut down "fighting like heroes."[15] The Sikhs set a fuse to the powder magazine in the fort, which soon exploded in an enormous column of fire and smoke. True to knight-errant form, Abbott now proposed a mass charge with swords down the mountainside into the retiring Sikhs, but the chiefs would not have it. Abbott estimated seventy-five

CHAPTER 7

Sikhs had been killed and 125 wounded throughout the day, as opposed to twelve of his own men.[16] Chattar Singh had freed a garrison of about 150 men from the fort before blowing it up, a force to which several weeks before Abbott had offered safe passage out of the fort with the honors of war, probably to get possession of the powder magazine. But most of Abbott's tribesmen were unwilling to fight yet again, and it is difficult for any military leader to win battles if his troops will not shoot at the enemy.

Still Chattar Singh dawdled. Abbott thought the Sikh general might now try to take the high ground at Sirikôt above the smoking ruins of the fort. With the Mashwaries unwilling to risk their villages and crops in the vicinity, Abbott could not stop Chattar Singh's forces if he advanced up the mountain, but there were no further offensive moves. "I slept in my cloak upon the field. And during the two following days and nights remained there under my umbrella, there being no tree to shade me, for the Sikh force continued encamped within sight, busied in burning their dead.... [A]t length they struck their tents and marched... to Attock."[17] Upon reaching Attock with his forces on October 20, Chattar Singh began a siege of the fort there, now under of the command of Lieutenant Herbert. Although he left no record of his strategy, it appears Chattar Singh's purpose was to relieve each of his garrisons in Hazāra in turn and then to seize Attock. He was either timid or overestimated the amount of time he had to consolidate his military position in the northern Punjab, however, as this series of maneuvers and minor engagements consumed several months.

From his position atop Sirikôt, on the western slope of the Gundgurh mountain ridge, Abbott observed Chattar Singh's siege of Attock. Months before, George Lawrence had anticipated at attack on Attock and purchased and burned most of the barges and ferries on the Indus in the area to prevent a future river crossing. Without boats, Chattar Singh could only shell the fort from the eastern side of the Indus. Unbeknownst to the British, he allied himself with the Afghan king, Dost Mohammed, by promising him the return of Peshawar, the former winter capital of the Durrani Empire. Abbott received reports from his scouts that Dost Mohammed was now marching south from Kabul with as many as twelve thousand men. Unsure whose side Dost Mohammed was going to be

Figure 7.2. A view of the Indus River at Attock in 2010, looking west from Abbott's camp on the western slope of the mountain at Sirikot. (PHOTOGRAPH BY AUTHOR)

on, Abbott wrote him a letter in friendly terms to ascertain his intentions. Abbott received a polite answer, requesting a private meeting, but before this could be arranged, the Afghan forces reached Attock, and Dost Mohammed's artillery opened fire on the fort, clearing up Abbott's uncertainty.

From his mountaintop redoubt, Abbott could make out the main body of Afghan troops across the Indus. "The dust also of the Doorani[18] camp of about 10,000 men (chiefly horsemen) could be seen beyond the Indus. The guns fired at the siege of Attock, thirty miles distant, were distinctly audible."[19] Upon his arrival, Dost Mohammed convened a large *jirga* of chiefs and mullahs, and declared himself "Ummîr ul Mumaneen," in Abbott's spelling, the "Leader of the Faithful" of all Muslims. Dost Mohammed had a special signet ring made with that inscription with which he began to seal all his orders.[20]

His brief reign in Peshawar was contested, however. Local power brokers were uneasy with Dost Mohammed's alliance with the Sikhs or saw their own political positions compromised. A few judged their lot better

CHAPTER 7

under the British, as their brief experience of British oversight had not been religiously offensive, financially burdensome, or politically intrusive. The Muslim tribesmen in the region were not mindless fanatics who automatically obeyed a call to jihad, as often later portrayed by the British, but cautious and thoughtful men who considered a broad spectrum of economic, political, and familial factors. Some joined Dost Mohammed; others did not. Abbott noted that "many of the Moollas in those parts are upright and sensible men," adding,

> *The most enlightened and most powerful of them all, a [mullah] of Kota in the Yusufzai*,[21] *refused all the overtures of Dost Muhummud to aid his Ghiza [jihad] with his extensive influence, although the Ameer waited upon him in person for the purpose. When presst by his disciples for the reasons of his denial, he is reported to have answered "Spit at the sky and what follows? You merely defile your own head. To what purpose . . . can Dost Muhummud and the Sikhs, whose feebleness we know, oppose a nation whose hand above covers all Hindoostan, and whose body none of us has seen?"*[22]

The Sikh garrison in Peshawar joined the rebellion on October 23, 1848.[23] The garrison of the Attock fort then defected, their families in the vicinity of Attock now under the control of the Afghan horsemen and their loyalties conflicted by the alliance. Lieutenant Herbert, commander of the fort, escaped with three loyal Muslim officers to a raft he had hidden for this contingency. When the war started, Abbott had sent the two British corporals of the sapper detachment in Hazāra to Herbert, but one of the men had drowned in the crossing of the Indus. The other British soldier, Corporal Carthy, was now delirious with fever in the fort and could not be gotten to the escape raft. Lieutenant Herbert sent the three Muslim officers off downriver on the raft and attempted to reach Abbott on foot with Corporal Carthy, but they were captured by Chattar Singh's cavalry.

Abbott had also sent Lieutenants Daniel Robinson of the Engineers and John Nicholson from his headquarters in Hazāra to join General Gough's army. With George Lawrence, Lieutenants Bowie and Herbert, and Corporal Carthy captured by the Sikhs and Lieutenants Robinson and Nicholson gone south to the main army, Abbott was now the only free Briton still north of the Chenab River.

On November 22, 1848, a large body of British cavalry was defeated by the Sikhs at the Battle of Ramnagar, where Colonel William Havelock

Figure 7.3. A British map of the Hazāra region from the 1860s enhanced by the author to show important locations, including Black Mountain and Abbott's camp, today the city of Abbottabad. (MAP FROM EDINBURGH GEOGRAPHICAL INSTITUTE WITH PLACE NAMES SUPERIMPOSED BY AUTHOR)

CHAPTER 7

(the brother of Sir Henry Havelock) and Brigadier General Charles Cureton were killed.[24] Abbott's secret agents who attended the next Attock Durbar of Dost Mohammed reported that Chattar Singh presented Dost Mohammed with the severed "heads of several Britons slain at ... Ramnaggur,"[25] one of them apparently that of Colonel Havelock. Abbott accurately notes that a British artillery piece was also captured at Ramnagar, which was considered at the time a military disgrace.[26]

For three months, from December 1848 to February 1849, Afghanistan briefly reclaimed its former winter capital at Peshawar from the British. With the fall of Attock, and with Dost Mohammed's Afghans now securing his rear, Chattar Singh finally felt free to proceed south to combine his army with the forces of the other ranking Sikh general in the war, his son Sher Singh. But he still delayed. Meanwhile, General Gough was reinforced at Lahore by an army sent up from Bombay and was on the move north. On January 13, 1849, Gough's army collided with Sher Singh's army in jungle terrain on the Jhelum River at Chilianwallah, resulting in one of the bloodiest and most confused battles in the history of British India.

After a daylong battle on January 13, 1848, which left 2,357 British[27] and an estimated 3,600 Sikhs killed or wounded, three days of torrential rain followed, which forced both armies to suspend combat operations. On January 17, Sher Singh proceeded north to link up with his father. Thus Chilianwallah was a strategic defeat for the British, whose objective had been to prevent the joining of the two Sikh armies. British superiority in numbers, artillery, and logistics was not decisive. As a direct result of his poor handling of his forces, Gough was relieved of command after Chilianwallah. Charles Napier, the man who annexed Sind, was sent from London to replace him, but Gough remained at the head of the army until Napier arrived.[28] During these months of December 1848 and January 1849 in Hazāra, there was little Abbott could do but attempt to harry Sikh supply lines and harass Sikh foraging raids in the district with those Hazārawals who remained loyal to him. The situation seemed bleak: "The first news of [Chilianwallah] reached me as I sat in the open-air on the hilltop at Srikote in durbar surrounded by my chiefs and mulliks. I was certain from the aspect of the messenger that the news he bore was unpleasant.... He had been disguised at the durbar of the Ammîr [Dost Mohammed] when Chattar Singh had brought the news of Chilianwallah.... The British, he said, had retreated, leaving on the field twenty guns."[29]

Chattar Singh's presence with his army in Attock in mid-January, however, is the telling factor in the war. His delay in moving south was militarily inexplicable, as were his sluggish movements in Hazāra from July to September the previous year. He was the leader of the Sikh rebellion that precipitated the Second Anglo-Sikh War, and as a field commander he was excessively timid. After Chilianwallah, he finally marched his army south toward the Jhelum together with eighteen hundred Afghan cavalrymen.

Meanwhile the political intrigues in Hazāra continued, as alliances shifted without warning. Some men remained loyal to Abbott throughout the entire campaign. Abbott's dear friend Saleh Mohammed, his rescuer from slavery during the Khiva expedition, came to join him against the Sikhs. Other friends too stayed close, worried about his well-being. As Abbott recounts their concerns, "Sometimes a few of my more loyal followers, Saleh Muhummud, Syed Goolam, Moolah Iradútt and others, conjecturing my loneliness, would drop into my tent with the affectionate hope of cheering me, attentions which were very precious."[30] Another man who allied himself with Abbott and remained a close friend was "my right hand chief, Mir Zaman Khan, son of the heroic defender of Nara."[31] Abbott relied on him the most for advice, saying of him, "His counsels I always trusted, because besides being true as steel ... [he] was quite fearless, and his judgment was never dazzled by the timidity which so often weakened that of my other advisors."[32] Abbott had taken an immediate liking to Mir Zaman Khan when they met a year and a half before, on his arrival in Hazāra in 1847:

> *The instant my eyes met the guileless and fearless gaze of Mir Zaman Khan, all idea of precaution vanished and I felt as confident of his good faith, at that first moment of acquaintance, as I afterwards felt throughout those eight months of anarchy when the Sikhs would have purchased my head with its weight in gold. He took his seat at my*

Chapter 7

feet on the carpet and the rest sat around. Mir Zaman Khan, by race a Yusufzye, by clan an Oothmanzye,[33] by family a Syudkaāni, was a man of remarkable appearance.... His countenance was massive, the nose aquiline; the brow broad; the eyes well opened, large, fearless and inviting confidence; he wore a strong mustache and a close black beard. His face was shadowed by an immense turban of blue-black cotton cloth; the ends sparkling with gold thread.... His age at the time may have been about 27.... His eyes met mine with an expression of confidence not to be mistaken.[34]

Another close confidant was Kulúndur Khan, responsible for Abbott's bodyguard of twelve matchlock men and the captain of his best marksmen. Kulúndur Khan too remained with Abbott until the day he left Hazāra. For security during the war, however, Abbott relied primarily on the customary obligation of the Mashwari tribe, on whose land he camped, under *Pashtunwali* to protect him as a matter of *malmastia* (hospitality), which included the commitment to guarantee the security of invited guests. Abbott selected the Mashwaries for their positive reputation for integrity in the district, as they held themselves to be a *Syed* tribe descended directly from the Prophet Mohammed. Any effort to kidnap or attack him, he believed, "would have obliged the whole clan ... to resist (however unwillingly) the capture of their guest."[35] Despite the large bounty on Abbott's head offered by the Sikhs, although they would not risk the destruction of their farms for him in battle, the Mashwaries never betrayed him.

Others would determine their interests lay elsewhere, and their choices sometimes defied Abbott's best leadership. His charisma was not unlimited. His greatest disappointment was Tarkhaili leader Khan-i-Zamman, who, after the suicidal charge of Ata Muhammud Khan at the Battle of Simulkund, became the head of the senior branch of the Tarkhaili clan. Abbott was aware of Khan-i-Zamman's conflicted interests but tried hard to keep him an ally. Knowing that Khan-i-Zamman had lived as an outlaw after the Sikhs confiscated his lands, Abbott had had his lands restored by the Lahore Durbar. Later, at a *jirga* of the chiefs of the valley, Abbott personally bestowed on him the ceremonial turban of the chief of the mountain, an act of great cultural significance.[36] Nevertheless, Khan-i-Zamman defected to the Afghans in January 1849.[37] So too did Goolam Khan, to whom Patrick Vans Agnew had restored a *jaghir*, or hereditary landholding, confiscated by the Sikhs, but Goolam Khan could persuade none of his clansmen to follow him. Such calculations of local actors in the Punjab were complex and often confounded British efforts to ensure reliable allies by means of legal patronage and the use of cultural idioms as they understood them.

Abbott never learned the given name of the Mullah of Kota in the Yusufzai lands who had defied Dost Mohammed, but the two men communicated throughout Abbott's tenure in Hazāra by means of the mullah's students, or *talibs*, who served also as his messengers. In January 1849, the mullah sent a messenger to Abbott to relate a vision in which he saw the Sikh army "stealing to the rear of the British force, confronting them, and threatening them with great disaster."[38] This Abbott understood to be intelligence gathered by the mullah's extensive network of informants expressed in the form of a vision, or dream, which is the idiom of communication of a charismatic mullah. Abbott immediately sent the warning to General Gough via courier, who, traveling thirty-five miles a day, took four days to reach the British camp.

Abbott's direct engagement with the Mullah of Kota was in stark contrast to the hands-off approach of later generations of British administrators. The figure of the charismatic mullah on the frontier became well known but little understood to later generations of British officials and officers, who by the 1870s had dubbed them "Mad Mullahs." In contrast to Abbott's friendship with the mullahs, most district officers despised them and generally refused contact with them. As Charles Allen notes, "Edwardes, Bellew and the British officers who came after them loathed these saiyyeds, imams, mullahs, maulvis, maulanas and Taliban in equal measure."[39] Here again, Abbott was cut from a different cloth.

In early February, Abbott's scouts intercepted a message from Goolam Hyder, a son of Dost Mohammed, indicating his intent to advance up the central valley of Hazāra for food and forage for his thirty-five hundred horsemen. To combat this new threat, Abbott determined to move eastwards to Shirivan, a table summit back in the center of Hazāra. From

Chapter 7

there he intended to direct guerilla operations against the Afghan prince's cavalry, although he had few mounted men of his own. On February 11, 1849, Abbott left Sirikôt and traveled up the valley of the Sirwan River toward Shirivan. They were overtaken at midday by an advanced patrol of Goolam Hyder's cavalry, but after a heated skirmish, Abbott's matchlock men eventually drove them off, indicating improving discipline on the defensive within Abbott's ranks.

Abbott's forces were now receiving a steady stream of reports that the Sikhs were winning the war further south and that the British were fleeing in defeat, but most of his men still remained with him. On February 12, they climbed to the tabletop of Shirivan amid shocking reports of Afghan plundering and rapine in the valley. "The people of Hazāra, who ... are truly religious," Abbott recalled, "were scandalized by the deeds of such 'champions of the crescent' engaged in a holy war."[40]

To the south, though, Sher Singh was running out of strategic options. His men were hungry. He did not dare move north out of the central Punjab where he had popular support. His father's months of delay in the Hazāra and at Attock were fatal to the cause. Since Chilianwallah, his troops were subsisting on a diet of cabbages and the occasional carrot. He decided to maneuver behind the British army by moving east and south across the Chenab, as the Mullah of Kota saw in his dream, planning to then circle west and finally north again to recross the Chenab in the rear of Gough's force. But the river was unexpectedly in flood, and his army was accidentally discovered by British irregular cavalry. Sher Singh withdrew to the little town of Gujarat, where on February 21, 1849, he was attacked by General Gough and decisively beaten.[41] Abbott's messenger to Gough with the mullah's vision arrived the next day. The battle ended the war before Napier reached his new command, and Gough was able to retire as a hero.[42]

On February 24, the chief of Abbott's intelligence department, Qazi (Judge) Abdul Gofar, came into Abbott's tent and announced, "The whole Doorani force has bolted suddenly from Hazāra, no one knows wherefore. They were all busy cooking their food. A courier from the army arrived. They dropped their food as if scalding hot, mounted their horses and were off."[43] The next day, a courier brought news of the British victory at Gujarat.

Early in March 1849, Abbott received a letter written in lemon juice as invisible ink from Mrs. George Lawrence in Rawalpindi, indicating she believed Chattar Singh intended to move her and the other British prisoners north as hostages. The knight-errant sprang into action. As he later recounted, "In less than an hour, I was in full march for Kyntla, a pass on that mountain ridge which overlook[ed] Rawalpindi.... I could distinctly see through my telescope . . . the remnants of that mighty Sikh host which had fled from Gujarat."[44] Here Abbott and his matchlock men succeeded in blocking the Kyntla pass, sealing off one possible escape route for Chattar Singh and his British hostages. Out of food, out of money, and out of options, Sher Singh and his father surrendered at Peshawar on March 12.[45] That day John Nicholson recognized the face of an old Sikh trooper in the ranks of the men surrendering their weapons. "How is this, friend?" Nicholson asked. "Did you not say you would drive us all into the sea?" "Ah, Sahib," replied the gaunt veteran, "there's no fighting upon a diet of cabbage."[46]

Mrs. Lawrence and the other captives were freed unharmed. The Second Anglo-Sikh War was over. Dost Mohammed and the Afghans fled north through the Khyber Pass, pursued all the way by "the flying general," Sir Walter Gilbert, and ten thousand men. Dost Mohammed later signed a treaty renouncing Afghan claims to the lands south of the Khyber. Peshawar never belonged to Afghanistan again. British soldiers received an average of £3 each in prize money, and Queen Victoria received the Koh-i-Noor diamond from the Sikhs.[47] Chattar Singh and Sher Singh were released to live on their own parole but were soon engaged in a new plot, arrested, and sent into exile.[48] Chattar Singh died in Calcutta in 1857, his son Sher Singh in Benares the following year.

For his part, Abbott received the thanks of the governor-general of India, Lord Dalhousie, the thanks of both houses of Parliament (a more formal recognition at the time than it sounds at this remove), and the Sikh War Medal. Oddly, Abbott was awarded the medal with the battle clasps for Chilianwallah and Goojerat, despite the fact that he was nowhere near either engagement. His service record shows that his service in the Hazāra was deemed the "equivalent" of these battles, so he was awarded them anyway. He was also promoted to brevet major on June 7, 1849.[49] Dalhousie noted,

Chapter 7

It is a gratifying spectacle to witness the intrepid bearing of this officer, in the midst of difficulties of no ordinary kind, not merely maintaining his position but offering a bold front, at one time to the Sikhs, at another to the Afghans, notwithstanding the religious fanatics who had been at work to induce his Muhummedan levies to desert his cause. He must have secured the attachment of the wild people among whom he was thrown by his mild and conciliatory demeanor in times of peace as well as by his gallantry as their leader in action, thereby enhancing the credit of our national character and preparing the way for an easy occupation of an almost impregnable country.[50]

Yet greater recognition, which Abbott's services again clearly merited, was refused by Dalhousie. In his letter recommending awards for the war to Sir John Hobhouse, president of the Board of Control for India in London, Dalhousie wrote, "Captain Abbott has shown great gallantry in Huzāra; and has kept himself a free man of the forest to the last. He has, however, several times incurred justly the censure of the Government. The utmost, therefore, I would ask for him would be a majority." The fact that Abbott was right all along did not matter to Dalhousie.

Dalhousie then went on in his letter for two pages praising his pet secretary, Henry Elliot, who spent the entire war ensconced in his office in Calcutta gallantly answering the mail. Dalhousie interceded strenuously to seek a knighthood for him, and Elliot was duly knighted for his high-quality stenography.[51] Even John Marshman, who was no fan of Abbott's, noted in 1867 that in comparison to the rewards granted to others, "the gallant Abbott, who had defended the fortress of Nara against fearful odds, down to the close of the campaign, was invidiously refused the honour due to his distinguished efforts and success."[52]

Dalhousie held a grudge against Abbott until the end of his administration as a result of Abbott's contretemps with Currie, for which he had censured Abbott in writing. He also censured Abbott for making direct contact with Dost Mohammed, which Dalhousie deemed inappropriate for a district officer.[53] He wrote to Henry Lawrence that Abbott had to be closely watched for "any manifestation of insubordination in conduct or language."[54] The entirety of Dalhousie's correspondence, particularly with his closest friend, George Couper,[55] reveals a man who, like Lord Ellenborough, was exceptionally vain and vindictive. It would have been difficult to find a man in all India who was more different from James Abbott than James Andrew Broun-Ramsay, 1st Marquess of Dalhousie. Dalhousie ridiculed what he termed "knight-erranting" and famously remarked that he did not allow his clerks in Government House in Calcutta to address him, because, he said, "no well-bred gentleman would address his game-keepers."[56] He was so egotistical that he wrote to Couper that he believed he was doing the directors of the East India Company a favor by serving as governor-general and noted that he owed them "neither gratitude nor courtesy beyond what is a matter of conventional expression."[57] Charles Napier, the man sent out to replace Gough and one of the finest military minds of the nineteenth century, detested Dalhousie, whom he referred to derisively as "the Laird o' Cockpen" and described as "a young Scotch lord with no head for governing empire."[58] To the snobbish aristocrat Dalhousie, Abbott's disrespect and ungentlemanly language in addressing Currie were unpardonable sins for which no amount of gallantry could atone.

In particular, the two men could scarcely have been further apart in their approaches to establishing a relationship with the Pashtun and other Muslim tribes of the frontier. Abbott lived among the people as one of them, as did one of Abbott's closest parallels in British colonial history, James Brooke, who lived in a similar manner among the native peoples of Sarawak.[59] Dalhousie created the policy that would become known as "butcher and bolt," a reprisal-based model of punitive raids against the Pashtun tribes characterized by collective punishment and indiscriminate violence. This approach of communal responsibility and communal punishment created the relationship of antagonism and mutual animosity with the Muslims on the Northwest Frontier, one that remained unchanged to the last day of British colonial rule in India.

In March 1851, Dalhousie wrote in regard to the Mohmand tribe near Peshawar that he had ordered "the C.-in-C. to take immediate measures against them, [and] if we can get at them, and wallop them well, burning and slaying a bit, it will quiet the frontier for a long time."[60] His plan for the tribes of the Khyber Pass, which he termed "a band of thieves," was to "sort" them out, adding, "I intend to disarm the whole while I am there, and every mother's son of them that comes down out of the hills after that, armed, shall be sent to work on the roads in the provinces."[61] If they won't take that hint, we will give them a touch of Avitabile again,[62] barring the impaling and skinning alive."[63] In September 1852, while Abbott was still in Hazāra, Dalhousie pronounced himself pleased with the recent punishment of the Ranizai tribesmen by Sir Colin Campbell, who "thrash[ed] them in May, and destroyed their whole valley, stoup and roup."[64] He wrote of "exterminating" the Pashtuns if they did not obey British policy.[65] When Abbott, in contrast, was asked the secret of his remarkable success in keeping the peace in the Hazāra, he replied simply that he "treated them as gentlemen."[66] Dalhousie's policy prescription for subjugating the tribes of the frontier was, he believed, enhanced by its element of divide and conquer: "We have succeeded in sowing dissensions among these hill-folk by allowing each tribe to make terms for itself, inducing, of course, suspicion from all the rest, and destroying union."[67] Dalhousie never swerved from his policy of violence against the peoples of the frontier. In September 1854, after Abbott had left the Hazāra, Dalhousie noted, "One of the Momund villages near the frontier won't pay. A small force has gone out to pound them. . . . The Momund villages . . . were stormed and destroyed."[68] He believed, with an epic lack of historical insight, that "these people will worry us for a time, but that one by one they will put their necks under our foot."[69] Unlike Abbott, he did not understand the culture of the mountains and was not interested in doing so.[70] Thus, within ten years of the first meaningful contact between them, the relationship between the Western world and the frontier tribes was poisoned beyond repair, and Dalhousie's bellicose policy laid the foundation for a century of colonial conflict on the Northwest Frontier.

To the misery and massive social disruption caused by all of this, Dalhousie was oblivious. Of more concern to him than the killing of the people of the region and the wanton destruction of their lands, homes, and crops was the loss of his horse. "My poor horse Maharajah is dead," he wrote Couper. "I have buried him among the flowers in the garden, poor fellow, and shall never see his like again."[71] When combined with his Doctrine of Lapse and the annexation of Oudh, which were major factors in the Great Mutiny of 1857, Dalhousie's policies remind the modern reader of F. Scott Fitzgerald's characters Tom and Daisy, of whom Fitzgerald wrote, "They were careless people.... [T]hey smashed up things and creatures and then retreated back into their money or their vast carelessness ... and let other people clean up the mess they had made."[72]

Abbott now entered the most significant chapter of his life. The next four years, from 1849 to 1853, challenge the standard histories of British rule on the Northwest Frontier and the historiography of Lawrence's Young Men. His methods not only were at odds with those deemed correct by the central administration in Calcutta but caused problems even for his friend and superior Henry Lawrence, who, in the tradition of Thomas Munro, John Malcolm, and Mountstuart Elphinstone, promoted a light footprint, cultural tolerance, self-governance, and peaceful coexistence.

After the war, Abbott stayed in the Hazāra, now a district of the Punjab, for four years as the deputy commissioner.[73] He became the de facto "King of Hazāra"[74] in an episode with few parallels in British colonial history, one that later British historians were at pains to tone down, recast, and shoehorn into the preferred narrative of the paternal and beloved district officer within the discourse of the empire of opinion.[75]

Other deputy commissioners lived in stockades. Abbott lived in a tent and moved regularly around the countryside. Henry Lawrence was a staunch advocate of local self-rule, as was Abbott. Abbott followed Lawrence's injunction to his subordinates that they not interfere "in the ordinary affairs of the people."[76] He took an evident pride in "his people,"[77] as he called them, writing that "they set themselves to the task of self-rule with an alacrity which created a system of order unequalled in the most highly civilized communities."[78] Abbott was proud of their character, which he romanticized as honest and noble. "They were a race of gentlemen," he wrote, "and when treated as such, were perfectly reliable."[79] He was touched by what he described as their "affectionate devotion."[80] "During the six years of my rule in Huzāra," Abbott noted, here including the Second Anglo-Sikh War, "I had but once to carry out a death sentence, and the columns of crimes in my returns were almost blank.... There was not a thief or beggar in the land; at least the only beggars were refugees from Cashmere.... When Sir Henry Lawrence on a visit to me gave out his weekly dole of 50 shillings worth of flour, there were none to take it."[81]

Abbott made it a point to be available to anyone at any time and did his best to eliminate bribery and corruption, the historical characteristics of governance failure in the region:

> *By holding my court daily in the open air, where it was impossible to hinder the access to me of even the meanest appellant, by encouraging the approach to me in my rides and walks of any who wished to address me, and by suffering no man to be driven from my door, even if my hands were too full to attend to him or I were at my meals or [bathing] I rendered it very difficult to withhold from me any occurrence in which the interest of individuals or of the community was concerned.... So that although I am not hardy enough to assert that no corruption was ever practiced, I rendered it very difficult, and the more so, that my Aumla or Native Staff were not men of our older Indian provinces, where dishonest practices have had root for a thousand years.*[82]

In this he closely mimicked the judicial practices of village mullahs, who were traditionally respected as judges and arbiters of disputes because of their impartiality and incorruptibility in open air hearings.

His situation in Hazāra was unique in the history of district officers. As noted earlier, the people of Hazāra credited him with ending their status as a vassal state of Jammu and Kashmir and bringing them under partial British protection as a monitored Sikh territory shortly after the First Anglo-Sikh War—an outcome that they attributed to his letters and recommendations to the Lahore Durbar. Abbott had already cut taxes in half across the board in the Hazāra, from two-thirds of a man's predicted income to one-third, a beneficence also attributed directly to him and not to any distant policy from faraway Lahore or Calcutta. Abbott interceded to secure the return of numerous tracts of land confiscated by the Sikhs to influential former local landholders, arranged for pensions for the victims of the village of Bukhur, and succored the important Mashwari leader,

Hussan Shah, wounded in the infamous night raid. These actions were all well known among the Hazārawals.

The outcome of the Second Anglo-Sikh War, in their eyes, freed them from the hated Sikhs altogether. In retribution for similar injunctions against the Sikh religion imposed by previous Muslim rulers of the Hazāra, the Sikhs had imposed curbs on the public practice of Islam. Abbott noted, "When first I entered Huzāra in 1847, any Sikh might with impunity take the life of any Mohummedan whom he found praying openly. It was death to sound the Mohummedan call to prayer or to kill an ox or a cow."[83] These prohibitions Abbott now swept away (as any district officer would have done). Just as importantly, he was seen by thousands of Hazāra men, as they interpreted his behavior from their way of fighting, as a leader contemptuous of death and danger in exposing himself continually to enemy fire on many occasions during their guerilla operations. This sangfroid simply reflected how British officers were expected at this time to act, as Abbott did as an artilleryman at the Siege of Bhurtpore, for example. But the tribesmen of the Hazāra did not know that, as apart from Nicholson and Robinson, they had no other experience of British officers for comparison. Furthermore, Abbott was the only British officer in the Punjab prior to the outbreak of the Second Anglo-Sikh War who remained at his post throughout the conflict, making him unique among postwar district officers in regard to his reputation among his citizens as well.

Thus Abbott's reputation was without parallel among district officers prior to his assumption of his new duties. He was seen differently from other district officers by the people of his district, not in a constructed British fantasy narrative of paternal overrule but as a practical reality. To them, he was literally a hero. There is ample proof of this from period indigenous sources. Thirty years after Abbott's death, another British administrator, Sir Olaf Caroë, traveled through the Hazāra while in official charge of the district for a few months in 1927. In the village of Khabbal, Caroë encountered a man named Qasim Khan, a Yusufzai Pashtun elder who had recently celebrated his one hundredth birthday. Qasim's memory was sharp; he remembered the epic flood of the Indus River in 1841 precisely. It was seventy-five years since James Abbott left the Hazāra, but Caroë, remembering the history of the district, asked Qasim Khan whether he remembered Abbott. Caroë recorded that the elder's eyes lit up. Indeed he did remember Abbott: Abbott arrived in the Hazāra when Qasim Khan was twenty. He told Caroë, "He was a little man with bristly hair on his face and kind eyes, and we loved him. He was hardly any taller than me (old Qasim was not much more than five feet in height!). I was at the *Jirga* when he asked us if we would stand and fight the Sikhs if he stood by us. We swore we would, and there were tears in our eyes, and a tear in Abbott Sahib's eye too. And we did! He was our father, and we were his children. There are no Angrez [English] like Abbott Sahib now."[84]

Qasim Khan's physical description of Abbott is accurate. Living in a small, remote village long before it had electricity or telegraph service, Qasim Khan can scarcely have known that Caroë briefly had some theoretical responsibility for his district, much less believe Caroë had any importance in his daily life. Indeed, as a celebrated centenarian elder, he was far more important in his village than Caroë might ever be, so he had nothing conceivable to gain in inventing or exaggerating this story among his peers for an unknown Englishman passing through his village, where the story he told would be endlessly repeated. Because Qasim Khan told his recollections publicly among his peers, it's clear that his having been with Abbott seventy years before was still regarded as an honor in the Hazāra. Similarly Hubert Watson, a settlement officer in the district, reported twenty years earlier in 1907 that scraps of paper with Abbott's handwriting were being used in the district as talismans of great value.[85]

Analysis of another period indigenous account, this one by a Muslim woman in the Hazāra, indicates that the Hazārawals at the time referred to Abbott simply as "the great man." Without understanding that the words were a reference to Abbott, Honoria Lawrence recorded a tale told by a blind Muslim woman: "A man met me and said 'Mother, why do you weep?' I answered 'Why should I not weep, when wicked men have stolen my child?' He answered, 'Is it not then your child of which notice is given in all our towns? Behold you will find her in the great man's camp. So here I have come [to Abbott's camp] and found my lost child.'"[86] This is a remarkable indigenous account for a number of reasons, including the modalities of the transmission of information of importance throughout populated areas—namely, that a lost child needed to be reunited with her mother, where the child currently was, and that thousands of people throughout the Hazāra were aware of this situation. Apropos of Abbott, the location of the missing child is given as being "in the great man's camp." Clearly this reference to James Abbott went over Honoria Lawrence's head, and she did not make the connection or remark on it. That (combined with the fact that she never intended her private journal to see the light of day) makes it obvious this is not an embellishment of Abbott's position among the people of the Hazāra. Clearly Abbott was referred to in this indigenous account as simply "the great man."

Later British historians like John Kaye sought to weave Abbott into the British narrative of the Paladins as part and parcel of the "respected and paternal British district administrator" narrative.[87] But at the time, Abbott was seen by his peers as exceptional. The later account left by Herbert Edwardes, who was briefly the deputy commissioner of the Hazāra after Abbott's departure,[88] makes clear that his lifestyle and reputation were considered extraordinary: "He ... literally lived among them as their patriarch—an out of door, under tree life. Every man, woman and child in the country knew him personally, and hastened from their occupations to salute him as he came their way. The children especially were his favorites. They used to go to 'Kaka [Uncle] Abbott' whenever their mouths watered for fruit or sugar plums. He spent all his subsistence on the people."[89] From this description, it is obvious that Abbott's life was different from that of not only Edwardes but all the other district officers in the Punjab as well, as Edwardes would not have considered such behavior worth recording had it been the norm. Among all the other Paladins, only Herbert Edwardes and Patrick Vans Agnew are known to have worn local dress. Nicholson, Mackeson, Herbert, Hodson, Robinson, and the three Lawrence brothers demonstrably did not. None of them lived permanently in a tent; Edwardes lived in a fort. Besides Abbott, only Edwardes and Nicholson learned Pashto.

Harold Lee encapsulates the paternal paradigm by noting of Lawrence's Young Men that their "individualist and militarist conceptions of righteous paternalist rule gave a flamboyant and free-wheeling flavour to the early British presence in the Punjab,"⁹⁰ but Abbott was clearly the odd man out. Alone among the district officers, he incurred Dalhousie's disapproval, and Dalhousie constantly urged Henry Lawrence to rein him in. In October 1849, he wrote to Sir John Hobhouse on the Board of Control in London, "I have requested [Lawrence] to pay especial attention to Huzāra. I do not understand and do not like Major Abbott's proceedings there."⁹¹ Dalhousie never wrote about any of the other Paladins to Lawrence or Hobhouse. Edwardes was perhaps closest to Abbott in terms of cultural assimilation, but Edwardes was a zealous Christian evangelist who spent much of his time in missionary work. Edwardes wrote that he hoped his book would "give my countrymen a juster conception of that department of the British-Indian Government which, in the intervals of peace ... sends [the political officer] forth beyond our boundaries to be the pioneer of Christian civilization in lands where Idolatry too often occupies the Temple."⁹²

Honoria Lawrence, the wife of Henry Lawrence, recorded a similar impression of Abbott. She was one of the most remarkable English women to set foot in colonial India. Well-read, perceptive, and highly intelligent, she was intrepid and adventurous, participating in life in India in a way that few British wives did. She was the first British woman to visit the Kashmir, for example, and the first to live in Nepal. As a result, she was an audacious and astute observer of India and British rule, usually much more so than the men around her. Unlike many writers who were aware their words would be published, she was candid and unsparing in her private journals, as she never considered they might become public. Indeed, they did not for seventy years after her death. As did Qasim Khan and Herbert Edwardes, she also noted the patriarchal relationship:

> *Among these people Major Abbott lives as a patriarch. It is delightful to see a British officer loved and respected as he is, and the province he administers, larger than all Wales, so peaceable and prosperous. I do not mean he is perfect, for he has some failings that make it difficult to deal with him officially, and he gives Papa [her husband] more trouble than many a man of not a tenth part the merit. The more so because Papa has so high a regard for him. Abbott is morbidly sensitive, and*

Figure 7.4. This study by British artist John Gantz (1772–1853), "Study of a Fakir" (watercolor over pencil), circa 1850, depicts a Muslim fakir with white robes, staff, and white cap, all garments and accoutrements worn by James Abbott in the Hazāra. Gantz was an East India Company draftsman. (PUBLIC DOMAIN)

has lived so long without coming into contact with other educated minds that he cannot comprehend any view other than his own.[93]

Henry Lawrence, too, saw Abbott as different from the other district officers, responding to one of Dalhousie frequent missives on Abbott on November 5, 1849, that "Abbott lives among them more as a patriarch than as a magistrate.... [T]here are defects in his system, but on the whole, I am satisfied that no other man could, for the present, keep the peace in this country as cheaply as he can."[94] It is noteworthy that Lawrence refers to Abbott's governance as "*his* system," clearly marking his methods as different from the norm.

Honoria Lawrence described his physical appearance at this time almost exactly as Qasim Khan did seventy years later: "He is about forty, small make with eager black eyes and well-marked features. I suppose it is many years since shears or razor approached him, and his hair and beard are silver white. A broad-brimmed white hat, coat and trousers made after the taste of a Hazāra tailor, a spiked staff about seven foot long, and the whole man alive with energy, a remarkably sweet and gentle voice."[95] In addition to the three indigenous voices recorded in chapter 6, these five contemporary accounts, three by his peers (Watson, Edwardes, and Lawrence) and two by Hazārawals in the district at the time (Qasim Khan and the blind Muslim woman), present a remarkable picture of Abbott in the Hazāra. The long untrimmed white hair and beard worn in the style of an Indian fakir rather than a British officer, his long, white, flowing robes, and the broad-brimmed white hat worn by some fakirs (such as those in his own cult following) are strikingly similar to images of Muslim fakirs and mullahs in the frontier region at this time. White garments and turbans continue to mark the mullah in parts of northern Pakistan and southern Afghanistan today. It is unlikely to have been a coincidence with respect to its local cultural significance. Abbott, astute to Muslim culture by this point as few Britons in India were, almost certainly made a conscious choice of white precisely for this religious connotation.

Contemporary British references to him as a patriarch are also striking. None of Lawrence's other Young Men were ever described using this term. In devoutly Christian mid-nineteenth-century British India, his peers would almost certainly have understood and used the word "patriarch" more in its now archaic biblical sense of one of the progenitors of the twelve tribes of Israel, such as Jacob, Isaac, or Abraham, or by extension a person who was the founder and leader of a tradition, such as a large tribe or clan, than in its modern connotation of a man who rules a family. In using the term "patriarch" in referring to Abbott in the Hazāra, they intended the term more in the Old Testament sense to mean a prophetic leader rather than a paterfamilias.

Already by August 1849, Dalhousie was sufficiently concerned about Abbott's reputation as a charismatic leader in the Hazāra to write to Henry Lawrence that Abbott "must not be permitted to set up Hazāra as a small kingdom of his own."[96] In fact he did just that. The Hazārawals called him *Kaka Sahib*, or often just *Kaka* Abbott,[97] literally "Uncle Abbott," but the highest term of genuine affection that rural mountain Pashtuns can bestow.[98] By now Abbott spoke both Pashto and Hindko[99] fluently.

After the war, Abbott immediately embarked on a huge reforestation program to replace the timber cut by the Sikhs, hiring men of the district to plant "tens of thousands" of new trees.[100] He had a disdain for the bureaucratic paperwork of the office:

> *None ever had ... the means of information of all passing in my district that I possessed [by] the intimacy of the relations which had grown up between myself and the people, ere the influx of the paraphernalia of overcivilization had shut the* ruler *up a prisoner in his Kucherry to fabricate for the service of white-ants and cockroaches ... figured statements utterly unreliable instead of having both his ears and his mental faculties at the service of* his people *and of the government he served.*[101]

His use of the words "ruler" and "his people" here in describing his position is telling.

Abbott's last military campaign came in the last days of his reign in the Hazāra. Two East India Company tax agents, a Mr. Carne and Mr. Tapp, came to the Hazāra late in 1852 to study the smuggling of salt into the Punjab.[102] Abbott warned them against proceeding north, as the

CHAPTER 7

Black Mountain borderlands they intended to visit were bad country, and while he could likely travel there unmolested, it would be as dangerous for two unknown British tourists then as it would be today.

They ignored his advice and went north to study the extension of the Company's salt line. They were on their way back south when they were ambushed and murdered by men of the Hassanzai clan of the Yusufzai Pashtuns.[103] The Hassanzai were in no way affected by the salt line, and the crime had nothing to do with Carne and Tapp's official duties. It was simply murder. The crime was actually committed on the tribal land of the Pashtun Turnoulee tribe, who wanted nothing to do with the crime or its consequences, and one of their leaders, a friend of Abbott's named Khan Jehandad, did what he could to assist in the capture of the killers. This in turn led to an escalating blood feud between the Turnoulee and Hassanzai tribes.[104]

The Hassanzai clan elders, bound by *Pashtunwali*, the unwritten Pashtun code of social behavior, were honor bound under the rule of *nanawatey*, or asylum, to protect the killers who sought refuge among them, and they refused to turn over the murderers to the British.[105] Under Dalhousie's policy of retribution, the next step, which became increasingly well choreographed over the next half century, was a punitive expedition against the Hassanzai. To protect his clan from British punishment, which he surely knew was coming, and already at war with the Turnoulee clan, Hassanzai leader Zaman Shah now negotiated a *ghund*, or alliance, with the Muslim sect in the north of the Hazāra that the British called the Hindustani Fanatics.[106] This group came to play an important role in Abbott's life, and their spiritual descendants in the modern Taliban are still leaders in the politics of the region today.

The Hindustani Fanatics, so-called because they originated in India (Hindustan), were a Muslim cult founded by Syed Ahmed Shah of Rai Bareilly.[107] He was killed in 1831, but his movement lived on. Syed Ahmed Shah called his sect the Tariqa-i-Muhammadiyya, or roughly "The Mystical Path of the Prophet." Within the context of the *pirimuridi* (teacher-student) tradition of the transmission of religious knowledge in the region, the militantly purist and superficially anti-Sufist doctrines of the movement represented a startling schism from those of Syed

Ahmed Shah's own teacher, Shah Ismael, whose peaceful group, the al-Muwahhidun (Unitarians) preached tolerance and coexistence.[108]

The British understanding of the movement, which it also referred to as the "Wahhabi Fanatics," was rather simplistic and heterogeneous.[109] The Wahhabi and anti-Sufi labels that British officers applied to the group elided a far more complicated reality. Doctrinally Sufism and Wahhabism (loosely defined as strict Islamic purism) do stand in opposition, but after Syed Ahmed Shah was killed at the Battle of Balakot in 1831, many of his followers were given sanctuary by Akhund Ghaffur,[110] the Akhund of Swat,[111] who is regarded as one of the greatest Sufi *pirs* (teachers) in South Asian history.[112] Syed Ahmed Shah, the "Wahhabist," and Akhund Ghaffur, the Sufi *pir*, were in fact friends.

In 1852, the movement had both allies and enemies in the area around Sitana, and these were highly commutative. Some of its tenets, such as the requirement that local tribesmen marry their daughters at fifteen to the movement's disciples without a bride price, for example, created significant animosity.[113] By allying himself with the Hindustani Fanatics movement, the man responsible for protecting Carne and Tapp's killers, Hassanzai clan leader Zaman Shah, demonstrated again how contextual and permutable tribal relations with other groups could be.

Abbott, who was familiar with the terrain, planned the campaign, building a model of the mountain and briefing the other two column commanders on their respective routes up the mountain.[114] Lieutenant Colonel Robert Napier[115] was in command of the right column; Abbott himself commanded the center column comprised of local indigenous forces, including two companies of "police" and eleven light field guns; and Captain W. W. Davidson, an officer of irregular cavalry, was in command of the left column. An artillery battery of four guns from the 5th Troop of the 1st Brigade of Horse Artillery was attached under the command of Captain Augustine Fitzgerald.[116] In December 1852, the Black Mountain Expedition got underway under the overall command of Lieutenant Colonel Frederick Mackeson, the district commissioner at Peshawar and, as such, technically entitled to command. However, it was Abbott's district, and he resented the intrusion into what he felt should have been handled under his overall command.[117] Some sharp fighting

Chapter 7

Figure 7.5. An 1888 print of Black Mountain looking eastward, with a tributary of the Indus River in the foreground, by an unknown British artist. (BRITISHBATTLES.COM)

occurred on the flanks of Black Mountain on December 29, as the Hassanzais had good defensive positions and knew they were literally fighting for their homes.[118] Abbott and his men met stiff resistance about half way to the summit, where they encountered the main body of about six hundred Hassanzai matchlock men.[119] A lot of musket balls were zipping through the trees, and a number of Abbott's men fell. Instead of continuing straight ahead, he ordered a textbook flanking maneuver and turned the Hassanzai positions, forcing them to retreat.[120] The next three days, December 30 and 31, 1852, and New Year's Day 1853, were spent in carrying out Dalhousie's policy of demolishing all the Hassanzai villages in the region.[121] Zaman Shah was caught and exiled to the Pulki plain, but after four years he was pardoned and his confiscated lands were restored.

On the following day, January 2, 1853, a reduced force with Mackeson in command and Abbott serving as his deputy moved against the Tariqa-i Muhammadiyya (Hindustani Fanatics) position at Kôtla, where they had seized a fort belonging to the Khan of Amb. The British force moved west across the Indus, then proceeded south to the village of Kôtla. An assault force under Abbott's command forded the Indus on the morning of January 7, 1853, and attacked the fort held by the Tariqa-i Muhammadiyya at Kotkai.[122] The garrison, estimated at between two hundred and three hundred men, retreated without firing a shot. The troops of the Khan of Amb pursued them, killing thirty.[123] British casualties for the entire campaign numbered fifteen dead or wounded.[124] The Tariqa-i Muhammadiyya camp at Sitana was destroyed, but the inhabitants were already gone. Abbott was in favor of pressing on to capture or kill them all, but Mackeson was content to call it a day, so the British force retired south. It was the last battle of Abbott's life.

Abbott was right again: Mackeson left the mission half done, and conflict with the Tariqa-i Muhammadiyya lasted another fifty years. It may also have cost Mackeson his life. Nine months after the Battle of Kotkai, on September 10, 1853, he was stabbed in the chest while sitting on his verandah in Peshawar by a man described by the British as a "Muslim religious fanatic," and he died thirty hours later. The killer came from Swat and may have been affiliated with Tariqa-i Muhammadiyya.[125] He was never identified.

Lord Dalhousie took a typical view of the Black Mountain Expedition. On November 20, 1852, he first noted the disturbance: "There is a vagabond in Hazārah bumptious, but it will be nothing serious," he wrote to Couper.[126] After the campaign Dalhousie reiterated his policy in another letter to Couper: "In Hazārah the row I told you of is over. . . . Mackeson drove the rebel into the snow, when, finding it uncomfortable, he surrendered. So that is over, and well done."[127]

Henry Lawrence's philosophy of administration on the Northwest Frontier, as it came to be known, was always in stark opposition to Dalhousie's.[128] Lawrence championed, as had Charles Metcalfe, John Malcolm, Mountstuart Elphinstone, and Thomas Munro before him,[129] a culturally sensitive approach of local self-administration that respected the people and their traditions as the easiest, least expensive, and most efficient means of keeping the peace and collecting the taxes. James Abbott was also an adherent of this school of thought, as were all of Lawrence's other Young Men. Abbott and Henry Lawrence saw eye to eye on almost everything,

CHAPTER 7

and indeed by 1853, they had been good friends for thirty years. They had studied together at Addiscombe, marched together to Kandahar, surveyed adjoining districts as survey team leaders, shared a love of poetry and Sir Walter Scott, and even started a literary magazine together. Certainly Abbott could be vexing at times, submitting the bare minimum of official paperwork and sometimes not even that, for which he was on occasion chastised. But Lawrence was a statesman and knew how to lead and motivate Abbott without confrontation. The two men never had a serious contretemps, as Abbott had, for example, with Currie. As long as Lawrence was in the Punjab, he ran interference with the authorities in Calcutta for his friend and tolerated Abbott's growing eccentricity.

Lawrence was publicly less tolerant of several of his other subordinates in the Punjab. Herbert Edwardes he openly criticized. Edwardes, Lawrence noted in a letter to Currie, "did not give [Gulab Singh] much reason to admire the presence of Politicals.... [H]e seemed to have taken him to book in a domineering if not positively offensive manner.... [T]he worst of his case is that he sticks offensively to his own opinions."[130] Lawrence was similarly harsh in his criticism of another district officer, Robert Cust in Ambala, calling him "more disliked by the people than any other District Officer."[131] The British settlement officer outside Rawalpindi in Kallar, Mr. Carnac, too, got the sharp side of Lawrence's pen: in February 1852 Lawrence found Carnac "ensconced in the upper room of a fort making his settlement instead of being in a tent in the midst of the people."[132] In the midst of the people was just where he found Abbott two weeks later in the Hazāra. "After all the screeching [in Rawalpindi]," Lawrence wrote to James Thomason, the Lieutenant Governor of the Northwest Provinces, "it was pleasant... to enter Hazāra and find Abbott looked on as a protector instead of a mere tax gatherer."[133] Thus Lawrence was not in the business of myth making about those who worked for him, and many, if not most, of the Paladins came in for a dose of his criticism from time to time. Any imputation that Lawrence conspired with Dalhousie to effect Abbott's removal from the Hazāra, as Harold Lee has suggested, for example, is simply wrong.[134] Henry Lawrence remained faithful to his friend James Abbott throughout his life, and there is no archival evidence to the contrary.

In point of fact, Lawrence was forced out of the Punjab before Abbott was. By 1852, Henry and his younger brother John were at loggerheads. They worked side by side, but their relationship had been increasingly antagonistic for several years, as their views on administering the Punjab became almost diametrically opposed. It was clear by 1852 that one of them had to go. Henry wanted to stay. Dalhousie offered either one of them the plum position of Resident at Hyderabad and adroitly maneuvered Henry into making a halfhearted suggestion in December 1852 that he would be willing to go. Dalhousie pounced on the suggestion, accepted it as Henry's resignation, then, opprobrious to the last, switched the job offered to that of Resident at Rajputana, a far less desirable and less well-paid position.

In January 1853, Abbott's friend John Nicholson received a letter from Henry Lawrence informing him that Lawrence was leaving the Punjab for Rajputana. Abbott's disfavor in Calcutta as a result of his eccentric rule in Hazāra was no secret to the other Paladins. Nicholson wrote back to Lawrence expressing a desire to work for him in Rajputana and adding astutely, "I am afraid poor little Abbott will soon be driven out" of the Punjab as well.[135] And so he was. On February 7, 1853, Henry Lawrence left the Punjab. Without Lawrence in Lahore as Abbott's guardian angel, Dalhousie lost no time in removing the King of Hazāra.[136] At this juncture in his life, Abbott bears a remarkable similarity to a figure in literature, Joseph Conrad's character Kurtz in *Heart of Darkness*. Like Kurtz, Abbott had been sent as an agent for his colonial company to its remotest outpost in the jungle. Both men became all powerful and even worshipped among the indigenous people in the process. Both were profoundly changed by the primitivism of the wilderness. Both Abbott and Kurtz were colonial petite bourgeoisie who were transformed for a short time into kings. Conrad wrote that because Kurtz's father was half French and his mother was half English, "all Europe went into the making of Kurtz."[137] So too, surely, did all of European mercantilism go into the making of James Abbott, whose father was mostly of Armenian, Italian, and Greek heritage and whose mother was Scottish.

Conrad wrote of Kurtz that after his arrival in his remote station, his "ascendancy was extraordinary. The camps of these people surrounded the place, and the chiefs came every day to see him" and added that "they adored him."[138] Both British and indigenous eyewitnesses in this period of Abbott's life are explicit in observing the same about him. Both men, significantly, were poets. At one point in his narrative, Conrad has the Russian harlequin say of Kurtz, "You ought to have heard him recite poetry—his own too it was, he told me! Poetry! Oh, he enlarged my mind."[139] This idea of expanded consciousness suggests that Kurtz possessed the knowledge of the arcane and mystical—or that of a Muslim mystic, as the Hazārawals saw Abbott, a man "with a heart like a fakir's."[140]

The change wrought on the colonizer by the colony, rather than vice versa, was Conrad's central point in *Heart of Darkness*. Conrad wrote that Kurtz's "soul was mad. Being alone in the wilderness, it had looked within itself, and ... it had gone mad."[141] Conrad specifically says it was not his mind but his *soul* that went mad. Kurtz was not literally insane but spiritually deranged as a result of exposure to the wilderness of the colonies, a metaphor for all of European colonialism. Abbott, too, was profoundly changed by his experience in the wilds of Hazāra. In the wilderness around him he saw plots and "combinations" everywhere. For a short time in 1851, the officer of the Madras Artillery, Lieutenant George Pearse, observed Abbott in the Hazāra and saw this slide into paranoia. In addition to identifying Abbott as a deity of the Nicholseynites noted earlier, Pearse later gently said of Abbott, "He lived in a world of plot and kept many spies."[142] Certainly walking around the wild lands at the farthest limits of British influence with a seven-foot staff, flowing white robes, a white hat the size of a sombrero, long flowing white hair, and a long white beard was considered eccentric, to say the least.

In the latter half of 1852, Abbott's suspicions of plots caused him to take into custody—or to take hostage, depending on one's point of view—and confine several chiefs from the Khagan region under a kind of permanent house arrest, from which they eventually escaped and complained to Frederick Mackeson in Peshawar. This was not putting heads on poles, as Kurtz did, but arrest without charge and indefinite detention without trial were not in the British legal canon. As with Kurtz, despite his extraordinary and unprecedented success at his remote station, Abbott's methods had also become "unsound," and he had to be removed.[143] His monarchical rule in the Hazāra and his eccentricity were too much for the aristocratic Dalhousie, who already disliked him for his "ungentlemanly" behavior. A trivial disagreement with Mackeson after the expedition against the Hindustani Fanatics provided the pretext for Abbott's transfer. By March 1853, Captain Herbert Edwardes had orders to relieve Abbott at Hazāra, and Abbott was on his way out.

Before he left, Abbott did something else extraordinary. He took most of his life savings and threw a party for three days and three nights for the entire populace of the Hazāra.[144] According to Edwardes, "His last act was to invite all the country—not the neighbors, but all Hazāra—to a farewell feast on the Nara Hill; and there for three days and nights he might be seen walking among the groups of guests and hecatombs[145] of pots and cauldrons—the kind and courteous host of a whole people."[146] As many as fifty thousand people came to see him off. When the party was over, he rode his horse to the border of the Hazāra accompanied, like Kurtz followed by the people of the jungle who wanted him to stay, by a multitude of wailing and crying Hazārawals, and never returned.[147] After he left, Herbert Edwardes named the village growing up on the spot that had been Abbott's base camp Abbottabad. It remains one of only two towns in all of formerly British India still named for a Briton.[148]

8

Endings

1854–1896

When James Abbott left the Punjab in the fall of 1854, almost half his life remained before him, but the part for which he would be remembered was largely over. The Honourable East India Company, at the ripe old age of 254, had less than four years left in control of India, although few guessed it at the time. Abbott still had one great adventure before him: he would play a key role in preventing the Great Mutiny of 1857 from beginning in Calcutta.

When he left the Hazāra, Abbott was at last out of debt, and after the farewell party he had £1,200 left in savings.[1] Considering that he had now been on active service for thirty years, it was not an overly large sum.[2] He applied for a furlough to go to England, but his account book for the Black Mountain campaign had not been forwarded by Frederick Mackeson to Calcutta before the district commissioner was murdered, and the regulations stipulated that no officer could go on leave with any financial ledgers still open. For six months, from May to October 1854, he remained in the Punjab, repairing and replacing boundary markers from Shahpoor to the Jhelum. He visited his brother Saunders, who, despite the grapeshot still in his shoulder from Ferozepore, was now the deputy commissioner at Hashiarpoor. James traveled with Saunders and his wife to Dhurmsālā, a hill sanatorium near Kôt Kāngra.

While he was waiting for permission to go on leave to England, an event occurred that, perhaps more than any other, demonstrates his genuine devotion and dedication to his indigenous friends. Fourteen years earlier, on the shore of the Caspian, he had been rescued from slavery among the Kazakhs and Turkmens by the remarkable Afghan Saleh Mohammed. They kept in touch with letters, and in 1848, Saleh Mohammed traveled from Kandahar to Hazāra to be with Abbott during the Second Anglo-Sikh War. Saleh Mohammed had spent many of the years since they met working for the British, but in 1854, in exile from Herat, he was in poor health and destitute. Abbott badly wanted to go to England to see his elderly and ailing mother again before she died, but his friendship and his debt to Saleh Mohammed outweighed that. Abbott immediately gave him £400, a third of his savings, equivalent in 2021 to almost £40,000. Instead of going to England, he took leave to procure a British pension for Saleh Mohammed for his services to the East India Company. As a result of Abbott's petition, his Afghan friend was granted an annual pension of £180 for life, equivalent to about £17,200 per year in 2021. It was larger than Abbott's good service and wound pensions combined would garner upon his own retirement.[3] Their friendship continued for many years, during which Saleh Mohammed often visited Abbott for long talks, which sometimes went on far into the night.

On one occasion, Saleh Mohammed came to see Abbott in Delhi in 1860 with an interesting request:

> *He was very anxious to become a Freemason. . . . He said that a Freemason acquired a sudden enlightenment which the toil of a man's life could not supply. I assured him that on the contrary, some of the greatest blockheads of my acquaintance were Freemasons and had certainly learnt nothing worth knowing. He would not believe this. He said a Persian [he knew] had become a Freemason and had at once relinquished his daily prayers and all other forms of religion . . . and had declared that he has been set free from all such burdens by the marvelous light shed in upon his mind in the Feramôsh Khana—The house of oblivion—For Persians of course suppose the word Freemason to be their word Feramôsh (forgetful). . . . There was however no lodge at Delhi so that he could not here be indoctrinated.*[4]

CHAPTER 8

In October 1854, Abbott traveled to Calcutta, where he met with Governor-General Lord Dalhousie, who "showed me much kind attention and kept me in conversation whenever he met me upon subjects familiar to my experience. The Russian war[5] was then threatening, and my knowledge of the countries between Russia and our Indian frontier was often consulted."[6] Dalhousie was the man most responsible for Abbott's going unrecognized and unrewarded for his actions in Hazāra, but Abbott never knew this. While in Calcutta, he was assigned as the assistant to the agent for the Saugor and Narbudda Territories, an area seized from the Marathas at the conclusion of the Third Anglo-Maratha War in 1818.[7] On November 28, 1854, he was promoted to lieutenant colonel.[8] Abbott remained in Calcutta for eight months until Herbert Edwardes, now reassigned from Hazāra to Peshawar to replace the murdered Frederick Mackeson, discovered Abbott's account book for the Black Mountain campaign in Mackeson's office "thrown carelessly into one of his private drawers."[9]

Living in Calcutta cost Abbott twice his monthly salary, even with his thrifty lifestyle, which was a further drain on his modest savings. In the spring of 1855, before Abbott left Calcutta for Saugor and Narbudda, Dalhousie offered him instead a transfer from political work to a position Abbott had once expressed an interest in: Superintendent of the East India Company's Gunpowder Agency at Ishapoor.[10] After some consideration, he accepted the position but later regretted it: "My mind wanted repose after all the wear and anxiety it had gone through. But my decision proved a mistake, and I regard the ... years I spent at Ishapoor as the dullest blank in my life."[11] Nevertheless, the decision may also have saved his life. The Saugor and Narbudda region was a center of rebellion during the Mutiny of 1857, and a number of British officers were slain there.[12]

The assignment to the gunpowder works, which supplied all the gunpowder to the Bengal Army, has been wrongly interpreted as a kind of exile or punishment for his disputes with his superiors. Abbott had already been assigned to another political position at Saugor and Narbudda, however, and chose this new position over that one. The superintendent's position was boring, certainly, in comparison to political work, but it was a well-regarded and well-compensated assignment. Abbott's predecessor in the job was a full colonel, and his successor was none other than the celebrated Victorian hero Sir Vincent Eyre, who survived the retreat from Kabul during the First Anglo-Afghan War as a hostage and became a household name during the Great Mutiny. Thus the superintendence of the gunpowder works was not a kind of political Devil's Island for officers in exile but a very respectable position. Nevertheless Abbott left an assignment in the political service to accept it and was never able to get back in.

Taking up his new assignment at Ishapoor in the spring of 1855, he set to work with the same conscientious energy and professionalism he demonstrated in all his other assignments. Abbott experimented with the formula and process for producing the gunpowder, which was generally inferior to European explosives, and after getting the necessary permission, he made several improvements to its explosive power. He made a point of inspecting the interior of at least one of the forty work sheds at the facility every day for three years, sleeping away from the factory only one night during that period—and that night was a result of official duty, not personal time off.[13] Prior to his arrival, the facility averaged one accidental explosion every fifteen months; while Abbott was there, there were none.[14] Two weeks after he left, another major explosion rocked the works.

He seems to have missed being surrounded by people in Hazāra. He recalled in 1880 that apart from an occasional visitor, this was an isolated time in his life. "My position was very lonely, for being three miles from the nearest station, not many would take the trouble to call upon a lonely widower."[15] It is Abbott's observations of the state of the Bengal Army and his views of the causes of the Great Mutiny of 1857 that make these three years of his life of historical interest in particular. His service in the vicinity of Calcutta from 1855 to 1858 also sheds interesting light on the plots by sepoys to take Fort William, an aspect of the Mutiny not often reflected in the voluminous literature on the events of 1857. These occurred before the outbreaks of mutiny in Meerut and elsewhere, and had the sepoys been successful in provoking a general rising in Calcutta, the history of the Mutiny might have been different.

In February 1856, Dalhousie was replaced as governor-general by Lord Canning. Abbott spent the year at the gunpowder works. For

Chapter 8

several months at the end of 1856, grassroots unease among the sepoys of the Bengal Army over the nature of impregnated paper cartridges for the new Enfield rifle had been spreading. The experimental all-in-one ammunition packets, which contained both powder and shot, felt stiff and waxy. The round paper packet was to be torn open during the loading drill to pour the powder inside down the muzzle of the rifle, followed by the bullet, which was inside at the bottom of the packet. Initially the loading procedure called for this to be done by tearing the cartridge open with one's teeth. It was rumored among the sepoys that the manufacturing process of the packets involved tallow derived from cows or pigs, biting into which would be defiling to Hindus and Muslims, respectively. Following alerts to the issue by a number of officers, steps were taken to ensure the manufacturing process was pure, and no improper cartridges were ever issued. As a further palliative, the loading-drill procedure was amended to tearing the new cartridges open with one's fingers instead, so that even if the cartridges were impure, which they were not, the contact would not be polluting or defiling. Although there were local misjudgments, the problem overall at the strategic level was by no means mishandled. But it was a rare issue that could incite both Muslim and Hindu sepoys alike, and as such it was ideal for pernicious disinformation by agitators. Whether the concerns were genuine or not may be judged by the fact that captured stocks of the new cartridges were later used with alacrity by the rebelling sepoys against British forces during the Mutiny.

On the night of January 24, 1857, the first sepoy plot to capture Fort William unfolded. Abbott recorded that the telegraph office at the main sepoy barracks at Barrackpore was burned to the ground. Arson of military buildings at this time appears to have been widespread and underreported. The next day, a *havildar* (native sergeant) of the guard at Fort William reported a conversation he heard in the barracks washroom between two sepoys that there was to be a mutiny that night to seize the arsenal and take over the fort. The British detachment at the fort consisted of some two hundred men whose arms were stored in the armory, and the nearest reinforcements for Fort William were at Barrackpore, sixteen miles away. In the event of an emergency, they would have been called for by telegraph, now prevented by the suspected arson at Barrackpore. Countermeasures were taken immediately at the fort and the plot failed.[16] News of it was initially suppressed. An Englishwoman at Gwalior, Mrs. R. M. Coopland, noted, "Things had been kept so quiet that we did not hear of the first disturbances at Barrackpore . . . till the middle of February."[17]

During this period, Abbott remained obsessed with plots and conspiracies and was on a kind of personal high alert. By January 1857 there was a widespread sense among British officers that all was not well with the Bengal Army, so Abbott was not alone in his concern, although few Britons anticipated a widespread sepoy rebellion. Abbott was never the type to be passive about his suspicions. Throughout 1856 and early 1857, he still employed his own private spies, a habit retained from Hazāra. Early in 1856, on his daily three-mile ride from Ishapoor to Barrackpore, he observed considerable activity around a small shrine to Shiva where "the excitement was at times so great that once I sent my groom to enquire what it was about, but the . . . man could not get me information, and not being aware [at that time] of any agitation in the native army, I did not think it worthwhile to press the enquiry farther."[18] A year later, however, after the plot at Barrackpore, Abbott wrote, "It struck me that information of its nature might be obtained at this place of assembly, and . . . I sent there occasionally an agent in disguise."[19] He also took aside the *jemadar* (native officer) of his forty-man sepoy guard detachment at the gunpowder works and spoke with him privately. Despite what Abbott noted as *bhae-bundee* (brotherhood among soldiers),

> *The old careworn native officer confessed to me . . . that he feared something was wrong in the Army. . . . [A]ll kinds of rumors were circulated, no one knew how. . . . The night after the combustion of the telegraphic bungalow [at Barrackpore] he had been called up by some men of the regiment who desired him to be on the alert, as news was expected. . . . [H]e and others had sat up accordingly. . . . [M]essengers were going to and fro and men talked in whispers. At length someone had come into their hut . . . and said that nothing would be done that night, on which they had all dispersed to their houses.*[20]

Chapter 8

Abbott immediately reported this intelligence to the officer commanding at Barrackpore, General John Hearsey. The *jemadar* was sent to Hearsey, who disregarded Abbott's plea that the man be interviewed in private and interrogated him publicly in the presence of a half dozen native orderlies.[21] "This was not the way to encourage men to come forward with information," Abbott noted with understatement.[22] Abbott's informant, Jemadar Durriow, told Hearsey about the midnight meeting, noting specifically that the British officers were to be killed. Durriow identified the men he knew at the meeting but indicated that most had covered their faces with cloth masks "leaving only a small part of their faces exposed."[23] Durriow was terrified by the interview and subsequently went into the hospital with real or feigned insanity.

British control over the Bengal Army was beginning to unravel. The 34th Bengal Native Infantry (BNI) regiment at Barrackpore was due to relieve the 19th BNI at Berhampur. On February 24, a typical advance party of the 34th went up to Berhampur to plan for the transition. The men of the two regiments mingled with the usual comradeship of such meetings. On February 26, sepoys of the 19th BNI at Berhampur refused to accept any cartridges of any type to perform firing drills. The officers of the 19th wisely decided not to press the matter. In early March, the 19th BNI, now seen as a deeply troubled unit, was marched toward Barrackpore. The advance party of the 34th was later implicated as a source of their discontent.

In March 1857 another plot to seize Fort William was discovered. A subedar of the 34th BNI led a plan to bring three companies of the 34th down the Hooghly River in boats to Cooli Bazaar just below Fort William. The three companies involved formed the guard detachment of the lieutenant governor. The plan called for the remaining companies of the 34th at Barrackpore to rise, murder their British officers, and then march to Fort William to rendezvous with the three companies arriving by boat. The plot fell apart when the lieutenant governor's schedule changed, and he and his three mutinous guard companies went elsewhere. The plot was uncovered, and the ringleader was sentenced to deportation. James's brother Augustus, then inspector general of ordnance in Calcutta, remarked, "The presence of a goose had saved Rome;

the absence of a gander, Calcutta."[24] The 34th BNI, however, had still more malcontents.

The disgraced 19th BNI was now en route south to Barrackpore. Two days before it arrived, on the afternoon of March 29, 1857, a Hindu sepoy of seven years' service in the 34th BNI named Mangal Pandey went berserk at Barrackpore, possibly while high on *bhang*.[25] Pandey marched up and down in front of the guardroom, shouting to his comrades to join him, and vowing to shoot the first British officer he saw. If he wasn't on drugs, he was a bad marksman. He shot at and missed at close range both of the first two Britons on the scene, Sergeant Major James Hewson and Lieutenant Henry Baugh. He managed to hit Baugh's horse, bringing down horse and rider. Hewson ordered the *jemadar* of the guard to seize Pandey. He refused. Hewson was then struck from behind by a musket butt and went down. Pandey drew his tulwar. In the ensuing melee, Hewson, Baugh, and Muslim sepoy Shaikh Paltu, who went to Baugh's aid, were all wounded by Pandey's sword. Paltu courageously attacked Pandey barehanded and wrestled with him despite death threats from the guards, keeping him away from the wounded Hewson and Baugh. All three wounded men had stumbled back a short distance while Pandey was reloading when General Hearsey himself rode up. Pandey took aim at Hearsey, changed his mind, and, in his last mortal act of poor marksmanship, tried to shoot himself. He missed that shot, too, the bullet from his rifle just grazing his chest and setting fire to his tunic. He was arrested and sent to the hospital under guard.

Two days later, on March 31, following deliberations by a formal court of inquiry into the refusal of the 19th BNI to accept orders while at Berhampur, that regiment was disbanded. Its men were permitted to keep their uniforms and given an allowance for their travel back to their homes.

Pandey was patched up, interrogated, and brought before a general court-martial presided over by Subedar Major Jowahir Lall Tewary and a jury of fourteen indigenous officers. During both his interrogation and his trial, he largely remained silent, saying only that he had taken *bhang* recently and had acted alone. He was sentenced to death. At dawn on April 8, Abbott, who came under the military authority of General Hearsey at Barrackpore, witnessed Pandey's execution: "It seemed very uncertain, whether the rebels would suffer their champion to be hanged without a struggle. The sentence, however, was carried out without disturbance. The wing[26] of the 34th B.N.I. to which Mangal Pandey had belonged was disbanded, being first disarmed, and the men . . . were allowed to go free and spread the mutiny far and wide."[27]

In late March 1857, Abbott imagined a conspiracy involving the Maharaja of Gwalior, who happened to visit Calcutta at that time. Abbott was convinced the timing was more than a coincidence, and he tried unsuccessfully to convince the governor-general, Lord Canning, that the maharaja's plan for a large outdoor party was nefarious. He was more successful in convincing Canning of the need to muzzle the press, and his argument that the Indian press was being used for sedition and the Anglo-Indian press was inadvertently leaking military secrets eventually led Canning to issue Act XV of June 13, 1857, the so-called Gagging Act, which applied equally to both indigenous and Anglo-Indian publishers, "much to the disgust of the latter."[28]

On April 21, Jemadar Ishwari Prasad, the native officer who had refused Hewson's order to seize Mangal Pandey, was also hanged.[29] Hewson and Baugh recovered from their wounds. Sepoy Shaikh Paltu was promoted to *havildar* (sergeant) on the spot by Hearsey and subsequently to *jemadar*, but he was murdered in the Barrackpore cantonment in early May.[30] On May 4, the remainder of the 34th was disbanded.[31] Six weeks after the Pandey incident, on May 10, 1857, the sepoy garrison at Meerut, 930 miles northwest of Calcutta, mutinied. There was no apparent connection to Mangal Pandey, and none of the Meerut sepoys who were subsequently captured and interrogated mentioned him.[32] Meerut is generally considered to be the starting point of the Great Mutiny of 1857, which raged in North-Central India that summer, although disaffection at Barrackpore in the 34th BNI was clearly just as bad. Most of the Meerut mutineers made for Delhi, with a vague plan of reinstating the Mughal emperor to rule India, but from the start there was no coherent political strategy among the mutineers. The events that followed are a contentious subject to say the least. As Thomas Metcalf notes, "The events of 1857 have long been the subject of bitter controversy, and have provoked more impassioned literature than any other single event in Indian history."[33]

The Bengal Army did not mutiny all at once; nor did the mutiny spread outward from the first outbreak of violence in Meerut in a predictable wave. Rather, individual regiments mutinied randomly, without any discernible pattern or obvious temporal connections, throughout the summer across the north-central region of the country, known as the Gangetic Plain. This lack of coherence factors heavily in the history of the events. The mutineers were overwhelmingly upper-caste Hindus and Rajputs recruited from the Gangetic Plain, including a large concentration of men from Oudh, the province annexed by Dalhousie in 1856 under his Doctrine of Lapse.

The local pattern of mutiny was all too common, and the particulars were often grisly. Mutinying regiments frequently massacred their officers, the officers' families, and any European civilians they found. Within Bengal, some regiments did remain loyal, but the majority, including fifty-four of the seventy-five regular native infantry regiments (72 percent), all ten regular native cavalry regiments, and the bulk of the irregular forces, both cavalry and infantry, mutinied. All of those regiments in the Bengal Army comprised predominantly of Gurkhas, Sikhs, and Punjabis, however, remained loyal, as did virtually the entire Madras and Bombay armies, which has served ever since as a kind of academic firewall against more provocative interpretations of the Mutiny by Indian nationalists seeking to portray it as a war of national independence. As Rudrangshu Mukherjee notes of Mangal Pandey, however, the mutineers "had no notion of patriotism or even India."[34]

Abbott personally played no direct role in the suppression of the Mutiny, but Calcutta in the summer of 1857 was in a state of near panic.[35] British civilians, men and women alike, were arming themselves in anticipation of the mutiny reaching the city. Gun sellers did a brisk business, and women's learning to shoot briefly became the height of fashion. Abbott remained at his post as superintendent of the gunpowder works until he was transferred on April 1, 1858. The closest he came to being a casualty of the Mutiny occurred when he was teaching a young woman, at her insistence, how to use a pistol. The woman accidently pulled the

Figure 8.1. Hand-tinted portrait photograph of James Abbott as a major in full dress artillery uniform, circa 1854, by an unknown photographer, probably in Delhi. (BRITISH LIBRARY BOARD)

trigger at the wrong time, and the bullet passed through Abbott's clothes. Once again his remarkable luck saved him.

Shortly after his change of command at Ishapoor, Abbott was ordered to march a company of European artillery recruits up country from Calcutta to Meerut, which he did from April to June 1858.[36] Technically, this might have entitled him to the Indian Mutiny Medal, as the route of march traversed the area around Delhi where mopping-up operations were taking place. However, he was not awarded the medal, even under the expanded criteria established in 1868, and his name does not appear on the official list of recipients, strong evidence that he was not engaged in any hostilities against the rebels.[37] The city of Delhi had long since been recaptured from the mutineers on September 21, 1857. Abbott's friend and comrade in arms from the Hazāra campaigns and the Second Anglo-Sikh War, John Nicholson, was wounded leading the final assault on Delhi and died of his wounds two days later. The city of Lucknow, where his friend Henry Lawrence was killed early in the siege, was recaptured in March 1858. The last organized force of mutineers was defeated in Gwalior on June 20, 1858, a hint perhaps that Abbott's suspicions about the Maharaja of Gwalior before the outbreak of the Mutiny may not have been entirely unfounded. On July 8, 1858, a proclamation was made, and the rebellion officially ended, although antiguerilla operations continued for some time against small bands of former sepoys roving the countryside as partisans or bandits, depending on one's point of view. During the Mutiny, the Punjab largely remained quiet. A Rajput leader in Sahiwal, southwest of Lahore, named Ahmad Khan Kharral led a short-lived insurrection, one sepoy regiment stationed at Ferozepur and three sepoy regiments in Jullundur mutinied and headed to Delhi, and there were small acts of resistance in Rawalpindi, Jhelum, and Sialkot. But overall, the Punjab was a bulwark of resistance to the Mutiny.[38] The Hazāra District remained completely peaceful and loyal to the British.

The Mutiny changed British India forever. It is also the terminus of the evolution of Abbott's perceptions of India and its people. The shock wave that struck North-Central India in the summer of 1857 continued to reverberate for decades and "touched off the most traumatic experience of Britain's imperial century."[39] In the unprecedented enormity of

CHAPTER 8

the violence, in its sheer incomprehensible brutality, and in the sense that the known order of things had changed forever, 1857 had an effect on the Victorian mind not dissimilar to that which the events of September 11, 2001, have on the modern American mind. The Great Mutiny, as it came to be known in British history, profoundly changed not only British policy toward India and affected policy toward the remainder of the empire but also contributed to the reshaping of British public opinion toward the non-Anglo-Saxon world in general, "a watershed for the British in India, and indeed for British Imperialism."[40]

It would be difficult to overstate the enormity of the impact the mutiny had on British consciousness, both in India and the metropole. In 1857, at the garrisons at Jhansi, Meerut, Cawnpore, and many smaller stations, not only British soldiers but British women, children, and civilian

THE BRITISH LION'S VENGEANCE ON THE BENGAL TIGER.

Figure 8.2. The *Punch* cartoon "The British Lion's Vengeance on the Bengal Tiger," from August 22, 1857, was subsequently made into a popular print. It launched the career of the artist, John Tenniel, who later illustrated *Alice's Adventures in Wonderland*. The cartoon received international attention, causing the *New York Times* to remark in September 1857 that the image was "emblematic of a near universal British desire for revenge." (PUNCH MAGAZINE, AUGUST 22, 1857)

personnel were slaughtered in cold blood by the sepoys. The mass murders at Cawnpore, where British women and children were hacked apart en masse with butcher knives and thrown, often while still alive, down a stone well in the Cawnpore bazaar, were then, and are still, particularly shocking.[41] "Cawnpore Well" remained a popular tattoo among British troops in India and Burma throughout World War II. These killings literally stunned the British public at home. Victorian "Prince of Preachers" Charles Spurgeon called Hindus "a mass of the rankest filth that ever imagination could have conceived" in a sermon to twenty-five thousand followers at the Crystal Palace and urged a national "crusade" to kill them "by their thousands."[42]

In India itself, the atrocities not infrequently drove British soldiers and civil servants who visited Cawnpore temporarily insane, "almost hysterical with rage and pity."[43] A contemporary witness, Viscount Garnet Wolseley, wrote, "A more sickening, a more maddening sight no Englishman has ever looked upon.... [A]n all absorbing craving for ruthless vengeance ... was deep in all hearts."[44] The mass murder of women and children could scarcely have been more calculated to inflame Victorian sentiment. As Metcalf notes, "Nothing could arouse such a frenzy of hatred in the Victorian Englishman as to see his womenfolk, so long safe from foreign invaders and hedged round by sentiment and chivalry, hacked to pieces by barbarous ruffians."[45] Christopher Hibbert adds, "For the mid-nineteenth century British mind this ruthless murder of women and children was a crime of unspeakable, blasphemous enormity. Englishmen regarded women in a light quite different from that in which Indians did, as creatures not merely of another sex but almost ... of another form of creation, as in T.X. Huxley's phrase, 'angels above them.'"[46] Interestingly, although Abbott's own perception of women fits into Huxley's description, there is no mention anywhere in his writing of the massacres and atrocities. Most Britons reacted with a sense of betrayal tinged with racism. It was beyond comprehension that Indians could be so vicious in their faithlessness to the people who, the British believed, had spent compassionate generations helping them. As Metcalf notes, Victorians at home "simply could not conceive of anyone consciously rejecting the benefits of British rule. Indeed they were at a loss to account for the uprising at all, except on the

CHAPTER 8

Figure 8.3. The massacre of British survivors of the siege of the Cawnpore garrison at the ghats (boat docks) on the Ganges River on June 27, 1857, depicted in a tinted lithograph by T. Packer, published by Stannard and Dixon of London in October 1857. About two hundred survivors of this incident, almost all women and children, were subsequently hacked to death with a meat cleaver in the infamous Bibighar (House of the Ladies) or Cawnpore Well Massacre on July 15, 1857. (NATIONAL ARMY MUSEUM)

ground that the Indian people were ignorant and credulous, like savages or children."[47]

The suppression of the uprising was grim work. British bloodthirstiness in its prosecution was no less than that of the mutineers, but they harmed no women or children deliberately. The military campaign of subduing the Mutiny might best be described as methodical and relentless, but the stoicism of British military and civilian personnel in many locations became a foundational trope for the British narrative of events that followed. Many of Abbott's former comrades in arms from the Punjab, including Henry Lawrence, John Nicholson, William Hodson, and Harry Lumsden, became household names in England as a result of the Mutiny. All of them except Lumsden were killed in the fighting.

An event of such enormity naturally triggered comprehensive investigations. The effects of the initial investigations and historical representations were immediate and profound. In the words of Percival Spear, "The Mutiny was the swan song of old India."[48] It was also the swan song of much of pre-Mutiny British policy in India, and it brought about a broad and deep set of policy changes. The first of these was the dissolution of the British East India Company. On November 1, 1858, a proclamation was read throughout British India to the effect that East India Company rule was abolished, and the British government would now rule India directly.[49] Determined to prevent the events of 1857–1858 from ever happening again, the ratio of British to indigenous troops was reset at 1:2, a major shift from the pre-Mutiny levels of 1:5 (or 1:6 when irregulars were counted). All artillery was placed in European hands, and changes were made to the ethnic and caste compositions of sepoy and *sowar* regiments to reduce the spread of potential future agitation.

More serious was the tectonic shift in relations between Britons and the peoples of India. As Abbott's journals illustrate, relations between the indigenous population and British military personnel had been steadily deteriorating in the three decades prior to the Mutiny. After the Mutiny, however, contact between them was virtually eliminated. As Byron Farwell notes, "The mutiny swept away what little social intercourse was left between Briton and Indian. Friendliness and hospitality became unnaturally strained or nonexistent. The knowledge of ways of life and ways of thinking which come with familiar daily intercourse disappeared."[50] More importantly, the way the people of India were viewed changed fundamentally. "The most important result of the Mutiny-Rebellion was the addition of hatred to indifference in the British attitude towards Indians," Ronald Hyam writes. "The 'mild Hindu' stereotype was replaced by a belief in his deceptiveness and cruelty."[51] These are almost the exact words Abbott used in 1880 to describe Hindus as a "race . . . proverbial for deceit and treachery."[52]

At the same time, the policy of "reforming" Indian institutions was largely reversed, and "religious and social reform came to an abrupt halt."[53] From a policy of reform intended to "civilize" the peoples of India through efficient administration, gradual annexation of the princely states, and

CHAPTER 8

ongoing legal and land reforms, conservatism immediately became the philosophy of governance. In Oudh, the large-scale *taluqdars* went almost literally overnight from being the enemy of progress to the heart of civil society. Land reforms in Oudh were reversed, and most landowners had their property restored in exchange for oaths of loyalty.

Finally, the mutiny and its interpretations helped shape British policies in other, more subtle ways. In concluding from the Mutiny that Indian society was conservative and best left as found, for example, Britain began to think of Asia more pessimistically as a region unreformable by enlightened Western governance. "This image," Metcalf writes, "generalized into a kind of imperial folklore, [which] was then used as evidence to support the theory of Oriental stagnation."[54]

An incident Abbott recorded when he was in Delhi soon after it was retaken from the mutineers highlights the conflicted evolution of his own attitude toward South Asians, which also sets him apart from most of his peers:

> *A long string of natives in single file were crossing the road leading across the Chundur Chokh or Main Bazar on their way to or from the Jumma. A British officer was [riding] a fiery horse at full speed down the Chundur Chokh. A tall Brahmin dresst in white . . . whether from deafness or absence of mind did not take flight with the rest, so that the horse was almost upon him ere with a violent jerk of the reins the [rider] could arrest him. A conscientious and humane man could have shuddered while he blamed his own culpable impetuosity. This officer slashed the unoffending man whose life he had imperiled over the face with his whip and then continued his headlong course to the peril of other passengers. The Brahmin thus outraged did not flinch from the furious blow nor utter a word of reproach. He stood upright, unmoved, with an air of dignity that would have become a king, turning upon his brutal assailant a glance not of reproach nor of anger but of ineffable superiority. The officer was not known to me, nor could I learn his name.*[55]

This assault on a Hindu pedestrian by a British officer that Abbott witnessed was no doubt a commonplace occurrence during and after the

Mutiny, when many Britons were in a murderous mood, and thousands of Bengalis were put to death with only the flimsiest of ad hoc judicial proceedings on the grounds of having somehow assisted the mutineers. Abbott's reaction to the incident—at once appalled by the British officer's actions and sympathetically admiring of the victim's courage and dignity—is remarkable. At a time when many of his countrymen were disgracing themselves with a kind of pathological vengeance, Abbott retained his humanity as an individual. Granted, he did not personally witness the atrocities against British women and children that had given rise to the spirit of retribution, but neither did many of Britain's most homicidal avenging angels, like Abbott's former comrade from the Punjab William Hodson, who had murdered the Mughal princes in cold blood some weeks before. Abbott demonstrated respect and humanity toward individual South Asians at a time when few Britons were, while still growing increasingly critical of them as an abstract group.

The remaining decade of Abbott's military service in India may be summarized briefly. All of it was in peacetime and in the regular army. Parliament passed the Government of India Act on August 2, 1858, and in November the British Crown took over control of India from the East India Company. The Company's army was amalgamated into the Royal Army, although not without significant discontent and a nonviolent mutiny among the European soldiery.[56] That summer of 1858, Abbott was stationed in Delhi, where he was assigned as officer in charge of artillery in the city. From August 1858 to November 1862, with amalgamation of the Bengal Artillery into the Royal Artillery in 1862, he was the commanding officer of the 16th Brigade of Royal Artillery in Jullundur and Delhi.

He was never able to really settle back into regimental duties and tried unsuccessfully several times to return to political work. In 1859, just five years after leaving Hazāra, he applied to Lord Canning for a political assignment but was advised that few such appointments were available at his rank. On February 16, 1861, he was promoted to the rank of colonel. In April 1861, he applied again for political work and was more firmly rebuffed by Canning, who noted in his reply that Abbott had left political work at his own request and was now, as a colonel with thirty-seven years' service, too senior for a political appointment in any event.

Figure 8.4. A photograph of James Abbott about the time of his retirement from the army, taken by photographer Cornelius Jabez Hughes (1819–1884) at Ryde, Isle of Wight, circa 1870. Hughes was one of the most prominent portrait photographers in Victorian England. After a long and successful career in London, he retired to the Isle of Wight, where this portrait was made. (BRITISH LIBRARY BOARD)

Thereafter, for three and a half years, from January 1863 to August 1866, he commanded the 5th Brigade of Royal Horse Artillery in Umballa. For a short spell he was acting commander of the Royal Artillery Division in Allahabad while the commanding general was on leave, during which time he doubled as the commanding officer of the Dinapore Brigade. On June 19, 1866, he was promoted to major general. It had taken him thirty years to rise in rank from lieutenant to major but only another eleven for promotion from major to major general. There is very little in his private journals from this period. Ten years after the Mutiny, after a final visit to his beloved Simla, he took furlough in October 1867 and returned to England.

This was the time in an officer's life when, in addition to promotions, honors were normally conferred. But Abbott's lack of caution when putting pen to paper was to cost him dearly one final time. In 1854, Abbott had published a third book in Calcutta, titled *Legends, Ballads, & c.* Unlike his previous works, which were released under the pen names of Snellius Schickhardus and Jedediah Bobson, *Legends, Ballads, & c* was simply published anonymously because Snellius Schickhardus's true identity in India was now too well known.[57] It was a mash-up of short stories, political satire, and some of his early Romantic poetry, including "The Reunion," written in 1829 in Karnaul; "Childhood," penned in Mhow in 1832; and "The Rose's Bower," written in Kandahar in April 1839. The prose segments are in a mordacious style and clearly written for an East India Company audience. Both the main text and endnotes were used to ridicule aspects of British society at large, the administration in India, and the clergy. *Legends, Ballads, & c* contains his best work of satire, a mock conversation between former governors-general William Bentinck, called "Bill," and Edward Law, 1st Earl of Ellenborough, referred to as "Ned."[58] It also contains one of Abbott's better pieces of fiction, "The Legend of Raja Sirikup," a short pseudo-historical essay about a legendarily wicked raja,[59] as well as a caustically satirical jab at the famous London sword maker Henry Hart, whom Abbott ridiculed as "Henry Hart the Tailor" in a faux advertisement.[60] And there it might have been forgotten entirely.

But unfortunately it also contained a singularly unpleasant and uncharacteristic piece of anti-Semitic doggerel in the form of a poem titled "The Caucasian." The target of the poem was none other than Abbott's old childhood roommate from Reverend Potticary's school in Blackheath, Benjamin Disraeli, who by 1854 had become a successful novelist and a prominent Conservative member of Parliament.

The title "The Caucasian" is a reference drawn from Disraeli's novel *Coningsby, or the New Generation*, published in 1844. Why Abbott felt the need to comment on it a decade later is unclear; there do not appear to be any subsequent editions of *Coningsby* published around this time. Disraeli used *Coningsby* to expound upon his very public and often repeated racist belief in the superiority of Jews over other races. As Bernard Glassman notes, in Disraeli's "scheme of thinking the Jews represented the superior race," and the character of Sidonia in *Coningsby* "exemplifies the qualities of a superior race that is so close to Disraeli's heart."[61] Disraeli held Jews to be the highest race within the Caucasian group and Caucasians to be superior to dark-skinned races. In *Coningsby*, the Jewish character Sidonia tells the astonished Mr. Coningsby that a majority of Europe's law, most of its literature and music, and much of its religion are the legacy of its Jewish population and that he, Coningsby, can be an honorary Jew because his race, also Caucasian, "is sufficiently pure."[62] In the words of Disraeli biographer Paul Smith, "It was that purity which gave [Jews] their ability to survive all persecution and constituted their title to look the nobility of England or anywhere else in the eye."[63] Disraeli was hounded all his life by anti-Semitism despite his conversion to Christianity and baptism at the age of twelve in 1817, and Glassman observes that he used Sidonia's commentary on "the power of the 'Hebrew intellect' to fight racism with racism."[64] It was apparently too much for Abbott, however. Rather than critique the merits of *Coningsby* as a novel or rebut Disraeli's racist beliefs on a personal basis, Abbott wrote an attack that went beyond the ad hominem to include an outburst of anti-Semitism that is unique in his voluminous writings. The reasons for this uncharacteristic attack are unclear. Nowhere else in Abbott's large written record does one find another hint of anti-Semitism; indeed, his philosemitic views are evident in much of his writing, both public and personal.

Disraeli was certainly a polarizing figure and was disliked by many, even without the stain of anti-Semitism, and his own racism did not help.

Robert Browning, for example, one of the greatest poets of the Victorian period who, like Abbott, often publicly expressed philosemitic views, personally despised Disraeli.⁶⁵ Disraeli's openly avowed racism made him a lightning rod for those with anti-Semitic views. Indeed, the perception that Jews regarded themselves as superior to other races was a recurrent theme running through anti-Semitism in nineteenth century. Professor Goldwin Smith of Oxford, a notorious anti-Semite, for example, wrote in 1881, "The Jew alone regards his race as superior to humanity."⁶⁶ Sir Richard Burton, the famed Victorian explorer and another East India Company officer, held conflicted and ambivalent views toward Jews.⁶⁷ In the words of biographer Fawn Brodie, Burton was "like many men who have difficulty with particular Jews and jump easily to an indictment of the whole people," against whom "his rage became generalized."⁶⁸ Burton, however, wisely did not publish his anti-Semitic manuscript *The Jew, the Gypsy and el Islam* during his lifetime out of concerns for his career.⁶⁹ Abbott, on the other hand, as always uniquely infatuated with his own poetry, once again let his pen and his certainty of his own correctness overwhelm his common sense as well as his own sense of decency. He published "The Caucasian" under a thin veil of anonymity in *Legends, Ballads & c.*, and the results were unfortunate.

"We had been reading *Coningsby*," Abbott wrote sarcastically in his forward to the piece, "the author of which so triumphantly proves that all virtue and all talent are confined to the Jewish race, who we all know, are the élite of [the] *Caucasus*."⁷⁰ He then relates in doggerel a fictitious occasion that occurs while the storyteller is reading *Coningsby* "at the window of our residence in Harley-street."⁷¹ A Caucasian rag collector passes by with his cart in the street below. The occupation of rag collector in the poem is an unsubtle repetition of a common epithet used against Disraeli and Jews in general in the Victorian era, "Ole Clothes," because Jews dominated the used-clothing trade in London.⁷² The rag collector entices the storyteller's maid Molly to part with a silver spoon.

Tis true the Arab* serves the Turk,
   The Moor, the Hun; the Perse, the Russ:
   The Jew does all your dirty work

Chapter 8

With his pure blood from Caucasus
The only harp ye skill to touch,[73]
Derives its name and frame from us:
Ben Nevis[74] *makes your mountains crouch,*
And Ben's a Jew from Caucasus
To bait the noble Lion King,
To yelp and snarl, and bark and fuss,
His foot-prints dig for hidden thing†
No cur like him from Caucasus

* I need not say that the Arab, Moor, and Persian are Caucasian races. The Turk, Hun and Russ Mongolian.
† See the speech of Benjamin on occasion of Sir Robert Peel having dined with some of the opposite party.[75]

Abbott wrote in a postscript to the poem that the apocryphal rag vendor is subsequently arrested for stealing the spoon, and the maid is fired. Abbott concludes this half poem, half essay with the comment, "The Caucasian proprietor of the spoon, on being taken into custody, proved to be of the Tribe of Benjamin, and of the family of Israel. We understand that he is author of the Psychological Antiquities of Monmouth-street[76]—so versatile is the genius of these Caucasians. It is remarkable that among the numerous and brilliant qualities of Caucasians, we find no mention by either author of honesty. Query: Did they forget to bring it with them from the Caucasus?"[77]

Even in the England of the 1850s, when vitriolic personal attacks and anti-Semitism in print were commonplace, "The Caucasian" was vulgar and ungentlemanly. Abbott had earlier published in *Narrative of a Journey from Heraut to Khiva, Moscow, and St. Petersburg* his philosemitic account of the remarkable generosity and honesty of the Jewish merchants in Merv and Khiva who assisted him fifteen years before. He had also made it a point to visit the synagogue in Cochin and attend there a Jewish wedding. Why, then, he chose to include this spiteful piece in *Legends, Ballads & c* is baffling. Whatever the reason, it was an ill-considered insult to a man rapidly rising to the highest political ranks in Britain. The identity of the author can scarcely have long been a mystery in either Calcutta or

London. Indeed, Disraeli made it his business to learn the identities of his anonymous tormenters and, like Ellenborough, was a notoriously vindictive Tory.[78] His memory was long, and he rarely missed an opportunity to use his power, political or literary, for revenge upon his enemies or to settle old scores—particularly those of an anti-Semitic nature. He pointedly used his novel *Lothair*, for example, published in 1870, to avenge himself on Goldwin Smith by introducing him as an easily identifiable character in the novel described as a "sedentary" man "of extreme opinions" and "a social parasite."[79] Twenty years before, in 1850, Smith had published a series of anonymous attacks on Disraeli in the *Morning Chronicle*, and he held views similar to those aired by Abbott in *The Caucasian* in 1854. Disraeli learned his identity and got his revenge twenty years later.

As it had in his bizarre letter to Sir John Hobhouse and his intemperate correspondence with Frederick Currie and Frederick Mackeson, Abbott's own pen again grievously wounded him when bullets, swords, cholera, cannonballs, mutinous sailors, rabid dogs, and mad elephants could not. Abbott's own nib was always his worst enemy. In June 1861, Queen Victoria created a new order of knighthood, the Order of the Star of India, to honor service to the Crown in British India. In the 1860s, the order was conferred thirty-four times, including sixteen times to Britons. After an initial wave of orders, however, only one Briton was appointed each year between 1866 and 1869. On June 1, 1867, John Lawrence, now viceroy of India, wrote from Simla to Sir Stafford Northcote, the Secretary of State for India, to recommend three men, Sir Robert Napier, Harry Lumsden, and James Abbott for appointment as Knights Commander of the Star of India (KCSI), noting, "I also recommend Major Gen[era]l James Abbott of the artillery to be made K.C.S.I. General Abbott was the officer who many years ago travelled from Herat through Khiva and Russia to England. During the second Sikh War he raised a small army in Huzāra in the Punjaub, and there maintained his position under very arduous cir[cumstan]ces during the campaign.... The appointment of these three officers to the Star of India would be very popular."[80]

All recommendations for knighthoods, after vetting by committee, were forwarded to the Queen at the discretion of the prime minister.

CHAPTER 8

Robert Napier was a personal favorite of Disraeli's, selected by him in August 1867 to lead the expedition to Abyssinia against Emperor Tewodros II of Ethiopia. Napier was made KCSI in September 1867, at a time when the prime minister, Edward Smith-Stanley, 14th Earl of Derby, was suffering severely from gout, using opium as a pain reliever, and relying heavily on his closest confidant in his cabinet, Chancellor of the Exchequer Benjamin Disraeli. Historians generally view Derby's third ministry as one dominated by Disraeli, who became prime minister in February 1868 when Derby was no longer able to continue in office. He rejected Abbott's nomination to the KCSI in 1868. Harry Lumsden's knighthood was approved later and conferred in 1873 when Disraeli was not in office.

"The Caucasian" came back to haunt him again in England. Abbott was made a Companion of the Bath, Military Division, on May 24, 1873,[81] the year *before* Disraeli became prime minister for the second time, but efforts on the part of friends in London to obtain for Abbott a knighthood at the time of his retirement from the army in October 1877 were unsuccessful. Ordinarily, a knighthood for a full general with a career as distinguished as Abbott's would have been a relatively routine matter. The reason for the snub is clear when one considers that Disraeli served his second term as prime minister from 1874 to 1880. Abbott was not knighted until 1894. Seldom has a piece of doggerel been so costly.

It would be pleasing to record that after so much tragedy, horror, and loss in forty years in India, James Abbott was able to find a happiness in his retirement in England that eluded him on active duty. Sadly, it was not to be. His relationship with his daughter was distant, and one last great tragedy awaited him. In India, Abbott had formed a close friendship with Captain and Mrs. Reymond de Montmorency, and he stood as godfather to both of the de Montmorency's daughters, Emma and Anna Matilda. Abbott wrote and visited the girls when he could, and Anna Matilda, or Maud as she was always known, remained in love with him all her life. In 1868 they became engaged. Her surviving letters show a woman supremely happy at being engaged, who obviously adored James Abbott. Her writing that year, when Abbott arrived back in England, is bubbly and overflowing with the enthusiasm of her emotions: "My own Dearest, our diamond of 2nd betrothal and first wedding has been flashing light in the darkness so wonderfully—It is quite a gem of a ring and reminds me of you so that I can't help thinking of you, my jewel of love and goodness.... Ever and always your own wife-to-be Maud 'Abbott.'"[82] Under the flap of the envelope is written "kisses." Both the envelope and the stationary have the monogram "MA," for "Maud Abbott," although they were not yet wed, and Maud was so excited about being married to James that she was not only already using the monogram but also already signing her letters "Maud Abbott." On October 24, 1868, when Abbott was sixty-one and Maude was thirty, they were married in England. The marriage of an older man to a younger woman known since childhood was not uncommon in Victorian times and was not always for the expected reasons. Edward Benson, the Archbishop of Canterbury from 1883 to 1896, for example, married Mary Sidgwick, whom he had known since she was seven, "to preserve himself from errant feelings in love" because he believed her "simple purity" would act as a restraint on his sexual urges.[83] Sadly James and Maud had just eighteen months together. In an appalling tragedy, on May 17, 1870, Maud died while giving birth to their son, Reymond de Montmorency Abbott. The grief of a man losing one wife in childbirth is difficult to imagine; the grief of losing two wives in childbirth is unimaginable.

By 1873, too, he was already estranged from his daughter, Margaret Ann, a rift that apparently never healed. There is nothing in the archives to suggest the cause. Perhaps Margaret Ann considered her father's second marriage a betrayal of her mother's memory. Margaret Ann was raised in England by her maternal great-aunt, Miss Petrie. James Abbott wrote his final will and testament in 1873, the text of which states, "My daughter, Margaret Harriet Anne, being provided for by a previous settlement, I do hereby give unto my only son ... all my real and personal estate."[84] Margaret Ann never married. In her will, it is clear that she possessed nothing of her father's belongings or images, but many of those of her maternal relatives, which were specifically identified and bequeathed individually. All her bequests were notably to other women identified as "spinsters" living near her in Middlesex. Her half brother Reymond is not mentioned in the document. There is no evidence in the archives of any

CHAPTER 8

correspondence between James and Margaret during the last thirty years of his life. She chose in her will not to be buried next to her father.

His relationship with his son was distant but cordial. By 1876 James Abbott was living on the Isle of Wight. At this time his son, Reymond, was six. His later letters convey a tone of sadness, a sense perhaps that he wished they were closer.[85] At the age of ten, according to British census records, Reymond was a "scholar" living on Bishops Down Park Road in Royal Tunbridge Wells. At sixteen, he was still in school and not living at home. Abbott wrote to him wistfully about India, religion, poetry, and his studies. A draft of an unsent letter in the archives, from E. Werge Thomas referring to an interview she conducted with Reymond Abbott in 1958, contains the comment that he told her that during his first six years, his father would not speak to him, suggesting that James was deeply disturbed by Maud's death and may have transferred blame onto Reymond for it.[86] Reymond went on to Cambridge. In 1911 he was single and a boarder in Kensington, London, with "private means." Like his sister, he never married.[87] Reymond was at Kings College in 1935 when he donated to Cambridge University the death mask of Charles XII that General Vasily Perovsky had given his father almost a century before. Reymond died on the Isle of Wight, in March 1963, at the age of ninety-three, the last living descendant of James Abbott.

John Kaye, the semiofficial historian of British India, wrote of James Abbott in 1872 that he was "of the true salt of the earth ... chivalrous, heroic, but somehow or other never thoroughly emerging from the shade."[88] Abbott was promoted to full general on October 1, 1877, on which date he finally retired from the active list of the British army.[89] Counting the two years in the military seminary at Addiscombe, he had been in uniform for fifty-six years. More than twenty years after Kaye's description was published, however, James Abbott finally did emerge from the shade. In recognition of his extraordinary service to Britain that was fifty years overdue, the knight-errant at last became a knight, made a Knight Commander of the Order of the Bath on May 26, 1894, at the age of eighty-seven.[90] Two and a half years later, after a long life of service, adventure, exploration, war, glory, and tragedy, as a soldier, diplomat, administrator, author, poet, and artist of the Company and Royal armies,

Figure 8.5. A photograph of James Abbott at the time of his knighthood in May 1894 at the age of eighty-seven by an unknown photographer. (BRITISH LIBRARY BOARD)

Chapter 8

General Sir James Abbott died at Ellerslie, Ryde, on the Isle of Wight, on October 6, 1896, at the age of eighty-nine.[91]

He outlived not only all his brothers and sisters and two wives but also all of his peers in the Great Game and the struggle for the Northwest Frontier as well. When Abbott died in 1896, his best friend D'Arcy Todd had been gone a half century, a suicide by enemy fire at the Battle of Ferozeshah in 1843. Alexander Burnes, too, was long dead in the streets of Kabul, killed by an angry mob in 1841. Charles Stoddart and Arthur Conolly, with whom Abbott had explored the ruins of Mandu, lay in unmarked graves in Bokhara, beheaded by the Emir of Bokhara in 1842. The redoubtable Captain Eldred Pottinger, defender of Herat and Abbott's companion in the city after the siege, survived the First Anglo-Afghan War only to die of disease in Hong Kong the same year. Patrick Vans Agnew, his colleague in the Hazāra before the Second Anglo-Sikh War, was slain together with Lieutenant W. A. Anderson in Multan in 1848. Frederick Mackeson was murdered days after Abbott left the Hazāra in 1853, and the adventurous, pioneering Lady Honoria Lawrence died of illness in India the next year. Her husband and Abbott's dear friend Henry Lawrence never got over the loss and was a different man after her death. He and Abbott's co-deity, John Nicholson, together with William Hodson and Henry Havelock, who served with Abbott's brother Frederick in Burma, all died in the Great Mutiny. James Broun-Ramsay, 1st Marquess of Dalhousie, died in Scotland in 1860. Fittingly, he was buried in the churchyard at Cockpen. James Outram, who relieved Abbott at Nimarr, died in London in broken health in 1863, less than two years after being appointed a Knight Commander of the Star of India. Richmond Shakespear, the man who received the credit and the knighthood for Abbott's diplomacy with the Khan of Khiva, died of bronchitis in India in 1861. Herbert Edwardes, Abbott's friend and, for a short time, his successor in the Hazāra who christened its capital Abbottabad, died in England in 1868, his health also ruined in India. The man Abbott called "Sir Fiddlesticks," Frederick Currie, died in London in 1875 after long service as Vice President of the Board of India. The youngest of the Lawrence brothers, John, served as Viceroy of India from 1864 to 1869 and was raised to the peerage as Baron Lawrence of the Punjab in 1869.

He died in England in 1879. Benjamin Disraeli died in 1881, having been defeated in the elections of 1880 by William Gladstone's Liberals, largely over the Second Anglo-Afghan War, which Abbott would have warned him against. Vincent Eyre, who relieved Abbott at Ishapoor, died in France the same year. George Lawrence, the third and eldest of the Lawrence brothers with whom Abbott served in the Punjab, died in London in 1884. So too did General John Reid Becher, the officer who replaced Herbert Edwardes in Abbottabad and the deputy commissioner of Hazāra from 1853 to 1859. Harry "Joe" Lumsden, who was fourteen years younger than Abbott, fought at Multan and later founded the Corps of Guides. He died in Aberdeenshire in August 1896. That October, James Abbott became the last of the Paladins to pass into history.

In many ways, James Abbott was the quintessential military officer of the East India Company of the nineteenth century. In terms of his background, as the orphan son of a bankrupted nabob channeled into a career in India, of his attitudes toward class, religion, women, and gentility, and of his tastes for poetry, the Romantic movement, and Sir Walter Scott, there were many like him. Yet he did extraordinary things and behaved in extraordinary ways. His trip through Central Asia to Khiva and beyond, his lifelong friendship with Saleh Mohammed, his life in his adopted village of Patalpanie, the eight months he served as very likely the first British guerilla leader of the modern era, and his reign for four years as the King of Hazāra mark him as an exceptional colonial figure of the nineteenth century. More than one thousand people were released from slavery and lived out their lives in freedom as a direct result of Abbott's interventions with the Khan of Khiva, Russian General Vasily Perovsky, and Russian Foreign Minister Count Karl Nesselrode. Abbott's last combat action was the Black Mountain campaign against the Hindustani Fanatics, the direct antecedents in religious doctrine of the modern-day Taliban. In a twist of fate, the Taliban sheltered al-Qaeda leader Osama bin Laden in Afghanistan from 1996 to 2001. Bin Laden was tracked down and killed in Abbottabad in 2011 not far from Black Mountain, bringing James Abbott's name into the news again. The town, which still bears Abbott's name, remains one of two in all of what was British India still named for an Englishman.

Figure 8.6. The last photograph of James Abbott, circa 1895, by an unknown photographer, shows him seated with a pith helmet on the ground next to him, holding a white dove. It is the only image of him that shows the wound received to his right hand on the shores of the Caspian Sea in 1840. (BRITISH LIBRARY BOARD)

Abbott's insight into the effects of William Bentinck's military reform of the Bengal Army is remarkable. His recognition that Bentinck's military reorganization fatally weakened the military chain of command within the entire Bengal Army by stripping regimental officers of virtually all authority over their soldiers holds considerable merit as a military analysis. By examining the ruinous impact of Bentinck's reforms on good order and military discipline in the Bengal regiments, Abbott introduces the collapse of senior military leadership *within* the Bengal Army prior to the Mutiny as a primary cause of the military decay that allowed the rebellion to occur. The self-fulfilling misunderstanding of caste, the over-reliance on upper-caste Brahmins, the toxic effects of the annexation of Oudh, and the reduced numbers of British officers in their regiments have all been studied before. The pernicious elimination of all military commanders' authority over their men that resulted from Bentinck's reforms to the Bengal Army has not. Abbott's insight greatly increases our understanding from a military perspective of how such a leadership failure could develop in interconnected ways.

Abbott's life and prodigious writings also cast a new light on some underquestioned assumptions about the deterioration of the relationship between Britons and the peoples of India in general in the first half of the nineteenth century. Abbott's observations show a dichotomy between Britons' actual, personal day-to-day behavior and the contemporaneous narrative of separation participated in by a broad swath of Britons in India at the time. Clearly words did not equate to deeds. The devolution of the language that Abbott also uses to describe indigenous peoples from 1824 to 1860 fits the same narrative of a breakdown in relations, but again his own behavior and that of many officers around him contradict the words. In actuality, Abbott made and retained remarkably close personal friendships with many Indians and Afghans and was deeply engaged with indigenous village culture almost until the events of 1857. A large majority of British officers in India maintained, in particular, monogamous relationships with South Asian women long after the introduction of the tropological discourse of segregation. While this narrative of cultural separation did lead gradually to a general deterioration of the relationship between colonizer and colonized in the first half of the nineteenth

Chapter 8

century, Abbott's life shows that this breakdown began well after much current historical writing suggests, with intercultural intermarriage and close personal relationships common well into the 1840s and in some cases far beyond, particularly in Burma.

Thus Abbott's life forces a reconsideration of the prevailing view that Britons and the peoples of India were separating as a result of ethnic and cultural differentiation as early as 1800. His account demonstrates there were as many exceptions to the trajectory of separation as there were adherents. Indeed, a study of period portraiture shows that most Britons in India sought deliberately and specifically to portray and define themselves for posterity as culturally attuned, knowledgeable, and integrated into indigenous life until the middle of the nineteenth century. Abbott's observations across this period demonstrate that the change in the relationship between ruler and subject did not take place uniformly or universally over space and time but piecemeal and sporadically. It shows that Britons often embodied contradictions, discarding prejudices on a personal basis and sometimes forming lasting individual relationships with the peoples of South Asia even into the mid-1850s, just as Abbott did throughout his life with Sammud Khan, Saleh Mohammed, Mir Zaman Khan, Kulúndur Khan, and indeed the entire population of Hazāra.

Most importantly, perhaps, Abbott's life shows that it is necessary to disaggregate his life from the trope of paternalist British officers on the Northwest Frontier and to examine this image more closely. Ironically, both the self-serving colonial British narrative of the district officer and the post-independence refutation of it inadvertently conspired to relegate Abbott's reign in the Hazāra District to obscurity. The quasi-official characterization of Abbott's service in Hazāra by British authors and contemporary colonial historians like Sir John Kaye as one largely conforming to the standard and tidy portrayal of the political officer in the Punjab under the Lawrences actually required major downplaying and recasting of his true position in Hazāra. The modern deconstruction of this narrative by recent historians also effectively marginalized Abbott's story. Ironically, in refuting the self-serving contemporary British portrayal of how they wanted to be seen as a group in history, modern scholars have also elided Abbott's extraordinary rule in the Hazāra and largely aggregated him together with the other Paladins. A district officer not unlike Joseph Conrad's protagonist in *Heart of Darkness* does not fit well into either the paternal "Paladins of the Punjab" British colonial narrative or the more recent counternarrative.

In fact, Abbott's rule in the Hazāra was the epitome of nonconformity. This was indeed privately acknowledged at the time by Dalhousie, Lawrence, Edwardes, and many others but kept out of the official histories. None of the other officers in the Punjab even attempted to replicate Abbott's extraordinary life among the people, which was considered eccentric in the extreme, as private, long-unpublished reminisces like those of Honoria Lawrence make clear. Abbott was actually perceived by his friend Henry Lawrence as possessing strange powers, not at all as a poster boy for the paternal district administration of the Punjab School. Lawrence's other Young Men lived in cantonments and acted like proper sahibs; Abbott lived in a tent and dressed like a Muslim fakir. Far from being a common figure in the British lexicon of paternalism and beloved district officers, Abbott was viewed as exceptional even by his contemporaries. And a substantial number of unimpeachable indigenous voices, male and female, also make clear that Abbott was genuinely the object of affection and respect from the Hazārawals. These voices are scattered over a half dozen accounts from diverse figures across seventy years and thousands of miles. Most of the recorders never met each other, and some, like Fredrick Burnaby, Richard Warburton, and Olaf Caroë, never met Abbott. Yet their descriptions of him are astonishingly consistent in depicting him as a holy man and a healer, elements well outside the standard British canon. In fact, Abbott would not have been nearly so successful in ruling his district if he had been typical of Lawrence's Young Men.

British figures like Lord Dalhousie and Hubert Watson used the word "king" in writing to describe him. For his part, Henry Lawrence glossed over his friend's irregularities and peculiarities in his reports to his superiors in Calcutta, but they grew increasingly concerned by other, backchannel reports of Abbott's unorthodox behavior. When he began arresting and detaining opposition leaders indefinitely without charge, "his system," as Lawrence called it, crossed over from eccentric to unacceptable. Abbott was ultimately seen by government not

Chapter 8

Figure 8.7. Watercolor by James Abbott titled *Rock of Aornos in Huzāra*, painted circa 1850. In the foreground are three mounted riders in shallow water, one dressed in red on the left of the group and two dressed in green facing him on the right, possibly representing Abbott himself, his late wife Margaret, and their daughter, Margaret Ann. (BRITISH LIBRARY BOARD)

as an obnoxious Paladin who could not keep his pen case shut but as a figure similar to the character of Kurtz in Joseph Conrad's *Heart of Darkness*. Like Kurtz, Abbott was a painter and writer from petit bourgeois origins acting as a company station master at the farthest reaches of empire, a man who ruled his own small kingdom with exceptional effectiveness and had actually caused the people to love him, but whose methods were ultimately seen in headquarters as "unsound" and necessitated his removal.

At the end of the day, however, the presence of the East India Company in India "was little more than an oil slick on the surface of the deep waters over which it briefly spread."[92] The peoples of India retained their agency and often found ways to manipulate the presence and imposed structures of the Company Raj to their advantage, as Shi'a Muslim women did with *Nikāḥ al-Mut'ah* and Bengal brahmins did with British interpretations of caste within the Bengal Army prior to the Mutiny.

So too did the peoples of the frontier, who were most often depicted as warlike tribesmen who respected the warrior attributes of the sahib. The epitome of this narrative is Kipling's "Ballad of East and West," deliberately written in the heptameters of the Anglo-Scottish border ballad to reinforce the invented parallels to Scottish Highlanders:

> *Oh, East is East, and West is West, and never the twain shall meet,*
> *Till Earth and Sky stand presently at God's great Judgment Seat;*
> *But there is neither East nor West, Border, nor Breed, nor Birth,*
> *When two strong men stand face to face, tho' they come from the ends of the earth.*[93]

In reality, most district officers on the frontier were more often the accidental beneficiaries of effective indigenous alternative governance systems than exemplars of administration. Two of them in particular, however, stood out from this pattern: John Nicholson and James Abbott. Nicholson was respected and feared as the God of Valor; Abbott was respected and loved as the Lord of Generosity.[94] But while Nicholson had an unusually powerful and violent personality, he remained within the methodological bounds of Company administration. Abbott, in contrast, did not. When apart from his peers, something within him broke free from his normally reserved, introspective, diffident, often obsequious, and sometimes quarrelsome official persona. He four times entered his own heart of darkness in South Asia—internally in dealing with depression and again after Margaret's tragic death and externally in both Khorezm and Hazāra—and returned each time. He was a diminutive man from an ordinary middle-class background who at times did extraordinary things.

In the bigger picture, because overall he was in many ways the stereotypical East India Company officer, his life raises important historical questions about many of the prevailing assumptions regarding Britons and the people of India under Company Raj and points to the need for more nuanced, less generalized interpretations of these relationships. It demonstrates that if there were at times arrogance and abuse of power, there were at times also kindness, self-sacrifice, and enduring friendships. There were base motives and self-interest, but these often existed side by

CHAPTER 8

side on a personal level with men like James Abbott who, in a different era in a different land, had a genuine desire to free slaves, give farmland back to the men who worked it, and safeguard the helpless. Despite the growing cultural and racial prejudices that surrounded him by the end of the Great Mutiny of 1857, at his best, James Abbott the knight-errant rose on occasion above his claustrophobic and classist social insecurity and retained a chivalric humanism at the ends of the earth. And in that sense, the ancient white-bearded Pashtun elders high up in their mountains were right: he had a heart like a fakir.

Appendix

Abbott the Artist

JAMES ABBOTT WAS A ROMANTIC, NOT A WARRIOR-POET BUT A POET-warrior. Although he lived two-thirds of his life during the reign of Queen Victoria, he was born in an earlier and very different time. His personality and his character were formed long before Britain's longest-reigning monarch assumed the throne on June 28, 1838. The term "Romantic" has been redefined many times since its inception in the Victorian era.[1] Abbott embodied the word largely in the sense attributed to it by Samuel Coleridge, as something improbable, wild, perhaps a little Gothic, something containing wondrous mystery, or in the sense given by *Oxford English Dictionary* at the time, "something which captivates the fancy."[2] To Abbott first and foremost it meant holding up that which was ideal, beautiful, and noble.

Romantic themes dominated early Anglo-Indian writing almost to the exclusion of other genres. In his *Survey of Anglo-Indian Fiction*, Bhupal Singh divides British writing in India into three periods, the first running from the tenure of Warren Hastings as governor-general, which began in 1773, to the Mutiny of 1857; the second from the Mutiny to the death of Queen Victoria in 1901; and the third constituting the period since then. "The novels of the first period," Singh concludes, "are mainly romances of Indian history."[3] However, most works of fiction deal with the travails of Anglo-Indians in India, and as Singh notes, "The number of novels in which the English are either altogether absent, or play a minor role, is comparatively small."[4] By far the most successful and most influential of these writers was the legendary Colonel Meadows Taylor, whose first book, *Confessions of a Thug*, published in 1840, was hugely popular both in the metropole and in India. As P. J. Marshall notes,

> The British in India fully shared in the Romantic aesthetic. Walter Scott, whose works were provided by the Company for libraries "in remote stations," enjoyed an enormous following in India. Even small European communities rigged up theatres. Large numbers of men and women sketched and painted Indian landscapes, usually within the established conventions of the Picturesque. Talented amateurs followed the lead of a small number of visiting professionals, so that it has been claimed that "at no time has one country been so extensively and minutely observed by artists from another." A small corpus of Anglo Indian poetry appeared in print.[5]

Poetry in the first half of the nineteenth century enjoyed a privileged place in English society. Literary criticism was in its infancy, and broad differences of opinion existed as to what constituted excellence in poetry. Yet poets and critics alike generally agreed on several points, including a consensus that poetry was the "greatest of all the arts," that it "must contain great ideas," that its object was truth, and that it was "a science with ascertainable laws, which, if correctly formulated, [are] universally valid in the sense in which the laws of science are valid."[6] Richard Altick notes, "Other things being equal, a poet outranked a novelist."[7] John Ruskin, in a critique of modern painting, wrote, "Painting is properly to be opposed to speaking and writing, but not to poetry. Both painting and speaking are methods of expression. Poetry is the use of either for the noblest purposes."[8] Poetry was to be valued, Abbott wrote to his son in 1878, "for beauty of thought, sentiment and imagery, rather than for the interest of the tale. . . . [T]he tale itself is quite subordinate to those considerations."[9]

Poetry contains the origins of Abbott's lifelong self-image as a knight-errant. Abbott recalled from when he was about ten, "The first poem I ever read was Dacien's literal translation of Homer's Iliad. . . . [A]fter the *Iliad* I pitched into *Orlando Furioso*, as done into English verse by Hoole.[10] It was in my Father's library and the Romantic adventures of Knight and Lady greatly captivated my fancy."[11] Abbott continues, "It was not I think until I was at Addiscombe [at fourteen] that I read the Lady of the Lake and was ... fully awake and alive to the power of poetry as an art. I no longer overvalued the story, but dwelt upon the *truth of the delineation* whether of nature or of passion."[12] Poetry for Abbott was an expression, above all, of truth, not in an objective sense but in the Aristotelian sense of poetry as the expression of the ideal.

Of critical interest in situating Abbott in the broader British imperium is the unmistakable confluence in his poetry of three central Romantic tropes. The first of these is the fascination in Britain with an idealized medieval past, a popularity that quickly grew beyond the borders of Britain to embrace past civilizations in Greece, Asia Minor, and elsewhere. The most important poets in shaping Abbott's artistic sensibilities were Sir Walter Scott (1771–1832), George Gordon (Lord) Byron (1788–1824), and Thomas Moore (1779–1852), all of whom were arguably best known for their work in this genre. The lost-civilization trope represented a turn toward an invented version of the past, putatively purer and more noble. Scott based many of his tales in this imagined version of the past, including *Ivanhoe*, *Tales of the Crusaders*,[13] and *Castle Dangerous*. His influence on Abbott is unmistakable; Abbott, for example, published his first piece of prose in the *East India United Services Journal*, "A Glance at Addiscombe," under the pen name Jedediah Bobson; Scott published a number of his early works anonymously under the non de plume Jedediah Cleishbotham.[14] The nexus of Abbott, Scott, Romanticism, and India was hardly a coincidence. Scott was enormously popular in India. As Douglas Peers notes, "Scott quickly became one of the most popular, if not the most popular novelist in India, where he was not only widely read but widely emulated by Anglo-Indians and Indians alike."[15] His books were routinely supplied to barracks libraries, where novels were otherwise rarely found. Scott was equally popular with enlisted men, officers, and Anglo-Indian women, and as Peers notes, he "had a significant impact" on other influential writers on India, including John Kaye, Robert Orme, and Phillip Taylor.[16] Not coincidentally, Henry Lawrence, who recruited Abbott as one of his Young Men or Paladins in the Punjab, published a novel derivative of Scott in 1845, which Abbott certainly read.[17] Scott's work enjoyed a particular popularity with East India Company officers,

APPENDIX

for whom his fusion of Romanticism, Orientalist subject matter, and veneration of the military struck a particular chord. As Peers notes, "He highlighted the aristocratic values and traits with which officers in India like to be associated. Company officers, in particular, were susceptible to such treatments for they were constantly being reminded that their commissions did not enjoy the same claim to status as those of their counterparts in the royal Army.... His love of feudal and medieval imagery was easily transferred to India where such images were often used in efforts both to capture the essence of Indian society and locate British officials within it."[18]

Scott's only work set partially in India was *The Surgeon's Daughter*, written and published in 1827 as the third and final tale in *Chronicles of the Canongate*.[19] It is considered among Scott's minor works, and he famously struggled to make the segment set in India sound authentic. Although Scott never visited India, he had extensive family connections to India, and many of his friends had long service there.[20] He drew heavily on historical works on Tipu Sultan, including James Scurry's captivity narrative,[21] but his most important source was a retired East India Company officer, Colonel James Ferguson (1778–1859), who acted as a sort of cultural advisor during the four months Scott was writing the novel. *The Surgeon's Daughter* was purportedly based on a true story, as were many of Scott's works, and tells the story of an innocent young woman, Menie Grey, lured into captivity in India by a heartless scoundrel, only to be saved at the last moment by a noble British officer with all the right sentiments. True to form for Scott, there is no happy ending; the scoundrel gets crushed to death by an elephant, but the British officer dies after saving the girl, and Menie keeps her vow to her savior never to marry. The Oriental genre in literature had already reached full pitch in England with the publication of Scott's epic poem *The Crusades* (1825), set in Syria, and *The Adventures of Haji Baba* (1824). As John Sutherland notes, "The Oriental tale was given its most characteristic turn by the enjoyably kitsch (and best-selling) *The Adventures of Haji Baba* (1824) and its successors."[22] Abbott was influenced by all of these.

This Romantic fascination with the Middle Ages continued seamlessly into the Victorian period. As Richard Altick notes, "Every major poet and every Victorian painter and sculptor of consequence repeatedly drew his inspiration from faraway times and places, most notably but by no means exclusively the age of classical antiquity and the Middle Ages."[23] Medieval ruins were of particular fascination to the public and provided an endless source of subject matter for poetry. They formed an integral part of what Alfred Lord Tennyson called "a passion for the past."[24] The passion for ruins was also infused into the young James Abbott, who spent much of his adult life in India exploring them. The interrelated British colonial trope of India as a civilization in decline also served as a fertile muse for Abbott's poetry.

After Scott, George Gordon (Lord) Byron (1788–1824) was the second of Abbott's three primary artistic influences. His characters introduced the literary audience to the "Byronic hero," a generically mysterious literary character typified as moody, often gloomy, intelligent but weary of the world, who often cut across the grain of what was considered socially acceptable. Byron was the acknowledged master of putting the sublime into verse and is remembered for bringing the Spenserian stanza into the nineteenth century. Abbott professed a dislike for Edmund Spenser's own *The Fairy Queen* written in the same meter, "tho' abounding in adventures of Knights and Damsels and told in the smoothest verse," because he could not feel the emotions, "anxieties, hopes & fears," he wrote. "But one or two poets have possessed this power—Homer, Shakespeare, Scott, Byron & Moore."[25]

The third author, Thomas Moore, may get the most credit for piquing the growing interest in the Orient in Britain. After the publication of *The Arabian Nights* in 1706,[26] the first subsequent work of literary importance in the Orientalist genre was *Vathek, an Arabian Tale*, written in French by William Beckford (1760–1844) and translated and published in 1786 by the Reverend Samuel Henley without Beckford's name.[27] In poetry, the interest in Eastern themes was then taken up by Robert Southey, who published the epic poems *Thalaba the Destroyer* in 1801 and the *Curse of Kehama* in 1810. The *Curse of Kehama* and Sydney Owenson's novel *The Missionary*, published in 1811, were among the first works set in India to appear in print in England.[28] Samuel Coleridge's famously opium-inspired "Kubla Khan," written in 1797 but first published in 1816 (at Byron's urging) in *Christabel, Kubla Khan, and the Pains of Sleep*, was set in a fantasy "pleasure dome" in "Tartary."[29] Byron wrote several of his own most acclaimed works in the genre, including four poems that became known as the *Oriental Tales* (sometimes given as the *Turkish Tales*): *The Giaour* (1813), *The Bride of Abydos* (1813), *The Corsair* (1814), and *Lara, a Tale* (1814), although the latter certainly had more in common with Scott's border tales than with the Orient. These all enjoyed commercial success, but it was with the publication of Thomas Moore's Eastern romance *Lalla Rookh* in 1817 when James Abbott was ten that the genre really took off in England. "Byron had given the world *Turkish Tales*," Roderick Cavaliero writes, "which were intended to inflame the beating heart of burgeoning love set in the land of the harem. Moore now did the same for Mughal and Persian India in *Lalla Rookh*."[30] In Moore's epic poem, Lalla Rookh is the daughter of the Mughal emperor Aurangzeb and the heroine of the connective narrative tale that pulls together four poems, *The Veiled Prophet of Khorasan, Paradise and the Peri, The Fire-Worshippers*,[31] and *The Light of the Harem*. Abbott's mother read it to him as a child. "For a long time" he recalled, "the Lady of the Lake and the Fireworshippers formed the great passion of my fancy—Ariosto had lost all his charms & my great ambition was to write a poem which should merit to be named with either of these beautiful compositions."[32] As Cavaliero notes in *Ottomania*, however, "Moore had never been anywhere East of London." Moore was no Orientalist, and his luxuriant vale of Cashmere filled with singing bulbuls and "Haram's half-caught glances" was based entirely on accounts found in books in the library of his patron, Lord Moira. Despite the copious footnotes, however, and Byron's praise that "the tone of the east has been perfectly preserved,"[33] the poem was, in Cavaliero's words, "no more orientally authentic than the Prince Regent's pavilion in Brighton."[34] It scarcely mattered; the book was an immediate best seller in England. As a result, Abbott arrived in India and began writing epic poetry at the height of a pan-European Oriental Renaissance. Not only English but French and German authors, too, were rediscovering inspiration in India. The German Orientalist Friedrich Schlegel had already written in 1800, "Im Orient müßen wir das höchste Romantische suchen [In the Orient we must seek the highest Romanticism]." An acolyte of Schlegel, Baron

APPENDIX

Ferdinand Eckstein was a German Jew who had converted to Catholicism and a Sanskritist who believed the ancient Sanskrit texts contained the pure revelation of God. Eckstein in turn influenced the French Romantic Victor-Marie Hugo (1802–1885) to write *Les Orientales*,[35] published in 1829, which Abbott, a great fan of poetry and fluent in French, certainly read. Eckstein also used his newspaper, *Le Catholique*, to encourage other authors and poets to seek inspiration from the "two prolific springs" of the Orient and the Middle Ages.[36] Many did so, including the French Romantic poet Alfred de Vigny, French poet and Second Republic politician Alphonse de Lamartine, and the great German Orientalist Friedrich Rückert, a professor of Oriental languages at the University of Erlangen, a master of thirty languages, and the author of *Nal und Damajanti, eine Indische Geschichte*, a translation from the Sanskrit epic *Mahabharata* of 303 pages, in 1828.[37]

Despite all the beauty of these inspirations, and for all the thousands of hours Abbott spent perfecting his rhymes, however, his poetry is generally leaden and easily forgettable. He struggled for greatness in poetry

Figure A.1. "Jehaz Ke Mhyl, Ruined City of Maandoo in Malwa," a pen-and-ink drawing by James Abbott dated 1835. (BRITISH LIBRARY BOARD)

but never reached it. Reviews of *Constance: A Tale*, published anonymously in 1877, were typically mixed. One critic described it as "a laboriously unsuccessful attempt at poetry."[38] *Allen's Indian Mail*, on the other hand, winked at Abbott by writing, "If it be true that the anonymous author is an old Bengal officer of high mark among the 'Politicals' of the old Punjab days ... we may congratulate him on the lays which he has intertwined with his laurels." The critique gently alluded to *Constance*'s quaint but venerable Byronic and Spenserian origins but praised the poem's "real merits" and noted that it was "marked by passages of great descriptive power and rich in utterances of genuine pathos."[39] The Sunday newspaper *John Bull* was more measured, observing, "Its literary merit is very unequal. Some of the descriptions of scenery ... are written with great power; but the narrative portion ... seldom passes, and does not always reach, mediocrity."[40] Other critics were kinder. The *Brighton Guardian* was laudatory in its praise of *Constance*, noting the author's "dramatic power" and "Byronic fire" and adding that the poet possessed a "gifted and cultivated fancy ... given to few ... with the grace which distinguishes our author."[41] Altogether Abbott wrote a dozen volumes of poetry and published six of them, including *T'Hakoorine, a Tale of Maandoo* (1841), *Tales of the Forest* (1853[42]), *Legends, Ballads, &c.* (1854), *Prometheus' Daughter* (1861), and *Allaoodeen* (1880), in addition to *Constance: A Tale* (1877), at least two of them at his own expense. None enjoyed any popular success. *Prometheus' Daughter*[43] was a typical example. The poem, written in the couplets that Abbott reserved for the narrative tale, plods on for 377 pages, a lugubrious, melancholic, and belabored attempt at an expression of sublimity and nobility, full of "cheerless woe," "melancholy descant," and noble brows burdened with "despair and gloom." Abbott occasionally livened up this overwrought gloom of cheerless woe and heart-wrung tears with some blood and gore, such as this verse:

> *I mark, like panther in his corse-strewn lair,*
> *In carnage riot high: his vengeful mood*
> *Unstill'd, unsated by that feast of blood:*
> *His mighty arm untir'd: terrific, grim*
> *E'en in retreat lends her gloom to him.*

APPENDIX

His armour black with gory stains imbued;
His sable steed bath'd saddle-deep in blood;
His sable plume unras'd of hostile brand;
The sword of ruin blazing in his hand;
As some black eagle from the carnage flies,
His strong wing dew'd with gore of sacrifice.[44]

As his use of expressions like "regurged" and "mutilated joy" suggest, Abbott had no real poetic talents and might be most charitably described as an enthusiastic amateur. His poetry and the notes that accompany it do, however, show him to have been extraordinarily literate, not only in classical Greek mythology, which he read in the original, but also in contemporary literature and poetry as well. Abbott's comments and literary allusions reflect a tremendously broad and deep intimacy with both classical and contemporary fiction and nonfiction. Many more of his poems were never published. *Hoomaioon* is an epic poem about the son of Babur, who succeeded his father to the Mughal throne in 1530 CE. It is, unlike Abbott's other works, written as a play with scenes and acts, of 242 handwritten pages.[45] *Perizad* is another extant manuscript, this one an epic Romantic poem offering an account of Alexander in Central Asia and India and ending, in the eighth canto, in Babylon with Alexander's death. Derived from Plutarch, the work was reviewed by Abbott as late as 1891, suggesting a continuing interest in having it published that was never realized. It is historically accurate and contains numerous marginalia and notes written in Greek. Another untitled and unpublished epic poem about Alexander in manuscript form runs to 215 pages.

Perhaps Abbott's best poetry was his first published book-length poem, *T'Hakoorine, a Tale of Maandoo*, first released in 1841. Critical reviews here too were mixed. The *Gentleman's Magazine* noted that the poem was "versified with spirit and ease, though sometimes deficient in correctness of rhyme, and too luxuriant in description."[46] The literary journal *Athenaeum* was less kind. The infamously acerbic literary critic there, Thomas Hervey, allowed that Abbott had some talent for description but criticized both his "determination to be Oriental in manner and tone" and his "involved and mystified" writing style.[47] Máire ni Fhlathúin notes that Abbott's publisher, Madden, intervened with the *Athenaeum* to seek a positive review for the work, which clearly did not have much effect.[48] The two publications were bitter rivals. The editor of the *Gentleman's Magazine* intensely disliked Hervey, writing in an obituary in 1859 that Hervey's criticism was "characterized by a causticity of censure and a costiveness of praise, scarcely worthy of a journal of high standing."[49] Three years before Abbott's death, a revised edition of *T'Hakoorine, a Tale of Maandoo* was published by in London by Kegan Paul with several added poems, including, fittingly, an ode to his dearest friend, titled "The Death of Major Elliot D'Arcy Todd."

Abbott's ventures into prose did not fare much better: He published a number of short pieces of satire and humor in the *East India United Services Journal* under the pen name Snellius Schickhardus prior to 1830, including "The Private Centinel [sic]," "Narrative of a Journey from Mhow in Malwa to Agra," "Journal of Lieut. C. Bannemore," and "Barrack Sketches." A satirical piece titled "Narrative of the Joudpore Countermarch" was published in the same journal during this period under the pseudonym of an enlisted artilleryman, Bombardier Charles Banneram. Abbott continued to publish doggerel in the *United Services Journal* in the 1830s, including a lengthy piece of fanciful humor titled simply "The Letters of Snellius Schickhardus."[50]

Two other works of fiction, *The Tomb of the First Homicide* and *The Recluse: A Tale of Maandoo*, at 203 and 400 pages, respectively, were bound as single copies but never published. Fragments survive of another novel about an English officer, Captain Adam of the Shah's Contingent who was left behind in Kabul at the time of the British retreat and nursed back to health by Begum Gool Behar, the beautiful daughter of an Afghan prince. In wooden prose and dialogue, Adam struggles to convince her to marry him, but she refuses because she doesn't want to burden him with an Afghan wife: "Let me not become a curse to him I would fain have served," the young woman tells him. "Let me not see him truly pining over a lot forced upon him by circumstances; and envying every man he sees happy in the possession of an English wife."[51]

Abbott's drawings and watercolor paintings, on the other hand, are well above average. They are skillfully created and reflect a talent for

APPENDIX

Figure A.2. Pencil-and-ink drawing of bathing ghats on the riverbank at Maheshwar (Indore) by James Abbott in 1842. On the original mounting Abbott wrote, "From Nature by General James Abbott 1842. Ghaut or stairs to the revered memory of the Mah-ratta Princess Ahilya Bae at Mhaiswa, Nimarr. Central India, drawn from a boat in the River Narbudda." (BRITISH LIBRARY BOARD)

composition and architectural rendering and perspective that was well developed. His pen-and-ink drawings of buildings and scenes in India show a keen eye for detail and often succeed in evoking a sense of mystery and intrigue in their subjects. A number of his watercolors survive in the British Library, and several of these are nicely composed and very capably painted with a pleasing color palette. Perhaps the best of his surviving paintings is *Rock of Aornos in Huzāra*, done in Hazāra in 1850, illustrated in chapter 8. As noted, many British officers sketched and painted as a hobby in India, but Abbott's work is better than most.

Abbott's style and literary instincts in both poetry and prose, however, found an increasingly negative critical reception over time—and Abbott was never one to compromise (or evolve) creatively with the times in response to it. As time progressed and attacks on Romanticism hardened, so, predictably, did Abbott's defense of it. As late as 1878, Abbott held firm to his Romantic sensibilities, writing to his son, "The advance of science [and] the wonderful creations of the mechanic have hardened the mind against the solicitations of fancy. The whirl of the railroad has left no time for the pleasures derived from reflection & has banished all the memories of the past to which the poet clings. He has no place in the world at present. But a revulsion may someday come, and thought, feeling & nature be again required of the poet."[52] Thus in James Abbott's poetry is seen part of his inner heart, an unreconstructed Romantic, at times an uncompromising and didactic moralist, a stubborn man untroubled by self-doubts regarding the correctness of his views who bristled at criticism, and, in later life, a man who clearly saw the world changing around him but saw himself as an old-fashioned knight-errant of an earlier, better time. By the time of Abbott's death at the end of the nineteenth century, Romanticism was a thing of the past. By the twentieth century, attacks on Romanticism and Romantic idealism, including those of Marxist materialists like Jerome McGann, zeroed in on the Aristotelian ideal as "escapism" from the "historical world" in works like Coleridge's masterpiece "Kubla Khan" "through imagination and poetry."[53] That, however, Abbott would have argued, was precisely the point: the modern world, as he saw it, had become sullied, degraded, and ignoble, and the purpose of the arts, and in particular the purpose of poetry, was to restore it.

Notes

Notes to Introduction
1. Badenach, *An Inquiry into the State of the Indian Army*, 38.
2. Kaye, *A History of the Sepoy War in India*, 1:31.
3. Allen, *Soldier Sahibs*, 206.
4. Parliamentary Papers, 1859, 5:364, quoted in P. J. Marshall, "British Society in India under the East India Company," *Modern Asian Studies* 31, no. 1 (February 1997): 93.
5. Sepoys: Plural of "sepoy," or *Sipâhi*, a native soldier in India.
6. Abbott, *Journals*, 1:1.
7. Houghton, *The Victorian Frame of Mind*, 137.
8. Ibid.

Notes to Chapter 1, Beginnings
1. For a general history of the Levant Company, see Wood, *A History of the Levant Company*; Epstein, *The English Levant Company*; Laidlaw, *The British in the Levant*.
2. Epstein, *The English Levant Company*, 159.
3. For a history of the Armenians in Ankara, see Kasparian, *The History of the Armenians of Angora and Stanos*.
4. von Haven, *Min Sundheds Forliis*, 202.
5. Mather, *Pashas, Traders and Travellers in the Islamic World*, 9.
6. Abbott, *Memoirs and Diary of Henry Abbott*, 1.
7. Laidlaw, *The British in the Levant*, 213.
8. Dalrymple, *White Mughals*, 26. Dalrymple rightly assumes that there were many more connubial relationships that were not formally codified in written wills.
9. *Nawab*: Hindi, a wealthy, powerful, or influential person.
10. Edwards, *The Nabobs at Home*, 178.
11. Price, *The Saddle Put on the Right Horse*, 60–61, 23.
12. Edwards, *The Nabobs at Home*, 13.
13. Cunningham, *The Letters of Horace Walpole*, 5:485. "Maccaroni" or "macaroni" was an eighteenth-century term for a dandy, a British gentleman who adopted foreign customs and manners.
14. Nechtman, *Nabobs, Empire and Identity in Eighteenth Century Britain*, 147.
15. Dalrymple, *White Moghuls*.
16. Holmes, *Sahib*, 505.
17. Edwards, *The Nabobs at Home*, 23–24.

18. Mrs. Monkland, *The Nabob at Home*. "Mrs. Monkland" was the nom de plume of the author of at least half a dozen books on life in India, including *Life in Calcutta* and *Elvira: The Nabob's Wife*, but her true identity is unknown.
19. Ibid., 90.
20. Marshall, "The Empire of the Officials," 57.
21. Abbott refers to it as "Hamptonshire," and it appears this way on some Victorian-era maps.
22. Abbott, *Journals*, 1:6.
23. Ibid., 38.
24. Ibid., 32.
25. Bourne, *Patronage and Society in Nineteenth Century England*, 101.
26. Ibid., 102.
27. Brodie, *The Devil Drives*, 33.
28. Morrison, *Lawrence of Lucknow*, 130.
29. Brodie, *The Devil Drives*, 38.
30. Wright, *Clean and Decent*, 138.
31. Cleanliness was not next to godliness in eighteenth- and early-nineteenth-century Britain. A doctor writing in 1801 noted that "most men resident in London and many ladies, though accustomed to wash their hands and faces daily, neglect washing their bodies from year to year" (Wright, *Clean and Decent*, 138). The nabobs and their male offspring were considered effeminate because they bathed often.
32. Hibbert, *Disraeli*, 8.
33. Abbott, *Journals*, 1:38.
34. Amelius Hood Bond was a rare example of a man who graduated from Addiscombe, was commissioned as an officer in the East India Company, and later transferred into the Royal (or "King's") Army. Cadet Papers, India Office Records, IOR/L/MIL/9/143/358–61, British Library.
35. Abbott, *Journals*, 1:41–2.
36. Sturm, *Reflections on the Works of God in Nature and Providence for Every Day of the Year*.
37. Abbott, *Journals*, 1:38.
38. Nechtman, *Nabobs*, 133.
39. Morden was founded by Sir John Morden in 1695 as a home for destitute merchants, and the primary donors in the 1700s were wealthy agents of the Levant Company who knew Jasper Abbott personally. The college provided housing, board, and a stipend of thirty shillings a month to thirty such men at a time. The Abbott family papers are sprinkled with references to Morden College in baptismal and marriage records, wills, and funerals.
40. The site where the Abbott home once stood is now part of the Euston Square underground station and shopping center.
41. Abbott, *Journals*, 1:39.
42. Bourne, *Patronage*, 94.
43. Ibid., 90–92.
44. Ibid., 94.

45. Steinbach, *Understanding the Victorians*, 124.
46. Thompson, *The Choice of a Profession*, 4.
47. Marshall, "The Empire of the Officials," 51.
48. Bourne, *Patronage*, 106, 181–82. Many years later, when James's brother Frederick returned from India to an appointment as the Superintendent of Addiscombe, he was asked by the East India Company's Board of Directors whether "the idea of going out to India [was] an agreeable one among the young gentlemen at Addiscombe." Absent an understanding, among the members of the board, of the reality that service in India was indeed often the avenue of last resort, the question would seem to make little sense. The fact that it was asked at all suggests how often East India Company officers were essentially dragooned into service by genteel poverty among nabob families. *Report from the Select Committee of the House of Lords on the Government of Indian Territories*, 648.
49. Bourne, *Patronage*, 181–82.
50. Marshall, "British Society in India under the East India Company."
51. Dodwell and Miles, *Alphabetical List*.
52. Possibly Sir James Brooke, Rajah of Sarawak. Brooke was an ensign in the Bengal Army at this time, but the dates and particulars do not match exactly.
53. Dodwell and Miles, *Alphabetical List*.
54. Heathcote, *The Indian Army*, 122–24.
55. Marshall, "British Society in India," 98.
56. Ibid., 99.
57. Quinney, *Sketches of a Soldier's Life in India*.
58. Abbott, *Journals*, 1:46.
59. Ibid., 1:48.
60. Bourne, *Patronage*, 103.
61. Abbott, *Journals*, 1:51.
62. Ibid.
63. Ibid., 52.
64. Stanley, *White Mutiny*, 27–28.
65. Abbott, *Journals*, 2:1.
66. Steinbach, *Understanding the Victorians*, 141–43.
67. Abbott, *Journals*, 1:121.
68. Altick, *Victorian People and Ideas*, 215.
69. Holmes, *Sahib*, 250.
70. Marshall, "British Society in India," 98.
71. Equivalent to approximately £4,000 in 2022 in real value.
72. Cavenagh, *Reminiscences of an Indian Official*, 3.
73. Fisher, *Counterflows to Colonialism*, 125.
74. Ali received an East India Company pension of £100 a year in 1816. Before departing England, he married an Anglican Englishwoman, Miss Biddy Timms, in March 1817, and they lived together in India until about 1830, when Mrs. Meer Hassan Ali returned to England and published her memoirs, *Observations on the Mussalmauns of India*. Fisher, *Counterflows to Colonialism*, 126–30; Ali, *Observations on the Mussalmauns of India*. Miss Timms was not alone in marrying a man from the subcontinent. The

Hindoostani Coffeehouse was opened in London in 1810 by an expatriate from India, Sake Dean Mahomet, who later opened a bath house in Brighton with his Irish wife and introduced shampooing to England. For more on his life, see Fisher, *The Travels of Dean Mohomet*. By 1800, the peoples of India were traveling to Great Britain in significant numbers. From lascars on the London docks to servants of nabobs in London and Cheltenham to entrepreneurs like Mahomet, the people of South Asia were not invisible in the metropole. See Fisher, *Counterflows to Colonialism*.

75. Lutfullah, *Autobiography of Lutfullah*, 389.
76. James, *Raj*, 131.
77. Abbott, *Journals*, 1:48.
78. Ibid., 52. Andrews seems to have grown increasingly demented in his last years, expelling students in groups for imagined offences. These students were virtually always reinstated by connections in London, but by 1822 the Board of Directors could no longer sweep his increasingly autocratic and erratic behavior under the carpet, and Andrews was sent into retirement.
79. Abbott, *Journals*, 2:102.
80. Ibid.
81. In the early nineteenth century, "intimate" meant "close" and had no sexual connotations. It meant then, as Miriam-Webster still partly defines it today, "marked by a warm friendship developing through long association."
82. Abbott, *Journals*, 2:103.
83. The trooping season from England to India ran from September to March, as it was thought that men needed to arrive in India in the "cool" season to have time to adapt to the climate.
84. De Courcy, *The Fishing Fleet*.
85. Marshall, "British Society in India," 106.
86. Steinbach, *Understanding the Victorians*, 113.
87. By "fame," Abbott certainly meant the word in the archaic Latinate sense of "reputation" (from the Latin *fama*, meaning "talk, rumor, report, reputation") and not in the current sense of "celebrity," that is, being famous.
88. Abbott, *Journals*, 2:124.

Notes to Chapter 2, Baptism of Fire

1. *Asiatic Journal and Monthly Register for British India and Its Dependencies* 16 (July 1823), 107.
2. Spelt: zinc or zinc alloy, used to make inexpensive metal objects such as candlesticks.
3. Of the fourteen East Indiamen listed in the *Asiatic Journal* for July 1823 as "Loading for India" in London, for example, including the *Mary*, none was over seven hundred tons.
4. Derived from the calculation for "real wage" or "real wealth" at the Measuring Worth website (www.measuringworth.com), recommended by the Economic History Association.

Notes

5. See, for example, Anonymous (A Lieutenant of the Bengal Establishment), *Cadet's Guide to India*, a copy of which James Abbott would almost certain have read if not owned. The author is believed to have been James Harriott.
6. Emma left England at age fourteen. Born on November 20, 1808, she passed her fifteenth birthday during the voyage.
7. Sister of then Governor General Auckland.
8. Rankin, *Shipmates*, 18.
9. The *Arniston* was not equipped with one of the modern ships' chronometers, and her loss was attributed to navigational error.
10. Holmes, *Sahib*, 109.
11. The soldiers on the HMS *Birkenhead* were ordered to stand at attention on deck as the ship sank to give the women and children a chance to get safely away, as there were not enough lifeboats for everyone on board. Under the command of Lieutenant Colonel Alexander Seton of the 74th Regiment of Foot, the men and their officers stayed in ranks as the ship broke up and sank. Their bravery inspired a poem by Rudyard Kipling and the introduction of the phrase "Birkenhead drill" to mean the practice of saving women and children first.
12. Sabdi and the lascars are excellent examples of the numerous peoples of the subcontinent in England at this time.
13. Rankin, *Shipmates*, 1–3.
14. Ibid., 18.
15. Ibid., 12.
16. Abbott, *Journals*, 2:131.
17. Ibid., 132.
18. Hervey, *A Soldier of the Company*, 8–9.
19. Williamson, *The General East India Guide and Vade-Mecum*, 33.
20. Hervey, *A Soldier of the Company*, 9.
21. Abbott, *Journals*, 2:134.
22. "Petty Officer" is a naval rank, a nautical term still in use today to refer to a senior enlisted man; thus, "petty" is not used here as an adjective but rather as part of a proper noun.
23. Anonymous [Harriott], *Cadet's Guide to India*, 14.
24. Ibid.
25. MacMullen, *Camp and Barrack-Room*, 309.
26. Ibid., 9.
27. Cannadine, *Ornamentalism*.
28. Abbott, *Journals*, 2:137.
29. Ibid.
30. Ibid.
31. Wilson, *Circumnavigators*, 22.
32. Cardigan, in particular, famously detested even queen's officers who had served in India, considering them no longer gentlemen, tainted by their service there.
33. Marshall, "British Society in India," 99.
34. Abbott, *Journals*, 2:139–40.

35. Ibid., 136.
36. Ibid., 138–39.
37. Hoopoo: a paddy bird common to India, which Abbott noted was considered by the peoples of India to be a symbol of wisdom, much like the owl in England.
38. Abbott, *Journals*, 2:140.
39. The notorious nautch did not live up to its prurient reputation. Thousands of Britons, men and women, attended nautches in the first forty years of the nineteenth century in hopes of being scandalized, but almost all were disappointed when the event turned out to be a kind of indoor Vaudeville show, complete with jugglers, ventriloquists, and fire-breathers. The dancing girls were a particular letdown. Writing in 1810, Maria Graham (later Maria, Lady Callcott) recorded, "Some of the women danced, but though they were pretty, and their motions rather graceful, I was disappointed after hearing so much about the nautch-girls of India" (Graham, *Journal of a Residence in India*, 136). Two years later, Lady Maria Nugent noted the dresses of the dancers were "made very full . . . concealing their shape very much" (Nugent, *A Journal from the Year 1811 till 1815*, 146). The redoubtable Bishop Reginald Heber, apparently attending to acquaint himself with sin, recorded instead that he "never saw public dancing in England so free from every thing approaching indecency" (Heber, *Narrative of a Journey through the Upper Provinces of India*, 1:47), while Elizabeth Fenton thought the dancer she saw made "frightful contortions" but did nothing salacious (Fenton, *A Journal of Mrs. Fenton*, 243).
40. Ibid., 147.
41. Maria Graham (1785–1842), born Maria Dundas, later Maria, Lady Callcott. Abbott's familiarity with Graham's book suggests he cast a wide net in his reading on India.
42. Graham, *Journal of a Residence in India*, 2.
43. MacMullen, *Camp and Barrack-Room*, 66.
44. Heber, *Narrative of a Journey through the Upper Provinces of India*, 4.
45. Shoes: archaic; thin slices.
46. *Kala jeera*, Hindi, meaning black cumin, from the family *bunium persicum*. In the Hooghly delta, however, the etymology is almost certainly from the Bengali *kalo jeera*, which instead refers to the family *Nigella sativa*, which is black onion seed. Nigella is a common ingredient of Bengali cuisine. The fact that Abbott knew what it was is a clear indication he had seen it used at home.
47. Sinha, *Colonial Masculinity*, 15.
48. Abbott, *Journals*, 2:155–56.
49. *Khidmatgar*: Hindi, literally "one who serves." In the sense Abbott used it at the time, it meant a Muslim servant whose duties included serving meals. *Hobson-Jobson* notes that this usage was "peculiar to the Bengal Presidency." Yule and Burnell, *Hobson-Jobson*, 486.
50. Abbott, *Journals*, 2:157.
51. James, *Raj*, 131.
52. Dalrymple, *White Moghuls*.
53. Abbott, *Journals*, 2:167. MacLeod was promoted to brigadier (general) shortly afterward and commanded the artillery during the 1826–1827 Siege of Bhurtpore.

54. Subedar: the senior Indian officer in an East Indian Army company, a military unit of approximately 120 men.
55. James, *Raj*, 132.
56. Ram, *From Sepoy to Subedar*, 14.
57. Later Sir Charles D'Oyly, 7th Baronet.
58. Griffin: an officer newly arrived in India, a greenhorn. Yule and Burnell, *Hobson-Jobson*, 395.
59. A Civilian and an Officer of the Bengal Establishment, *Tom Raw*, 261.
60. Ram, *From Sepoy to Subedar*, 14n13.
61. Marshall, "British Society in India," 93.
62. Abbott, *Journals*, 2:159–60.
63. *Sowar*: an indigenous cavalryman.
64. Smythe was cleared in his court-martial but resigned under pressure immediately afterward, perhaps part of a prearranged quid pro quo. James, *Raj*, 213.
65. Captain George Stack was also on Napier's staff at this time. Stack was a pioneer of the study of Sindi in Great Britain, composed a dictionary of Sindi, and administered Burton's exam in the language. It is impossible to assess, however, the extent to which Stack actually spoke the vernacular language. John Shakespear, the Hindustani instructor at Addiscombe, for example, composed the grammar of Hindustani used at Addiscombe for decades but could not speak a word of the language in conversation. Simons, *A Place for Pleasure*, 98–99. See also James, *Raj*, 213.
66. Venereal disease rates among British enlisted men for the years 1827 to 1833, for example, ranged from 16 percent of the force to 31 percent of the force each year, proof that at least a quarter of all British soldiers were frequenting prostitutes in the bazaar. There is also considerable evidence that British authorities encouraged monogamous relationships between enlisted men and indigenous women as both a means of reducing the rate of venereal disease and a way to reduce alcoholism by encouraging a more stable lifestyle. India Office Records, L.Mil 5/376, 120, 132–33, 232–33, British Library. Cited in James, *Raj*, 139.
67. MacMullen, *Camp and Barrack-Room*, 171.
68. Dalrymple, *White Mughals*.
69. Emily Eden, *Letters from India*, 1:324–25.
70. *Chatta*: Hindi, parasol. Sometimes rendered as *chatra* and even *chitree*. *Chatta* bearers, found in *Hobson-Jobson* as *chitree-burdars*, were a caste, engaged on a daily basis and employed by almost every Briton in India at this time, including noncommissioned officers in both the East India Company and Royal armies.
71. Abbott, *Journals*, 2:190–91.
72. Ibid., 168.
73. Hervey, *A Soldier of the Company*, 17.
74. Pogson, *Memoir of the Mutiny at Barrackpore*, 33.
75. Abbott, *Journals*, 2:170.
76. Ibid., 170–72.
77. MacMullen, *Camp and Barrack-Room*, 78.
78. Abbott, *Journals*, 2:171.

79. Ibid., 172–74.
80. The British victory in the First Anglo-Burmese War cost the lives of some fifteen thousand British and Indian soldiers and gave Britain territorial control of Assam, Manipur, Cachar, Jaintia, Arakan, and Tenasserim. The peace treaty levied an indemnity of £1 million and forced an agreement to open commerce. The indemnity, however, reimbursed the British treasury only a fraction of the cost of the war, which is estimated at up to £13 million. The equivalent sum in 2022, using the retail price calculator, would be £1.091 billion.
81. Abbott, *Journals*, 2:174.
82. *Hŭtti Hŭtti*: Hindi, "elephant! elephant!"
83. Abbott, *Journals*, 2:179–84.
84. Abbott was quite aware that this had been a very foolish thing to do, noting at the end of his lengthy account of it, "I have been very careful to whom I related this story of the elephant hunt [and] here pass my veto against its publication now or hereafter." Abbott, *Journals*, 2:184.
85. MacMullen, *Camp and Barrack-Room*, 175–76.
86. *Sowar*: a native cavalryman.
87. The Chāran clan of the Banjāra tribe of the Nimarr District, for example, an area which James Abbott would later come to know well, were highly regarded as porters, having been employed by both the Mughals and the Marathas. They were known to British officials as "a caste of carriers and drivers of pack-bullocks." Russell, *The Tribes and Castes of the Central Provinces of India*, 2:162.
88. Abbott, *Journals*, 2:186–87.
89. Overseas service was not in the *Seeur ul Mutu ukhireen*, and the high-caste Brahmin sepoys maintained that travel by ship to Burma would in all probability render it impossible for a high-caste Hindu to maintain the purity of his body, his clothing, and his food, thus defiling him and breaking his caste.
90. Abbott, *Journals*, 2:186–87.
91. The *Yajñopavitam*, or *zunnar*, the sacred cord worn by all Brahmins.
92. Pogson, *Memoir of the Mutiny at Barrackpore*, 35.
93. Ibid., 71.
94. Abbott, *Journals*, 2:186–87.
95. The first newspaper printed in Urdu appeared in 1822 as the *Jam-e-Jahan Numa*. It was published in Calcutta under the auspices of the East India Company. The same year, the first Persian-language newspaper was also published in Calcutta, the *Maraat-ul-Akhbar*. It was founded and edited by Raja Ram Mohan Raaey and may be considered the first independent Indian newspaper in a vernacular language, although Persian, as the official court language, was spoken chiefly among elites. The first newspaper in India published in Hindi was the *Samachar Sudha Varshan*, which first appeared in 1854. Many handwritten news sheets opposing the policies of the EICo were also circulated clandestinely. By 1857, the British had implemented four laws aimed at curbing the vernacular press, one of them at the urging of James Abbott himself.
96. *Budgerow*: An indigenous boat with oars at the rear and a cabin at the front, used for river movement in India.

97. Abbott, *Journals*, 2:188.
98. Marshall, "British Society in India," 94.
99. Peers, *Between Mars and Mammon*, 83.
100. Abbott never saw Clementine again. She died in childbirth a few years later. James Elphinstone died of disease two years after Clementine passed. The couple was survived by one son. Emma returned to England, where her ailment was cured by an unspecified "minor surgery." She never married.
101. Abbott, *Journals*, 2:194–96.
102. *Dak*: from Hindi *dāk*, meaning "quickly"; the system of mail or passenger transport by relays of bearers or horses stationed at intervals along the route.
103. Abbott, *Journals*, 2:208.
104. Malleson, *The Decisive Battles of India*, 344.
105. Abbott, *Journals*, 2:218.
106. Ibid., 218–19. Ochterlony was one of the truly exceptional figures of British India. He was fully assimilated into Mughal culture, keeping thirteen concubines and adopting a completely Indian lifestyle. To this day a pillar remains in Delhi to commemorate his life, one of the few such monuments to be retained in modern India.
107. Stubbs, *History of the Organization, Equipment, and War Services of the Regiment of Bengal Artillery*, 2:220.
108. Also somewhere along the gun line was a British gunner named James Lewis. Shortly after the battle, Lewis deserted and traveled to Afghanistan, where he assumed the name Charles Masson and became well known as an explorer, adventurer, and spy for the East India Company in Kabul, where he worked as a "news writer." Among his best-known books is his *Narrative of Various Journeys in Balochistan, Afghanistan, and the Punjab*.
109. The 2nd Battalion, to which Frederick Abbott was assigned, was still in Burma.
110. Lieutenant Colonel Henry Stark, commander of the Second Brigade, Horse Artillery, and Lieutenant Colonel Clements Brown, commander of the Third Brigade, Horse Artillery.
111. Abbott, *Journals*, 2:223.
112. Buckle, *Memoir of the Services of the Bengal Artillery*, 388.
113. *Golandaz*: literally, "bringer of round shot."
114. Buckle, *Memoir of the Services of the Bengal Artillery*, 391.
115. Anonymous, "The Siege of Bhurtpore," 433.
116. Abbott, *Journals*, 3:3.
117. Sita Ram, present at Bhurtpore with the 63rd BNI, recalled that "great numbers of the ... people of the city had been killed by shells." Ram, *From Sepoy to Subedar*, 72.
118. Abbott, *Journals*, 2:224.
119. Tunnels dug by engineers under the walls of the fort, filled with explosives, and detonated.
120. Anonymous, *Blackwood's Edinburgh Magazine*, 436.
121. James, *Raj*, 141.
122. The sum 41,50,000 (or 4,150,000 rupees in US notation) in 1830 would have been the equivalent of about $48,000,000 in 2022, using a basis rate of twenty-four pence or

two shillings for a silver rupee in 1830 and using the measuringworth.com tables to calculate approximate relative purchasing power.
123. Peers, *Between Mars and Mammon*, 203.
124. James, *Raj*, 141.

Notes to Chapter 3, Progress and Reform

1. Abbott frequently wrote for the *United Services Journal* in the 1830s under the pen name Snellius Schickhardus, sometimes referred to in articles written under his other pen names as "the Moon Man." The likely source of this pen name is a pair of lunar craters, the Snellius crater, named for Dutch astronomer Willebrord Snell (in Latin *Snellius*), and the Schickard crater, named for the German polymath Wilhelm Schickard (in Latin *Schickardus*). Wilhelm Schickard (1592–1635) was an Orientalist, theologian, linguist, mathematician, astronomer, and early pioneer of calculating machines for basic arithmetic operations. The *Monumenta Guerickiana*, the magazine of the Otto-von-Guericke Society at the University of Magdeburg, gives Schickhard as an accepted alternative spelling of the name, and it appeared this way occasionally in the nineteenth century. Abbott's book *Tales of the Forest: Containing The Lotus-Walker and The Spoiler's Doom* (London: James Madden, 1853) was also published under the pseudonym Snellius Schickhardus.

2. The original report never found its way into the East India Company archives for some reason. It was found in Calcutta by a friend some forty years after Abbott submitted it and was returned to him in 1878. Abbott, *Bareilly District Report*.

3. Marshall, "The Empire of the Officials," 48.

4. An army of 12,000 officers and men that was ordered to capture and subdue the Arakan peninsula at the beginning of 1825, for example, mustered only 3,240 effectives by September of that year, with 5,505 either hospitalized or on convalescent leave. The British second in command in Burma, Willoughby Cotton, dubbed the Siege of Bhurtpore a "champagne campaign" in a letter to Herbert Taylor in 1828. Taylor, *The Taylor Papers*, 223.

5. Peers, *Between Mars and Mammon*, 174.

6. La Nauze, "The Substance of Adam Smith's Attack on Mercantilism," 4:55; Marshall, "British Society in India," 96.

7. Arnold, *Oakfield; or, Fellowship of the East*, 231.

8. Stanley, *White Mutiny*, 27–28.

9. Marshall, "British Society in India," 96.

10. Ibid., 97.

11. Stanley, *White Mutiny*, 49–50.

12. Ibid., 51.

13. Marshall, "The Empire of the Officials," 50.

14. Peers, *Between Mars and Mammon*, 79.

15. Ibid.

16. Ibid., 173.

17. Alavi, *The Sepoys and the Company*, 90.

18. *Cafre* was a Portuguese term, derived from the Arabic *Qafr*, from which the word "Kaffir" was adopted. At the time the term was used in the article, it meant "Negro" or "Black," presumably in this case referring to soldiers of low social classes from Sri Lanka or the Andaman Islands.
19. Anonymous (W.W.), "Considerations on the Native Army and General Defense of India," 1–8.
20. Anonymous (S.S.), *United Services Journal and Naval and Military Magazine*, 28–40. The article is signed simply "S.S.," but there can be no doubt this is the abbreviation for Snellius Schickhardus, one of the noms de plume used by James Abbott in this publication. Even without the initials, the writing style and wide detours into the lore of Alexander the Great are unmistakably Abbott's.
21. Schickhardus, "An Apology for the Indian Army," 31.
22. Ibid., 37.
23. Ibid., 31.
24. Cannadine, *Ornamentalism*, 4.
25. Ibid., xix.
26. James, *Raj*, 236–37.
27. The so-called Doctrine of Lapse, first used in 1824 to annex the princely state of Kittur, allowed the British to take possession of any princely state in which the sovereign died without a legitimate male heir.
28. Anonymous (W.W.), "Considerations on the Native Army and General Defense of India," 1–8.
29. Schickhardus, "An Apology for the Indian Army," 33.
30. Ram, *From Sepoy to Subedar*, 24.
31. Abbott was not alone in defending the sepoy's reputation. Other articles also appeared at this time to continue a debate that the *United Services Journal* no doubt found good for circulation. See, for example, Anonymous (An Officer of the Bengal Infantry), "The Indian Army," 85–88.
32. Peers, *Between Mars and Mammon*, 173.
33. Lord Wellesley, 1st Marquess Wellesley, governor-general of India from 1798–1805.
34. The coronet is the uppermost part of the hoof, where the bone-like portion of the hoof meets the fur of the lower leg.
35. Abbott, *Journals*, 3: 4–5.
36. Abbott, *Journals*, 3: 13.
37. Lunar caustic: Silver nitrate, used in the 1800s as a cauterizing agent. *Luna* comes from the Greek word for the moon, thought by the ancient Greeks to be associated with silver.
38. *Mofussil*: The Bengal backcountry; that is, near wilderness.
39. Dutta, *Glimpses of European Life in 19th Century Bengal*, 95.
40. Hays, *Epidemics and Pandemics*, 217–26. How it spread was not understood. The means of transmission of cholera was first discovered by Dr. John Snow in London in 1854.
41. Abbott, *Journals*, 3: 39.

42. Abbott may well have encountered one of the remarkable figures of Afghan history, the American adventurer and soldier of fortune Josiah Harlan, in Karnal at this time. Harlan, a Quaker from Philadelphia, was then serving as a surgeon in the Bengal Artillery in Karnal, despite never having studied medicine. Macintyre, *The Man Who Would Be King*, 16–17.
43. Abbott, *Journals*, 3:33.
44. Ibid., 44–45.
45. Ibid., 35–39.
46. Abbott means *diwali*, which translates as "row of lamps."
47. Hikers commonly experience a sense of euphoria while climbing from hypoxia, or oxygen deficiency in the body. It is also known to disorient aircraft pilots when climbing in altitude.
48. Abbott, *Journals*, 3: 40–41, 44. After 1829, Abbott did not again return to Simla until thirty years later in 1859. He wrote, "My mind was haunted with its beauties.... [T]he poem *Constance*, was an attempt to depict those beauties in words and to convey to others some of the delight I had enjoyed from that mountain scenery." Ibid., 48.
49. Ibid., 45–46. Marianne Sarah Abbott (1808–1887) married Charles Scott Hadow (1801–1849) and had one son, Frederick Edward Hadow. Charles Hadow was a partner in Willis, Hadow and Co, wine merchants of Scot's Yard, Bush Lane, London, which also traded in India. Illustrating again how many Abbotts were present in the East, Marianne Abbott was the sister of Major General Herbert Abbott. They were the children of George Edward Abbott (d. 1822) and Anna Maria Stacy, who married in India. George Edward Abbott was the head assistant in the Calcutta General Post Office. George was the son of John Abbott, the British Consul at Aleppo and James Abbott's uncle. Herbert Abbott was yet another Abbott to become a major general in the Indian Army.
50. Tennyson, *Poems*, 2:96, line 39.
51. *Locus amoenus*: Latin, literally "pleasant place."
52. Kennedy, *The Magic Mountains*.
53. Abbott, *Journals*, 3:50–51.
54. Scott, *Rob Roy*, 2:62.
55. Ibid., 110.
56. Ibid.
57. For details on the charges and the trial, see *The Asiatic Journal and Monthly Register for British and Foreign India, China and Australasia*, 61–62.
58. Prior, Brennan, and Haines, "Bad Language," 93.
59. Colebrooke, "Letter from Sir Edward Colebrooke to Sir George Swinton, Chief Secretary to the Government in Calcutta," 207–8, 301.
60. Prior, Brennan, and Haines, "Bad Language," 109.
61. Pernau, *Bürger mit Turban*, 94.
62. The East India Company was, however, permitted to continue its trade with China for another ten years.
63. Marshall, "The Empire of the Officials," 51.
64. Collingham, *Imperial Bodies*, 60.
65. Marshall, "British Society in India," 93–96.

Notes

66. Ibid., 90.
67. Ibid., 92.
68. Ibid., 101.
69. Dalrymple, *White Moghuls*.
70. Ghosh, *Sex and the Family in Colonial India*, 38.
71. Memsahib: a middle- or upper-class British women in Bengal; a contraction of "Madam Sahib." Yule and Burnell, *Hobson-Jobson*, 576.
72. Ballhatchet, *Race, Sex and Class under the Raj*, 144.
73. Marshall, "British Society in India," 90.
74. Ibid.
75. Ghosh, *Sex and the Family in Colonial India*, 38, 40.
76. Holmes, *Sahib*, 436–457.
77. Ram, *From Sepoy to Subedar*, 24–25. Scholars have questioned the provenance of Ram's book, noting the number of standard British narratives, his Flashman-like engagement in most of the important battles of British India, and its similarity to period Romantic novels. Wagner, *The Great Fear of 1857*, 16.
78. Holmes, *Sahib*, 436.
79. For a detailed study of Shi'a Islam in colonial India, see Jones, *Shi'a Islam in Colonial India*.
80. Williamson, *The General East India Guide and Vade-Mecum*, 452.
81. Ghosh, *Sex and the Family in Colonial India*, 136–47.
82. "What the Data Tells Us about Love and Marriage in India," *BBC News*, December 8, 2021, www.bbc.com/news/world-asia-india-59530706.
83. Abbott, *Journals*, 3: 90.
84. Burton, *The Life of Sir Richard F. Burton*, 135.
85. Ghosh, *Sex and the Family in Colonial India*, 237.
86. Singh, *A Survey of Anglo-Indian Fiction*.
87. Princep, *The Baboo and Other Tales Descriptive of Society in India*, 1:114–15. Princep was an English printmaker and a civil servant who lived in India from 1822 to 1829. He died at sea in 1830 at the age of twenty-seven.
88. Abbott, notes for an unfinished novel; pages unnumbered, approximately forty pages present.
89. Later Sir Charles D'Oyly, 7th Baronet.
90. Wallace, "Calcutta in 1823," 326.
91. Ghosh, *Sex and the Family in Colonial India*, 41.
92. By this, Abbott meant a woman born of one British parent and one Indian parent.
93. Probably Colonel F. J. T. Johnson of the 3rd Light Cavalry. Skinner's Horse was also known at this time as the 3rd (Bengal) Cavalry. They wore distinctive yellow *kurtas* (long coats), which gave them the nickname "the yellow boys." Their coats and hats were similar to those commonly worn by *khidmatgars*. The men Abbott encountered in Simla were likely Skinner's Horse. Dodwell and Miles, *Alphabetical List*, 152–53.
94. Abbott, *Journals*, 3:46.
95. Skinner's Horse had a detachment of fifty-six troopers (out of a total of 656 *sowars* in the brigade) at Karnal.

96. Abbott, *Journals*, 3:47.
97. Heathcoat, *The Indian Army*, 40.
98. A quaint way of saying he subdued Abbott by grabbing hold of his genitals.
99. Abbott, *Journals*, 3:47–48.
100. Peers, *Between Mars and Mammon*, 211.
101. Stokes, *The English Utilitarians and India*.
102. Peers, *Between Mars and Mammon*.
103. As much as a quarter in some cases and for some ranks. Majors were especially hard hit.
104. Peers, *Between Mars and Mammon*, 223.
105. The great Agra Gun is thought to have been forged during the reign of either Akbar or Shah Jahan circa 1600 CE. Cooper, *The Anglo-Maratha Campaigns and the Contest for India*, 198.
106. Abbott, *Journals*, 3:13. The legend that Bentinck planned to break up the Taj Mahal to sell the marble circulated for decades. According to Bentinck's biographer, John Rosselli, the story began when Bentinck salvaged marble from the Red Fort in Agra and sold it to raise funds. Rosselli confirms Abbott's allegation that it was Bentinck who ordered the scraping of the Great Agra Gun. Rosselli, *Lord William Bentinck*, 283.
107. Sati or suttee: the practice of burning widows alive upon the funeral pyre of their husbands. Because under Hindu customary law, a widow inherited her husband's property and estates, the ritual murder of widows in this fashion had everything to do with estate inheritance (which reverted to the husband's family if the widow died) and nothing to do with the religious obligations it was wrapped up in.
108. "Bentinck to Charles Grant, Sir R. Campbell, Sir E. Barnes, Sir E. Ryan, J. G. Ravenshaw, and Others, 1832," in Papers of Lord William H. Cavendish Bentinck (1774–1839), Soldier, Politician and Statesman, Bentinck to Charles Grant, Sir R. Campbell, Sir E. Barnes, Sir E. Ryan, J. G. Ravenshaw, and Others 1832.
109. Rosselli, *Lord William Bentinck*, 318. This measure would, of course, have completely contradicted Bentinck's passion for budget cuts, as maintaining British troops in India was far more expensive than sepoys.
110. Cannadine, *Ornamentalism*.
111. Alavi, *The Sepoys and the Company*, 294.
112. Flogging was eventually reintroduced in certain specific cases after Bentinck's departure.
113. Sir John Malcolm, letters to Governor-General William Bentinck: "pride of caste": "Letter of January 27, 1830"; "unreliable": Letter of November 27, 1830.
114. Grant, *Observations on the State of Society among the Asiatic Subjects of Great Britain*, 45.
115. Hodgson, *Opinions on the Indian Army*, 117–18.
116. Napier, *Defects, Civil and Military, of the Indian Government*, 29.
117. Appendix 61, in *Evidence of Major General Birch, Military Secretary to Government of India to Royal Commission on Organisation of Indian Army*, 77.
118. Peers, *Between Mars and Mammon*, 85.

119. Ibid., 85–86.
120. Ibid., 79.

Notes to Chapter 4, D'Arcy Todd and the Revenue Survey

1. Abbott noted that Todd's head was shaved to allow cool damp cloths to be applied, a common part of the treatment in particular at this time for scarlet fever. Fullerton, *A Family Medical Guide*, 241.
2. Kaye, *The Lives of Indian Officers*, 300.
3. Abbott, *Journals*, 3:54.
4. Richards, "Passing the Love of Women," 93, 95–96.
5. Ibid.
6. Laidlaw, *The Poetical Works of Alain Chartier*, 393–409.
7. Richards, "Passing the Love of Women," 98.
8. Fone, *A Road to Stonewall*, 91.
9. Montaigne, *Complete Essays*, 137; Shelley, *Works*, 2:143; Hyam, *Britain's Imperial Century*, 141.
10. Richards, "Passing the Love of Women," 102.
11. The term "lascar" is generally associated with Indian sailors. However, there were also Indian artillerymen called "gun lascars" whose duties were the "manhandling and cleaning of guns, carriage of ammunition ... the construction of gun platforms, erecting batteries during siege warfare and throwing up protective earthworks around the guns. In fact the gun lascars did everything on and around the guns except aim and fire" (Butalia, *The Evolution of the Artillery in India*, 119). The men who performed these supporting roles were often called "powder monkeys" by artillery gunners in the nineteenth century.
12. Abbott, *Journals*, 3:57.
13. Ibid., 62–63.
14. Abbott meant *jemadar*, the lowest rank of indigenous officers.
15. Abbott, *Journals*, 3:61.
16. *Shootur sowar*: from Hindi, *shutur-sawar*, the rider of a dromedary or swift camel, attached to an official on a march in upper India. Wagenaar et al., *Allied Chambers Transliterated Hindi Hindi-English Dictionary*, 1125.
17. That is, ordered him.
18. This word does not appear in *Hobson-Jobson* and seems very archaic, referring to a mayor or man in charge of a village.
19. Abbott, *Journals*, 3:66.
20. Ibid.
21. Ibid., 57.
22. Roberdeau, "Calcutta in 1805," 64–65.
23. Patalpanie is a small but popular village in the Indore District of Madhya Pradesh, famous for its scenery and waterfalls and now a major tourist attraction.
24. Abbott, *Journals*, 3:91.
25. Ibid., 83.
26. Ibid.
27. *Dispression*: depression; a common misspelling in the nineteenth century.

28. Abbott, *Journals*, 3:83–84.
29. Flaherty, *The Midnight Disease*, 32.
30. Sutherland, *A Little History of Literature*, 98.
31. Burton, *The Anatomy of Melancholy*.
32. *Terrific*: at this time, the word meant "terrifying."
33. Abbott, *Journals*, 3:84.
34. Written under the nom de plume Jedediah Bobson.
35. India Office Records, European Manuscripts, Mss Eur F171/30, British Library. Loose, single-page note in Abbott's handwriting, dated January 27, 1894; inside the front cover of the bound original manuscript of *The Private Centinel* [*sic*].
36. Stanley, *White Mutiny*, 53.
37. Marshall, "British Society in India," 104–5.
38. The Revenue Survey of the North-Western Provinces conducted by the Revenue Service Branch of the Bengal government should not be confused with the Great Trigonometrical Survey of India, which was under the authority of the Surveyor General of India and was a far more ambitious undertaking that took sixty years to complete, beginning in 1802. Keay, *The Great Arc*.
39. Marshman, *History of India*, 372–73. For details of the surveying process and the names of most of the surveyors in this period, see Markham, "Second Period of the Topographical Surveys, 1823–1843," 81–86.
40. Madan, *Indian Cartography*, 105.
41. Madan, *Indian Cartography*, table on 106. In 1842, following the First Anglo-Afghan War, retrenchment resulted in the elimination of all the survey teams, and during the Great Mutiny of 1857, most of the district maps and land records completed prior to 1842 were destroyed.
42. Marshman, *The History of India*, 3:48–49.
43. Dutt, *The Economic History of India under Early British Rule*, 148.
44. Edwardes and Merivale, *Life of Sir Henry Lawrence*, 3rd ed., 88.
45. Stokes, *The English Utilitarians and India*, 114.
46. O'Malley, *The Indian Civil Service*, 61–62.
47. Both Bareilly and Shahjihanpoor districts were swept early into the Mutiny, and the civil stations at both were hard hit. At Bareilly, there had been sufficient warning, and the women and children were sent north to safety before the outbreak of violence. Seven men at the station, however, were massacred on May 31, 1857, when the 18th and 68th Bengal Native Infantry regiments mutinied. In Shahjihanpoor seven Britons, including two officers' wives, were murdered in church on Sunday morning, May 31 when the 28th BNI mutinied. For a full account of the rebellion at Bareilly and the names of the slain, see Anonymous, *Narrative of the Indian Mutinies of 1857*, 34–36. For an account of the massacre at Shahjihanpoor, see Forrest, *A History of the Indian Mutiny*, 311–13, and for the names of the men and women murdered there, see Blunt, *List of Inscriptions*, 104–5.
48. *Pargana* or *purgana*: an administrative division established by the Moghul government; a subdivision of a district.
49. Michael, "Making Territory Visible," 84.
50. Smyth and Thuillier, *A Manual of Surveying for India*, 605–17.

51. For greater detail on the technical aspects of the revenue survey mapping process, see Edney, *Mapping an Empire*.
52. *Mootsuddy*: from the Hindi *mutasaddi*, an accountant. See Yule and Burnell, *Hobson-Jobson*, 585. *Mootsuddies* were indigenous surveyors who measured with chains (also known as "chain men," made famous by Rudyard Kipling's novel *Kim*). They calculated angles and plotted their work entirely by eye.
53. Abbott, *Journals*, 3:110–11.
54. Ibid., 110.
55. *On the Origin of Species* was published on November 24, 1859.
56. For a good summary of this debate, see Sramek, *Gender, Morality, and Race in Company India*, 172n57.
57. "At the time, medical opinion generally favored the theory that diseases like typhoid and cholera were spread through the atmosphere by malign gases from decomposing organic material. Only in the early 1880s was this etiological theory displaced by the one that attributed disease to specific living organisms present in food and water." Altick, *Victorian People and Ideas*, 48. Abbott repeats this misconception about vapors on several occasions in his journals.
58. The Banjara, or Bunjara, were a nomadic group of Lambadi speakers thought to be of Persian origin. They kept cattle, traded salt, and found work in transporting goods.
59. The Kalandars are Muslim nomads, classified by the government of India today as "OBC," for "Other Backward Tribes." They continue to live in the forests of India and find work as entertainers with domesticated bears and sloths.
60. Abbott, Bareilly District Report.
61. Raychaudhuri, "Permanent Settlement in Operation," 167.
62. *Tehsildar*: a local revenue collector.
63. Abbott, *Journals*, 3:112.

Notes to Chapter 5, A Mission to Khiva

1. Farwell, *Mr. Kipling's Army*, 115.
2. Abbott at this time was still a brevet captain. This allowed him to wear the rank insignia of a captain and hold any positions requiring a captain's rank, while still receiving the pay of a lieutenant.
3. Hopkirk, *The Great Game*, 188–91.
4. Macrory, *Signal Catastrophe*, 66–82. The officer is believed to have been Jan Prosper Witkiewicz, using the Russified name Yan Viktorovich Vitkevich. A Lithuanian, Witkiewicz traveled in the uniform of a captain of Cossacks and reached Kabul in 1837 on a diplomatic mission from the tsar. He is thought to have committed suicide in Moscow in May 1839 after his return from Kabul, although conspiracy theories abounded.
5. Jasanoff, *Edge of Empire*, 311.
6. Macrory, *Signal Catastrophe*, 81–82.
7. Elphinstone, *An Account of the Kingdom of Cabaul*.
8. Macrory, *Signal Catastrophe*, 66.
9. Todd, "Observations on the Military Memoir of Cpt. Burnes on Afghanistan, 2 July, 1837."

10. Macrory, *Signal Catastrophe*, 81.
11. Hopkirk, *The Great Game*, 189.
12. MacNaughten paid the ultimate price for his folly, as would virtually the entire army of sixteen thousand soldiers, porters, and camp followers in the disastrous retreat from Kabul in 1842. MacNaughten did not live to witness it; he was murdered at an outdoor meeting with the Afghans near the British encampment before the retreat.
13. Ewans, *Afghanistan*, 45.
14. Macrory, *Signal Catastrophe*, 77.
15. Buckle, *Memoir of the Services of the Bengal Artillery*, 408.
16. Ibid., 409–10.
17. Abbott, *Journals*, 3:133–35.
18. Ibid., 135.
19. Ibid., 135–36.
20. Ibid., 136.
21. Buckle, *Memoir of the Services of the Bengal Artillery*, 410–11.
22. Lee, *Dictionary of National Biography (Supplement)*, 22:4.
23. Abbott, *Narrative of a Journey from Heraut to Khiva*, xv–xvi.
24. Napier, *The Conquest of Scinde*, 10–11.
25. Abbott, *Journal of March with Army from Kandahar to Herat*.
26. The fates of the members of the legation illustrate the difficulty of surviving a military career in India. After reaching Herat, Edward Conolly had orders to travel onward to Seistan to make a statistical survey and rough map of the area, which he accomplished successfully to considerable acclaim (Conolly, "Sketch of the Physical Geography of Seistan"). He was subsequently assigned as an aide-de-camp to General Robert Sale at Kabul, where he was killed early in the rebellion there. Lieutenant Henry Saunders survived multiple wounds in an assault on a fortress outside Herat a year later only to be killed at the Battle of Maharajpoor, the final battle of the Gwalior Campaign of 1843. Dr., later Sir, John Login was the man who later converted the last maharaja of the Sikh Empire, Duleep Singh (1838–1893), to Christianity. Lieutenant North later accompanied Eldred Pottinger to Kabul across Ghor, a route previously believed to be impassable. He and Dr. Ritchie, who evacuated Herat with Todd, appear to have survived the First Anglo-Afghan War. Eldred Pottinger survived the First Anglo-Afghan War as a captive of Dost Mohammed in Kabul only to die of fever on leave in Hong Kong a year later. Waller, *Beyond the Khyber Pass*, 283.
27. Abbott, *Journal of March with Army from Kandahar to Herat*, 32.
28. Ibid., 24.
29. Abbott's use of the phrase "the game he had been sent to play" is particularly interesting in regard to the etymology of the phrase "the Great Game." Abbott's friend, Arthur Conolly, with whom he spent much time exploring Mandu, is credited with coining the phrase "the Great Game" in a letter to his brother, Edward Conolly, with whom Abbott was now riding.
30. Abbott, *Journal of March with Army from Kandahar to Herat*, 25.
31. Ibid., 37.

Notes

32. In Greek mythology, Hades was divided into four regions. The deepest was Tartarus, an abyss that served as a dungeon for the torment of the souls of the wicked.
33. Ibid., 44–45. In an 1878 endnote to his journal of the march from Quetta to Kandahar, Abbott wrote that he had intended to publish an account of his trip from Ferozepore to Herat under the pseudonym Haji Bimbajie Khan. His intention to impersonate a Muslim and publish under an Indian pseudonym was never realized because his original journal of the journey from Ferozepore to Quetta was lost. Abbott, *Journal of a March from Quetta to Cundahar*, 35.
34. Olson and Shadle, *Historical Dictionary of the British Empire, A–J*, 372.
35. Hopkirk, *The Great Game*, 27–28.
36. Abbott, *Journal of March with Army from Kandahar to Herat*, 53–54.
37. Ibid.
38. Hopkirk, *The Great Game*, 204.
39. Ibid.
40. Ibid.
41. The first European to reach Khiva was apparently the Russian Captain Nikolai Muravyev, who published an account of his travels in *Journey to Khiva through the Turkoman Country*, first printed in Moscow in 1822. Muravyev, *Journey to Khiva through the Turkoman Country*.
42. Hopkirk, *The Great Game*, 125–28.
43. Ibid., 204–5.
44. Ibid.
45. Ibid.
46. Abbott renders the name "Sammud Khaun" throughout his books.
47. In 1840, a steward was an employee in charge of managing the household affairs of an estate; in a military context the term carried, in particular, responsibility for food preparation and provisions. Sammud Khan's role in Abbott's travels was a combination of valet, chamberlain, and orderly.
48. *Pir*: an Islamic honorific title for Sufis, meaning "teacher."
49. Abbott, *Journey from Heraut to Khiva*, 1:3–4.
50. Kamran was the nephew of Shah Shuja.
51. Which he indeed turned out to be, murdering Kamran and seizing the throne of Herat in 1844. Lodge, *The History of Nations*, 5:363.
52. It was widely believed that Yar Mohammed schemed by private correspondence with the emir of Bokhara to have both Stoddart and later Conolly arrested and imprisoned.
53. *Mirza*: from Persian (میرزا); by Abbott's time it retained a number of connotations, including nobleman, gentleman, scholar, scribe, and often simply "literate person."
54. Abbott, *Journey from Heraut to Khiva*, 10.
55. Here Abbott means *farash*, from Persian (फराश), meaning "servant or chamberlain."
56. Abbott, *Journal of a March from Quetta to Cundahar*, 3.
57. *Nazir*: Persian (نذیر), literally "supervisor, controller, surveillant."
58. Abbott, *Journey from Heraut to Khiva*, 177.
59. Vibart, *Addiscombe*, 372.

60. Whitteridge, *Charles Masson of Afghanistan*, 35–37. The British found that disguising oneself as a local, such as a caravan merchant or horse trader, was extraordinarily difficult, as even the slightest misstep, such as sneezing the wrong way, would result in discovery and quite possibly death. Few succeeded in pulling it off.
61. Abbott, *Journey from Heraut to Khiva*, 9.
62. The pseudonym of John Lewis.
63. Lee, *The "Ancient Supremacy,"* 145.
64. Queen Victoria assumed the throne in 1837 after the death of her uncle, William IV.
65. Abbott, *Journey from Heraut to Khiva*, 74. By "fame," Abbott certainly meant the word in the archaic Latinate sense of "reputation" (from the Latin *fama*, meaning "talk, rumor, report, reputation") and not in the current sense of "celebrity," that is, being famous.
66. It is generally accepted that he died of fever in Afghan Turkestan in 1825, although rumors persisted for many years that he died in Tibet in 1837. His traveling companion, George Trebeck, died of fever a day or two after Moorcroft.
67. Conolly, *Journey to the North of India*; Hopkirk, *The Great Game*, 128–30.
68. Mandu was the capital of the Ghilzai Sultanate of Malwa, founded by Mahmud Khan (1436–1469). By the seventeenth century it was abandoned. Abbott notes this in *Journey from Heraut to Khiva*, 2:132. For Abbott's description of his visit to the ruins with Arthur Conolly, see Abbott, *The Legend of Maandoo*, xvii–xviii.
69. This account of Abbott's trip to Khiva and beyond is largely drawn from his subsequent two-volume account, *Journey from Heraut to Khiva*. Abbott kept a journal for much of the trip, some of which survived and formed the basis for the books.
70. Hopkirk, *The Great Game*, 213.
71. Alexander, *A Carpet Ride to Khiva*, 21.
72. Hopkirk, *The Great Game*, 205–8.
73. Abbott, *Journey from Heraut to Khiva*, 1:112.
74. Joshua Marshman (1768–1837) was a prominent Christian missionary in Bengal during Abbott's first decade in India.
75. Marshman, *The History of India*, 3:400–1. The first edition was published in 1842. The second edition of 1869 was amended to include Abbott's name (spelled incorrectly). John Marshman (1794–1877) was primarily a missionary, but he was also an official Bengali translator and published *Guide to the Civil Law*, which, before the work of Macaulay, was the civil code of India.
76. That is, Monday, January 20, 1840.
77. Muhammad Yusuf Bek, known by his nom de plume as the poet "Bayani," wrote a history of Khiva, *Shajara-ye khorezmshahi* (Genealogy of the Khorezmian kings), from 1911 to 1914 under official instructions from the Khan of Khiva, Isfandiyar. However, Dr. Ron Sela of Indiana University notes that Bayani based his accounts on the earlier works of Munis and Agahi, except for the periods from 1846 to 1856 and 1864 onward. In particular, Agahi seems to have been the later historian. Only one copy of *Shajara-ye khorezmshahi* survives, as a manuscript in the Institute of Oriental Studies of the Academy of Sciences of Uzbekistan located in Tashkent. It is written in Chagatai, and

the manuscript number is 9596. Dr. Sela notes, "It was never edited nor published in its entirety." The folio numbers are 301b to 302a.
78. Munirov, *Munis, Ogahiy and Bayoniy's Historic Works*, 132.
79. Abbott, *Journey from Heraut to Khiva*, 1:93, footnote "†."
80. In the only known painting of him, a watercolor painted in 1841 by B. Baldwin, Abbott's left arm and hand are visible, bent at the elbow as if he is leaning on the arm of a chair, but the right hand is not seen..
81. Abbott, *Journey from Heraut to Khiva*, 322–23.
82. Too many eyewitness accounts by indigenous participants of the stoicism of British officers exist to dismiss such reportage as broad Victorian romanticizing of heroics. Arthur Conolly, for example, when standing before his open grave in Bokhara, was told to convert to Islam and his life would be spared. Indigenous eyewitnesses reported his reply was simply, "Do your work."
83. Abbott, *Journey from Heraut to Khiva*, 1:398.
84. His sextant was a source of danger; Abbott believed that to reveal its true purpose would have resulted in his being put to death for sorcery. Abbott told his captors it was a device for determining the direction of Mecca. The tiny notebook containing his correspondence with Fanny de Burgh and his route maps to Khiva survived.
85. Add Mss 38725, "Diary of Captain Arthur Conolly and Extracts of the Last Letters of Captain Arthur Conolly, Murdered at Bokhara in 1842," 60–74, India Office Records, British Library Collection.
86. Abbott, *Journey from Heraut to Khiva*, 2:295–96.
87. Sammud Khan also later worked for the British garrison in Kabul and also survived the First Anglo-Afghan War.
88. Ferrier, *Caravan Journeys and Wanderings in Persia, Afghanistan, Turkistan and Beloochistan*, 299.
89. Abbott's middle finger, which had been almost severed during the melee at the campsite, was amputated above the first knuckle by a Russian surgeon while Abbott was in Russia.
90. Abbott, *Journey from Heraut to Khiva*, 2:345.
91. Lee, *Dictionary of National Biography*, 56:427. The wound was considered equivalent to the complete loss of his sword hand, which was deemed equivalent to the loss of the use of a limb. The designated pension for this stipulated in the regulations was £200 for a captain, but the Pension Board ruled that because Abbott had been detached on *political* service and was not at the time on *military* service, the regulations did not technically apply. Nevertheless, to be charitable, Abbott was granted the lesser amount of £50, half that granted to a cadet for the loss of a limb.
92. Abbott, *Journals*, 3:100.
93. There are three known copies of the death mask of Charles XII in addition to the original, all of which show the bullet wound to his right temple which killed him. One copy in plaster is held by the Hunterian Museum and Art Gallery in Glasgow (GLAHM C.46). A second in plaster is held by the British Museum (OA.4275). According to university records, a third copy in bronze in Cambridge University's Fitzwilliam Museum (M.21B-1938) is the one given to Abbott by Perovsky. Abbott's son

Reymond gave the mask to the museum in 1938. The original bronze mask is held by a military society in Stockholm.

94. Abbott, *Journals*, 3:100.
95. Hobhouse, *Recollections of a Long Life*, 5:294–95.
96. Ibid.
97. In fact, D'Arcy Todd brought the manuscript out of Herat with him.
98. Abbott, *Journey from Heraut to Khiva*, vol. 1, Second Edition Preface.
99. Cooper, *England, with Sketches of Society in the Metropolis*, 164.
100. Richards, "Passing the Love of Women," 104.
101. *Monthly Review* (London), July 1843.
102. Ibid.
103. Ibid.
104. Ibid.
105. Ibid.
106. Burnes, *Travels into Bokhara*, vol. 1, frontispiece.
107. Abbott, *Journey from Heraut to Khiva*, vol. 1, frontispiece.
108. Six hundred Khivans held hostage by the Russians, four hundred Russian slaves held in Khorezm, the twenty Afghan women, and Umeer Beg.
109. Lee, *Dictionary of National Biography (Supplement)*, 22:4.
110. Lee, *Dictionary of National Biography*, vol. 56; Lee, *Dictionary of National Biography (Supplement)*, vol. 22.
111. Abbott, *Journey from Heraut to Khiva*, 2:245.
112. Ibid., 249.
113. Ibid. The 1840 production by Madame Vestris at Covent Garden was enormously popular and ran for many years. The production was padded extensively with singing and dancing and was considered the marvel of the age.
114. Schwab, *The Oriental Renaissance*, 43.
115. Abbott, *Journals*, 4:2.
116. Ibid., 11.
117. Calculated using the CPI Inflation Calculator provided by the officialdata.org website December 2021: www.officialdata.org/uk/inflation/1841?amount=100.
118. Abbott, *Journals*, 4:17.
119. Ibid.
120. Formerly part of Dutch Malabar on India's southwestern coast, ceded to the United Kingdom in the Anglo-Dutch Treaty of 1814 in exchange for the island of Bangka, east of Sumatra.
121. Cochin was home to a thriving Jewish community even in earlier Portuguese times. During the Inquisition, which was active in Cochin, the Jewish population was heavily persecuted.
122. Hervey, *A Soldier of the Company*, 97.
123. See, for example, Foltz, "Judaism and the Silk Route," 9–16.
124. Abbott, *Journals*, 4:39–40.
125. Lewis, *The Jews of Islam*; Gilbert, *In Ishmael's House*.
126. Abbott, *Journals*, 4:45.

127. Ibid.
128. Abbott, *Journey from Heraut to Khiva*, 1:45–46.
129. Abbott, *Journals*, 4:21.
130. Indeed, he was strongly advised by the directors to do so in late 1840. Kaye, *History of the War in Afghanistan in Three Volumes*, 3:32–33.
131. See, for example, Macrory, *Retreat from Kabul*.
132. Kaye, *Lives of Indian Officers*, 258.
133. Todd, "Observations on the Military Memoir of Cpt. Burnes on Afghanistan, 2 July, 1837."
134. Pottinger and Macrory, *The Ten-Rupee Jezail*, 98.
135. Abbott, *Journals*, 4:38.
136. Equivalent at that time to about £100. Abbott, *Journals*, 4:38.
137. Lee, *Dictionary of National Biography (Supplement)*, 22:4.
138. Abbott, *Journals*, 4:31.
139. Ibid.
140. Ibid., 33.
141. Abbott wrote the two volumes of *Journey from Heraut to Khiva* between September and December 1841 before going upcountry to Murwara.
142. Stephen, *Dictionary of National Biography*, 7:390.
143. Lee, *Dictionary of National Biography*, 56:427.
144. A regulation enacted on June 27, 1787, gave the district collectors in Bengal the powers of judge and magistrate. At the time of the permanent settlement in Bengal in 1793, however, the district collectors lost the judicial function. The powers were reinstated in 1831, and the title of the position thereafter was "district magistrate and collector."
145. Abbott, *Journals*, 4:41.
146. Lee, *Dictionary of National Biography*, 56:427.
147. Carey, *The Good Old Days of the Honorable John Company*, 59.
148. Abbott, *Journals*, 4:46.
149. Ibid., 91.
150. Lee, *Dictionary of National Biography*, 56:427.
151. The dates are inscribed on the back of one of Abbott's drawings in the British Library. "Cemetery Showing the Grave of Margaret Abbott Surmounted by a Column, Asirgarh," British Library Online Gallery, http://www.bl.uk/onlinegallery/onlineex/apac/other/019wdz000003451u00000000.html (accessed March 18, 2013).
152. Abbott, *Journals*, 4:92.

Notes to Chapter 6, A New Beginning

1. Aristotle, *Poetics*, 20.
2. Cleghorn, "The Pitfalls in Thinking Big: Megalomania," 607–8.
3. "We have no right to seize Sind, yet we shall do so, and a very advantageous, useful and humane piece of rascality it will be." The comment was made as a diary entry. Napier, *The Conquest of Sindh*, 5.

NOTES

4. Later General Sir James Outram, a hero of the Indian Mutiny and an enduring Victorian icon.

5. Ellenborough was a High Tory and a mean-spirited man who worked tirelessly to harm his enemies, of whom there were many. In 1812, he had radical author Daniel Eaton imprisoned for selling *Age of Reason*. The poet Percy Bysshe Shelley memorably published "A Letter to Lord Ellenborough" in response. Ellenborough also persecuted and imprisoned radical politicians William Cobbett and Henry Hunt in what were essentially political witch hunts. He also notably destroyed the life and career of Royal Navy officer Thomas Cochrane, 10th Earl of Dundonald, over trumped-up charges in the Great Stock Exchange fraud affair of 1814. (Three lord chancellors reviewed the trial and determined that Cochrane should have been found not guilty; he was subsequently reinstated.) Cordingly, *Cochrane the Dauntless*.

6. Outram soon took furlough to England on the grounds of poor health and, upon Ellenborough's replacement, took the position of resident at Sattara, a far more lucrative assignment.

7. Abbott, *Journals*, 5:8.

8. Ibid., 8–9.

9. There were military insane asylums in India for enlisted men who went mad, while officers were usually invalided home to England to be confined in more genteel asylums there.

10. Abbott, *Journals*, 5:10.

11. Commonly spelled in reports Hidgellee.

12. There were 1,046 miles of embankments at this time. House of Commons, "Report of Return to the Honourable the East India Company," August 1851, 75.

13. A *lak* is equal to one hundred thousand (written "1,00,000" in the Indian numbering system); sixty *laks* would be six million rupees or, at that time, £600,000.

14. The cause was not established until 1898, when Scottish physician Sir Ronald Ross of the Indian Medical Service in Calcutta demonstrated the full life cycle of the malaria parasite in mosquitoes, for which he was awarded the 1902 Nobel Prize in Medicine.

15. Abbott, *Journals*, 5:15. Saunders was not permanently disabled, but some of the shot remained in his shoulder until his death in 1894.

16. Ibid., 19.

17. Ibid., 17.

18. Charpoy: Hindi and Urdu, from *Charpaya*, "four footed"; a lightweight Indian bed strung with tapes from head to foot and side to side. Yule and Burnell, *Hobson-Jobson*, 185.

19. Abbott, *Journals*, 5:19.

20. Featherstone, *At Them with the Bayonet!*, 58.

21. Abbott, *Journals*, 19–20.

22. Ibid., 58.

23. The European mercenaries were initially hired by Ranjit Singh. After his death in 1839, many were maintained by the Sikh regent, Maharani Jindan Khaur, mother of the infant maharaja Duleep Singh. Featherstone notes that "as late as 1844, there were 12 French officers, 4 Italian, 1 Prussian, 2 Greek, 7 Anglo-Indian, 1 Scotsman, 3 English, 3

NOTES

Americans, 3 Germans and 2 Spaniards, with a solitary Russian." Featherstone, *At Them with the Bayonet!*, 10.
24. Abbott, *Journals*, 5:22.
25. Singh, *Empire of the Sikhs*, 232.
26. Ibid., 246.
27. Ibid., 232.
28. The Treaty of Bhairowal was signed ten months later in December 1846. It gave the British considerably greater direct supervision of the Punjab during the minority of the maharaja, followed by British withdrawal in 1854. As a result of the Treaty of Bhairowal, Henry Lawrence officially became the Resident at Lahore and Agent to the Governor-General for the Northwest Frontier. This designation was altered again on March 6, 1848, to that of Resident at Lahore and Chief Commissioner of the Cis- and Trans-Sutlej states.
29. Allen, *Soldier Sahibs*, 78.
30. *Journals and Diaries of the Assistants of the Agent*.
31. Lieutenant Robinson's record of his survey of Hazāra also survives at the National Archives of India in New Delhi. "Robinson Military Survey of Hazara," M (Manuscript) 398, RP (Report) 12, SI. No. 533 (old number M-398). The report provides detail on the boundary survey detachment. Besides Robinson, there were two European assistants, three "native surveyors," and fifty *klassizs*, a term used both for tent pitchers and chain men employed by a surveyor. From the Hindi *khalāsī*, in turn from the Arabic *khalās*, a tent pitcher.
32. *Diwan*: from the Persian *divan* (ديوان), a chief treasury official, finance minister, or prime minister in some Indian states.
33. Abbott, *Journals*, 5:30.
34. Ibid., 31–22; italics added.
35. Postern: a secondary door or gate, particularly in a fortification such as a city wall or castle curtain wall. Posterns were often located in a concealed location, allowing the occupants to come and go inconspicuously. In the event of a siege, a postern could act as a sally port, allowing defenders to make a sortie against the besiegers.
36. Later General Sir William Olpherts, VC GCB. Known as "Hellfire Jack" Olpherts, he was a hero of the Great Mutiny, earning the Victoria Cross for the relief of Lucknow. He rose to be Colonel Commandant of the Royal Artillery in 1888, the highest-ranking artilleryman in Great Britain.
37. Abbott, *Journals*, 5:33–34; italics added.
38. Geological Survey of India, *Records of the Geological Survey of India*, vol. 10–12, part 1, 20–21.
39. Abbott, *Journals*, 5:53–4.
40. Oberoi, *The Construction of Religious Boundaries* 274.
41. Allen, *Soldier Sahibs*, 131.
42. Watson, *Gazetteer of the Hazara District*, 134.
43. Abbott, *Journals*, 5:48.
44. *Sardar*: in this instance, a subgovernor.

45. Written in the mid-1850s, this is Abbott's first use of the word "race" to denote a separate group of humans, as opposed to a holistic "human race." Abbott, *Journals*, 5:48–9; italics added.
46. *Mehmandar*: an official courier appointed to escort an important traveler; used in Persian-speaking countries and the Indian subcontinent.
47. Abbott, *Journals*, 5:50–1.
48. Ibid., 50.
49. Allen, *Soldier Sahibs*, 133.
50. *Russoom*: customary perquisites attached to the office of the zamindar in the form of supplemental taxes. Rickards, *India or Facts Submitted to Illustrate the Character and Condition of the Native Inhabitants*, 2:33.
51. *Nuzzerana*: from *nuzzur*, money payable by a lessee in consideration of a lease. Sutherland, *The Weekly Reporter*, 13:307.
52. "Inclosure 1 in No. 13, Captain Abbott to the Acting Resident," in Parliament of Great Britain, *Papers Relating to the Punjab*, 71.
53. Parliament of Great Britain, *Papers Relating to the Punjab*, 71.
54. Caroë, *The Pathans*, 345.
55. Hyam, *Britain's Imperial Century*, 135–48. See also Hyam, *Empire and Sexuality*, 467.
56. Barrier, "The Punjab Government and Communal Politics," 523–539.
57. Lieutenant General Reynell Taylor, CB, CSI (1822–1886), another of Henry Lawrence's Young Men, was a veteran of the Sikh Wars; he was wounded at Moodkie and later became Commandant of the Corps of Guides. He was known as the "Bayard of the Punjab."
58. Lieutenant General Sir Harry "Joe" Lumsden (1821–1896) fought in both Sikh Wars, was wounded at Sabraon, and is best remembered as the founder of the Corps of Guides.
59. *Journals and Diaries of the Assistants of the Agent*, 62.
60. Abbott, *Journals*, 5:48.
61. Written in the 1850s looking back on this period in his life, this is another early use of the term "race" by Abbott to refer to a specific group of people. *Journals and Diaries of the Assistants of the Agent*, 90.
62. Abbott, *Journals*, 5:57.
63. Ibid.
64. The Mashwari tribe in the Hazāra was a highly respected lineal descent group, most of whose members claimed to be *Syeds*, that is, to have direct ancestry from the Prophet Mohammed. In northern Pakistan and Afghanistan, this genealogical claim often confers a special honorific status as a potential peacekeeper, interlocutor, or negotiator.
65. In Central and South Asia, articles of clothing such as robes of honor, or *kel'at*, are vested with enormous symbolic importance and are the embodiment of the authority of the giver. The bestowal of a robe of honor was usually done by a superior to a subordinate as an indication of special favor by literally imparting part of the superior's power upon the recipient. British authorities seldom understood the huge hidden significance of the gift of *kel'at*, but Abbott clearly did. Gordon, *Robes of Honor*.
66. Abbott, *Journals*, 5:61.

Notes

67. "Inclosure 1 in No. 10," in Parliament of Great Britain, *Papers Relating to the Punjab*, 54–55.
68. Abbott, *Journals*, 5:62.
69. "Inclosure 2 in No. 16," in Parliament of Great Britain, *Papers Relating to the Punjab*, 81.
70. Abbott regularly used the word "prejudice" to mean "superstition."
71. This is a wonderful example of Abbott replacing "native superstition" with nineteenth-century British scientific quackery. Abbott, *Journals*, 5:74.
72. Abbott, *Journals*, 5:75.
73. That is, seeds, such as beans, peas, lentils, and chickpeas, which are normally cooked before eating. Archeologists have located the oldest use of pulse in the world a few miles from where Abbott was camped, in the Ravi River valley of the Punjab, dating to circa 3300 BCE.
74. Abbott, *Journals*, 5:74.
75. Abbott, "Hazara and Its Place in the Second Sikh War," 111.
76. Ibid., 186 (footnote).
77. Letters from Brigadier John Nicholson to Sir James Abbott, India Office Records, European Manuscripts, Mss Eur F171/18, British Library.
78. Flinders, *Cult of a Dark Hero*, 186.
79. Dalrymple, *The Last Moghul*, 187.
80. Allen, *Soldier Sahibs*, 62.
81. The *Nikal Seyn*, or *Nikal Seyni* cult. The worship of John Nicholson and James Abbott was relatively short-lived in its primary form, but elements of it survived into the 1980s. Tarin, "Tending to the Dead Sahibs."
82. Wilberforce, An Unrecorded Chapter of the Indian Mutiny, 25.
83. British Library, India Office Records, European Manuscripts, Mss Eur F417/7, "Papers of Lt. Gen. George Godfrey Pearse," 180–85.
84. Ibid., 184.
85. Urdu: سندھ ساگر دوآب, written by Abbott as Sind Sagur Doaba.
86. Urdu: حسَن ابدال.
87. The poem (later a popular song) "Bendemeer's Stream" appears in *Lalla Rookh* by Thomas Moore, first published in 1817 (contained in Part Two of "The Story of the Veiled Prophet of Khorassan"). It is a nostalgic piece about a place where the writer was happy in childhood. *Lalla Rookh*, a classic of orientalist Romance writing, was enormously popular with East India Company officers, including, obviously, Nicholson.
88. *Gosyne* or *gosain*: from Sanskrit: गोस्वामी (gōswāmī), "lord of senses"; an ascetic.
89. Abbott, "Hazara and Its Place in the Second Sikh War," "Appendix G The Nickolsynie Sect."
90. Ibid. The pencil note in the upper left hand corner of the first page of Appendix A, dated August 1887, suggests Abbott was still editing the manuscript for publication at this time.
91. Tarin, "Tending to the Dead Sahibs."
92. Abbott, *Journals*, 5:77.

93. *Jayt, Jayt'h, Jeth,* or *Jayth* is the third month in the Sikh calendar, known as the *Nanakshahi* calendar. It coincides with May/June of the Western/Georgian/Julian calendar.
94. Abbott, *Journals,* 5:77.
95. Attributed to Georges Clemenceau in Suarez, *Soixante anneés d'histoire française,* 181.
96. Lawrence, "Punjaub 1848/9 Nicholson's Letters one from Major George Lawrence."
97. Chattar Singh, as the Hazāra had just reverted from Jammu and Kashmir control to that of the Sikh state, although the exact day of the transfer is unclear.
98. Abbott, *Journals,* 5:58.
99. Ibid., 56.
100. Burton, *The First and Second Sikh Wars* 46–49.
101. *Wallah* was a useful word derived from Hindi, "denoting a person who does any act, performs any function, or is charged with any duty or belongs to any trade or profession." Yule and Burnell, *Hobson-Jobson,* 239.
102. Nyhan and Reifler, "When Corrections Fail," 303–30.
103. Letter dated August 12, 1848, "Punjaub 1848/9 Nicholson's Letters One from Major George Lawrence," India Office Records, European Manuscripts, Mss Eur F171/24, British Library.
104. Hubert Watson, *Gazetteer of the Hazara District,* 138.
105. "Obituary from the *Standard,*" India Office Records, European Manuscripts, Mss Eur E277/6, British Library.
106. Webster, *A Dictionary of the English Language,* 371, 282.
107. Watson, Fowler, and Fowler, *The Concise Oxford Dictionary of Current English, Seventh Edition,* 603. The first edition was published in 1911.
108. The *Nikal Seyn,* or *Nikal Seyni* cult. The worship of John Nicholson and James Abbott was relatively short-lived in its primary form, but elements of it survived into the 1980s. Tarin, "Tending to the Dead Sahibs."
109. Warburton's mother was a Pashtun, married to a British officer.
110. Warburton, *Eighteen Years in the Khyber,* 316–17.
111. Burnaby, *Ride to Khiva,* 299–300.
112. "Hindustani Fanatics" and "Wahabi Fanatics" were British terms applied to a religious colony established near Sitana in the northern Punjab by Syed Ahmed Shah around 1818. They practiced an austere form of Islam. Ahmed Shah called for a jihad, or holy war, against the British. Abbott encountered them later.
113. Harold Lee, *Brothers in the Raj,* 229.
114. Later General Sir George Lawrence (1804–1884). The eldest of the three Lawrence brothers, he was then Assistant to the Resident for the Rajputana District.
115. "Inclosure 29 in No. 27, the Secretary to the Government of India to the Resident at Lahore," in Parliament of Great Britain, *Papers Relating to the Punjab,* 175.
116. Ibid., 176.
117. "Letter from James Abbott to the Resident at Lahore," No. 287, Huzāra, May 10, India Office Records, European Manuscripts, Mss Eur F171/17, British Library.

118. Lee, *Brothers in the Raj*, 228–29.
119. Ibid., 229.
120. Allen, *Soldier Sahibs*, 151.
121. Abbott, *Journals*, 5:81.
122. James Abbott in Hazāra to Frederick Currie in Lahore, June 17, 1848.
123. Frederick Currie in Lahore to James Abbott in Hazāra, June 23, 1848.
124. "Inclosure 23 in No. 29, the Resident at Lahore to the Secretary to the Government of India," in Parliament of Great Britain, *Papers Relating to the Punjab*, 218.
125. Frederick Currie in Lahore to William Elliot in Calcutta.
126. William Elliot in Calcutta to Frederick Currie in Lahore.
127. Frederick Currie to Lord Dalhousie, August 12, 1848, "Inclosure 13 in No. 35, the Resident at Lahore to the Secretary to the Government of India," in Parliament of Great Britain, *Papers Relating to the Punjab*, 279.
128. Ibid., 280.
129. Trotter, *The Life of John Nicholson*, 78.
130. "Punjaub 1848/9 Nicholson's Letters One from Major George Lawrence," India Office Records, European Manuscripts, Mss Eur F171/24, British Library.

Notes to Chapter 7, The Man Who Was King

1. Farwell, *Queen Victoria's Little Wars*, 32–33.
2. The phrase "lions led by asses" is first attributed to a British soldier in the Crimea in 1853.
3. Abbott, "Hazara and Its Place in the First Sikh War."
4. Irving and de Rhé-Philipe identify him as "Viennese American." Kennedy was killed on Chattar Singh's orders on August 6, 1848, while defending his guns in Haripur. Allen, *Soldier Sahibs*, 163; Irving and De Rhé-Philipe, *A List of Inscriptions on Christian Tombs or Monuments in the Punjab, North-West Frontier Province*, 3.
5. Abbott, *Huzāra*, 310–11.
6. Ibid., 296.
7. Ibid., 344.
8. Ibid., 285–86.
9. Ibid.
10. Ibid., 289; Watson, *Gazetteer of the Hazara District*, 150.
11. Abbott, *Huzāra*, 285–86.
12. John Dollond (1706–1761) was a prominent optician and maker of telescopes in London. The company remained in business for many years.
13. Abbott, *Huzāra*, 290.
14. Burton, *The First and Second Sikh Wars*, 76.
15. Abbott, *Huzāra*, 291.
16. Burton, *The First and Second Sikh Wars*, 76.
17. Abbott, *Huzāra*, 290.
18. Doorani: Abbott means Afghan; Dost Mohammed was of the Durrani Pashtun confederation of tribes, which historically provided almost all of Afghanistan's kings, and the words "Durrani" and "Afghan" at this time meant roughly the same thing to the

British. The Afghan empire that had once conquered Delhi is known historically as the Durrani Empire.
19. Abbott, *Huzāra*, 310–11.
20. Ibid., 337–38.
21. Yusufzai: the region north of Peshawar inhabited by Pashtuns of the Yusufzai tribal group. Kota was a village in the district of Swat, about 150 miles northwest of the center of Hazāra District. Today Kota is an administrative unit of Union Council of Swat District in Khyber Pakhtunkhwa province of Pakistan.
22. Abbott, *Huzāra*, 338–39. The historical identity of the Mullah of Kota is unknown.
23. Burton, *The First and Second Sikh Wars*, 76.
24. Ibid., 83. General Cureton was one the rare officers who enlisted as a private and rose through the ranks to general.
25. Abbott, *Huzāra*, 318.
26. Burton, *The First and Second Sikh Wars*, 83. The British claimed they "spiked" the gun, meaning it was rendered unserviceable by hammering a metal spike into the fuse hole of the cannon and shearing it off.
27. Farwell, *Queen Victoria's Little Wars*, 58.
28. Ibid.
29. This was accurate; the British left nineteen guns on the field, which they had captured from the Sikhs on January 13 when British forces stormed the Sikh artillery lines. Abbott, *Huzāra*, 325.
30. Ibid., 314.
31. Ibid., 258.
32. Ibid., 345–46.
33. Utmanzai. The Utmanzai are a clan of the Mandanr branch of the Yusufzai tribe in the Huzāra. The Syudkaāni family is one of four main extended *khels*, or patriarchal groups, in the Torbela-Khalsa tracts of Hazāra. Balfour, *The Cyclopædia of India and of Eastern and Southern Asia*, 2:214–15; Wylly, *Tribes of Central Asia from the Black Mountain to Waziristan*, 65.
34. Abbott, *Huzāra*, 8–9.
35. Ibid., 337.
36. Ibid., 367.
37. After the Afghans fled north, Khan-i-Zamann became an outcast and lived with his son across the Indus, where he died several months later.
38. Abbott, *Huzāra*, 342.
39. Allen, *God's Terrorists*, 18.
40. Abbott, *Huzāra*, 344.
41. Om Prakash, *History of Anglo-Sikh Wars*, 278. British losses were ninety-six killed and seven hundred wounded. Anesthetics were used during this battle for the first time. Farwell, *Queen Victoria's Little Wars*, 59.
42. Prakash, *History of Anglo-Sikh Wars*, 267.
43. Abbott, *Huzāra*, 355.
44. Ibid., 357.
45. Burton, *The First and Second Sikh Wars*, 129.

46. Trotter, *The Life of John Nicholson*, 119–20.
47. Farwell, *Queen Victoria's Little Wars*, 60.
48. Prakash, *History of Anglo-Sikh Wars*, 298.
49. Lee, *Dictionary of National Biography (Supplement)*, 22:5.
50. Academy, *A Weekly Review of Literature, Science, and Art*, 283–84.
51. Dalhousie in Calcutta to Hobhouse in London, "The Governor-General to the President 6 April 1849."
52. Marshman, *The History of India*, 2:350.
53. Watson, *Gazetteer of the Hazara District*, 152.
54. Lee, *Brothers in the Raj*, 263.
55. Sir George Couper, twenty-four years older than Dalhousie, had served as an aide-de-camp to Dalhousie's father, General the Earl of Dalhousie, as a captain in the 82nd Highlanders in the Peninsular Wars from 1812 to 1814.
56. Knight-erranting: "Lord Dalhousie to George Couper August 18, 1853," in Broun-Ramsay, *Private Letters of the Marquess of Dalhousie*, 262. Game keepers: "Lord Dalhousie to George Couper August 18, 1853, October 22nd, 1854," in ibid., 326.
57. "Lord Dalhousie to George Couper January 1853," in ibid., 241.
58. Prakash, *History of Anglo-Sikh Wars*, 295–96. The "Laird o' Cockpen" was a very old Scottish tune dating back to at least 1692. It gained popularity again in England in the late 1840s when the poet Carolina Oliphant, Lady Nairne (1766–1845), wrote new lyrics. The first verse was

> The Laird o' Cockpen, he's proud and he's great,
> His mind is ta'en up wi' the things o' the state;
> He wanted a wife his braw [fine or splendid] house to keep,
> But favour [a badge or ribbon worn or given to indicate loyalty to a knight by a lady] wi' wooin' was fashious [troublesome or vexatious] to seek.

59. James Abbott and James Brooke had a remarkable amount in common. Both of their parents married in India, their fathers were both East India Company agents, and their mothers were both of Scottish descent with remote connections to royalty. Both fathers had a direct ancestor who had been lord mayor of London; both of their eldest brothers died in India. Both had older brothers in the East India Company Army, and both men were officers in the Bengal Army. Brooke was fighting in Burma while Abbott was at Barrackpore. Brooke was shot through the lung leading a cavalry charge in January 1825 and invalided to England to recover. Runciman, *The White Rajahs*, 46–47.
60. Broun-Ramsay, *Private Letters of the Marquess of Dalhousie*, 179.
61. That is, arrested, put in chains, and made to work on the chain gangs used to improve the frontier roads.
62. Paolo Crescenzo Martino Avitabile, or Abu Tabela (1791–1850), was an Italian soldier of fortune who, as a civilian administrator hired by Ranjit Singh, served as the governor of Peshawar from 1834 to 1843 using methods introduced by Tamerlane. Henry Lawrence said of him that he "acts as a savage among savage men, instead of showing them that a Christian can wield the iron scepter without staining it by needless cruelty." Gardner, *Soldier and Traveller* [sic], 319.

63. "Lord Dalhousie to George Couper March 1851," in Broun-Ramsay, *Private Letters of the Marquess of Dalhousie*, 155, 179.
64. Stoup and roup: Completely, entirely, absolutely; from the archaic Scottish expression "frae stoop to roop." "Lord Dalhousie to George Couper September 1852," in Broun-Ramsay, *Private Letters of the Marquess of Dalhousie*, 223.
65. Ibid.
66. "Knowledge of Local Vernaculars," 143.
67. "Lord Dalhousie to George Couper September 1852," in Broun-Ramsay, *Private Letters of the Marquess of Dalhousie*, 223.
68. "Lord Dalhousie to George Couper September 1854," in ibid., 321.
69. Broun-Ramsay, *Private Letters of the Marquess of Dalhousie*, 281.
70. "Lord Dalhousie to George Couper December 1853," in ibid., 281.
71. "Lord Dalhousie to George Couper October 1853," in ibid., 268.
72. Fitzgerald, *The Great Gatsby*, 142.
73. Allen, *Soldier Sahibs*, 202.
74. Watson, *Gazetteer of the Hazara District*, 156.
75. "King of Hazāra": Watson, *Gazetteer of the Hazara District*, 156.
76. Lee, *Brothers in the Raj*, 146.
77. Abbott, *Huzāra*, 375–76.
78. Ibid., 375.
79. Ibid.
80. Ibid., preface, 2.
81. Ibid., 364, 375–76.
82. Ibid., 376.
83. Ibid., 110.
84. Caroë, *Pathans*, 341.
85. Watson, *Gazetteer of the Hazara District*, 157.
86. Lawrence, *The Journals of Honoria Lawrence*, 223.
87. See, for example, the handling of the Paladins in Kaye, *Lives of Indian Officers*.
88. Herbert Edwardes was called away by the murder of Colonel Mackeson within a few months of taking over as the district commissioner of Hazāra. He was replaced by Colonel John Reid Becher. Colonel Becher (later general) was an officer in the Bengal Cavalry. He was born in 1819, educated at Bruce Castle and Addiscombe, and entered service in India in the Bengal Engineers in 1839. Becher is one of the lesser-known officers of the "Punjab School," but he had a distinguished career both in the military and political service, fighting at Ferozepore, Ali Masjid, and Sabraon, where he was severely wounded. He was the deputy commissioner of Hazāra from 1853 to 1859. Becher retired in 1866 and passed away in 1884. Buckland, *Dictionary of Indian Biography*, 32.
89. Edwardes, *Memorials of the Life and Letters of Major General Sir Herbert B. Edwardes by His Wife*, 222. The book consists of letters and journals written by Edwardes published posthumously by his wife.
90. Lee, *Brothers in the Raj*, 144.

91. Dalhousie in Calcutta to Hobhouse in London, "The Governor General to the President 6 October 1849," in Broun-Ramsay, *Private Letters of the Marquess of Dalhousie*, 265.
92. Edwardes, *A Year on the Punjab Frontier in 1848–9*, 1:xi.
93. Lawrence, *The Journals of Honoria Lawrence*, 221. She referred to her husband as "Papa."
94. Henry Lawrence to Lord Dalhousie 5 November, 1849, "Lord Dalhousie's Letters to and from Sir Henry Lawrence."
95. Lawrence, *The Journals of Honoria Lawrence*, 221.
96. Lee, *Brothers in the Raj*, 263.
97. Edwardes, *Memorials of the Life and Letters of Major General Sir Herbert B. Edwardes by His Wife*, 221.
98. Spain, *The Way of the Pathans*. Only once, while serving as the State Department political officer in Paktika Province of Afghanistan in 2005, did a Pashtun friend at the office of the Ministry for Tribal Affairs call me *Kaka*. It was the highlight of the assignment.
99. Hindko: a language of the Punjab.
100. Lawrence, *The Journals of Honoria Lawrence*, 221.
101. Abbott, *Huzāra*, 375–76; italics added.
102. Wylly, *Tribes of Central Asia*, 32.
103. Nevill, *Campaigns on the North-West Frontier*, 22.
104. India Foreign and Political Department, *Selections form the Records of the Indian Government (Foreign Department) Report, No. XII, Showing the Relations of the British Government with the Tribes, Independent and Dependent, on the Northwest Frontier of the Punjaub* (Calcutta: Thomas Jones, 1856), 4.
105. Caroë, *Pathans*, 351. This same unwritten code was what prevented Mullah Omar and the Taliban from turning Osama bin Laden over to American authorities after the terrorist attacks of September 11, 2001. Johnson and Mason, "Understanding the Taliban and Insurgency in Afghanistan."
106. Nevill, *Campaigns on the North-West Frontier*, 26.
107. The name is also sometimes rendered as Sayyid Ahmad Brelvi or Barelvi, a reference to his home village of Barelvi. Religious leaders were often identified with their villages (e.g., the Mullah of Kota).
108. The transmission of Islamic knowledge in the region is done through the *pirimuridi* system (teacher-student), in which the student literally seeks to become a virtual clone of his teacher.
109. Hopkins and Marsden, *Fragments of the Afghan Frontier*, 83.
110. Akhund Ghaffur (1793–1878), the Akhund of Swat (Pashto: اخوند عبدالغفور), was commonly known as Saidu Baba (Pashto: سيدو بابا).
111. *Akhund*: a Muslim cleric. The Akhund of Swat is a hereditary title.
112. Haroon, *Frontier of Faith*, 33–64.
113. Families in the region have for a millennium recognized the bride price as compensation for the costs of feeding and raising daughters prior to their loss as economic units at marriage. A daughter is, in effect, a living savings account that is cashed out

upon her transfer to another family. In cultures that privilege males and undervalue females, the bride price has long been a deterrent to female infanticide.

114. Vibart, *Addiscombe*, 372.
115. Subsequently 1st Baron Napier of Magdala (1810–1890).
116. Stubbs, Francis, *History of the Organization, Equipment, and War Services of the Regiment of Bengal Artillery, Volume 3*. London: W. H. Allen & Co., Ltd, 1895, 472.
117. Allen, *Soldier Sahibs*, 204.
118. Nevill, *Campaigns on the North-West Frontier*, 21–26.
119. Wylly, *Tribes of Central Asia*, 35.
120. Nevill, *Campaigns on the North-West Frontier*, 21–26.
121. Ibid.
122. Vibart, *Addiscombe*, 371.
123. Ibid.
124. Intelligence Branch, Army Headquarters India, *Frontier and Overseas Expeditions from India in 7 Volumes*, 1:110.
125. Altogether the British sent some twenty expeditions against the movement, finally suppressing it in 1870 with the trials and deportation of a large number of Tariqa-i Muhammadiyya to the British penal colony in the Andaman and Nicobar Islands. The movement got its revenge two years later, in 1872, when the viceroy, Lord Mayo, was fatally stabbed by a Tariqa-i Muhammadiyya adherent while visiting the penal colony at Port Blair. Sen, *Disciplining Punishment*.
126. "Lord Dalhousie to George Couper November 20, 1852," in Broun-Ramsay, *Private Letters of the Marquess of Dalhousie*, 232.
127. "Lord Dalhousie to George Couper December 5, 1852," in ibid., 234.
128. Lee, *Brothers in the Raj*, 383.
129. Ibid., 3–4.
130. Henry Lawrence, "Henry Lawrence to Frederick Currie 6 November 1846," Henry Lawrence Papers, India Office Records, European Manuscripts, Mss Eur F85/6, 62, British Library.
131. Henry Lawrence, "Henry Lawrence to George Edmonstone 21 March 1850," India Office Records, European Manuscripts, Mss Eur F85/9/264, British Library.
132. Henry Lawrence, "Henry Lawrence to Lord Dalhousie 31 January 1852," India Office Records, European Manuscripts, Mss Eur F85/11B/282, British Library.
133. Henry Lawrence, "Henry Lawrence to James Thomason 13 February 1852," India Office Records, European Manuscripts, Mss Eur F85/11B/290, British Library.
134. Lee, *Brothers in the Raj*, 271.
135. Trotter, *The Life of John Nicholson*, 151.
136. Watson, *Gazetteer of the Hazara District*, 156.
137. Conrad, *Heart of Darkness*, 71–72.
138. Ibid., 83, 80.
139. Ibid., 91.
140. Warburton, *Eighteen Years in the Khyber*, 317.
141. Conrad, *Heart of Darkness*, 95.
142. Watson, *Gazetteer of the Hazara District*, 146.

143. Conrad, *Heart of Darkness*, 99.
144. Edwardes, *Memorials of the Life and Letters of Major General Sir Herbert B. Edwardes by His Wife*, 221–222.
145. Hecatombs: in ancient Greece and Rome, a sacrifice to the gods, originally consisting of one hundred oxen or cattle.
146. Edwardes, *Memorials of the Life and Letters of Major-General Sir Herbert B. Edwardes by His Wife*, 222.
147. Watson, *Gazetteer of the Hazara District*, 157.
148. The other is Jacobabad, in Sindh Province, named for Brigadier General John Jacob CB (January 11, 1812–December 6, 1858). Jacob, the founder of the town, raised two regiments of cavalry, which were named Jacob's Horse. Unlike Abbott, Jacob planned and lived in the town that bears his name, laying out the roads and building hundreds of miles of irrigation canals.

Notes to Chapter 8, Endings

1. Abbott, *Journals*, 7:3.
2. Measured by the historic standard of living, which tracks the relative ability to purchase goods such as food, shelter, and clothing, this represents a sum of £115,000 in 2022.
3. Abbott was granted a good service pension of £100 upon leaving India and had been receiving a wound pension since the 1840s of £50, a total of £150 per annum, so Saleh Mohammed received a 20 percent higher pension than General Abbott.
4. James Abbott, "Delhi February 27, 1860," *Commonplace Books*, vol. 1, India Office Records, European manuscripts, Mss Eur F171/47-53, 204, British Library.
5. The Crimean War.
6. Abbott, *Journals*, 7:2–3.
7. "Military Service Record of James Abbott," India Office Records, European Manuscripts, Mss Eur E277/1, British Library.
8. Ibid.
9. Abbott, *Journals*, 7:3.
10. Ibid.
11. Ibid., 4.
12. Mukharya, *Revolt of 1857*.
13. Abbott, *Journals*, 7:5.
14. Ibid., 5–6.
15. Ibid.
16. Ibid., 12–13. There were at that time five sepoy regiments at Barrackpore.
17. Coopland, *A Lady's Escape from Gwalior and Life in the Fort of Agra during the Mutinies of 1857*, 76.
18. Abbott, *Journals*, 7:10.
19. Ibid.
20. Ibid., 14.
21. Ibid.
22. Ibid.

23. Sarup, *The Trial of Mangal Pandey*, 38.
24. Abbott, *Journals*, 7:15. An interesting indication of how well schooled many East India Company officers were in the classics. According to Livy, the geese in the temple of Juno on Capitoline Hill saved Rome from the Gauls around 390 BC by cackling when disturbed by the Gauls' night attack on the city.
25. *Bhang*: Hindi, a drug derived from marijuana popular with Hindu sepoys.
26. Wing: a term in the Indian Army for a battalion.
27. Abbott, *Journals*, 7:23–25. In fact, many former sepoys from the disbanded wing of the 34th went north and joined the mutineers in Delhi, where a number were later arrested and executed.
28. Tickell, *Terrorism, Insurgency and Indian-English Literature*, 84.
29. All mutineers were subsequently called "pandies" by the British during the Mutiny.
30. Wagner, *The Great Fear of 1857: Rumours, Conspiracies and the Making of the Indian Mutiny*, 97.
31. Heathcote, *The Military in British India*, 91–92.
32. Mukherjee, *Mangal Pandey*, 52.
33. Metcalf, *The Aftermath of Revolt*, 47.
34. Mukherjee, *Mangal Pandey*, 52.
35. An exhaustive list of officers of the Bengal Artillery "who served in the suppression of the rebellion in India 1857–1859" lists no Abbotts. Appendix B in Stubbs, *History of the Bengal Artillery*, 3:459–464.
36. Ibid.
37. The Indian Mutiny Medal was instituted in 1858 for anyone in the military who was involved in military operations to suppress the Mutiny. In 1868, the criteria for the award were expanded to include everyone who had "borne arms" or who had been under fire, including civilians. Approximately 290,000 medals were awarded. Even under the expanded criteria, none of the Abbott brothers in India qualified for the medal.
38. Cave-Browne, *The Punjab and Delhi in 1857*, vol. 1.
39. Hyam, *Britain's Imperial Century*, 134.
40. Farwell, *Armies of the Raj*, 64.
41. The massacre of British civilians at the Jokhun Bagh in Jhansi was every bit as horrific as the massacre of innocents at Cawnpore, but it was Cawnpore that was to be remembered by Britons well into the twentieth century. In the same way the terrible images of civilian jetliners slamming into the World Trade Center's towers have become etched in the collective post-9/11 consciousness, the vivid descriptions and depictions of the scene at the Bibighar or the "Cawnpore Well" took on a iconic nature for Victorians.
42. Paxman, *The Victorians*, 198.
43. Hibbert, *The Great Mutiny*, 209.
44. Wolesley, *The Story of a Soldier's Life*, 272–273.
45. Metcalf, *The Aftermath of Revolt*, 290.
46. Hibbert, *The Great Mutiny*, 209–210.
47. Metcalf, *The Aftermath of Revolt*, 75.
48. Spear, *India*, 270.
49. Gardner, *The East India Company*, 292.

Notes

50. Farwell, *Armies of the Raj*, 64.
51. Hyam, *Britain's Imperial Century*, 141.
52. Abbott, *Journals*, 7:18–19.
53. Hyam, *Britain's Imperial Century*, 142.
54. Metcalf, *The Aftermath of Revolt*, 326.
55. James Abbott, *Commonplace Book Six*, India Office Records, European Manuscripts, Mss Eur F/171/52, 21, British Library.
56. Stanley, *White Mutiny*.
57. Abbott had himself given away the secret, if it was one, by referring to Snellius Schickhardus as his "friend" in the notes to *T'Hakoorine* published under his own name in 1841. Abbott, *T'Hakoorine, a Tale of Maandoo*.
58. Lord Ellenborough served as governor-general of India from 1842 to 1844. "Ned" is the common English nickname for Edward or Edmund.
59. Schickhardus, *Tales of the Forest*, 88–124.
60. Ibid., 85.
61. Glassman, *Benjamin Disraeli*, 50–51.
62. Disraeli, *Coningsby, or the New Generation*, 252.
63. Smith, *Disraeli*, 68–69. In his comprehensive travels, Sidonia visited and examined many Jewish communities of the world.
64. Glassman, *Disraeli*, 51.
65. Ibid., 92.
66. Ibid.
67. Kennedy, *The Highly Civilized Man*.
68. Brodie, *The Devil Drives*, 265.
69. It was published posthumously in 1898.
70. Anonymous (Abbott), *Legends, Ballads, & c*, 24; italics in the original.
71. Ibid. Why Abbott chose London's Harley Street is unclear, but in 1854 William Gladstone, then chancellor of the exchequer, lived there.
72. Hurd and Young, *Disraeli*, 18.
73. The reference to the harp here is obscure; possibly it is a reference to a line in Disraeli's earlier novel, *Vivian Grey*, first published in 1827: "Though his harp was golden and his throne of ivory, his feelings were not less keen, and his conviction not less complete." The book may have come to Abbott's attention at the time of the writing of *The Caucasian* because the revised edition of *Vivian Grey* was published in 1853, the year before *Legends, Ballads & c*. Disraeli, *Vivian Grey*, 165.
74. Ben Nevis is a mountain in Scotland. It doubtless appears at this time in Abbott's verse because in 1847 it was confirmed by an ordnance survey to be the highest mountain in Great Britain.
75. This is a reference to Disraeli's famous speech on March 17, 1845, addressing Prime Minister Sir Robert Peel in the House of Commons, saying, "A Conservative government is an organized hypocrisy." Disraeli, *Selected Speeches of the Late Right Honourable the Earl of Beaconsfield*, 1:81.
76. Monmouth Street is a reference to Charles Dickens's *Meditations in Monmouth-Street*. Dickens particularly liked Monmouth Street, which was famous in Abbott's time

as part of a London district where one could find antique garments. Most of the vendors there were Jews, who dominated the rag trade in London at the time. Abbott appears to have coined the phrase "psychological antiquities," at least in print. It does not appear in print again until 1909, when pioneering British psychologist William McDougall (1871–1938) used the phrase "the museum of psychological antiquities" in *A Textbook of Psychology* while at Harvard. Abbott obviously uses the term disparagingly to characterize Disraeli's thinking as full of outmoded ideas. McDougall, *A Textbook of Psychology*, 127.

77. Anonymous (Abbott), *Legends, Ballads, & c*, 29.
78. Hurd and Young, *Disraeli*, 179.
79. Ibid.
80. "Letter from John Lawrence to Stafford Northcote June 1, 1867," India Office Records, European Manuscripts, Mss Eur F90/32a no. 34, British Library.
81. Lee, *Dictionary of National Biography (Supplement)*, 22:4.
82. "Letter from Maud de Montmorency to James Abbott, undated," India Office Records, European Manuscripts, Mss Eur E277/3, British Library.
83. Goodman, *How to Be a Victorian*, 417–18.
84. "Last Will and Testament of James Abbott," India Office Records, European Manuscripts, Mss Eur F171/112, British Library.
85. "Letter from James Abbott to Raymond Abbott, Ellerslie, Sept 26, 1886," India Office Records, European Manuscripts, Mss Eur E277/3, British Library.
86. "Notes of Interview by E. Werge Thomas with Raymond Abbott in 1958," India Office Records, European Manuscripts, Mss Eur F171/99/2, British Library.
87. British Census Records.
88. Kaye, *A History of the Sepoy War in India*, 1:31.
89. Ibid.
90. Ibid.
91. Ibid.
92. Marshall, "British Immigration into India in the Nineteenth Century," 195.
93. Kipling, "Ballad of East and West."
94. "Papers of Lt.-Gen. George Godfrey Pearse," India Office Records, European Manuscripts, Mss Eur F417/7, 180–85, British Library.

Notes to Appendix Abbott the Artist

1. The artists later grouped together as Romantics were in their own day referred to as the Lake School. William Wordsworth (1770–1850) is often thought of today as one of the foremost Romantic poets, but in its earliest use as a description of an artistic school, in 1863, the term "Romantic" expressly excluded Wordsworth, whose antiromanticism was a regular theme of early-nineteenth-century literary criticism. In the words of early Romantic historian Henry Beers, Wordsworth was "absolutely unromantic" in comparison to the twin icons of the genre in Abbott's early years, Sir Walter Scott (1771–1832) and Samuel Coleridge (1772–1834). Beers, *A History of English Romanticism in the Nineteenth Century*, 51–54.
2. *Oxford English Dictionary*.

3. Singh, *A Survey of Anglo-Indian Fiction*, 1. Abbott's *T'Hakoorine* is mentioned in the bibliography but not discussed in the work. The survey is remarkable for the number of contemporary books dealing with the subject of love and marriage between Britons and the peoples of India and for the degree to which women novelists were successful in this genre.

4. Ibid., 283.
5. Marshall, "The Empire of the Officials," 52.
6. Warren, *English Poetic Theory*, 6–7.
7. Altick, *Victorian People and Ideas*, 279.
8. Ruskin, *Modern Painters*, 3:31.
9. James Abbott, unpublished letter to his son, India Office Records, European Manuscripts, Mss Eur E277/3, British Library.
10. *Orlando Furioso* or *The Madness of Orlando*, by Ludovico Ariosto, first appeared in its complete form in 1532. An epic set in the Middle Ages, it is one of the longest poems in literature at nearly thirty-nine thousand lines. It is filled with fantasy, knights, sea monsters, female warriors, and even a trip to the moon. The engraving from the tale of *Ruggiero Rescuing Angelica*, by Gustave Doré, of a knight riding a griffon to rescue a naked maiden in bondage from a dragon suggests why it might have captured the adolescent imagination.
11. James Thomson (1700–1748) was a Scottish poet perhaps best remembered for writing the words for the song "Rule Britannia!" His magnus opus, *The Seasons*, became the basis for Franz Joseph Haydn's oratorio of the same name.
12. Abbott, *Journals*, 1:123–24; italics added.
13. *Tales of the Crusaders* comprises two separate books, *The Betrothed* and *The Talisman*, both published in 1825.
14. The etymology of Bobson as a pen name used by Abbott is more obscure. There was a well-publicized legal incident involving a Scottish laird named Carruthers of Dormont, whose wife gave birth to an illegitimate girl named Elizabeth. Scott related the story to Lady Abercorn in a letter in May 1813. At a legal hearing at which Scott was acting as clerk, Elizabeth was sent to reside with a farmer named Bobson. Bobson at the time was a stout, hearty, and not uncommon Midlothian name, but the reason for Abbott's using it is a mystery.
15. Peers, "Conquest Narratives," 245.
16. Ibid.
17. Lawrence, *Adventures of an Officer in the Punjaub* [Vol. 1.]; Lawrence, *Adventures of an Officer in the Service of Ranjeet Singh* [Vol. 2.]. Intended as one book in two volumes, the books actually have differing titles, although the volume numbering is present.
18. Peers, "Conquest Narratives," 245.
19. Scott, *The Surgeon's Daughter*.
20. Scott's eldest brother, Robert, served in the Royal Navy and the East India Company and died in India in 1824, Abbott's first year in country. Robert's son Walter, later General Walter Scott, supervised the Survey of Scind, which employed Sir Richard Burton.

21. Scurry, *Captivity, Sufferings, and Escape of James Scurry*. Appearing in print in the first year of Abbott's service, this is undoubtedly a book that he would have read.
22. Sutherland, "The Novel," 342.
23. Altick, *Victorian People and Ideas*, 276.
24. Tennyson, *Tiresias, and Other Poems*, 53.
25. Abbott, *Autobiography*, Mss Eur F171/33/1.
26. The first English-language translation of the Arabian Nights was published anonymously in London in 1706 by the firm of A. Bell under the title *Arabian Nights Entertainments*. It was a retranslation of the French version, *Les mille et une nuits*, which was translated from the Arabic by Antoine de Galland and published by Barbin in Paris in 1704. The volume enjoyed some popularity, but the English reading public was not immediately swept away by any great wave of enthusiasm for Eastern tales.
27. Beckford, *An Arabian Tale*. Beckford was believed in his day to be the richest commoner in England.
28. Sydney Owenson, later Lady Morgan, is known to have influenced both Shelley and Moore.
29. The historical Kublai Khan was the grandson of Chinghiz Khan and founder of the Yuan Dynasty (1271–1368).
30. Cavaliero, *Ottomania*, xix.
31. For centuries, the Zoroastrians (today the Parsees) were inaccurately called fire-worshippers. The third story in *Lalla Rookh* recounts the doomed love of Hinda and Hafed, a leader of Zoroastrians fighting the Arab conquest of Persia.
32. Abbott, *Autobiography*, Mss Eur F171/33/1.
33. Byron, *Letters*, 5:249–50: letter to Moore, July 10, 1817, cited in Kelly, *Ireland's Minstrel*, 136.
34. Cavaliero, *Ottomania*, 150–51.
35. Hugo, *Les Orientales*.
36. Quoted in Schwab, *The Oriental Renaissance*, 12.
37. Rückert, *Nal und Damajanti*. It seems unlikely that Abbott read *Nal und Damajanti*, however, as there remains no English translation, and Abbott did not speak German.
38. *The Athenaeum*, No. 2631, March 30, 1878.
39. *Allen's Indian Mail*, January 28, 1878, 76.
40. *John Bull*, December 15, 1877, 805.
41. *Brighton Guardian*, "New Looks," December 26, 1877, 2.
42. Published under the pen name Snellius Schickhardus, it contains a large number of endnotes with subject matter also covering the ethnology and ornithology of India.
43. Prometheus—the Titan in Greek mythology who stole fire from Zeus, gave it to humans, and in punishment was chained to a rock to have an eagle eat his liver every day and have the liver regenerate itself every night—was a favorite of the Romantic movement, for whom he represented rebellion against authority.
44. Abbott, *Prometheus' Daughter*, 300–301.
45. Abbott, *Hoomaioon*, Mss Eur F171/41.
46. *The Gentleman's Magazine* (London: F. Jefferies, July 1841), 64.
47. Thomas Hervey, *Athenaeum* (London: W. Lewer, March 20, 1841), 220–21.

48. Máire ni Fhlathúin, ed., *The Poetry of British India, 1780–1905* (Milton Park, UK: Routledge, 2011), 1:58.
49. P. D. Edwards, "Hervey, Thomas Kibble (1799–1859)," *Oxford Dictionary of National Biography* (Oxford: Oxford University Press, 2004).
50. *East India United Services Journal*, No. 22, April 1836.
51. Abbott, Notes for an Unfinished Novel, Mss Eur F171/40.
52. James Abbott to Reymond Abbott, 1878, Mss Eur E277/3.
53. Wu, *A Companion to Romanticism*, 8.

BIBLIOGRAPHY

JAMES ABBOTT, PUBLISHED WORKS
Legends, Ballads, & c. Calcutta: Sanders, Cones & Co., 1854.
Constance: A Tale. London: Smith, Elder & Co., 1877.
The Legend of Mandoo. London: Keegan, Paul, Trench, Trübner & Co., 1893.
Narrative of a Journey from Heraut to Khiva, Moscow, and St. Petersburg. London: William H. Allen & Co., 1843.
Prometheus' Daughter, a Poem. London: Smith, Elder & Co., 1861.
T'Hakoorine, a Tale of Mandoo. London: J. Madden and Co., 1841.

JAMES ABBOTT, MANUSCRIPTS AND CORRESPONDENCE
Bareilly District Report. India Office Collection, European Manuscripts, Mss Eur F171/21. British Library.
Chiefs of the Hazara Memorandum. India Office Collection, European Manuscripts, Mss Eur C120. British Library.
First Expedition against Black Mountain Hazara. 1853 manuscript, India Office Collection, European Manuscripts, Mss Eur C210. British Library.
Hazara and Its Place in the Second Sikh War, Vol. 1. India Office Collection, European Manuscripts, Mss Eur C225/1. British Library.
Hazara and Its Place in the Second Sikh War, Vol. 2. India Office Collection, European Manuscripts, Mss Eur C225/2. British Library.
Huzāra and Its Place in the First Sikh War. India Office Records, European Manuscripts, Mss Eur C225, 266. British Library.
James Abbott in Hazara to Frederick Currie in Lahore, June 17, 1848. Foreign Department Proceedings for the Years 1840–1849. M & I October 1848, No. S 283–287, Cons S.C. "Copies, No. 15." National Archives of India, New Delhi.
James Abbott to Reymond Abbott, 1878. India Office Records, European Manuscripts, Mss Eur E277/3. British Library.
Journal of a March from Quetta to Cundahar. India Office Records, European Manuscripts, Mss Eur F171/22. British Library.
Journal of March with Army from Kandahar to Herat. 1849, India Office Records, European Manuscripts, Mss Eur F171/22, 24. British Library.
Journals of James Abbott. India Office Records, European Manuscripts, Mss Eur F171/33/1-7. British Library.
Military Service Record. India Office Collection, European Manuscripts, Mss Eur E277/1. British Library.

BIBLIOGRAPHY

Notebooks of James Abbott. India Office Records, European Manuscripts, Mss Eur F171/47-53. British Library.
Notes for an unfinished novel. India Office Records, European Manuscripts, Mss Eur F171/40. British Library.
Official Correspondence between James Abbott and EICo Officials. India Office Collection, European Manuscripts, Mss Eur A45. British Library.
Sketches and Watercolors of James Abbott, India Office Collection, European Manuscripts, Mss Eur F171/119. British Library.
Wahabi Fanatics. India Office Records, European Manuscripts, Mss Eur F171/32. British Library.

Primary Sources

A Civilian and an Officer on the Bengal Establishment [Charles D'Oyly]. *Tom Raw, the Griffin, a Burlesque Poem*. London: R. Ackermann, 1828.
Abbott, Augustus. *The Afghan War*. London: R. Bentley and Son, 1879.
Abbott, Henry. *A Journal, with Occasional Remarks, Made on a Trip from Aleppo to Bussora, across the Grand Desert of Arabia*. Calcutta: Joseph Cooper, 1789.
———. *Memoirs and Diary of Henry Abbott*. India Office Select Materials, European Manuscripts, Mss Eur B412, British Library.
Ali, Mrs. Meer Hassan [Biddy Timms]. *Observations on the Mussulmauns of India*. London: Parbury, Allen and Co., 1832.
Anderson, William. *The Blue Pamphlet*. London: J. Ridgway, 1858.
———. *Narrative*. India Office Collection, European Manuscripts, Eur Mss C703. British Library.
Anonymous. "The Siege of Bhurtpore." *Blackwood's Edinburgh Magazine* 23 (January 1828).
Anonymous. *Narrative of the Indian Mutinies of 1857*. Madras: Asylum Press, 1858.
Anonymous (A Lieutenant of the Bengal Establishment) [James Harriott]. *Cadet's Guide to India, by a Bengal Lieutenant*. London: Black, Kingsbury, Parbury and Allen, 1820.
Anonymous (An Officer of the Bengal Infantry). "The Indian Army." In *United Services Journal and Naval and Military Magazine*. Part I. London: Richard Bentley, 1833.
Anonymous [James Abbott]. *Legends, Ballads, & c.* Calcutta: Sanders, Cones & Co., 1854.
Anonymous (S. S.) [James Abbott]. *United Services Journal and Naval and Military Magazine*. Part I. London: Henry Colburn and Richard Bentley, 1832.
Anonymous (W. W.). "Considerations on the Native Army and General Defense of India." *United Services Journal and Naval and Military Magazine*. Part III. London: Henry Colburn and Richard Bentley, 1831.
Arnold, William. *Oakfield; or, Fellowship in the East*. Boston: Ticknor and Fields, 1855.
Asiatic Journal and Monthly Register for British and Foreign India, China and Australasia 9 (September–December 1832).
Badenach, Walter. *Inquiry into the State of the Indian Army, with Suggestions for Its Improvement, & c.* London: William Clowes for J. Murray, 1826.

BIBLIOGRAPHY

Bellew, Francis. *Memoirs of a Griffin*. London: W. H. Allen & Co., 1843.
Board of Revenue, North-Western Provinces (India). *Selections from Revenue Records, North-West Provinces*. Vol. 2: *A.D. 1822–1833*. Allahabad: North-Western Provinces Government Press, 1872.
Broun-Ramsay, James, Lord Dalhousie. *Private Letters of the Marquess of Dalhousie*. Edited by J. G. A. Baird. Edinburgh: William Blackwood and Sons, 1910.
Buckle, Capt. E. *Memoir of the Services of the Bengal Artillery*. London: W. H. Allen, 1852.
Burnaby, Capt. Fredrick. *Ride to Khiva*. London: Cassell, Petter & Galpin, 1877.
Burnes, Alexander. *Travels into Bokhara*. 3 vols. London: John Murray, 1834.
Cave-Browne, John. *The Punjab and Delhi in 1857, Being a Narrative of the Measures by Which the Punjab Was Saved and Delhi Recovered during the Indian Mutiny*. Vol. 1. London: William Blackwood & Sons, 1861.
Cavenagh, Gen. Orfeur. *Reminiscences of an Indian Official*. London: W. H. Allen & Co., 1884.
Coghill, Col. Kendal Josiah William. "Letters Written by Col. Kendal Coghill (1832–1919)." National Army Museum. Accession Number 1971-12-39-2-1, "Papers and Letters of Lt. Kendall Coghill, Bengal European Regiment, 1851–1861." Coghill to Joey, March 2, 1851.
Colebrook, Edward. "Letter from Sir Edward Colebrooke to Sir George Swinton, Chief Secretary to the Government in Calcutta." India Office Records, F4, *Records of the Board of Commissioners for the Affairs of India: Board's Collections* 1339. British Library.
Colvin, John. "Notice of the Peculiar Tenets Held by the Followers of Syed Ahmed, Taken Chiefly from the 'Sirát-úl-Mustaquin,' a Principal Treatise of That Sect, Written by Moulavi Mahommed Ismail." *Journal of the Asiatic Society of Bengal* 1, no. 11 (November 1832).
Conolly, Arthur. *Journey to the North of India, Overland from England, through Russia, Persia and Affghaunistan*. London: Richard Bentley, 1834.
Coopland, R. M. *A Lady's Escape from Gwalior* and *Life in the Fort of Agra during the Mutinies of 1857*. London: Smith, Elder & Co, 1859).
Cunningham, P., ed. *The Letters of Horace Walpole: Earl of Oxford*. London: Henry G. Bohn, 1861.
Currie, Frederick, in Lahore, to James Abbott in Hazara, June 23, 1848. Foreign Department Proceedings for the Years 1840–1849. M & I October 1848, No. S 283-287, Cons S.C., "No. 280." National Archives of India, New Delhi.
Currie, Frederick, in Lahore, to William Elliot in Calcutta. Foreign Department Proceedings for the Years 1840–1849. M & I October 1848, No. S 283-287, Cons S.C. "Consultation 7 Oct, No. 283-4, Copy No. 134." National Archives of India, New Delhi.
Dalhousie, in Calcutta, to Hobhouse in London. "The Governor-General to the President 6 April 1849." India Office Records, European Manuscripts, Mss Eur F213/124-9. British Library.

Bibliography

"The Defects of the Indian Army." *Monthly Review*, Article 7 (January–April 1827). London: Bradbury & Co.

Dodwell, Edward, and James Miles, eds. *Alphabetical List of the Officers of the Indian Army, with the Dates of Their Respective Promotion, Retirement, Resignation, or Death, Whether in India or in Europe, from the Year 1760 to the Year 1834 Inclusive, Corrected to September 30, 1837*. London: Longman, Orme & Brown, 1838.

D'Oyly, Charles, and Capt. Thomas Williamson. *The European in India*. London: Edward Orme, 1813.

Durand, Henry Marion. *The First Afghan War and Its Causes*. London: Longmans, Green, and Co., 1879.

Eden, Emily. *Letters from India*. Vol. 1. London: Richard Bentley and Son, 1872.

Edwardes, Herbert. *Memorials of the Life and Letters of Major General Sir Herbert B. Edwardes by His Wife*. Edited by Emma Edwards. London: K. Paul, Trench & Co., 1886.

———. *A Year on the Punjab Frontier in 1848–9*. London: R. Bentley, 1851.

Edwardes, Herbert, and Herman Merivale. *Life of Sir Henry Lawrence*. 3rd ed. London: Smith, Elder & Co., 1873.

Elliot, William, in Calcutta, to Frederick Currie in Lahore. Foreign Department Proceedings for the Years 1840–1849. M & I October 1848, No. S 283-287, Cons S.C. "Foreign 1848 Dept. Secret Consultation 7 Oct No. 287." National Archives of India, New Delhi.

Elphinstone, Mountstuart. *An Account of the Kingdom of Cabaul*. New Delhi: Munsharam Manoharial Publishers, 1998 (originally published 1815).

Fenton, Elizabeth. *The Journal of Mrs. Fenton: A Narrative of Her Life in India, the Isle of France (Mauritius) and Tasmania during the Years 1826–1830*. London: Edward Arnold, 1901.

Ferrier, Joseph Pierre. *Caravan Journeys and Wanderings in Persia*. London: J. Murray, 1857.

Gardner, Alexander. *Soldier and Traveller* [sic]. London: William Blackwood and Sons, 1848.

Graham, Maria. *Journal of a Residence in India*. Edinburgh: George Ramsay and Company, 1813.

Grant, Charles. *Observations on the State of Society among the Asiatic Subjects of Great Britain*. London: House of Commons, 1813.

Grant, James. *Incidents in the Sepoy War, 1857–58*. Boston: Adamant Media, 2006.

Harriott, John. *Struggles through Life, Exemplified in the Various Travels and Adventures in Europe, Asia, Africa and America, of Lieutenant John Harriott*. London: Black, Parry and Kingsbury, 1807.

Heber, Reginald. *Narrative of a Journey through the Upper Provinces of India*. London: John Murray, 1828.

House of Commons. "Report of Return to the Honourable the East India Company." August 1851.

Jacob, John. *The Views and Opinions of Brigadier-General John Jacob*. London: Smith, Elder & Co., 1851.

BIBLIOGRAPHY

Jacquemont, Victor. "Calcutta in 1829." In *Calcutta in the 19th Century*, edited by P. Thankappan Nair. Calcutta: Firma KLM Private Limited, 1989.
Kaye, John. *The Administration of the East India Company: A History of Indian Progress*. 2nd ed. London: Richard Bentley, 1853.
———. *A History of the Sepoy War in India: 1857–1858*. London: W. H. Allen, 1872.
———. *History of the War in Afghanistan*. London: Wm. Allen, 1857.
Kipling, Rudyard. "Ballad of East and West." In *Barrack-Room Ballads and Other Verses*. Leipzig: Heinemann & Balestier Ltd. Of London, 1889.
"Knowledge of Local Vernaculars." *Allen's Indian Mail* 30, no. 1009 (February 13, 1872).
Lawrence, George. "Punjaub 1848/9 Nicholson's Letters One from Major George Lawrence." Letter dated August 12, 1848. India Office Records, European Manuscripts, Mss Eur F171/24. British Library.
Lawrence, Henry. *Adventures of an Officer in the Punjaub*. [Vol. 1.] London: Henry Colburn 1846.
———. *Adventures of an Officer in the Service of Ranjeet Singh*. [Vol. 2.] London: Henry Colburn, 1845.
Lawrence, Henry, to Lord Dalhousie. "Lord Dalhousie's Letters to and from Sir Henry Lawrence." November 5, 1849. India Office Records, European Manuscripts, Mss Eur F85/45/B. British Library.
Lawrence, Honoria. *The Journals of Honoria Lawrence*. Edited by John Lawrence and Audrey Woodiwiss. London: Hodder & Stoughton, 1980.
Lawrence, John. "Letter from John Lawrence to Stafford Northcote June 1, 1867." India Office Records, European Manuscripts, Mss Eur F90/32a no. 34. British Library.
Lowrie, John. *Two Years in Upper India*. New York: R. Carter and Brothers, 1850.
Lutfullah. *Autobiography of Lutfullah: A Mohamedan Gentleman*. Edited by Edward Eastwick. London: Smith, Elder and Co., 1858.
MacMullen, John. *Camp and Barrack-Room; Or, the British Army as It Is*. London: Chapman & Hall, 1846.
Malcolm, Sir John. "Letter to Governor-General William Bentinck, January 27, 1830." India Office Records, European Manuscripts, Mss Eur F4/1287/51585. British Library.
———. "Letter to Governor-General William Bentinck, November 27, 1830." India Office Records, European Manuscripts, Mss Eur F4/1287/51585. British Library.
Masson, Charles. *Narrative of Various Journeys in Balochistan, Afghanistan, and the Punjab*. London: R. Bentley, 1844.
McDougall, William. *A Textbook of Psychology*. London: Methuen & Co, 1909.
Merivale, Herman. *Life of Sir Henry Lawrence*. London: Smith Elder & Co., 1873.
Mill, James. *Principles of Political Economy: With Some of Their Applications to Social Philosophy*. London: Longmans, Green, Reader, and Dyer, 1871.
Monkland, Mrs. [pseud.]. *The Nabob at Home; or, the Return to England*. New York: Harper & Brothers, 1842.
Morris, Henry. *Edwardes: The Hero of Multan; The Peacemaker among Wild Afghan Tribes; the True Friend of India; the Earnest Christian*. London: Christian Literature Society, 1895.

BIBLIOGRAPHY

Napier, Charles. *The Conquest of Scinde, with some Introductory Passages in the Life of Major General Sir Charles James Napier.* London: T. & W. Boone, 1845.
Nugent, Maria. *A Journal from the Year 1811 till 1815, Including a Voyage to and Residence in India.* Vol. 1. London: T. and W. Boone, 1839.
Papers of Lord William H. Cavendish Bentinck (1774–1839), Soldier, Politician, and Statesman. Nottingham University Library, Department of Manuscripts and Special Collections, File Pw Jf 2685/1-3.
Parliament of Great Britain. *Papers Relating to the Punjab: 1847–1849.* London: Harrison and Son, 1849.
Pococke, Richard. *A Description of the East and Some Other Countries.* Vol. 2. London: W. Boyer, 1745.
Pogson, Wredenhall. *Memoir of the Mutiny at Barrackpore.* Serampore: Serampore Press, 1833.
Price, Joseph. *The Saddle Put on the Right Horse.* London: John Stockdale, 1783.
Quinney, Staff Sgt. Thomas. *Sketches of a Soldier's Life in India.* Glasgow: David Robertson, 1853.
Ram, Subedar Sita. *From Sepoy to Subedar.* Edited by James Lunt. Delhi: Vikas Publications, 1970.
Rankin, Agnes. *Shipmates.* Kendal, UK: Titus Wilson and Son, 1967.
Report from the Select Committee of the House of Lords on the Government of Indian Territories. Shannon: Irish University Press, 1853.
Rickards, R. *India or Facts Submitted to Illustrate the Character and Condition of the Native Inhabitants.* London: Smith, Elder & Company, 1832.
Roberdeau, I. H. T. "Calcutta in 1805." In *Calcutta in the 19th Century*, edited by P. Thankappan Nair. Calcutta: Firma KLM Private, 1989.
"Robinson Military Survey of Hazara." M (Manuscript) 398, RP (Report) 12, SI. No. 533 (old number M-398). National Archives of India, New Delhi.
Sale, Lady Florentia. *A Journal of the Disasters in Affghanistan, 1841–2.* London: John Murray, 1844.
———. *A Journal of the First Afghan War.* Oxford: Oxford University Press, 2002.
Schickhardus, Snellius (James Abbott). "An Apology for the Indian Army." In *United Services Journal and Naval and Military Magazine.* Part I. London: Henry Colburn and Richard Bentley, 1832.
———. *Tales of the Forest.* London: James Madden, 1853.
Scott, Walter. *Rob Roy: The Complete Works of Walter Scott in Six Volumes*. New York: Connor and Cooke, 1833.
———. *The Surgeon's Daughter.* Edinburgh: Adam and Charles Black, 1827.
Scurry, James. *Captivity, Sufferings, and Escape of James Scurry: Who Was Detained a Prisoner during Ten Years, in the Dominions of Hyder Ali and Tippoo Saib.* London: Henry Fisher, 1824.
Sellon, Edward. *The Ups and Downs of Life.* Hertfordshire, UK: Wordsworth Editions, 1999 (reprint of London: William Dugdale, 1867).
Shipp, Lt. John. *Memoirs of the Extraordinary Military Career of John Shipp.* London: T. Fisher Unwin, 1829.

———. *Memoirs of Lt. John Shipp*. London: Hurst, Chance, and Co., 1830.
Smith, Paul. *Disraeli: A Brief Life*. Cambridge: University of Cambridge, 1996.
Smyth, Ralph, and Henry Thuillier. *A Manual of Surveying for India*. Calcutta: W. Thacker & Co., 1851.
Solvyns, François Baltazard. *Les Hindous*. Paris: Chez l'auteur & H. Nicolle, 1808.
Stocqueler, Joachim. *The British Officer: His Position, Duties, Emoluments, and Privileges*. London: Smith, Elder and Co., 1851.
———. *The Old Field Officer: The Military and Sporting Adventures of Major Worthington*. Edinburgh: Adam and Charles Black, 1853.
Symonds, John. *Memoirs*. Edited by Phyllis Grosskurth. Chicago: University of Chicago Press, 1986.
Todd, D'Arcy. "Observations on the Military Memoir of Cpt. Burnes on Afghanistan, 2 July, 1837." India Office Records, Letters and Enclosures from Persia, L/PS/9, 102: folios 420–463. British Library.
Vibart, Henry Meredith. *Addiscombe: Its Heroes and Men of Note*. London: Archibald Constable and Co., 1894.
Wallace, Lt. Robert. "Calcutta in 1823." In *Calcutta in the 19th Century*, edited by P. Thankappan Nair. Calcutta: Firma KLM Private, 1989.
Wilberforce, Reginald. *An Unrecorded Chapter of the Indian Mutiny*. London: John Murray, 1894.
Williamson, Thomas. *The General East India Guide and Vade-Mecum*. London: Kingsbury, Parbury and Allen, 1825.
Wolesley, Garnet. *The Story of a Soldier's Life*. London: A. Constable & Co., 1904.
Wollaston, John Ramsden. *Journals and Diaries of the Assistants to the Agent, Governor-General North-West Frontier and Resident at Lahore, 1846–1849: Political Diaries, Journals, ... and Records of British India before 1857*. Lahore: Sang-e-Meel Publications, 2006.

Secondary Sources

Ahmed, Akbar. *Pieces of Green: The Sociology of Change in Pakistan, 1964–1974*. Karachi: Royal Book Co., 1977.
Akram, Javid. *1998 District Census Report of Abbottabad*. Islamabad: Government of Pakistan, Population Census Organisation, Statistics Division, 1998.
Alavi, Seema. *The Sepoys and the Company*. New Delhi: Oxford University Press, 1995.
Alexander, Christopher. *A Carpet Ride to Khiva*. London: Icon Books, 2010.
Allen, Charles. *God's Terrorists*. Cambridge, MA: Da Capo Press, 2006.
———. *Soldier Sahibs*. London: Abacus Books, 2001.
Allen's Indian Mail. "Constance." London: Wm. H. Allen, Vol. 26, January 28, 1878.
Allworth, Edward. *The Modern Uzbeks: From the 14th Century to the Present: A Cultural History*. Stanford. CA: Hoover Institute Press, 1990.
Altick, Richard. *Victorian People and Ideas*. New York: W. W. Norton & Co., 1973.
Anderson, Benedict. *Imagined Communities: Reflections on the Origin and Spread of Nationalism*. London: Verso, 2006.

Bibliography

Anderson, Gerald, ed. *Biographical Dictionary of Christian Missions*. Grand Rapids: Wm. B. Eerdmans Publishing, 1999.

Anonymous. *The Poetical Register and Repository of Fugitive Poetry for 1810–1811*. London: F. C. and J. Rivington, 1814.

Arnold, David. *Colonizing the Body: State Medicine and Epidemic Disease in 19th C. India*. Berkeley: University of California Press, 1993.

Balfour, Edward. *The Cyclopaedia of India and of Eastern and Southern Asia*. Vol. 2. London: Bernard Quaritch, 1885.

Ballhatchet, Kenneth. *Race, Sex and Class under the Raj*. Houndmills, UK: Palgrave Macmillan, 1980.

Barat, Amiya. *The Bengal Native Infantry: Its Organization and Discipline, 1796–1852*. Calcutta: Firma K. L. Mukhopadhyay, 1962.

Barrier, N. Gerald. "The Punjab Government and Communal Politics, 1870–1908." *Journal of Asian Studies* 27, no. 3 (May 1968).

Barthorp, Michael. *Afghan Wars and the Northwest Frontier, 1839–1947*. London: Cassel, 1982.

Bayly, C. A. *Empire and Information. Intelligence Gathering and Social Communication in India, 1780–1870*. Cambridge: Cambridge University Press, 2000.

———. *Imperial Meridian: The British Empire and the World, 1780–1830*. White Plains, NY: Longman, 1989.

———. *Indian Society and the Making of the Raj*. Cambridge: Cambridge University Press, 1990.

Beckford, William. *An Arabian Tale, from an Unpublished Manuscript*. London: J. Johnson in St. Paul's Churchyard, 1786.

Beers, Henry. *A History of English Romanticism in the Nineteenth Century*. London: Keegan, Paul, Trench, Trübner, 1899.

Blunt, Edward. *List of Inscriptions on Christian Tombs and Tablets of Historical Interest in the United Provinces of Agra and Oudh*. Allahabad: United Provinces Government Press, 1911.

Brighton Guardian. "New Looks." Sussex, UK, December 26, 1877.

Bourne, J. M. *Patronage and Society in Nineteenth Century England*. London: Edward Arnold, 1986.

Brodie, Fawn. *The Devil Drives: A Life of Sir Richard Burton*. New York: W. W. Norton and Co., 1967.

Buckland, C. E. *Dictionary of Indian Biography*. London: Swan Sonnenschein & Co., 1906.

Burton, Isabella. *The Life of Sir Richard F. Burton, K.C.M.G., F.R.G.S*. London: Chapman & Hall, 1893.

Burton, Reginald. *The First and Second Sikh Wars*. Delhi: Government Central Branch Press, 1911.

Burton, Robert. *The Anatomy of Melancholy*. London: B. Blake, 1838.

Butalia, Romesh. *The Evolution of the Artillery in India: From the Battle of Plassey (1757) to the Revolt of 1857*. New Delhi: Allied Publishers, 1998.

Cannadine, David. *Ornamentalism: How the British Saw Their Empire*. New York: Oxford University Press, 2002.
Carey, W. H. *The Good Old Days of the Honorable John Company*. Calcutta: D. C. Kerr, 1906.
Caroë, Olaf. *The Pathans*. New York: St. Martin's Press, 1958.
Cavaliero, Roderick. *Ottomania*. London: J. B. Taurus & Co., 2010.
Chandler, Alice. *A Dream of Order: The Medieval Ideal in 19th Century English Literature*. Lincoln: University of Nebraska Press, 1970.
Choudhury, Pranab Chandra Roy, and Lewis O'Malley. *Santal Parganas*. New Delhi: Logos Press, 1999; originally published as a *Bengal District Gazetteer* in 1910.
Cleghorn, R. A. "The Pitfalls in Thinking Big: Megalomania." *Psychiatric Quarterly* 38 (October 1964).
Colley, Linda. *Captives: Britain, Empire, and the World, 1600–1850*. New York: Pantheon Books, 2002.
Collingham, E. M. *Imperial Bodies: The Physical Experience of the Raj, c. 1800–1947*. Cambridge, UK: Polity Press, 2001.
Conolly, Edward. "Sketch of the Physical Geography of Seistan." *Journal of the Asiatic Society of Bengal* (1840).
Conrad, Joseph. *Heart of Darkness*. London: William Blackwood and Sons, 1902.
Cooper, James Fennimore. *England, with Sketches of Society in the Metropolis*. Paris: Baudry's European Library, 1837.
Cooper, Randolf. *The Anglo-Maratha Campaigns and the Contest for India*. Cambridge: Cambridge University Press, 2003.
Cordingly, David. *Cochrane the Dauntless: The Life and Adventures of Thomas Cochrane*. New York: Bloomsbury Publishing, 2007.
Creighton, Louise. *Life and Letters of Mandell Creighton*. Vol. 1. London: Longman's, Green & Co., 1904.
Curtain, Philip. *Death by Migration: Europe's Encounter with the Tropical World in the Nineteenth Century*. New York: Cambridge University Press, 1989.
Dalrymple, William. *The Last Moghul: The Fall of a Dynasty, Delhi, 1857*. London: Bloomsbury, 2006.
———. *White Moghuls*. New York: Penguin Group, 2002.
David, Saul. *The Indian Mutiny*. London: Penguin Books, 2002.
Davis, Henry William Carless. *The Great Game in Asia, 1800–1844*. London: Published for the British Academy by H. Milford, Oxford University Press, 1927.
Davis, Ralph. *Aleppo and Devonshire Square: English Traders in the Levant in the Eighteenth Century*. London: Routledge, 1967.
De Courcy, Anne. *The Fishing Fleet: Husband Hunting in the Raj*. London: Weidenfeld & Nicolson, 2012.
DeLong-Bas, Natana. "Wahhabism." Oxford Bibliographies Online Research Guide. https://www.oxfordbibliographies.com/view/document/obo-9780195390155/obo-9780195390155-0091.xml?rskey=t3zkbC&result=1&q=Wahhabism%5C#firstMatch.
Dickens, Charles, ed. *Household Words* 16 (July 4, 1857). London: Ward, Lock and Tyler.

Bibliography

Disraeli, Benjamin. *Coningsby, or the New Generation.* London: Longmans Green & Co., 1844.

———. *Selected Speeches of the Late Right Honourable the Earl of Beaconsfield.* Edited by T. E. Kebbel. Vol. 1. London: Longmans Publishing, 1882.

———. *Vivian Grey.* New York: George Routledge & Sons, 1853.

Docherty, Paddy. *The Khyber Pass: A History of Empire and Invasion.* New York: Sterling Publishing, 2008.

Dutt, Romesh Chunder. *The Economic History of India under Early British Rule.* London: Rutledge and Kegan Paul, 1950.

Dutta, Abhijit. *Glimpses of European Life in 19th Century Bengal.* Calcutta: Minerva Associates, 1995.

Edney, Matthew. "British Military Education, Map-Making and Military Map-Mindedness in the Late Enlightenment." *Cartographic Journal* 31, no. 1 (1994).

———. *Mapping an Empire: The Geographical Construction of British India, 1765–1843.* Chicago: University of Chicago Press, 1999.

———. "The Patronage of Science and Creation of Imperial Space: The British Mapping of India, 1799–1843." *Cartographica* 30, no. 1 (1993).

Edwards, Michael. *The Nabobs at Home.* London: Constable and Company, 1991.

Edwards, P. D. "Hervey, Thomas Kibble (1799–1859)." *Oxford Dictionary of National Biography.* Oxford: Oxford University Press, 2004.

Edwards, W. "Conservatism in Human Information Processing." In *Formal Representation of Human Judgment*, edited by B. Kleinmuntz. New York: John Wiley & Sons, 1968.

Epstein, Mortimer. *The English Levant Company: Its Foundation and Its History to 1640.* London: George Routledge and Sons, 1908.

Evidence of Major General Birch, Military Secretary to Government of India to Royal Commission on Organisation of Indian Army. London, 1859.

Ewans, Martin. *Afghanistan: A Short History of Its People and Politics.* New York: Harper Collins, 2002.

Farwell, Byron. *Armies of the Raj: From the Mutiny to Independence, 1858–1947.* New York: W. W. Norton & Company, 1989.

———. *Mr. Kipling's Army.* New York: W. W. Norton & Co., 1981.

———. *Queen Victoria's Little Wars.* New York: W. W. Norton & Co, 1972.

Featherstone, Donald. *At Them with the Bayonet! The First Sikh War.* London: Jarrolds, 1968.

ni Fhlathúin, Máire, ed. *The Poetry of British India, 1780–1905.* Vol. 1. Milton Park, UK: Routledge, 2011.

Fisher, Michael. *Counterflows to Colonialism.* Delhi: Permanent Black, 2006.

———, ed. *The Travels of Dean Mahomet.* Berkeley: University of California Press, 1997.

Fitzgerald, F. Scott. *The Great Gatsby.* Oxford: Oxford University Press, 1998.

Flaherty, Alice. *The Midnight Disease.* Boston: Mifflin Harcourt, 2005.

Flinders, Stuart. *Cult of a Dark Hero.* London: I. B. Taurus, 2018.

Foltz, Richard. "Judaism and the Silk Route." *History Teacher* 32, no. 1 (November 1998).

Fone, Bryan. *A Road to Stonewall.* New York: Twayne Publishers, 1995.

BIBLIOGRAPHY

Forbes, Archibald. *Britain in Afghanistan: The First Afghan War, 1839–42*. London: Leonaur, 2007.

Forrest, George. *A History of the Indian Mutiny, 1857–58*. Edinburgh: William Blackwood, 1904.

Fredericks, Pierce. *Sepoy and the Cossack*. Cleveland, OH: World Publishing Co., 1971.

Fullerton, George. *A Family Medical Guide*. London: Chapman & Hall, 1871.

Gaborieau, Marc. "A Nineteenth-Century Indian 'Wahabi' Tract against the Cult of Muslim Saints: *Al-Balagh al-Mubin*." In *Muslim Shrines in India: Their Character, History and Significance*, edited by Christian Troll. Delhi: Oxford University Press, 1989.

Gardner, Brian. *The East India Company*. New York: Barnes & Noble Books, 1997.

Geological Survey of India. *Records of the Geological Survey of India*. Vol. 10–12, Part 1. Calcutta: Government Printing Office, 1876.

Ghosh, Durba. *Sex and the Family in Colonial India: The Making of Empire*. Cambridge: Cambridge University Press, 2006.

Gilbert, A. N. "Recruitment and Reform in the East India Company Army, 1760–1800." *Journal of British Studies* 15, no. 1 (1975).

Gilbert, Martin. *In Ishmael's House: A History of Jews in Muslim Lands*. New Haven, CT: Yale University Press, 2011.

Gilmore, Mark. *Ruling Caste*. New York: Farrar, Straus and Giroux, 2007.

Girouard, Mark. *The Return to Camelot: Chivalry and the English Gentleman*. New Haven, CT: Yale University Press, 1981.

Glassman, Bernard. *Benjamin Disraeli: The Fabricated Jew in Myth and Memory*. Studies in Judaism Series. Lanham, MD: University Press of America, 2002.

Gooch, G., and A. Ward. *The Cambridge History of British Foreign Policy, 1783–1919*. Cambridge: Cambridge University Press, 1922.

Goodman, Ruth. *How to Be a Victorian*. London: Penguin Books, 2013.

Gordon, Stewart, ed. *Robes of Honour: Khilat in Pre-colonial and Colonial India*. New Delhi: Oxford University Press, 2003.

Gough, Charles. *The Sikhs and the Sikh Wars: The Rise, Conquest and Annexation of the Punjab State*. London: A. D. Innes & Co., 1897.

Green, Nile. *Islam and the Army in Colonial India: Sepoy Religion in the Service of Empire*. Cambridge: Cambridge University Press, 2009.

Grimble, Arthur. *Return to the Islands*. New York: William Morrow & Company, 1957.

Gupta, Hari Ram. *Punjab, Central Asia, and the First Afghan War: Based on Mohan Lal's Observations*. Chandigarh, India: Panjab University Press, 1987.

Haigh, R. H. *"Nickalsain": The Life and Times of John Nicholson, Brigadier-General in the Army of the Honourable East India Company, 1822–1857*. Manhattan, KS: Military Affairs/Aerospace Historian Publications, 1980.

Haroon, Sana. *Frontier of Faith: Islam in the Indo-Afghan Borderland*. New York: Columbia University Press, 2007.

Harrison, Mark. *Climate and Constitutions: Health, Race, Environment and British Imperialism in India, 1600–1850*. New York: Oxford University Press, 1999.

Bibliography

Hays, J. N. *Epidemics and Pandemics: Their Effect on Human History*. Santa Barbara, CA: ABC-CLIO, 2005.
Heathcote, T. A. *The Indian Army: The Garrison of British Imperial India, 1822–1922*. Newton Abbott, UK: David & Charles, 1974.
———. *The Military in British India: The Development of British Land Forces in South Asia, 1600–1947*. Manchester, UK: Manchester University Press, 1995.
Hervey, Albert. *A Soldier of the Company: Life of an Indian Ensign, 1833–43*. London: Michael Joseph, 1988.
Hibbert, Christopher. *Disraeli: A Personal History*. London: Harper Perennial, 2005.
———. *The Great Mutiny: India 1857*. New York: Penguin Books, 1983.
The Great Mutiny. Middlesex, UK: Penguin Books, 1983.
Hobbes, Thomas. *Leviathan; or The Matter, Forme and Power of a Common Wealth Ecclesiasticall and Civil*. Cambridge: Cambridge University Press, 1904.
Hobhouse, John (Baron John Cam Hobhouse Broughton). *Recollections of a Long Life*. Vol. 5. New York: Charles Scribner & Sons, 1911.
Hochschild, Adam. "Mr. Kurtz, I Presume." *New Yorker*. April 7, 1997.
Hodgson, John. *Opinions on the Indian Army*. London: W. H. Allen & Co., 1857.
Holdsworth, T. W. E. *Campaign of the Indus: In a Series of Letters from an Officer of the Bombay Division*. Charleston, SC: Bibliobazaar, 2007.
Holmes, Richard. *Sahib: The British Soldier in India, 1750–1914*. London: Harper Collins, 2005.
Hopkins, Benjamin, and Magnus Marsden. *Fragments of the Afghan Frontier*. New York: Columbia University Press, 2011.
Hopkins, Hugh. *Sublime Vagabond: The Life of Joseph Wolff—Missionary Extraordinary*. Worthing, UK: Churchman, 1984.
Hopkirk, Peter. *The Great Game*. New York: Kodansha America, 1994.
Houghton, Walter. *The Victorian Frame of Mind*. New Haven, CT: Yale University Press, 1985.
Hugo, Victor. *Les Orientales*. Paris: Hector Bossange, 1829.
Hurd, Douglas, and Edward Young, *Disraeli, or The Two Lives*. London: Weidenfeld and Nicolson, 2013.
Hyam, Ronald. *Britain's Imperial Century, 1815–1914*. New York: Palgrave Macmillan, 2002.
———. *Empire and Sexuality: The British Experience*. Manchester, UK: Manchester University Press, 1990.
Intelligence Branch, Army Headquarters India. *Frontier and Overseas Expeditions from India in 7 Volumes*. Vol. 1: *Tribes North of the Kabul River*. Simla: Government Monotype Press, 1907.
Irving, Miles, and George William De Rhé-Philipe. *A List of Inscriptions on Christian Tombs or Monuments in the Punjab, North-West Frontier Province, Kashmir, and Afghanistan Possessing Historical or Archaeological Interest*. Part 1. Lahore: Punjab Government Press, 1910.
James, Lawrence. *Raj: The Making and Unmaking of British India*. New York: St. Martin's Griffin, 1997.

Jasanoff, Maya. *Edge of Empire: Lives, Culture, and Conquest in the East, 1750–1850*. New York: Alfred A. Knopf, 2005.
Jenkyns, Richard. *The Victorians and Ancient Greece*. Oxford, UK: Basil Blackwell, 1981.
John Bull. "Constance." London: Theodore Hook, December 15, 1877.
Johnson, Thomas, and Chris Mason. "Understanding the Taliban and Insurgency in Afghanistan." *Orbis* (winter 2007).
Jones, Justin. *Shi'a Islam in Colonial India: Religion, Community and Sectarianism*. Cambridge: Cambridge University Press, 2012.
Kaye, John. *History of the War in Afghanistan in Three Volumes*. Vol. 3. London: W. H. Allen & Co, 1878.
———. *The Lives of Indian Officers*. London: A. Strahan & Co., 1867.
———. *Lives of Indian Officers*. London: J. J. Keliher, 1904.
Keay, John. *The Great Arc: The Dramatic Tale of How India Was Mapped and Everest Was Named*. New York: HarperCollins, 2000.
Kelly, Linda. *Ireland's Minstrel: A Life of Tom Moore, Poet Patriot and Byron's Friend*. London: I. B. Taurus, 2007.
Kennedy, Dane. *The Highly Civilized Man: Richard Burton and the Victorian World*. Cambridge, MA: Harvard University Press, 2007.
———. *The Magic Mountains: Hill Stations and the British Raj*. Berkeley: University of California Press, 1996.
Kinderman, Peter, and Richard Bentall. "Causal Attributions in Paranoia and Depression: Internal, Personal, and Situational Attributions for Negative Events." *Journal of Abnormal Psychology* 106, no. 2 (May 1997).
Kolff, Dirk. *Naukar, Rajput and Sepoy: The Ethnohistory of the Military Labor Market in Hindustan, 1450–1850*. Cambridge: Cambridge University Press, 1990.
Kuran, Timur, and Cass Sunstein. "Availability Cascades and Risk Regulation." *Stanford Law Review* 51, no. 4 (1999).
La Nauze, J. A. "The Substance of Adam Smith's Attack on Mercantilism." In *Adam Smith: Critical Assessments*, ed. John Wood. London: Routledge, 1984.
Laidlaw, Christine. *The British in the Levant: Trade and Perceptions of the Ottoman Empire in the Eighteenth Century*. London: I. B. Taurus Publishers, 2010.
Laidlaw, J. C. *The Poetical Works of Alain Chartier*. Cambridge: Cambridge University Press, 1974.
Lake, Marilyn, and Henry Reynolds. *Drawing the Global Color Line*. New York: Cambridge University Press, 2008.
Lawrence, Henry. India Office Records, European Manuscripts, Mss Eur E277/6, "Obituary from the *Standard*." British Library.
Lawson, Philip, and Jim Phillips. "Our Execrable Banditti: Perceptions of Nabobs in Mid-Eighteenth-Century Britain." *Albion: A Quarterly Journal Concerned with British Studies* 16, no. 3 (autumn 1984): 225–241.
Leak, Nigel. *British Romantic Writers and the East: Anxieties of Empire*. Cambridge: Cambridge University Press, 1993.
Lee, Harold. *Brothers in the Raj: The Lives of John and Henry Lawrence*. New York: Oxford University Press, 2002.

BIBLIOGRAPHY

Lee, Jonathan. *The "Ancient Supremacy": Bukhara, Afghanistan and the Battle for Balkh, 1731–1901*. Boston: Brill Academic Publishers, 1996.
Lee, Sydney, ed. *Dictionary of National Biography*. Vol. 56. New York: MacMillan Company, 1898.
———. *Dictionary of National Biography (Supplement)*. Vol. 22. London: Smith, Elder, & Co., 1901.
Lee-Warner, William. *The Life of the Marquess of Dalhousie, K.T.* Vol. 1. London: MacMillan and Co., 1904.
Lewis, Bernard. *The Jews of Islam*. Princeton, NJ: Princeton University Press, 1987.
Lodge, Henry Cabot, ed. *The History of Nations*. Vol. 5: *India and Persia*. New York: P. F. Collier and Son, 1913.
Macintyre, Ben. *The Man Who Would Be King: The First American in Afghanistan*. New York: Farrar, Straus and Giroux, 2003.
Macrory, Patrick. *Retreat from Kabul: The Catastrophic British Defeat in Afghanistan, 1842*. Guilford, CT: Lyons Press, 2007.
———. *Signal Catastrophe*. London: Hodder and Stoughton, 1966.
Madan, P. L. *Indian Cartography, a Historical Perspective*. New Delhi, Manohar Publishers, 1997.
Mahomet, Dean. *The Travels of Dean Mahomet*. Edited by Michael H. Fisher. Berkeley: University of California Press, 1997.
Mahood, Linda. *Magdalenes: Prostitution in the Nineteenth Century*. London: Routledge, 1990.
Makdisi, Saree. *Romantic Imperialism: Universal Empire and the Culture of Modernity*. New York: Cambridge University Press, 1998.
Malleson, George. *The Decisive Battles of India, 1746–1849 Inclusive*. London: W. H. Allen & Co., 1888.
Manz, Beatrice. "Central Asian Uprisings in the Nineteenth Century: Ferghana under the Russians." *Russian Review* 46, no. 3 (July 1987).
Markham, Clements. "Second Period of the Topographical Surveys, 1823–1843." Chapter 6 in *A Memoir of the Indian Surveys*. London: W. H. Allen, 1878.
Marshall, P. J. *Bengal: The British Bridgehead, Eastern India, 1740–1828*. Cambridge: Cambridge University Press, 2006.
———. "British Immigration into India in the Nineteenth Century." *Itinerario* 14 (1990).
———. "British Society in India under the East India Company." *Modern Asian Studies* 31, no. 1 (February 1997).
———. *East India Fortunes: The British in Bengal in the Eighteenth Century*. Oxford: Clarendon Press, 1976.
———. "The Empire of the Officials." In *Romantic Representations of British India*, edited by Michael Franklin. New York: Routledge, 2006.
Marshman, John. *The History of India, from the Earliest Period to the Close of Lord Dalhousie's Administration*. Vol. 3. London: Longmans, Green, Reader & Dyer, 1869.
———. *History of India from the Earliest Period to the Close of the East India Company's Government*. Edinburgh: William Blackwood and Sons, 1876.

Bibliography

Mason, Philip. *A Matter of Honor: An Account of the Indian Army, Its Officers and Men.* London: Jonathan Cape Publishing, 1974.
Mather, James. *Pashas, Traders and Travelers in the Islamic World.* New Haven, CT: Yale University Press, 2009.
McMunn, Maj. G. F. *The Armies of India.* London: Adam and Charles Black, 1911.
Metcalf, Thomas. *The Aftermath of Revolt: India, 1856–1870.* Princeton, NJ: Princeton University Press, 1964.
———. "From Raja to Landlord: The Oudh Talukdars, 1850–1870." In *Land Control and Social Structure in Indian History,* edited by Robert Frykenberg. Madison: University of Wisconsin Press, 1969.
Meyer, Karl, and Shareen Blair. *Tournament of Shadows: The Great Game and the Race for Empire in Central Asia.* New York: Perseus Books Group, 2006.
Michael, B. A. "Making Territory Visible: The Revenue Surveys of Colonial South Asia." *Imago Mundi* 59, no. 1 (2007).
Mikics, David. *A New Handbook of Literary Terms.* New Haven, CT: Yale University Press, 2007.
Moir, Zawahir, and Martin Moir. "Old District Records in Pakistan." *Modern Asian Studies* 24, no. 1 (February 1990).
Montaigne, Michel de. *Complete Essays.* Stanford, CA: Stanford University Press, 1958.
Morgan, Gerald. *Anglo-Russian Rivalry in Central Asia.* New York: Routledge, 1981.
Morrison, J. L. *Lawrence of Lucknow.* London: G. Bell, 1934.
Mukharya, P. S. *Revolt of 1857: Saugor and Narbudda Territory.* Delhi: Sharada Publishing House, 2001.
Mukherjee, Rudrangshu. *Mangal Pandey: Brave Martyr or Accidental Hero?* New Delhi: Penguin Books India, 2005.
Munirov, Q. *Munis, Ogahii va Bayoning tarikhi asarlari* [Munis, Ogahiy and Bayoniy's historic works]. Tashkent: UzSSR Fanlar Akedemiyasi Nashriyoti, 1960.
Munro, Alistair. *Delusional Disorder: Paranoia and Related Illnesses.* Cambridge: Cambridge University Press, 2004.
Muravyev, Nikolai. *Journey to Khiva through the Turkoman Country.* London: Oguz Press, 1977.
Naeem, Nadhra Shahbaz. "Life at the Lahore Darbār: 1799–1839." *South Asian Studies* 25, no. 2 (January–June 2010).
Nanda, Bikram, and Mohammed Talib. "Soul of the Soulless: An Analysis of Pir-Murid Relationships in Sufi Discourse." In *Muslim Shrines in India: Their Character, History and Significance,* edited by Christian Troll. Delhi: Oxford University Press, 1989.
Napier, Charles. *The Conquest of Sindh.* California: Sani Hussain Panhwar, 2009.
———. *Defects, Civil and Military, of the Indian Government.* London: John Murray, 1853.
Nechtman, Tillman. *Nabobs, Empire and Identity in Eighteenth-Century Britain.* New York: Cambridge University Press, 2010.
Nevill, Hugh. *Campaigns on the North-West Frontier.* Nashville, TN: Battery Press, 1912.
Newbury, Colin. *Patrons, Clients and Empire: Chieftaincy and Over-Rule.* New York: Oxford University Press, 2003.

Norris, J. A. *The First Afghan War, 1838–1842*. Cambridge: Cambridge University Press, 1967.
Nyhan, Brendan, and Jason Reifler. "When Corrections Fail: The Persistence of Political Misperceptions." *Political Behavior* 32, no. 2 (2010).
Oberoi, Harjot. *The Construction of Religious Boundaries: Culture, Identity, and Diversity in the Sikh Tradition*. Chicago: University of Chicago Press, 1994.
Olson, James, and Robert Shadle, eds. *Historical Dictionary of the British Empire, A–J*. Westport, CT: Greenwood Press, 1996.
O'Malley, L. S. S. *The Indian Civil Service, 1601–1930*. London: Frank Cass & Co., 1965.
Patmore, Derek. *The Life and Times of Coventry Patmore*. London: Constable, 1949.
Paxman, Jeremy. *The Victorians: Britain through the Paintings of the Age*. London: BBC Books, 2009.
Pearse, George. "On the Excavation of a Large Raised Stone Circle or Barrow Near the Village of Wurreegaon, One Mile from the Military Station of Kamptee, Central Provinces of India." *Journal of the Ethnological Society of London* 1 (1869).
Pearson, Hesketh. *The Hero of Delhi: A Life of John Nicholson, Saviour of India, and a History of His Wars*. London: Penguin Books UK, 1930.
Peers, Douglas. *Between Mars and Mammon: Colonial Armies and the Garrison State in India, 1819–1835*. London: Taurus Academic Studies, 1995.
———. "Colonial Knowledge and the Military in India, 1780–1860." *Journal of Imperial and Commonwealth History* 33, no. 2 (2005): 157–80.
———. "Conquest Narratives: Romanticism, Orientalism and Intertextuality in the Indian Writings of Sir Walter Scott and Robert Orme." In *Romantic Representations of British India*, edited by Michael Franklin. New York: Routledge, 2006.
Pennel, T. L. *Among the Wild Tribes of the Afghan Frontier*. Whitefish, MT: Kessinger Publishing, 1997 (reprint of 1909 edition).
Pernau, Margrit. *Bürger mit Turban, Muslime in Delhi im 19. Jahrhundert*. Göttingen: Vandenhoeck & Ruprecht, 2008.
Peters, Rudolph. "Erneuerungsbewegungen im Islam vom 18. Bis zum 20. Jahrhundert und die Rolle des Islams in der neuen Geschichte: Antikolonialismus und Nationalismus." In *Der Islam in der Gegenwart*, edited by Werner Ende, Udo Steinbach, and Renate Laut. Munich: Verlag C. H. Beck oHG, 1996.
Pollock, J. C. *Way to Glory*. London: John Murray, 1957.
Porter, Bernard. *The Absent-Minded Imperialists*. Oxford: Oxford University Press, 2004.
———. *The Lion's Share*. Harlow, UK: Pearson Education Limited, 2004.
Pottinger, George, and Patrick Macrory. *The Ten-Rupee Jezail: Figures in the First Afghan War, 1838–1842*. Norwich, UK: Michael Russell Publishing, 1993.
Pottinger, George. *The Afghan Connection: The Extraordinary Adventures of Major Eldred Pottinger*. Edinburgh: Scottish Academic Press 1983.
Prakash, Om. *History of Anglo-Sikh Wars*. New Delhi: Anmol Publications, 2004.
Princep, Augustus. *The Baboo and Other Tales Descriptive of Society in India*. 2 vols. London: Smith & Elder, 1834.

Prior, Katherine, Lance Brennan, and Robin Haines. "Bad Language: The Role of English, Persian and Other Esoteric Tongues in the Dismissal of Sir Edward Colebrooke as Resident of Delhi in 1829." *Modern Asian Studies* 35 (2001).
Raychaudhuri, Tapan. "Permanent Settlement in Operation: Bakarganj District, East Bengal." In *Land Control and Social Structure in Indian History*, edited by Robert Frykenberg. Madison: University of Wisconsin Press, 1969.
Richards, Jeffrey. "Passing the Love of Women: Manly Love and Victorian Society." In *Manliness and Morality: Middle-Class Masculinity in Britain and America, 1800–1940*, edited by J. A. Mangan and James Walvin. Oxford, UK: Alden University Press, 1987.
Rosselli, John. *Lord William Bentinck: The Making of a Liberal Imperialist, 1774–1839.* London: Chatto and Windus for Sussex University Press, 1974.
Rückert, Friedrich. *Nal und Damajanti, eine Indische Geschichte.* Frankfurt a.M.: Johann David Sauerländer, 1828.
Runciman, Steven. *The White Rajahs: A History of Sarawak from 1841 to 1946.* Cambridge: Cambridge University Press, 1960.
Ruskin, John. *Modern Painters.* Vol. 3. Reprint ed. Whitefish, MT: Kessinger Publishing, 2005.
Russell, Robert. *The Tribes and Castes of the Central Provinces of India.* Vol. 2. London: MacMillan and Co., 1916.
Sarup, Leela, ed., *The Trial of Mangal Pandey: State Papers.* New Delhi: Niyogi Books, 2007.
Schofield, Victoria. *Afghan Frontier: Feuding and Fighting in Central Asia.* London: Taurus Park Paperbacks, 2003.
Schwab, Raymond. *The Oriental Renaissance: Europe's Rediscovery of India and the East, 1680–1880*, translated by G. Petterson-Black and V. Reinking. New York: Columbia University Press, 1984.
Sen, Satadru. *Disciplining Punishment: Colonialism and Convict Society in the Andaman Islands.* New Delhi: Oxford University Press, 2000.
Shelley, Percy Blythe. *Works.* Edited by Roger Ingpen and Walter Peck. Vol. 2. London: Scribner's, 1930.
Simons, Geoffrey. *A Place for Pleasure: The History of the Brothel.* Lewes, UK: Harwood-Smart Publishing Co., 1975.
Singh, Bhupal. *A Survey of Anglo-Indian Fiction.* London: Curzon Press, 1974.
Singh, Jyoti Rai Patwant. *Empire of the Sikhs: The Life and Times of Maharaja Ranjit Singh.* London: Peter Own Publishers, 2008.
Sinha, Mrinalini. *Colonial Masculinity: The "Manly Englishman" and the "Effeminate Bengali" in the Late Nineteenth Century.* New York: St. Martin's Press, 1995.
Skinner, James. *Military Memoir of Lieut-Col. James Skinner.* Edited by C. B. Baillie Fraser. London: Smith, Elder & Co., 1851.
Spain, James. *The Way of the Pathans.* London: Oxford University Press, 1972.
Spear, Percival. *India.* Ann Arbor: University of Michigan Press, 1961.
———. *The Nabobs: A Study of the Social Life of the English in Eighteenth Century India.* London: Curzon, 1980 (first published 1932).

BIBLIOGRAPHY

Sramek, Joseph. *Gender, Morality, and Race in Company India, 1765–1858.* New York: Palgrave Macmillan, 2011.
Stanley, Peter. *White Mutiny: British Military Culture in India.* London: C. Hurst & Co. Publishers, 1998.
Steinbach, Susie. *Understanding the Victorians: Politics, Culture and Society in Nineteenth-Century Britain.* Oxon, UK: Routledge Publishing, 2012.
Stephen, Leslie, ed. *Dictionary of National Biography.* Vol. 7. Oxford: Oxford University Press, 1973.
Stokes, Eric. *The English Utilitarians and India.* Oxford: Oxford University Press, 1959.
———. *The Peasant Armed: The Indian Rebellion of 1857.* Oxford, UK: Clarendon Press, 1986.
Stubbs, Francis. *History of the Bengal Artillery.* Vol. 3. London: W. H. Allen & Co., 1895.
———. *History of the Organization, Equipment, and War Services of the Regiment of Bengal Artillery.* Vol. 2: War Services. London: Henry S. King & Co., 1877.
Sturm, Christoph Christian. *Reflections on the Works of God in Nature and Providence for Every Day of the Year,* translated by Adam Clarke. London: Richard Edwards Publishers, 1810.
Suarez, Georges. *Soixante anneés d'histoire française.* Paris, Editions de France, 1932.
Sutherland, David. *The Weekly Reporter: Appellate High Court.* Vol. 13. Calcutta: D. E. Cranenburgh, 1892.
Sutherland, John. *A Little History of Literature.* London: Yale University Press, 2013.
———. "The Novel." In *A Companion to Romanticism,* edited by John Wu. Oxford, UK: Blackwell Publishers, 1998.
Tarin, Omer. "Tending to the Dead Sahibs." Unpublished ethnological research paper, South Asian Studies Seminar, South Asian Studies Institute, University of the Punjab, Lahore, Pakistan, 2006.
Tarin, Omer, and Sarkees Najmuddin, *Saddah: A Journal of the Humanities* (Pakistan) 12, no. 2 (summer 1999).
———. "Five Early Military Graves (c. 1853-1888) at the Old Christian (Anglican) Cemetery, Abbottabad, Pakistan," *The Kipling Journal.* London: The Kipling Society, Volume 84, Number 339, December 2010, 35-52.
Taylor, Herbert. *The Taylor Papers.* London: Longman, Green & Co., 1923.
Tennyson, Alfred. "The Ancient Sage." In *Tiresias, and Other Poems.* London: MacMillan and Co., 1885.
———. *Poems by Alfred Tennyson, in Two Volumes.* Vol. 2. Boston: William D. Ticknor, 1842.
———. *Tiresias, and Other Poems.* London: MacMillan and Co., 1885.
Thompson, Henry. *The Choice of a Profession. A Concise Account and Comparative Review of the English Professions.* London: Chapman & Hall, 1857.
Thompson, Henry Frederick. *Intrigues of a Nabob: Or, Bengal the Fittest Soil for the Growth of Lust, Injustice and Dishonesty.* Bishopsgate, UK: Printed for the author, 1780.
Tickell, Alex. *Terrorism, Insurgency and Indian-English Literature, 1830–1947.* New York: Routledge, 2012.

Tosh, John. *Manliness and Masculinities in Nineteenth Century Britain*. Harlow, UK: Pearson Education, 2005.
Trotter, Capt. Lionel. *The Life of John Nicholson, Soldier and Administrator, Based on Private and Hitherto Unpublished Documents, With Portraits and Maps*. London: J. Murray, 1898.
Turner, Frank. *The Greek Heritage in Victorian Britain*. New Haven, CT: Yale University Press, 1981.
Vlami, Despina. "Entrepreneurship and Relational Capital in a Levantine Context: Bartholomew Edward Abbott, the 'Father of the Levant Company' in Thessaloniki." In *Historical Review* 6 (2009): 129–64.
Von Haven, Frederik Christian. *Min Sundheds Forliis: Rejsejournal fra Den Arabiske Rejse 1760–1763* [The loss of my health: travel journal from the Arabian expedition], ed. Anne Hansen and Stig Rasmussen. Copenhagen: Forlaget Vandkusten, 2005.
Wagenaar, H. W., S. S. Parikh, D. F. Plukker, and R. Veldhuijzen van Zanten, eds. *Allied Chambers Transliterated Hindi Hindi-English Dictionary*. New Delhi: Allied Publishers, 1993.
Wagner, Kim. *The Great Fear of 1857: Rumours, Conspiracies and the Making of the Indian Mutiny*. Witney, UK: Peter Lang, 2010.
Waller, John. *Beyond the Khyber Pass: The Road to British Disaster in the First Afghan War*. New York: Random House, 1990.
Warburg, Gabriel. "From Sufism to Fundamentalism: The Mahdiyya and the Wahhabiyya." *Middle Eastern Studies* 45, no. 4 (2009).
Warburton, Richard. *Eighteen Years in the Khyber*. London: John Murray, 1900.
Warren, Alba, Jr. *English Poetic Theory, 1825–1865*. Princeton, NJ: Princeton University Press, 1950.
Watson, Henry, Francis Fowler, and George Fowler, eds. *The Concise Oxford Dictionary of Current English*. 7th ed. Oxford, UK: Clarendon Press, 1919.
Watson, Hubert. *Gazetteer of the Hazara District*. London: Chatto & Windus, 1908.
Webster, Noah, ed. *A Dictionary of the English Language*. New York: Huntington and Savage, Mason and Law, 1850.
Webster, Noah, and John Walker. *An American Dictionary of the English Language, Exhibiting the Origin, Orthography, Pronunciation and Definition of Words*. New York: N. and J. White, 1834.
Whitteridge, Gordon. *Charles Masson of Afghanistan*. Bangkok: Orchid Press, 2002.
Wilkinson, Theon. *Two Monsoons: The Life and Death of Europeans in India*. London: Duckworth, 1976.
Wilson, Derek. *Circumnavigators*. New York: Robinson Publishing, 2003.
Wilson, W. J. *History of the Madras Army*. Vol. 3. Madras: E. Keyes for the Government Press, 1883.
Winokur, George. "Delusional Disorder (Paranoia)." *Comprehensive Psychiatry* 18, no. 6 (November–December 1977).
Wolseley, Garnet. *Story of Soldier's Life*. London: Archibald Constable & Co., 1904.
Wood, A. C. *A History of the Levant Company*. Oxford: Oxford University Press, 1935.

Wright, Lawrence. *Clean and Decent: The Fascinating History of the Bathroom and the WC*. London: Routledge & Kegan Paul, 1960.
Wu, Duncan, ed. *A Companion to Romanticism*. Oxford: Blackwell Publishing, 1998.
Wylly, H. C. *Tribes of Central Asia from the Black Mountain to Waziristan*. London: MacMillan & Co., 1912.
Yule, Henry, and Arthur Burnell. *Hobson-Jobson: A Dictionary of Colloquial Anglo-Indian Words and Phrases*. London: John Murray, 1903.

Index

Page references for figures are italicized.

A

Abbott, Anna-Matilda (Maud), 153, 165, 272–74, 334n82
Abbott, Augustus, 6, 8, 10–11, 14, 17, 54, 56, 59, 68, 71–72, 83, 111, 114, 136, 254
Abbott, Clementina, 6, 14, 20, 54
Abbott, Edward, 6, 10
Abbott, Emma, 6, 20–24, 34, 54, 85, 301n56, 305n100
Abbott, Frederick, 6, 8, 11, 17, 20, 22, 24, 28, 34, 36, 39, 48, 75–76, 170, 276, 299, 305n109
Abbott, Henry Sr., 1, 2, 4, 6, 9, 10, 11, 297n6
Abbott, Henry Jr., 6, 130, 138
Abbott, Keith, 6
Abbott, Margaret (mother of James), 2, 11
Abbott, Margaret (sister of James), 6
Abbott, Margaret (wife of James), 152–54, 156, 157, 159
Abbott, Margaret Ann (daughter of James), 156, 162–63, 273, 282
Abbott, Marianne, 16, 71–72, 74–75, 308n48
Abbott, Morris, 1
Abbott, Reymond, 138, 273–74, 318n93
Abbott, Saunders, 6, 74, 97, 111, 116, 166–67, 248, 320n15
Abbottabad, city of, xiv, xviii, 221, 247, 276–77
Addiscombe, military academy, 8, 10–11, 14–15, 17–20, 25, 30, 34, 39, 48–49, 94, 104, 114, 117, 132, 244, 274, 287, 298n34, 99n48, 303n65, 328n88
Agra, city of, 53–54, 59, 68–70, 89, 294, 310n106, 331n17
Aleppo, city of, 1–3, 308n49
Ali, Meer Hassan, 18, 299n74
Ali, Meer Hassan, Mrs., nee Biddy Timms, 299n74
amalgamation, of EICO Army and Royal Army, 265
Amherst, Lord William, Governor-General, 52, 55, 68, 88–89
Anderson, W. A., 195, 197, 203, 276
Andrews, James, 17–19, 300n78
Arniston, wreck of, 25, 301n9
Attariwala, Chattar Singh. See Singh, Chattar.
Auckland, Lord Governor General (George Eden, 1st Earl of Auckland), 110, 112–13, 127, 151–52, 301
Avitabile, Paolo, 230, 327n62

358

Index

B

Bareilly, district of, 60, 103, 107–9, 183, 240, 306n2, 312n47, 313n60

Barrackpoor, mutiny at, 51

Becher, John, 277, 328n88

Bedford, James, 102

Beg, Umeer. See Umeer Beg.

Bengal Army, xviii, xx, 13–14, 40, 63–64, 66, 68, 90–91, 93, 161, 172, 174–75, 189, 250–54, 257, 279, 282, 299, 327

Bengal Presidency, xv–xvi, 161, 302n49

Benson, Archbishop Edward, 273

Benson's School, at Hounslow, ix, 10–11

Bentinck, William Governor-General xx, 68, 77, 88–93, 102–6, 110, 113, 175, 267, 279, 310n106

Bharatpore. See Bhurtpore, 55

Bhurtpore, Battle of, xix, 55–63, 68, 84, 112, 171, 233, 302, 305–6

Bird, Robert, 103, 105

Birkenhead, wreck of, 25, 301n11

Black Mountain, xi, 221, 240–43, 248, 250, 277

Blackheath, ix, 6–10, 14, 16, 75, 268. See also Paragon.

Brahmaputra River, 51

British East India Company. See East India Company.

Brooke, James, 13, 229, 299n52, 327n59

Browning, Robert, 269

Burma, xvii, 49, 51, 55, 60–61, 63, 68, 80, 261, 276, 280, 304n80, 304n89, 305n109, 306n4, 327n59

Burnaby, Frederick, 200, 281, 324

Burnes, Alexander, 123, 142–43, 145, 153, 276, 318n106

Burton, Isabella, 83

Burton, Richard, 8, 42, 83, 101, 269, 303n65, 335n20

C

Calcutta, city of, ix, xii, xix, 1–2, 8–9, 14, 20, 22, 32, 34, 36–39, 52, 60, 72, 82, 106, 110, 142, 151–54, 156, 160, 162–66, 184, 188, 196–97, 207–9, 214, 227–29, 231–32, 244–45, 248, 250–51, 254–57, 259, 267, 270, 281, 298n18, 304n95, 306n2, 308n49, 320n14

Campbell, Archibald, 63

Campbell, Colin, 230

Canara, Colonel, pseudonym, 214

Canning, Charles (1st Earl Canning) Governor-General, 251, 256, 265

Cardigan, 7th Earl of (Thomas Brudenell), 31, 301n32

Carmichael-Smith, George, 45

Caroë, Olaf, 233–34, 281, 322, 329n105

caste, in India, 30–31, 43–44, 51, 66, 69, 89–93, 160–61, 163, 174–75, 189, 263, 279, 282, 303n70, 304n87

Cavenagh, Orfeur, 18, 299

Cawnpore, city of, xi, 54, 111, 163–64, 173, 260–62, 332n41

Cawnpore Well, massacre site, 261–62, 332

Charlton, East Indiaman, 25

Chartier, Alain, 95, 311
Cherenjeet Regiment, of Sikh Army, 209, 211
Chilianwallah, Battle of, 222–23, 226–27
Churenjeet Regiment. See Cherenjeet Regiment.
cholera, in India, 70, 145, 164, 203, 271, 307n40, 313n57
Clive, Robert (1st Baron Clive), Governor-General, 24, 104–5
Cochin, former Dutch colony of, 149, 151, 270, 318n120
Colebrooke, Edward, 75, 77
Coleridge, Samuel, 94, 285, 289, 296, 334
College School at Taunton, 14
Combermere, 1st Viscount (Stapleton Cotton), 63
Conolly, Arthur, 107, 116, 119, 123, 133, 137, 276, 314n29, 316n68, 317n82
Conolly, Edward, 116, 314
Conrad, Joseph, xix, 245–46, 281–82
Cooper, James Fennimore, 143, 310, 318
Cornwallis, Charles, Governor-General (1st Marquess Cornwallis), 103–5
Couper, George, 229–30, 243, 327–28
Cureton, Charles, 222, 326n24
Currie, Frederick, 192–93, 196–97, 201–4, 206–11, 214, 228–29, 244, 271, 276
Cust, Robert, 244

D

D'Oyly, Charles ix, 40–41, 84–85, 303n57, 309n89
Dalhousie, Lord (James Broun-Ramsay), Governor-General xviii, 202–3, 207, 209, 214, 227–31, 236, 238–40, 242–45, 247, 250–51, 257, 276, 281, 327n55
Dalzell, Robert, 51–53, 63
de Burgh, Fanny, nee Case, 16, 74–76, 142, 317n84
Delafosse, Charles Reverend, 8
Delhi, city of, xiv, xix, 55, 75, 135, 171, 249, 256, 258–59, 264–65, 305n106, 326n18, 332n27
de Montmorency, family, 99, 153, 165, 272–73
de Montmorency, Anna Matilda (aka Maud). See Abbott, Anna Matilda.
desertions, sepoy, 54, 63, 209
Dick, Robert, 168
Disraeli, Benjamin, 9, 118, 151, 268–69, 271–72, 277, 333n73, 333n75, 334n76
Doctrine of Lapse, 66, 230, 257, 307n27
Dost Mohammed. See Mohammed, Dost.
Dum Dum, artillery garrison, 39–40, 42, 45, 47–49, 51, 53, 156, 163, 166

E

Earl of Abergavenny, wreck of, 25
East India Company, xv–xx, 1–2, 4, 8, 10, 12–17, 20–21, 25, 31, 39,

48, 50–52, 55, 60–64, 65, 66, 68, 77, 83–84, 88, 90, 108, 112–13, 115, 137, 139, 161, 165, 168–70, 190, 193, 207, 211, 229, 237, 239, 248–50, 263, 265, 267, 269, 277, 282–83, 287–88, 298n34, 299n48, 303n70, 304n95, 305n108, 308n62, 323n87, 327n59, 332n24, 335n20
Eden, Emily, 25, 43
Edwards, Lieutenant, 69–70, 218, 220
Edwardes, Herbert, xviii, 47–48, 184, 190, 195, 201, 203–4, 225, 235–36, 238, 244, 247, 250, 276–77, 281, 328n88
Ellenborough, 1st Earl of (Edward Law), Governor-General, 40, 67, 102, 116, 152, 162–63, 197, 229, 267, 271, 320n5, 320n6, 333n58
Elliot, William, 209, 325
Elphinstone, Mountstuart, 54, 103, 113, 231, 243
embankments. See Hidgellee.
Evans, Mary, 94
evangelism, in India, 16, 47, 146
Eyre, Vincent, 251, 277

F
Fane, Henry, 115
Ferguson, James, 166, 288
Ferguson, Margaret. See Abbott, Margaret (wife of James).
Ferozeshah, Battle of, 156, 166–67, 169, 276
flogging, as punishment, 28, 91, 310n112
Fort William (Calcutta), 37, 39, 51, 209, 251–52, 254

Freemasonry, in India, 249

G
Gagging Act, in India, 256
Gascoigne, William, 2
Ghaffur, Akhund, 241, 329n110
Gilbert, Walter, 227
Gladstone, William, 277, 333n71
Gough, Hugh, 167–68, 213, 220, 222, 225–26, 229
Government of India Act of 1833, 77
Government of India Act of 1858, 265
Graham, Maria, 34–35, 302n41
Graham, Thomas, 35
Grant, Charles, 91
Great Game, xviii–xix, 118, 136, 143, 276, 314n29
Great Mutiny of 1857, xv, xix–xx, 66, 68, 80, 89–90, 104, 106, 160, 172, 175, 199, 231, 248, 250–51, 256, 260, 276, 284–85, 312, 321, 332n37
Greene, Godfrey, 163
Gujarat, Battle of, 226–27
Guildford, wreck of, 25
gunpowder works, at Ishapore, 250–51, 253, 257
Gwalior, city of, 69, 253, 256, 259, 314n26
Gwalior, Maharaja of, 256, 259

H
Hardinge, Henry (1st Viscount Hardinge), Governor-General, x, 102, 167–70, 177
Haripur, village of, 179, 214, 325n4
Harlan, Josiah, 308n42

Harrison, John, 24
Harripur, village of. See Haripur.
Hassel, Christopher, 102
Havelock, Henry, 222, 276
Havelock, William, 221–22, 276
von Haven, Frederick, 1, 297
Hazara, district of, x, xiv, 181, 321n31, 324n97, 326n21, 326n33, 328n88
Hearsey, John, 254–56
Heber, Bishop Reginald, 35, 302n39
Herat, city of, x, 113–14, 116–22, 124–27, 131, 134, 136–38, 140, 142, 144, 151–52, 249, 271, 276, 314n26, 315n51, 318n97
Herbert, Lieutenant, 195, 218, 220, 320n11, 320n12
Hidgellee, sea embankments at, 163, 165–66, 169, 320
Hindustani Fanatics, xviii, 201, 240–42, 247, 277, 324n112, 330n125
Hindustani, language, 18, 303
Hobhouse, John, 139–41, 148, 228, 236, 271
Hodson, William, 13, 170, 235, 262, 265, 276
hookah, use of in India, xix, 40–41
Hooghly River, ix, 34–35, 156, 165, 254, 302n46
Hugo, Victor-Marie, 291
Hussan Shah. See Shah, Hussan.
hydrophobia, in India. See rabies.

I
intercultural marriage in India. See marriage, intercultural, in India.

Ishapoor. See Ishapore.
Ishapore, Gunpowder Agency. See Ishapore, gunpowder works.
Ishapore, gunpowder works, 250–51, 253, 259, 277

J
Jaipur, city of, 97
Jammu, Kashmir, 169–71, 177–80, 182, 194, 204, 232, 324n97. See also Kashmir.

K
Kabul, city of, 83, 111, 113, 120, 136–37, 149, 151, 218, 251, 276, 294, 305n108, 313n4, 314n12, 314n26, 317n87
Kandahar, city of, 20, 115–16, 121–22, 137, 148–49, 244, 249, 267, 315n3
Karnal, town of, 70–72, 74, 82, 86, 88, 94–95, 97, 99, 110–12, 114, 308–9
Kashmir (and Jammu), 168–71, 177–80, 194, 201, 204, 213, 232, 236, 324n97. See also Jammu.
Kean, John, 115
Kent, wreck of, 25
Khalsa, 169, 204, 206, 213
Khan-i-Zamman, 188, 224–25
Khan, Kulúnder, 217, 224, 280
Khan, Mir Zaman, 223–24, 280
Khan of Khiva, x, 119–20, 124–25, 128, 130, 136, 140, 144, 276–77, 316n77
Khan, Qasim, 233–34, 236, 238

INDEX

Khan, Sammud, x, 120–21, 124, 129,
    132–33, 136, 138–39, 141–42,
    144–46, 148–49, 280, 315n46,
    317n87
Khaur, Maharani Jindan, 204,
    206, 320
khidmatgar, also spelled khitmatgar,
    occupation and dress of, ix, 39,
    85, 87, 100, 302n49, 309n93
Khiva, city of, vii, ix–x, xix, 19, 74, 76,
    112–13, 115, 117–31, 133–34,
    136–45, 147–51, 153–54, 157,
    165, 182, 200, 223, 270–71,
    276–77, 315n41, 316n69,
    316n77, 318n108
Kipling, Rudyard, 283, 301, 313n52
Koh-i-Noor diamond, 227
Kôt Kangra, fortress of, x, 173, 177
Kota, Mullah of. See Mullah of Kota.
Kulúndur Khan. See Khan, Kulúndur.

L
Lahore, city of, 169–71, 176–80,
    182–83, 188, 193–97, 201–4,
    206, 209–11, 214, 222, 224, 232,
    245, 259, 321n8
Lahore, Treaty of, 169, 196
Lahore Durbar, 178, 182, 188,
    194–97, 203–4, 206, 224, 232
Lawrence, George, 201, 203, 214, 218,
    220, 227, 277, 324n114
Lawrence, Henry, xix, 8, 19, 48, 104,
    114, 122, 170–71, 175–76, 178,
    182–85, 188, 192, 196, 198,
    201, 228, 231–32, 236, 238–39,
    243–45, 259, 262, 276, 281, 287,
    321n28, 322n57, 327n63

Lawrence, Honoria, 114, 190, 198,
    234–36, 238, 276, 281, 328–29
Lawrence, John, 271
Levant Company, 1–3, 297n1, 298n39
Login, John, 116, 314n26
London, city of, 1–4, 6, 9, 11, 35, 37,
    88, 112, 123, 130, 139, 142,
    152–53, 162, 222, 228, 236, 267,
    269, 271–72, 274, 276, 277, 290,
    294, 298n31, 300n74, 78, 3,
    307n40, 308n48, 325, 327n59,
    333n7, 334n334, 336n26
Lumsden, Harry (aka Joe), 262,
    271–72, 277, 322n58
Lunt, James, 40

M
Macaulay, Thomas, 37, 316n75
Mackeson, Frederick, 235, 241–43,
    246–48, 250, 271, 276, 328n88
Macleod, Alexander, 40, 43, 53, 67,
    302n53
MacMullen, John, 29–31, 35, 42, 47,
    50, 301–4
Mackenzie, James, 105
Mackenzie, Holt, 103
MacNaughten, William, 113, 151,
    314n12
MacNeil, John, 117
Maharaja of Gwalior. See Gwalior,
    Maharaja of.
Mahomet, Dean, 146, 300n74
Malcolm, John, 91, 103, 231, 243
Mann, Horace, 4
marriage, intercultural, in India, xvi,
    40, 42, 79, 81–84, 147, 280,
    335n3

Marshman, John, 127, 228, 316n75
Marshman, Joshua, 127, 316n74
Mary, East Indiaman, 22–23, 26, 28, 30, 32–34, 37, 300n3
Masonry. See Freemasonry.
Masson, Charles, 305n108, 316n60
Meerut, city of, ix, 55, 87, 251, 256–57, 259–60
Merv, city of, 131, 134, 136–37, 150, 200, 270
Metcalfe, Charles, 95, 103, 105, 113, 243
Mhow, city of, 95, 97, 99–102, 110, 112, 153, 159, 267, 294
Mill, James, 103
Mill, John Stuart, 104
Mir Zaman Khan. See Khan, Mir Zaman.
Mohammed, Dost, 111–13, 188, 218–20, 222–23, 225, 227–28, 314n26, 325n18
Mohammed, Saleh, x, 134–37, 142, 149, 223, 249, 277, 280, 331n3
Monkland, Mrs., pseudonym, 4, 298n18
Moorcroft, William, 123, 316n66
Moore, Thomas, 287, 289–90, 323n87
Morden College, 10, 298n39
Mullah of Kota, 225–26, 326n22, 329n107
Mulraj of Multan, 195
Multan, city and siege of, 184, 195, 197, 201–4, 206, 210–11, 276–77
Munirov, Quwāmidden, 128
Munro, Thomas, 103, 105, 231, 243
Mutiny of 1857. See Great Mutiny of 1857.

N

Napier, Charles, 42, 91, 116, 161, 222, 229
Napier, Robert, 241, 271–72
Nath, Raja Deena, x, 176, 185
Neptune, East Indiaman, 1
Nesselrode, Karl, 139, 143–44, 277
Nicholson, John, 184, 188, 190–93, 195–98, 201, 214–16, 220–21, 227, 233, 235, 245, 259, 262, 276, 283, 323n81, 323n87, 324n108
Nicolas I, Tsar, 138–39
Nikāḥ al-Mut'ah, marriage form, 42, 81–82, 282
Nimarr, district of, xi, 153–54, 156, 158, 162–63, 276, 295, 304n87

O

Ochterlony, David, xx, 53, 55, 305n36
Olpherts, William, 176, 321n36
Oudh, province of, 104, 230, 257, 264, 279
Outram, James, 162, 276, 320n4, 320n6

P

Paladins, group, 184, 193, 196–97, 201–4, 235–36, 244–45, 277, 281, 287, 328n87. See also Young Men.
Palmerston, 3rd Viscount (John Henry Temple), 112, 139–40
Paltu, Shaikh, 256–57
panchayats, in India, 177
Pandey, Mangal, 255–57, 332n29
Paragon, ix, 6–10, 14, 16, 75, 268. See also Blackheath.

INDEX

Patalpanie, village of, 99–101, 110, 277, 311n23
Pearse, George, 190–91, 246
Perovsky, Vasily, 119–20, 127, 138, 140, 143, 190, 274, 277, 317n93
Pogson, Wrendenhall, 45, 51–53
Potticary, John and school, 8, 10, 268
Pottinger, Eldred, 113, 116–17, 122–23, 152, 276, 314n26
Powney, Richard, 42
Prema Conspiracy, 178, 193, 204
Price, Joseph, 2
Princep, Augustus, 83, 309n87
Pulki Brigade, of Sikh Army, 207, 210–11

Q
Qasim Khan of Khabbal. See Khan, Qasim.
Queen Victoria, 123, 227, 271, 285, 316n64
Quinney, Thomas, 14

R
rabies, incidence of in India, 70
race, conceptions of, xvii, 30, 34, 79, 108–9, 146, 179, 182, 186, 224, 231, 263, 268–69, 322n45, 322n61
Radhanite, trading network in Central Asia, 150
Ram, Sita, 40, 67, 305n117, 309n77
Ramnagar, Battle of, 221–22
Revenue Survey, of Northwest India, vii, 94–95, 97, 99, 101–3, 105–7, 109, 111, 114, 183, 186, 188, 312n38, 312n41, 313n51

Robinson, Daniel, 193, 201, 214, 220–21, 233, 235, 321n31
Romantic Movement of literature, 277, 336n43
Romanticism. See Romantic Movement.

S
Sabraon, Battle of, 167–69, 322, 328
Saleh Mohammed. See Mohammed, Saleh.
Sammud Khan. See Khan, Sammud.
Schlegel, Friedrich, 290
Scott, Eliza, 37, 39, 51
Scott, Walter, 14, 21, 75, 95, 159, 186, 244, 277, 286–90, 334n1, 335n14, 335n20
sea embankments. See Hidgellee.
Seeur ul Mutu ukhireen, 50, 304n89
Shah, Hussan, 187, 213, 233
Shah, Syed Ahmed, 240–41, 324n112
Shah, Zaman, 240–42
Shahjihanpoor, district of, 108–9, 112, 312
Shakespear, John, 18, 303n65
Shakespear, Richmond, 114, 116, 127–28, 130, 140, 144–45, 276
Sheil, Justin, 137
Shikarpore, mutiny at, 50
Sikh Army. See Khalsa.
Simla, city of, ix, 71–74, 76, 84, 87, 132, 267, 271, 308n48, 309n93
Simulkund, Battle of, 188, 216–17, 224
Sind, region, 161–62, 166, 191, 222, 319n3
Singh, Balwant, 55

365

Singh, Chattar, x, 186, 194, 201, 205–7, 209–16, 218, 220, 222–23, 227, 324n97, 325n4
Singh, Gulab, 168–69, 171, 178–80, 182, 186, 194–95, 197, 204, 213, 244
Singh, Duleep, 169, 204, 206, 314n26, 320n23
Singh, Raja Ranjit, 161, 166, 204, 320n23, 327n62
Singh, Sher, son of Chattar, 201, 206, 211, 222, 226–27
Smith-Stanley, Edward (14th Earl of Derby), 272
Smyth, Ralph, ix, 45, 106–7
Spurgeen, Charles, 261
Stirling, Edward, 123
Stoddart, Charles, 121, 123, 125–26, 137, 276, 315n52
Stuart, Charles, 53, 78
Sujah ul Mulk, Shah, 111, 113–15, 120, 315n50
Survey of India, trigonometric, 101, 312

T
Tariqa-i-Muhammadiyya. See Hindustani Fanatics.
Taylor, Meadows, 285
Taylor, Reynell, 184, 322n57
Tennyson, Alfred (1st Baron Tennyson), 72, 289
Thackeray, William Makepeace, 4
Third Anglo-Maratha War (1818), 250
Thomason, James, 244, 330
Thompson, George, 102

Thompson, Henry, 12
Thuillier, Henry, ix, 106–7
Timms, Biddy, 299n74
Todd, D'Arcy, vii, ix, 19–20, 48, 56, 94–97, 99, 101–3, 105, 107, 109, 111, 113–18, 120, 134, 136, 140, 144, 151–53, 156, 166, 276, 294, 311n1, 314n26, 318n97
Treaty of Lahore, 169, 196
Trebeck, George, 123, 316n66
Trevelyan, Charles, 8
Trigonometric Survey of India. See Survey of India, trigonometric.
Tsar Nicolas I. See Nicolas I.

U
Umeer Beg, British agent in Khiva, 130–31, 137, 144, 318n108
United Services Journal, 60, 62, 64, 101–2, 287, 294, 306n1, 307n20

V
vans Agnew, Patrick, 184, 193–95, 197, 203, 225, 235, 276
Vellore, mutiny at, 49
Victoria, Queen, 123, 227, 271, 285, 316n64

W
Wahhabi Fanatics. See Hindustani Fanatics.
Walpole, Horace, 4, 297
Warburton, Richard, 199, 281, 324n109
Warwick School, 8
Watson, Hubert, 234, 281

Wellington, 1st Duke of (Arthur Wellesley), 55–56, 113, 162, 212
Werge-Thomas, Evelyn, xiv, 274, 334n86
Wesley, Richard, 68
Wheeler, Hugh, 172, 175
Whish, William, 201
Wilberforce, Reginald, 191
Williamson, Thomas, 28, 81
witchcraft, belief in, in India, 154
Wolseley, Garnet (1st Viscount Wolseley), 184, 261

Woodrooffe, George, 56, 58

Y

Young Men, Henry Lawrence's, xix, 6, 11, 15–16, 48, 184, 186, 193, 196, 198, 203, 231, 235, 238, 243, 281, 287, 322n57. See also Paladins.

Z

Zaman Shah. See Shah, Zaman.

About the Author

Chris Mason is currently professor of national security affairs and director of the Study of Internal Conflict (SOIC) at the US Army War College in Carlisle, Pennsylvania. He researches, writes, and teaches in the fields of civil wars and insurgencies and modern and historical India. A former US Navy officer, Dr. Mason has published extensively on South Asia, focusing on Afghanistan, India, and the nineteenth- and twentieth-century borderlands between them. He is a retired Foreign Service officer and holds a PhD in imperial and colonial history from the George Washington University in Washington, DC.

www.ingramcontent.com/pod-product-compliance
Lightning Source LLC
Chambersburg PA
CBHW022008300426
44117CB00005B/76